THE
Vegetable Encylopedia
AND
Gardener's Guide

BY

VICTOR A. TIEDJENS

Associate Professor of Vegetable Gardening
New Jersey State Agricultural Experiment Station
Rutgers University

Illustrated by

TABEA HOFMANN

AVENEL BOOKS
A Division of Crown Publishers, Inc.
New York

Preface

In planning the VEGETABLE ENCYCLOPEDIA AND GARDENER'S GUIDE, every effort has been made to present in the most convenient form all the information which will be useful to the home vegetable grower.

For ready reference, Part I is an "Encyclopedia of Vegetables," including in alphabetical order all the commonly grown vegetables and also a large number of less familiar vegetables which are valuable as foods and which add interest and variety to the vegetable garden.

Each vegetable is first fully described, and then there are sections on soil requirements, cultural directions, the prevention and cure of plant diseases, and the avoidance of insect pests.

Recognizing the steadily increasing interest in growing herbs, Part II is a very complete "Encyclopedia of Herbs." Here also the arrangement is alphabetical. The very full discussion of each herb should encourage many users of this book to assign a special part of their vegetable gardens to a group of favorite herbs which are so welcome in the kitchen for flavoring and seasoning.

Both Part I and Part II are fully provided with cross references, so that the user of the book who looks up a vegetable or herb under one of its alternative names will immediately be referred to the page on which he will find the plant in which he is interested.

Part III is called "The Gardener's Guide." This valuable division of the book brings together all the important general instructions and suggestions which apply to vegetable gardens as a whole. Such matters as preparation of the soil, use of fertilizers, selection of seed, choice of varieties, vitamin content, growing plants in coldframes and hotbeds, transplanting of seedlings, handling of tools and equipment, and construction and use of frames and greenhouses are among the many matters presented. A Glossary of technical terms is placed at the end of the book for ready reference.

The various vegetables are illustrated by exceptionally effective and useful drawings, and the skillful drawings of the herbs make possible instant identification of herb plants. These illustrations, as well as the diagrams and sketches of equipment in Part III, are the work of Tabea Hofmann.

I am grateful to Francis C. Coulter, author of *A Manual of Vegetable Gardening*, and the publishers, Doubleday, Doran & Co., for permission to reprint the following material from that book: the three garden plans included in this book in the section on "Planning the Garden," the illustrations of familiar weeds, included here in the section on "Controlling Weeds in the Garden," the illustrations of well-known insect pests in the section on "Controlling Garden Pests" (all these illustrations also by Tabea Hofmann), the description of the pH scale in the section on "Judging and Improving the Soil," the "Table of Spring and Fall Frost Dates," and the list of "State Agricultural Experiment Stations."

I wish to express my appreciation to my co-partner and wife, who gave so freely of her time and displayed such unlimited patience to make possible the preparation of the manuscript for this book.

VICTOR A. TIEDJENS

Contents

CONTENTS

Glossary

PART I
The Encyclopedia of Vegetables

The Encyclopedia of Vegetables

Adsuki Bean

See Beans

Air Potato

See Yams

Arrowroot

See in Part II (Herbs)

Artichoke

DESCRIPTION: Globe artichoke (*Cynara scolymus*) is of Old World origin, having been grown in Southern Asia before the Christian Era. It is a large vigorous plant resembling the thistle with its coarse spiney long leaves. The plants may grow to a height of six

feet, with three-foot leaves growing out from the stems. Globe artichoke is prized for its flower buds, which are eaten in salads or are cooked in salt water and eaten as a cooked vegetable. The flower buds are produced, terminally, on the stem and on branches originating at the base of the leaves, and are two to three inches across. The artichoke is generally considered to be a cultivated form of cardoon. The plant is a perennial and, once established, will produce buds for three or four years or as long as the plants remain alive. (*See also* Jerusalem Artichoke.)

TYPES AND VARIETIES: There are a number of types which differ in the size and shape of the bud. The conical-bud type, more widely grown in Europe than in this country, is represented by the following varieties: Thistle or Prickley artichoke, Violet artichoke, and French or Green French artichoke. The globular-headed type is generally grown in this country as well as in Europe. Its varieties include the Green or White Globe, the Red Dutch, the Violet Bud (probably the same as the Green Globe), and the Giant Bud. The Green Globe is generally offered by the seed trade as the best variety for general garden purposes.

SOIL AND CLIMATIC REQUIREMENTS: The Globe artichoke is very sensitive to cold weather and for this reason the commercial crop is grown in those sections of the United States where the ground does not freeze. When grown in states with killing frosts, the plants must be protected by heavy mulches or grown in large tubs which can be moved to a protected place during the dormant season when the tops die down. The soil must be very fertile, well drained, rich in organic matter, and well sup-

3

plied with liming material. If grown on sandy soils that are low in fertility, the plants must be well supplied with manure or be side-dressed with liquid fertilizer at least three times during the growing season. The plants occupy the ground for five or six years and all subsurface preparation of the soil must be made before the plants are set. For this reason it is a good practice to dig the soil to a depth of two feet and mix lime, manure, and some superphosphate with the soil as it is worked over. Then the soil is permitted to settle in place—perhaps by soaking with water—for several weeks before the plants are set. This requires some additional labor but is well worth the effort in terms of the number of buds that can be harvested from a few plants.

CULTURAL DIRECTIONS: A small packet of seed will produce enough plants for a number of gardens. Five or six plants will be sufficient in the small garden. The seeds should be sown in a four-inch pot of good garden soil and when the seedlings are two inches high they should be transplanted to individual four-inch pots. The seed is sown about the middle of February and can be germinated in a south window where the temperature does not go below 60 degrees. The plants are set in the garden when the soil has been thoroughly warmed and there is no danger of frost. If the plants can be set on the south side of a building, they have a better chance of living through the winter, because they can be protected more easily. The plants should be set two feet apart in rows which are four feet apart. They should not be set in the middle of the garden where they

will interfere with the garden plowing. The plants should be set without disturbing the roots any more than is necessary to remove the pot. The ball of earth is set in the ground with a starter solution. A quart of the solution should be poured around the ball of soil before the garden soil is firmed around the plants. These plants, with a little care and water if the soil dries out too much, will produce buds the first year of planting. Seed may be sown directly in the garden soil after it is warm, but the plants will not then blossom the first year. Beds can also be established by setting in sprouts from an old bed. As soon as the sprouts come up in the spring and are four to eight inches long, they can be broken from the old plants and set in for a new planting. When a bed is to be renewed it should be replanted by means of the sprouts. In this way sprouts can be selected from the plants which produce the largest and best shaped buds. Commercial growers prefer this method because plants grown from seed will vary considerably in the size of the buds. The commercial grower wants a uniform lot of buds.

The artichoke requires a good supply of water and, if the soil becomes too dry, it should be thoroughly soaked. Gardeners near the seashore should gather seaweed and place it around the plants. This makes a good mulch and also supplies some potash. Wood ashes are good to put around the plants toward fall or during the winter when the plants are dormant. The tops die down and should be removed cleanly so that the stump of the stem does not offer an avenue for disease infection, which works into the crown.

INSECTS AND DISEASES: The plants are remarkably free from diseases and, if they are grown in well-drained soil, the crown rots will cause very little difficulty. Plant lice or aphids sometimes cause some trouble when they occur in large numbers on the undersides of the young leaves, but they can be easily controlled by dusting with a nicotine dust. The larvae of the Plume Moth often cause trouble in commercial plantations by feeding on the buds and sometimes working into the interior. In the garden, however, they will probably cause little trouble.

GENERAL RECOMMENDATIONS: The buds should be harvested when they are still compact and before they give any sign of opening. The flower parts and the short stems are tender at this stage. They should be placed in the icebox as soon as picked, to be chilled before they lose their delicate flavor. They probably have a higher flavor if picked in the evening rather than in the morning. The sprouts around old plants can also be used for salads or cooked as asparagus is.

Gardeners should try the Globe Artichoke. It offers variety and has a fine flavor. Even though most of the crop is grown in the localities of high temperatures, the quality is much better in the cooler sections and with a little care the plants can be grown even where the soil freezes. It is also an interesting plant for the hobbyist to work with. There are tremendous possibilities of improving the varieties, for the man who wishes to take the time and has the patience can obtain a lot of satisfaction from developing hardier or better tasting varieties, or spineless varieties, or new varieties in size and color of the buds.

The seed is very much mixed because the plants are cross-pollinated and ordinary selection will do much to improve varieties.

Asparagus

DESCRIPTION: Asparagus (*Asparagus officinalis*) was grown as a food plant by European and Asiatic peoples long before the Christian Era. It is now the common garden variety grown in practically all parts of the world. It is a vigorous-growing bushy plant with finely divided or rudimentary leaves on long heavily branched stems. The stems die down every year, while the fleshy roots increase in size and number from year to year. A bed properly established in a garden should last a lifetime, if given proper care. The species probably originated from the wild asparagus

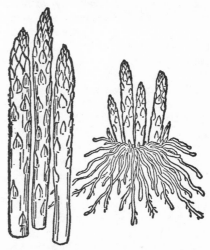

that grows in the Caucasian regions and Siberia, probably being introduced into America by the Colonists. It is widely grown in the United States in large quantities and appears on our markets from late winter to midsummer.

TYPES AND VARIETIES: There are some eight or ten different species of asparagus which are largely grown for ornamental purposes but have been used as sources of food by Mediterranean peoples. Usually the tender sprouts are used, but in some cases the fleshy roots were used, and a few species produce a tuber which was used. None of them compare with the present garden variety in yield or flavor or palatability. The Washington varieties are generally grown in the United States; the number of selections by growers offered for sale are probably all of the Washington strain. This variety was developed by the United States Department of Agriculture as rust-resistant, to take the place of a number of French and German varieties which were being gradually killed out by the asparagus rust. Commercial varieties are all rust-resistant. There are many areas in the United States where asparagus which seems to have withstood the rust epidemics is growing wild, probably having escaped from plantings of the older European varieties. One of these areas is the sandy loam country of central Wisconsin, where the plants grow wild in fence rows, throughout the wooded areas, and along railroad rights of way. These plants probably would serve as a source of seed for some very good plantings, since natural selection has doubtless eliminated the weak plants. An opportunity for someone to develop a good variety! There is now only one desirable variety: the Mary Washington or some strain from this variety.

SOIL AND CLIMATIC REQUIREMENTS: Asparagus reaches its greatest degree of perfection in the northern states, where the winters are cold. In such sections the plants are very hardy and will compete with weeds or other plants. However, those are not the areas where our commercial crop is grown. Most of our asparagus is grown in the warmer climates of the coastal plain and southern states, where growers are limited in their yields by weather too warm for best results. Under such conditions, it is necessary to pamper the plants to get even average yields. Asparagus is particularly suited to the sands and sandy loam soils but will grow well in the heavier soils with proper care. Asparagus requires heavy applications of liming materials and responds more to applications of pulverized limestone than to fertilizer. Most soils in which asparagus is grown are altogether too acid to get good yields. It is possible to grow 1000 crates of asparagus to the acre, and yet the average yield is less than 100 crates. Much of this shortage in yield can be attributed to high winter temperatures and a lack of sufficient lime.

Asparagus beds when once established may last for fifty or more years if properly cared for and if sufficient lime is added every year to satisfy the needs of the plants. The importance of magnesium liming material cannot be over-emphasized. The areas where asparagus grows wild are limestone areas. To prepare the soil for the asparagus bed, 20 pounds of pulverized limestone and 3 pounds of superphosphate should be worked into the soil to a depth of 18 inches to 2 feet, for every 100 square feet. If the soil is heavy and has considerable clay in it, even more should be added. Wood ashes are quite satisfactory for liming, but they may not carry sufficient magnesium unless they are used fresh from the stove or fireplace. Very heavy soils are not well suited for asparagus but, if well drained, can be improved by adding large quantities of limestone and even hard coal cinders or sand to the soil and mixing them thoroughly. If manure is available, it should be mixed with the soil to a depth of at least 18 inches. If good, partially decomposed compost is available, it will help to give the plants a quick start. Fertilizer need not be applied until the plants are well established, and then they should be fed with a liquid fertilizer.

CULTURAL DIRECTIONS: There are several ways in which an asparagus planting can be made. The method depends on the time of the year that the bed is planned. The quickest method is to buy roots from a grower and set them in the soil as early in the spring as possible. A 100-foot row containing 50 plants or an 8 × 25 foot bed will give sufficient asparagus for the average family and leave some to can. The best arrangement is to plant a row along one side of the garden, between the flower and vegetable gardens where the summer brush of the asparagus will make a very effective background for the flower garden, or in some out-of-the-way place where it will least interfere with soil-preparation practices in the other part of the garden.

The first operation is to dig a trench in the previously prepared soil. This trench should be 10 inches deep in the lighter types of soil and 8 inches deep in the heavier soils. After the trench is dug 5 pounds of pulverized limestone and one pound of superphosphate should be spread along the bottom of the furrow,

where it should be thoroughly mixed with the soil. Then the roots of the asparagus plants should be spread out and placed on a small mound not over an inch high in such a way that the flesh roots are spread and the buds or the crown are on top. These crowns are placed two feet apart, so that 50 plants will occupy a 100-foot row. Then the roots are covered with two inches of soil. As the plants become established, more soil is gradually filled in around the plants to keep the weeds from growing. All the soil is finally filled in by the middle of August. To fill in the soil too soon may kill the plants. Such a row, once established, will last for many years if properly cared for.

Roots can also be set closer together in the row, but such crowding shortens the usefulness of the bed and causes the spears to become spindly. A bed may be established by digging four parallel trenches two feet apart from center to center. The roots are then set in the adjacent rows so that the plants are staggered in the bed. A bed established in this manner requires much hand weeding.

There are times when it is impossible to get one-year-old roots or roots of any kind. In this case it is necessary to grow the roots from seed. One method is to plant a small packet of seed in a row in the garden. The best assurance of good roots is to plant the seed in several flower pots in late winter and keep them in a warm place until the seed germinates. This requires from two to three weeks. Then the pots should be set in a window where the plants will get as much sunlight as possible. As soon as the soil can be worked in the garden, the seedlings should be transplanted in a row, three inches apart. These can be easily weeded and cared for. When seed is planted in the open in the cool soil, it takes so long to germinate that the weeds practically cover the ground before it is possible to see the rows of asparagus seedlings. A common practice is to plant radish seed with the asparagus seed. The radish seed will germinate quickly, indicating the location of the row, and the radishes will be ready to pull before asparagus seedlings are crowded.

Such seedlings are cared for until frost and are dug the following spring for setting in the permanent location. There will be many more roots than will be needed. Fifty of the largest roots that have a good distribution of buds should be selected and planted in the bed. The other roots are thrown away. Although it takes a year longer to start a bed from seed than from roots, the permanent bed so started will be much more productive. Roots bought from growers are not selected and therefore include a large number of low producing ones. If it is possible to get selected roots by paying more for them, it is a good investment.

If a person has a sunny place where he can grow roots during the winter, it is possible to sow seed in deep flats in the late summer and grow them as long as possible out-of-doors and then bring them in and grow them at a temperature of 55 degrees all winter. These plants can be transplanted to the permanent positions in the early spring and by careful weeding and hoeing will produce an excellent bed. The plants should not be grown with too much water. It is well to keep the soil rather dry unless the air is very dry. The plants should be at least two inches apart either way.

It is possible to cut spears for a few weeks the second year, if the plants have been well grown and cared for. The third year, the beds can be cut until the middle of June and in subsequent years until the first of July. The vigor and number of stalks should determine how much the plants should be cut. It must be kept in mind that the crop harvested will depend on the vigor of the summer brush; this brush should not be removed until the plants are dead.

The plants should have at least 1000 pounds of limestone applied around them over a period of four or five years, or three to five pounds for each of the 50 plants every spring when the soil is spaded over and loosened above the crowns. They should not be injured with the shovel. The crowns should not be hilled up during the summer, because it will cause them to work to the surface. Any mulching material that can be applied around the plants will be helpful, but it should not be put on early in the spring with the idea of controlling the weeds. A mulch of finely divided material over the crowns about the first of June will keep down weeds and permit the spears to come through. It will also keep the ground loose, so that the spears will come through straight. Liquid fertilizer should be applied around the plants as the summer brush is allowed to grow. Wood ashes may be strewn around the asparagus plants or over the beds during the winter. The best way to determine the amount of fertilizer to apply is to make an application according to directions on the seed package and not use any more unless the brush does not look vigorous and green. The brush should be higher than one's head by the middle of August. If manure is available, it should be spread over the bed in the fall and worked into the soil in the spring. Chicken manure should be put on after the cutting season—after the first of July. Four hundred pounds of superphosphate should be mixed with every load of chicken manure used in the garden.

INSECTS AND DISEASES: There are a few diseases of asparagus, but the home gardener can do nothing about them. Asparagus rust is one of the diseases that kills out plants, but the present varieties are all selections out of a rust-resistant variety. There is nothing that can be done if rust appears on the stalks. It is a good practice to keep the plants cut off clean when the beds are being cut. All volunteer plants that happen to be growing in waste places should be kept down. In this way the rust spores do not have a chance to develop early in the season and any infection that might take place after the first of July will do very little harm. There are a few crown rots that affect the underground parts of the plant. These often occur in soils that tend to remain moist or that are heavy and inadequately aerated. Good cultural practices will help to control them. Keeping the soil well-limed and being careful not to put chemical fertilizer directly over the tops of the crowns will tend to prevent such diseases from developing.

Insects may be a serious pest. There are several asparagus beetles that may cause considerable damage. The most serious one is the common asparagus beetle. It is $\frac{1}{4}$-inch long, has a slender body, blue-black with a yellow section just back of the head, and wings of lemon yellow and dark blue. The larva or grub is gray in color and feeds on the leaves. The long slender eggs are often seen on the spear when it is cut. The grubs hatch out as the brush develops, and the leaves are eaten off as fast as they are grown. It gives the plants a skinned appearance. People sometimes run their chickens in the asparagus bed, because the chickens will eat enough of the beetles to keep them under control. The twelve-spotted asparagus beetle has a broader back and is orange-red in color. Each wing cover has six black dots distributed over it. This species feeds on the young shoots and, after the brush is grown, on the berries of the female plants. By keeping all the spears cut during the harvesting season, the beetles can be starved out. If a few plants are allowed to grow, the beetles will congregate on the brush and the plants can be dusted with an arsenical or rotenone dust. If there are but few plants, it is often quicker to shake them so that the larvae fall off. They are so sluggish that they will die before they can return to the plants. Japanese beetles are a serious pest in some localities during July. Commercial growers dust the brush with lime to repel the beetles. Some growers cut their asparagus two weeks longer than usual, because they say it does no more damage to the roots than if the Japanese beetles eat off the tops.

GENERAL RECOMMENDATIONS: There are some special cultural practices, much discussed by the small gardener, which should be debunked. There is a general idea that salt is good for asparagus. Salt will stimulate the growth of asparagus plants the first year of application, but the effect soon wears off and the soil is irreparably damaged. Salt application kicks out calcium and potash from the colloidal matter in the soil. Calcium and potassium are beneficial to the asparagus plant and, on soils that are not too well supplied with these elements, enough are eliminated from the soil colloids to give the asparagus an added push. In other words, the nutrients are released so that the plants can absorb them. However, this will only happen for a year or so; then the soil is in worse condition than ever, and it may take several years to bring it back to its normal fertility. This colloidal matter, which resembles a thin film of jelly, surrounds the tiny soil particles and is the basis for the potential fertility of the soil. If the colloidal matter is thoroughly saturated with calcium the soil is productive. If it is saturated with soda from the soil, it becomes very unproductive. Thus for the few extra first-year spears obtainable by adding salt, enough damage may be done to cut the yield materially for several years after.

There is a general idea that when asparagus is planted it should be set very deep—15 inches or more. This was a practice when white or blanched asparagus was desired. The spears were cut 8 to 10 inches below the surface and some growers even hilled up the rows to keep them white. We know now that green asparagus is more tender, better flavored, and richer in vitamins. Now

it is cut just below the surface of the ground and there is no need to plant it deep. The closer the roots are planted to the surface, the bigger the yield will be, and the sooner the spears can be cut.

There is an idea that asparagus trenches should be dug deep enough to permit the burying of a large number of tin cans and other roughage, as well as wood, before the roots are set in. The idea back of this was to improve the aeration in heavy soils. There are better ways of improving the soil. Sand or cinders may be mixed with the soil if it is too heavy. Thoroughly mixing pulverized limestone with the soil will do much to improve aeration. Brush or twigs of various sizes buried in the heavy soil will serve as organic matter. Sawdust, if mixed with limestone, can be mixed to considerable depths and will have lasting value. A person can afford to spend considerable time and labor on the bed, because it is the only chance one has of fixing up the subsoil for years to come. The practice of digging a trench two feet wide and three feet deep, mixing manure and superphosphate with the removed soil, then replacing it before the roots are set, seems like a lot of work, but it is conducive to exceptional yields. A rose bed, grown in a shale soil so hard that all of it required picking before it could be shoveled, responded so well to this treatment that after seven years it was still the envy of the neighborhood. Any perennial plant will respond to such treatment; asparagus will respond more than any, because it needs so much oxygen for its roots. A bed that is put in with such preparation can be expected to last a lifetime, if it is limed and fertilized occasionally. Asparagus produces berries or seed on the female plants. These berries will weaken the plant if a heavy crop is set, and it is just as well to take them off as soon as they are formed. The twelve-spotted asparagus beetle will do this if left alone. In that sense the beetle does more good than harm.

Asparagus spears are harvested by cutting when they are six to eight inches tall. They are carefully cut just below the surface of the ground in such a manner that buds not yet visible will not be injured. The spear yield from a plant may be halved if the buds below the surface are injured; the spears may come up crooked or may not come up at all. There is no limit to the number of spears that may be harvested from a plant, except the heredity capacity of the plants themselves. Plants have been known to produce over a hundred spears during a cutting season. Fifty times 100 means 5000 spears or 420 bunches. The average spear yield from a bed of 50 plants will probably be closer to 42. Even this is a big yield for commercial beds.

When asparagus spears are cut they should be chilled at once or placed in the ice-box, unless they are to be cooked immediately after cutting. Asparagus experiences rapid vegetative changes which are responsible for the quick growth of the spears. When the spears are cut, these changes continue, altering the sugars and soluble proteins to simpler compounds which are bitter to the taste. Chilling the spear arrests these chemical changes and preserves the sugars, giving to the spear that delicate, sweet flavor that only those who have eaten asparagus immediately after cutting know.

Asparagus Bean

The asparagus bean (*Vigna sesquipedalis*), sometimes called YARDLONG BEAN, is named after its tremendously long pods and is grown more as a curiosity than for food. Although it produces a heavy vine

growth, it does not yield well. The leaves are medium in size, but the pods are two to three feet long, producing a small seed every inch of the way. For cultural directions, *see* Beans.

Banana Squash
See Squash

Barbe de Capuchin
See Chicory

Bean, Lima
See Lima Bean

Beans

DESCRIPTION: The common bean (*Phaseolus vulgaris*) embraces the wide variety of garden beans, known as SNAP BEANS, STRINGLESS or STRING BEANS, GREEN BEANS, or WAX BEANS;

the FIELD BEANS, which are shelled and dried and include the red KIDNEY BEANS and the small NAVY BEANS; and the Spanish FRIJOLES as well as the French HARICOTS. The term kidney bean, sometimes used to designate the entire species, is here used in the limited American sense to specify only the large, purplish-brown, characteristically kidney-shaped field bean. Some varieties of the common bean, often classified as HORTICULTURAL BEANS, are used either for their immature pods, like the snap beans, or for their ripe seeds, like the field beans.

The bean was found in cultivation by the American Indians when America was discovered and from here has been taken to all parts of

used as a rotation crop for soil-improvement, the vines being plowed under to fertilize the succeeding crop.

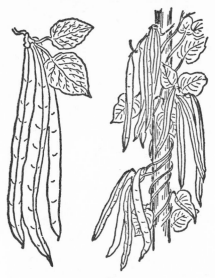

POLE BEANS

The flowers are white, pink, yellow, or red. The plants range in habit of growth from low and bushy to tall and climbing, and are accordingly classified as "bush" or "pole" varieties.

There are a number of other beans closely enough related in habits of growth and cultural requirements to be grouped with the common varieties. The SCARLET RUNNER BEAN and the TEPARY BEAN as well as a few species of less importance are of this kind. Although the LIMA BEAN belongs to this group, it is so important and so specifically cultivated as to warrant separate description under its own name.

For beans of other genera, *see* Asparagus bean; Broad bean; Castorbean; Cowpea; Hyacinth bean; Jack bean; Soya bean; and Velvet bean.

BUSH BEANS

the world. It is one of our most popular vegetables, upwards of 500 varieties being in cultivation. It is a legume, able to obtain its nitrogen from the air, and is therefore often

GARDEN BEANS: These are the snap, string, green, or wax beans commonly grown in the kitchen garden for their immature edible pods. They include both the green-pod and wax- or yellow-pod varieties. Both are available in either the bush or pole varieties, although the bush varieties are by far the most popular, because they are grown with so little effort. The following varieties are suggested for the small garden:

Bush green-pod: Bountiful, Stringless Green-Pod.

Bush yellow-pod: Stringless Wax, Yellow Bountiful.

WAX BEANS

Pole green-pod: Kentucky Wonder, Rust-Resistant Kentucky Wonder.

Pole yellow-pod: Kentucky Wonder Wax, Golden Cluster Wax.

FIELD BEANS: These include the navy and kidney beans, which are harvested when ripe and eaten as dried beans. They include all sizes from the small navy or pea bean, which has a white seed, to the large kidney bean, which is a half inch long and red in color. Although they are usually grown as bush beans, there are a number of pole or twin-

KIDNEY BEAN

ing types which have either white or colored seeds. Example: White Marrowfat, Red Kidney, Navy.

HORTICULTURAL BEANS: These comprise a number of varieties which are grown for either the green pod or the ripe beans. Suggested varieties are:

Bush: Dwarf Horticultural, French Horticultural.

Pole: Horticultural, Cranberry Bean.

FRIJOLE BEAN: Sometimes called Spanish frijole, this bean is commonly seen and used in Mexico and the southwestern states, where only the Tepary bean exceeds it in popularity and yield. It was probably introduced from the Mediterranean countries by the early Spanish missionaries. The Red Indian and the Bayou are two common varieties. The bean is small but flat, resembling the small kidney bean. Like the Tepary, it is well adapted to the peculiar climate of the region. It is grown as a dry shell bean, but is not particularly suited for the small gardener, for the pods are not edible and the seeds are too small to be used as green shell beans.

SCARLET RUNNER BEAN (*Phaseolus coccineus or multiflorus*): This plant is as ornamental as it is useful for food purposes. It is a climber, like the pole beans, and produces scarlet flowers on long racemes, which are very showy, making the plant ideal for covering unsightly spots in the garden. It is often grown on the side of buildings on wire netting or strings. The leaves are very similar to the snap or kidney pole beans. When grown for ornamental purposes, it should be fertilized and provided with moisture in order to grow larger vines, and it may be grown in partial shade, but seed probably will not set. The pods, which grow about five inches long, have three to five large seeds in them—fully as good as the Lima beans. The plant wants full sun to produce seed, but they mature in climates too cool and too short to mature Lima beans. The fully mature seeds, being brown or red and black, are not so attractive upon the table as those that are picked and shelled green. In the northern climates, where the plants are grown as annuals, they mature in 65 days. In the tropics or climates where the root lives over, they produce tubers or rootstocks. The Scarlet Runner is generally grown in northern Europe, although it probably had its origin in Mexico or tropical America. The Dutch Caseknife bean is a variety that has white flowers.

TEPARY BEAN (*Phaseolus acutifolius*): This is a small-seeded bush bean that has been adapted to the exacting climate of the southwestern states, where it produces large yields in comparison with other field beans. The pods are small and the seeds, about the size of the Navy bean, may be either white, brown, yellow, or even spotted. The cultivated varieties are the result of a breeding program by the Arizona Experiment Station on a wild variety of bean growing in the canyons of the southwestern states and in Mexico and possibly once generally cultivated by the American Indians. Tepary beans have the quality to withstand extremes of heat and drought. They will grow on a wide variety of soils, growing rather erect on poor soil and very bushy on the fertile soils with abundant moisture. The cultural practices are similar to those for the snap bean or the Navy bean. Tepary beans are used entirely as dry seed or shell beans.

SPECIES OF LESS IMPORTANCE: The following species of the genus *Phaseolus*, although all edible beans, are not grown in important quantities in the United States. They are included here only in the interests of the hobbyist, who may find that some of them, upon closer inspection, are only varieties of more common species: *P. aconitifolius Jacq.* or MOTH BEAN and *P. adenanthus*, both grown in India; *P. asellus, P. derassus*, and *P. pallar*, all grown in Chile; *P. calcaratus* or RICE BEAN, a pole bean grown in the Orient; *P. radiatus*, the ADSUKI BEAN, found in the Mississippi Valley; *P. retusus*, the PRAIRIE BEAN of Western America; and *P. triolobus* and *P. tuberosus*, both of China.

SOIL AND CLIMATIC REQUIREMENTS: Bush and pole beans are annuals and will grow in any locality where there is at least 50 days between spring and fall frosts, although they prefer warm days and bright sunshine. Some form of bean is suited to practically any climate prevailing in the

United States. The plant is very sensitive to cold and will freeze at the least sign of frost. Beans will grow on very poor soils, providing there is sufficient moisture. They grow on any well-limed and well-drained soil, including all types from the sands to the loams. They do not grow well on low-lying land where the moisture of the air is comparatively high. Under those conditions, there are a number of diseases which will kill the plants before they mature their pods. Furthermore, the night temperature may be so low on such soils that the growth will be stunted. Seeds of many varieties will decay in low ground.

Beans are considered soil-building crops and should not be fertilized with much nitrogen if the soil is at all fertile. If they get some nitrogen to start with, they will get the remainder from the air by means of bacteria which live in the nodules on the fine roots. By carefully digging up a plant, these nodules will be seen as knotty growths the size of large peas. If the plants are fertilized with nitrogen, they will not have these nodules on the roots, and the assumption is that they will get no nitrogen from the air. Sometimes it is necessary to inoculate the seeds with the bacteria before they are planted. They need an abundance of lime in the soil, so that the roots can function and forage throughout the soil. Under such conditions they will need very little fertilizer, particularly if the soil is well supplied with organic matter and has grown crops before.

Beans should be grown in such a manner that they will produce a moderately heavy vine-growth in order to get long tender pods. For

this reason, the snap beans are grown on slightly more fertile soil than the field beans. A good practice is to plant the beans in furrows and pour a starter or transplanting solution over them before they are covered with soil. This small amount of fertilizer very often is enough to mature the crop. Beans respond to water on particularly dry soil.

Pole beans will do much better on the heavier soils and will respond to more fertilizer. One or two side-applications of liquid fertilizer as the pods begin to set, and another when the first pods are picked, will greatly increase the yield.

Horticultural beans require more fertility than the snap beans. They do not grow as well in the southern states, because the high temperatures tend to blast the flowers. They do well in temperate sections where the soil is well-limed. These varieties have lost much favor among gardeners, because their lime requirements have not been recognized.

CULTURAL DIRECTIONS: Snap beans will mature in 50 to 60 days and will continue to yield pods for three weeks or more, depending on the growing season. The seed is sown in drills one inch deep and the plants should stand three inches apart in the row. The rows should be at least two feet apart. Where only two rows are grown, they may be placed closer and then worked from the outside. Light sandy soils cannot support as many plants in a given area as the heavy soils, and the seed must be planted deeper than in heavy soil. On loose sand, the seed may be planted two inches deep. Seeds will germinate two to three days earlier in the spring if soaked overnight before sown. Pouring transplanting solution over the seed before it is covered with soil will hasten its germination. Plantings should be made at weekly intervals or, if both the green-pod and wax varieties are to be grown, there is sufficient difference in time of maturity to warrant omission of the second planting of green beans. Successive plantings can be made until the first of August. This will insure a continuous bean crop until autumn frost. Plants should be kept picked, because if any of the pods mature the plant will die.

A half pound of seed will plant a 100-foot row; by making successive plantings, a 50-foot row will be enough for each planting. For a large family, more may be desired, but only if the garden is large, because a wider variety is better than too much of one thing.

Pole beans are planted in hills 18 inches to two feet apart, and the rows are usually three feet apart. A half dozen seeds are planted in the place around a pole and the seedlings are thinned to three to each pole. Pole beans require 65 to 70 days to mature and will continue to produce pods up to frost-time, providing the vines are kept growing and are free of bean beetles. Thus there is no need to make successive plantings, unless the first planting is made so early that there is danger of late frost catching the first seedlings. Three weeks can be gained by early planting, but it is a good safeguard to make plantings of seed at weekly intervals so that the last planting will definitely escape the latest frost. If they are not frozen, the extra seedlings can be pulled out. Pole beans require more attention than bush beans. The poles must be pro-vided, and the plants may have to be wrapped around the poles occasionally in windy weather.

Dwarf Horticultural beans were quite generally grown in the New England states at one time for their green shell-beans. Diseases and poor yields have gradually eliminated them from our markets and gardens, except in certain localities.

Weeding and cultivation is the same for all types of beans. Weeds should be kept from offering competition for water or plant nutrients. On the other hand cultivation should not be deep, as the root system of the bean plant is not too plentiful and, if the roots are torn off, there is not sufficient time to make more new roots. Any cultivator that is used should not go deeper than an inch. The only reason for cultivating is to kill weeds and these can be killed by merely scraping the surface of the soil. The idea of keeping a dust mulch to conserve moisture is an exploded theory. The plants should be close enough so that when they are full-grown they will cover the ground. During the spring while the plants are making their growth, there is usually enough moisture in the soil. A shove hoe with a sweep on it makes a fine cultivator for beans. Weeds not more than an inch tall can be knocked over with the back of the garden rake and the soil loosened enough to cover them. An hour thus spent with a rake is as good as three weeks of hoeing and cultivating after the weeds have grown to a height of six or more inches. Gardeners don't appreciate this and then complain what a terrible job it is to weed the garden. Remember that weeds will germinate more quickly than vegetable seeds; the time to kill them is when they are just coming through the ground.

Pole beans can be mulched to good advantage. They are planted far enough apart and occupy the ground long enough so that it is really worth while to place a mulch around the hills and between the rows before the weeds have started to grow. If weeds get a head start before the mulching material is applied, they will grow up through the mulch and it will take a lot of hand labor to get rid of them. Weeds, grass clippings, sawdust or dry hay or straw are suitable for the purpose of mulching.

INSECTS AND DISEASES: Diseases of beans are more or less prevalent according to weather conditions. Moist, foggy, or rainy weather brings on bean rust and anthracnose. These diseases are particularly bad if the plants are grown too close together or are grown too luxuriantly, as is the case on fertile soils that are well supplied with moisture. For this reason beans do better on the light sandy types of soil. A soil well supplied with calcium and magnesium, in other words with lime, will tend to prevent severe infestations of diseases. The bean rust is avoided by growing the rust-resistant varieties.

Insects are not serious, if the Mexican bean beetle is kept in control. This beetle is easy to kill and yet, if permitted to breed, will ruin a bean plant in a couple of days. The mature beetles come out of the ground early in the season, when the leaves are full size, and lay masses of yellow eggs on the undersides of the leaves. These hatch out into a woolly, orange-yellow larvae with black spots. They have a tremendous appetite and will soon eat up a leaf. As soon as they are seen, they should be dusted with a rotenone dust; they can also be killed with a calcium arsenate dust, but this should not be applied after the pods begin to form. Care should be taken to get the dust on the underside of the leaves. Unless the dust comes in contact with the larvae, it will do no good. It is advantageous to have a small hand duster for this purpose, since its curved spout will shoot the dust up under the leaves without requiring that one get under the leaves with the duster. Whenever small holes are seen in the leaves, the bean beetle should be looked for and the egg masses, if visible, can be picked off. This requires some patience but can be done during inspection of the plants.

GENERAL RECOMMENDATIONS: Beans grown for the edible pod should be harvested when the pods are well formed but before the bean-shape has produced bulges in the pod. If the pods are to be shelled, they should not be picked until the seed has reached its maximum size. When they are picked, preferably in the evening, they should be chilled to maintain their flavor and palatability. If allowed to stand in the sun, they will wilt and lose their freshness. If they are to be canned or frozen, they should be immediately placed in cold water and disposed of as soon as possible. Freezing or canning only preserves the flavor, but does not improve it. Poor quality when frozen will come out poor quality.

In small gardens, pole beans can be easily handled by running wires across the garden from several directions about seven feet from the ground. The beans are then trained up on strings attached to the wires. They may also be trained up on woven wire, if planted beside a building or hedge which offers some protection from wind. Pole beans can be made to serve a double purpose, if they can be grown over an arbor where they will produce shade as well as a crop of beans. An occasional Scarlet Runner bean among the other plants will make for attractiveness because of its long chains of scarlet flowers.

Beans do not transplant well, because they have a tap root which if once disturbed will not re-establish itself. However, it is possible to gain several weeks on a few beans by planting them in pots or veneer bands which will permit transfer to the garden without disturbing the roots. The plants may have three or four true leaves when transplanted. A bean plant will grow almost to the flowering stage without any fertilizer, because of the large amount of stored food in the large seeds.

Beets

DESCRIPTION: The garden beet (*Beta vulgaris, var, crassa*) is probably a native of the Eastern Mediterranean countries but it is grown generally all over the world. It is very hardy and one of our more popular vegetable crops. It is an herbaceous plant that produces a fleshy root the first year and the seed stalk the second year. In the northern states, however, the beet root must be harvested in the fall and stored until spring, if they are to be set out to produce seed. The seed is really a ball containing three to seven very small kidney-shaped seeds. The flowers, produced on a long, branched stalk,

are green in color and very inconspicuous. The home gardener is primarily interested in the fleshy root and the leaves.

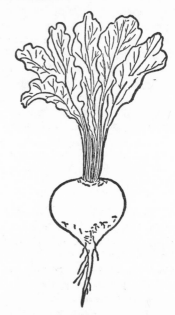

TYPES AND VARIETIES: There are three types of beets, but only one is particularly palatable for humans. Stock beets or MANGELS are too coarse for human food but produce a tremendous amount of feed for chickens in the subsistence garden. SUGAR BEETS, large and rather coarse in texture, contain 15 to 22 percent sugar and are the source of a large part of the sugar which we use on our tables. They may be grown for chickens in the small garden.

Garden beets are a small, red type, probably developed by selection from the large stock beet. There are two general sub-types: the long, tapering, turnip-rooted type and the short or ball type. A flat type is usually classed with the ball type. They vary somewhat in inside color. The ideal color is a full dark red with no white stripes. A few varieties of each are as follows:

Turnip-rooted type: Crosby's Egyptian, Winter Keeper.

Ball or Globe type: Red Ball, Detroit Dark Red.

Flat type: Early Wonder, Flat Egyptian.

SOIL AND CLIMATIC REQUIREMENTS: High quality beets are grown in cool climates where the air is not too dry. In high temperatures, they become woody and stringy when mature. In cool climates, they store large quantities of sugar, which can be detected when they are eaten raw.

Beets require very fertile soils that are well drained and well supplied with lime. They are very sensitive to toxic material in the soil. An abundance of lime tends to counteract the toxic elements. Hardwood ashes are particularly good when applied to beet ground, because they contain considerable potash and lime. The soil should be well limed to a depth of two feet for best results. The texture of the soil is not so important. The ground should be well fertilized with potash, or the beets will grow large tops but no fleshy taproots. Heavy soils, however, are not so likely to run short of potash. Lack of phosphorous or nitrogen will stunt the growth and produce a deep red color in the foliage, and too little boron in the soil may cause beets, when cooked, to show black spots throughout the tissue and have a bitter taste. A quarter of a teaspoon of borax in a twelve-quart pail of water, poured along the row in a stream the size of a lead pencil, will prevent this, if a similar precaution has been taken in previous years.

On well-manured ground there will be no trouble in growing beets. If chemical fertilizer is used, a 5–10–10 mixture should be spread over the ground at the rate of three pounds to 100 square feet of ground and spaded under. Side-dressings of liquid fertilizer will also grow good beets.

CULTURAL DIRECTIONS: Beet seed may be sown in flats about three or four weeks before the soil warms up in the spring. The seedlings can then be transplanted to the garden soil, one to two inches apart in the row. These will be ready to pick in five weeks. Alternate plants should be pulled first, to make room for the later plants. Seed may be sown in the open ground as soon as it can be worked. If the gardener has some means of grinding the balls that contain the beet seed without crushing the seed itself, he can save himself much labor of thinning the seedlings when they come up. Otherwise, there will be three or more seedlings in a place, and these must be thinned to a single seedling. Seed released from the balls can be planted at an even spacing of an inch apart. Even if the ground pulp is planted with the seed, there will be little need for thinning. If the small beets when a half inch in diameter are pulled for greens, enough plants can be removed to give the others a chance to grow freely. It is a good idea to make plantings every two weeks in order to have tender beets available throughout the summer. It requires from 55 to 65 days for beets to mature. Plantings may be made up to the middle of July and still be matured. If these suggestions are followed, only a short row need be planted at one time.

In order to be of high quality, beets

should be grown rapidly. If once slowed down in growth, they are apt to be woody. In dry weather, watering is necessary to maintain constant growth. They should be kept weeded. Radish seed sown with the beet seed will germinate before the weeds get started and the ground can be hoed even before the beets are up. A good practice, if the gardener will not neglect it, is to make a ridge an inch high above the seed and in ten days level it off with the back of the rake. This will save a tremendous amount of trouble in weeding the plants. If the ground is kept raked between the rows so that the ground always has a loose-soil covering, weeds will give very little trouble.

For pickling or canning, beets are pulled when about an inch to two inches in diameter. The smaller beets are more tender and it is often better to plant them thick enough so that they will not grow too large. For canning purposes, they are often planted in bands three or four inches wide, but in weedy ground this may give some trouble because of the hand labor needed to control the weeds.

DISEASES AND INSECTS: Diseases do not give much trouble if the ground is properly limed and fertilized. Insects may cause some trouble, especially if the beets are grown for greens. As the leaves get older, the beet-leaf miner may show its presence by burrowing through the leaf in an aimless fashion and leaving burrows which can be seen by holding the leaf to the sun. The small worm can itself be seen, unless the leaf is so old that the worm has pupated and left. These miners make the leaves unpalatable, but there is not much that can be done about them.

GENERAL RECOMMENDATIONS: Beets can be stored for the winter, and some people grow them late in the season and store them for winter use in addition to starting the summer crop early in the spring. They can be stored by digging just before the ground freezes, cutting off the tops a half inch from the beet, and covering the roots with dry sand. If a cool root cellar is available, they will keep in baskets or hampers without any protection. The tops can be cut up for chickens.

Sugar beets are not generally grown in the garden, but because of their value for chicken feed or for the family cow there is no reason why the person who has a glorified vegetable garden should not grow them. They are easily grown, like the mangel beet, and produce from 10 to 25 tons of roughage per acre, plus as many roots as can be accommodated in a limited storage space. They are planted in rows three feet apart and the plants are thinned to stand at least six inches apart. Sugar- and stock-beet crops should have a place on the subsistence farm where land is inexpensive and where the gardener wishes to get as large a part of his living as possible from the land. Both crops require a well-limed soil and will grow very well with the animal manure that would be available on such a farm.

Black Oyster Plant
See Scorzonera

Black Salsify
See Scorzonera

Broad Bean
Broad bean (*Vicia faba*), sometimes called FAVA or FABA BEAN, is a

vigorous bushy plant with large, flat, more or less angular seeds, square stems, and large, dull-white flowers with dark blue spots on the lips. It produces large thick pods which may grow to be 15 inches long. It grows much larger than the bush Lima bean, but matures earlier by several weeks, and does its best in the cooler, moister regions. It is more generally grown in northern Europe than in the United States, where it has not done so well, because of the hot summers and bad infestations of insects. It does particularly well in parts of Canada where the summers are cool but the growing season is long enough to mature the seeds. It is one of the oldest beans in cultivation, having been grown at least 5000 years ago by the Chinese, who still grow it for food and forage.

Broccoli

DESCRIPTION: Broccoli (*Brassica oleracea, var. italica*) is a member of the cabbage family and an annual

that produces flowers and seeds the same year. It produces bunches of flowering buds on the terminal stems as well as on branches which continue to be formed throughout the fall months. These buds are a great delicacy. Because of the high vitamin content, even the young leaves are eaten as well as the tender parts of the stem. Broccoli is probably the forerunner of cauliflower and was developed to its high degree of perfection by the Danish gardeners. The plants are coarse and grow to a height of four feet.

TYPES AND VARIETIES: Broccoli is the branching type of inflorescence and should not be confused with cauliflower which is not branching. It is referred to as Sprouting or Italian broccoli or as CALABRESE. It matures in 80 days and will continue to produce buds for a month or more. Two varieties generally grown are Calabrese and Propageno.

SOIL AND CLIMATIC REQUIREMENTS: Broccoli does better in cool weather, particularly cool nights, after the heads begin to form. It is usually grown as a fall crop, following an early crop of spinach or snap beans. The plants are grown during late summer and the heads are harvested from October to late November or until the ground freezes. They are very hardy and will stand light freezes. They require a very fertile soil that supplies an abundance of water but is well-drained, contains a large amount of organic matter, and is well supplied and sweetened with lime. On the light sandy soils, the crop may be grown with a good layer of mulching material. The soil should be well supplied with manure or chemical nutrients. Growers usually apply a ton of 5–10–10 fertilizer per acre and plow it under. The gardener will find that if the plants are set with a starter solution and given two or three feedings of liquid fertilizer they probably will get all the nutrients that they need. The side-dressings should be made before the buds are ready to be harvested.

CULTURAL DIRECTIONS: Broccoli seed can be sown indoors in the northern states and transplanted to the garden as soon as the ground can be worked. The larger seedlings will probably be ready to cut by the middle of July. They do not do so well in hot summer temperatures unless they receive considerable water. Generally seed can be planted for the late crop any time up to the first of July. The plants grow large and should be planted at least 2 feet apart in rows which should be 3 feet apart. The ground should be kept clean of weeds but not deeply cultivated.

INSECTS AND DISEASES: Broccoli is subject to the same diseases that are common to other members of the cabbage family. In acid or poorly limed soils, the plants may be affected by club root, which deforms the roots and prevents proper feeding. Blackleg also affects the stems and kills the plants. There are a number of remedies suggested for the commercial grower, but they are usually too much trouble for the small gardener. He should have a few extra plants to replace those he loses. By having the soil well-limed and moving the location of the eight or ten plants every year, he will probably have very little trouble. Insects will prove troublesome. The plants should be dusted with a rotenone dust to kill the cabbage worm which will eat the leaves. Plant lice or aphids may cause trouble in cool weather. If they are seen early, they can be sprayed with Black Leaf 40. Otherwise they may have to be cut out, as they are apt to congregate on a few plants. If they get into the heads, it is almost impossible to reach them with a spray or dust. In that case, they can be cleaned off by placing the heads in salt water after they are cut. The heads should be cut into small pieces and dropped into a fairly strong salt solution for a short time; the aphids will leave the stems and float on the top of the water where they can be poured off as the broccoli is drained. Usually a few rinsings of water will remove the excess salt. A small amount of salt will improve the flavor of the broccoli.

GENERAL RECOMMENDATIONS: Broccoli is an excellent vegetable that is becoming more popular every year. It has a very high food value and, if the gardener has not tried it, he should set out a few plants at his earliest opportunity. When the stems and buds are cooked, they become tender in a few minutes. Most people will cook it too much and the heads will fall apart and much of its flavor be lost. It is usually served with melted butter. It is readily accessible on our markets but much of it is not fresh when we get it. It is quite perishable and should be eaten directly from the garden to be appreciated. When harvested, it should not be left where it will get too warm. It is better to cut it near mealtime or else chill it in the refrigerator. Broccoli is being canned and much of it is being preserved by the quick-freeze method. The frozen product, if fresh when frozen, is almost as good as that which is used directly from the garden. The tender leaves are sometimes canned separately and are widely used in animal-food preparations because of their high vitamin content. Broccoli cannot be stored like some of the other members of the cabbage family, unless the gardener is equipped to freeze it with his own equipment.

Brussels Sprouts

DESCRIPTION: Brussels sprouts (*Brassica oleracea, var. gemmifera*), another member of the cabbage family, is grown for its miniature buds, produced in the axils of the leaves. It is a biennial and is grown in some

sections of the United States. It is one of the older types of vegetables, having been grown in this country for a century and in Europe probably several hundred years. It is a tall, erect, non-branching plant with rather large, long, slender, and ruffled leaves. The buds are one to two inches across.

TYPES AND VARIETIES: There are two varieties generally grown: the Danish and the Long Island Improved.

SOIL AND CLIMATIC REQUIREMENTS: It is a cool-season crop and develops best as a fall crop. It requires a fairly heavy well-drained soil that is well limed and contains considerable organic matter. It does best with a good supply of moisture; the commercial crop is often grown on the lower-lying soils. Animal manures are excellent fertilizer for the crop, which does not grow well on the sandy soils unless it has a dense subsoil.

CULTURAL DIRECTIONS: The seed should be sown in the open ground about June first. When the seedlings are three inches high, they should be transplanted to rows three feet apart and at least two feet apart in the row. Four or five plants will probably produce enough sprouts for the average family unless it has an exceptional liking for the vegetable. The plants are fairly hardy and the flavor of the sprouts is improved by a light freeze. They respond to the same fertilizer treatment that other members of the cabbage family do. Insects and diseases are controlled as for broccoli (which see).

SPECIAL RECOMMENDATIONS: The lower leaves should be removed from the stem as the sprouts begin to mature. Maturity is reached in 120 days.

Bur Gherkin
See Cucumber; Gourds

Butter Leaves
See Orach

Cabbage

DESCRIPTION: The common heading cabbage (*Brassica oleracea, var. capitata Linn.*) produces a round, pointed, or flat head the first year and a seedstalk the second year. It is probably the most popular member of the cabbage family, being grown in all parts of the world. The wild form of cabbage probably was known to ancient peoples a long time before Christ, although it is not definitely known whether the cabbage mentioned in ancient times was the heading type or the wild form having only a head of loose leaves. Its greatest development probably took place in Europe. The stem is short and terminates in a large bud, which is the edible portion of the plant. This bud or head may weigh anywhere from 2 to 50 pounds, depending on the type and variety.

Cabbage is a popular vegetable because it can be used as well in the raw state as in the preserved or cooked state and because it is high in minerals and vitamins. Its outer leaves are generally green, while the inner leaves are white. The vitamins are more abundant in the green leaves. It has a mild flavor, probably enjoyed by more people than that of any other vegetable. It is also an ideal food for animals, and people who have a flock of chickens find it an ideal green food for winter feeding.

TYPES AND VARIETIES: Cabbage is divided into early or late, smooth- or crinkly-leaved, green or purple, and conical-, round-, or flat-headed varieties, in various combinations, as follows:
Early, Smooth, Green Varieties
    Conical heads: Jersey Wakefield; Yellows Resistant.
    Round heads: Copenhagen; Golden Acre.
    Flat Heads: Improved Allhead (not very early); Early Flat Dutch.

Late, Smooth, Green Varieties
    Conical heads: Charleston Wakefield (not very early, for no truly late conical heads exist).

FLAT DUTCH CABBAGE

    Round heads: Danish Ballhead; Succession.
    Flat heads: Late Flat Dutch; Wisconsin Hollander.
Crinkly Varieties (all green and all flat-headed)
    Early: Cornell Early Savoy.
    Late: Perfection Drumhead Savoy.

SAVOY CABBAGE

Purple Varieties (all smooth and all round-headed)
    Late: Danish Round Red; Mammoth Red Rock.

The early varieties require about 65 or 70 days to form a head, while the latest varieties require 120 days. There are varieties that mature in between, often referred to as midseason varieties, and a large number of other varieties; but they are mostly selections in the above groups.

SOIL AND CLIMATIC REQUIREMENTS: Because of its leafy growth and peculiar formation, cabbage requires a cool moist climate with an abundance of sunlight. It wants a soil that is fertile and that will supply a good amount of moisture. Cabbage does well on the heavier types of soil that have a high water table but are well drained at the surface. It will not grow in swampy ground. It requires an abundance of organic matter in the soil and animal manures are an ideal source of fertilizer. Even sandy soils, if well manured and supplied with organic matter, will grow cabbage. The round-headed early varieties, which make small heads, are best grown on the sandy soils. They are also the varieties that should be grown in the early spring. Cabbage is very hardy and will withstand rather severe freezes, although it should not be left in the ground until the ground freezes. Since cabbage can be grown in practically any climate that has three months of summer, it is adapted to all sections of the United States.

CULTURAL DIRECTIONS: Cabbage seed should be planted in good soil in a flower pot during the latter part of February, or about four weeks before the plants can be safely set in the garden. When the seedlings come up, they can be set in separate pots so that transplanting to the garden will not disturb the roots. However, cabbage seedlings can be transplanted rather easily, as the plants make new roots immediately. It is probably better to decide on a single variety for the spring planting and make about three plantings of that, rather than to plant simultaneously several varieties that mature at different times. One packet of seed will plant all that is needed. As soon as the ground can be worked, a planting should be made in the open ground. About July first, a planting of a late large-heading variety should be made for winter storage. Sometimes people of a community cooperate, and one person will grow enough plants for several of the neighbors. This simplifies the planting and saves seed during times when it may be scarce. If cooked cabbage is an acceptable dish, a few plants of red cabbage should be set. The Savoy type should be included for salad purposes. It is particularly good for cole slaw and is highly nutritious. The heads should be used as soon as they begin to get firm, because the early varieties do not hold up long after they are once formed, probably because the temperature is high when the heads mature. In the cool weather of fall, heads will remain firm for several weeks.

The plants are set two feet apart in the row and the rows should be at least three feet apart. An ideal place for cabbage is some corner of the garden where the ground has been spaded in the fall and has had a chance to freeze and settle down. When the plants are set in the garden, the ground around the roots should be saturated with liquid fertilizer. The soil should not be packed around the roots but simply filled in around the plant. The liquid causes the soil gradually to fill in around the roots. Any packing that is done when the soil is wet will puddle it and prevent the plants from getting started. They should be given several side-dressings with liquid fertilizer during the growing season. If the soil gets extremely dry, it should be thoroughly soaked once a week. It should not be lightly sprinkled. The ground must be wet to a depth of six inches. Sprinkling lightly every evening does more damage than good. If the soil has enough lime, the roots will have gone down three feet or more and probably will get moisture from deep in the subsoil. Cabbage should be cleanly cultivated, but the roots should not be disturbed in killing the weeds.

INSECTS AND DISEASES: Cabbage has several bad insects and diseases. The cabbage maggot is the larva of a small black fly that lays its eggs on the stem just above the surface of the ground. The eggs hatch in five or six days and the maggots crawl down the stem and feed on the tap root just below the surface. They will kill the plant in a short time. By careful looking two or three days after the plants are set, the eggs may be discovered. If they are rubbed off, no other control measures need be resorted to, and for a half dozen plants this is a practical method. Another method is to fit a small piece of tar paper around the stem at the base in order to discourage the flies from laying eggs. Summer plantings are not bothered by the maggots.

The green cabbage worm is the larva of the white butterfly and feeds on the leaves of the cabbage. The eggs are laid at the base of the leaves. The worms are not noticeable when first hatched and will probably have done much damage before they are first seen. Their presence is first evidenced by small round holes eaten into the leaf. They are very easy to kill by dusting with a rotenone dust —an insect poison harmless to animals and humans. The cabbage looper also is a green worm that feeds on the leaves. It gets its name from the manner in which it loops up its back as it crawls. It can be controlled by the same dust.

Cabbage aphids or plant lice make their appearance in cool weather and disappear in hot weather. They are a serious pest and may be so plentiful as to stunt the leaves and growing points. They should be killed by spraying the young leaves and growing tips with a solution of Black Leaf No. 40 or Nicotine Sulphate during the heat of the day, and an attempt should be made to clean the plants before they start to make a head. Sometimes a fine, forceful spray from the hose will discourage them sufficiently to make the pest negligible.

In the southern states, the Harlequin cabbage bug often becomes a bad pest. It sucks the juices from the plant tissue and in so doing injects a poison that will stunt the growth of the plant. The bugs are hard to kill, and for a few plants it is practical to pick them off. The rotenone dust used for cabbage worms will get some of them. They should be considered when the garden is spaded, and all rubbish and leaves should be cleaned up in order to give the bugs no place to hibernate.

There are a number of diseases that may cause considerable damage, but no special treatment is available to the small gardener for combatting them. Club root occurs in acid soil and is held in check by keeping an abundance of limestone in the soil. Blackleg is a rot that works in the stem and will kill the plants. This can be detected when the plants are set in the soil, particularly if they have been grown in individual pots, by the black and somewhat shrunken appearance of the stems. They should not be planted if blackleg is present.

GENERAL RECOMMENDATIONS: If cabbage is to be stored, it should be' cut so that most of the stem is left on the head. The injured leaves should be removed and the whole head placed in a large paper bag. The cabbage may then be placed in a cold cellar and, if possible, hung from the ceiling, stem up. The heads can, of course, be wrapped in waxed paper and placed on shelves, but they should not be piled one upon the other. Cabbages may also be placed in trenches out of doors. The whole plants should be pulled up and the roots set in loose soil in the bottom of the trench. Enough straw should be packed over the tops of the heads to prevent freezing, and the straw should be covered with boards so that water will be shed.

People who like sauerkraut make it in the early fall, when the cabbage is harvested. A ten- or twenty-gallon keg or crock is provided and the cabbage is cut into fine shreds and packed into the crock. There are special kraut cutters for this purpose. Two inches of cabbage is shredded into the crock and covered with a handful of salt. This is continued until the crock is filled. A heavy plunger should be available to stomp the cabbage until the juice comes above the shredded leaves. A circular board that fits freely inside the crock is then heavily weighted upon the

kraut to keep the cabbage pressed below the level of the juice. The cabbage is permitted to ferment in a warm place for a month or more, and is then stored in a cool cellar. The kraut may be used directly from the crock as long as it is kept immersed in its own liquid. Needless to say, the greatest cleanliness should be observed to obtain the best quality. Any molds which start a growth around the board or the top of the crock should be washed off. The kraut is preserved by the acidity built up by its own fermentation, and the flavor is better than can be obtained in a can.

Calabrese

See Broccoli

Cantaloupe

See under Melons

Cardoon

DESCRIPTION: Cardoon (*Cynara cardunculus*) is a perennial plant similar to the Globe artichoke and is grown for its fleshy leaves. It is a native of the Mediterranean and is generally grown in Europe for its bleached leafstalks, which are used in salads, or for winter use as a boiled vegetable. Cardoon is grown to some extent in our southern states and is often seen in our northern markets packed in yard-long boxes to accommodate the long leafstalks. Although the plants are not hardy in the northern states, the plants may be grown there as annuals. The seed is sown where the plants are to be grown, as soon as the ground is warm and danger of frost is past. The hills in which the seed is sown should be two feet apart and the seedlings thinned to one in a hill. They require a good soil and should receive water if the soil gets exceptionally dry. The leafstalks become pithy with lack of water. About the middle of September, the leaves are tied together and wrapped with a tough paper to bleach the leaves, or, if the leaves are not too

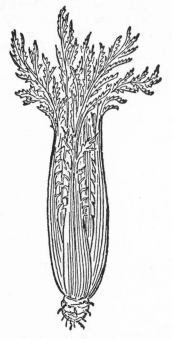

long, soil may be heaped around the plants in a manner similar to that used for bleaching celery (which see). So protected, the plants will not suffer from frost and can be harvested rather late in the season. It requires at least a month to bleach the leaves. If the plants are dug and set in a pit for protection against freezing weather, they can be removed as needed long into early winter. The best quality for salad purposes probably will be obtained where the leaves can be harvested directly from the garden. In the southern states, where the plants will live over as a perennial, the leaves are much fleshier and longer and they must be harvested in the field, for the old roots must stay in the ground for succeeding crops.

Carrot

DESCRIPTION: Carrots (*Daucus carota, var. sativa*) are among the most popular and nutritious vegetables grown. The smaller and earlier types, which are of high quality, are grown for human consumption, while the large-rooted late varieties are grown for stock feed. The carrot, as we know it, is supposed to have originated from the wild carrot, often called QUEEN ANNE'S LACE—one of the worst weeds we have to contend with, particularly in abandoned meadow land. In cultivated ground it does not give so much trouble. Since the wild carrot and the cultivated form will cross if grown near to one another, carrot seed must be produced in areas where the wild carrot does not grow. Roots produced from seed developed where cross-fertilization has been possible will show a certain number of the characteristic white roots of the wild carrot, which are of little value for food.

TYPES AND VARIETIES: The varieties of carrots may be grouped into six rather distinct types according to shape and size of the root:

The French Forcing or Earliest Short Horn type is the smallest and earliest carrot that is grown. The root is almost as thick as it is long, has a golden, orange-red color, and matures in 60 to 68 days. The mature root is not much larger than a good sized plum. This is a good garden variety of high quality and particularly suited where the surface soil is shallow.

The Oxheart type, of orange-red color, is a third longer than it is broad and tapers gradually toward the tip. It matures in 70 to 80 days. The small-to-medium-sized roots, approximating three inches in length, are good for bunch carrots but better suited as cut carrots for storing.

The Chantenay type is probably the most important for the canning industry and as a bushel carrot for storage. It has better quality than the Oxheart type. At one time it was the principal carrot used for bunching but is gradually being replaced by the longer varieties. The 4-inch root is

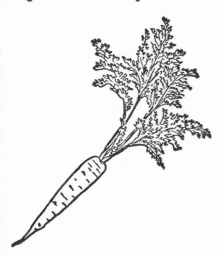

about two and a half times as long as it is broad and tapers gradually to a blunt tip. Like the types described above, the Chantenay is better suited to the shallow soils with a gravelly subsoil than are the long varieties. It requires approximately 78 days to mature but may be pulled ten days earlier.

The Danvers Half Long is just what its name implies. It is not so thick as the Chantenay and grows to

about seven inches in length, or about two thirds the length of the True Danvers type which has given way to other long slender types. The Danvers Half Long has been a very popular type in the New England areas, where it was grown for bunch as well as bushel carrots. It tapers gradually to a rather sharp point, in contrast to the Chantenay type. Carrots of higher quality are taking its place where the soil is deep enough to grow a long straight root. It requires 75 to 80 days to mature.

The Nantes is a half-long type and probably should be included in the Danvers group, but because of its characteristic shape and particularly high quality deserves special consideration. It is an ideal bunching carrot and is quite generally grown in the midwestern states in the market-gardening sections. It grows to a length of 8 inches and is cylindrical in shape, being almost as broad near the tip as it is at the butt end. It is much higher in sugar-content than some of the other varieties. It requires 70 days to mature and has rather an inconspicuous core. The color is orange-red.

The long slender type is represented by such varieties as Hutchinson, Morses Bunching, Imperator, and Streamliner. These carrots average 11 inches long and are of particularly high quality. When mature, the roots are orange-red in color. If pulled when half grown, they are apt to be light in color, particularly in heavy soil or soil that lacks calcium and potash. These varieties should never be grown in a shallow soil. They require a deep soil that is well limed and sufficiently open to offer no obstruction to the down-growth of the slender, slightly tapering roots. They should not be grown in rocky or gravelly soil. If the root does not make a free growth, it turns to one side, and a bunch of crooked long carrots is less attractive than a bunch of short stubby ones. Many soils have a dense subsoil, and growers who have tried these long varieties on such soils have been disappointed. Most of the carrots grown for market on the West Coast are varieties of this group. They require 85 to 95 days to mature.

For the small garden, the Nantes type is probably the best suited, because it is a medium-long root that has high quality and matures almost as quickly as the earliest types. For the farm or subsistence garden, where carrots are also to be used for chickens, rabbits, or other animals, a larger type, such as the Hutchinson, might be better, because it combines high quality with ample yields and can be eaten both by humans and by animals. For strictly animal-feeding purposes, some of the coarser varieties will yield more per square foot. There is a large, White Belgian variety that has been grown for animal feed, but because vitamin-content is associated with yellow coloring the orange varieties are now more generally grown.

SOIL AND CLIMATIC REQUIREMENTS: Carrots are a fairly hardy plant, adaptable to both the warmer and the cooler sections of the United States. They will withstand light freezes but not severe ones. They like a sandy loam soil that is well limed and sufficiently open for the taproot to grow straight down without interference. The soil should be well supplied with organic matter, preferably well-rotted material or leaf mold. If there is danger of the surface packing after a rain, a covering of grass clippings or other finely chopped material should be scattered over the row. Usually a well-limed soil does not require this special treatment. If the soil is fertile, a single side-dressing of liquid fertilizer will satisfy the needs of the plants; otherwise two side-dressings may be needed.

CULTURAL DIRECTIONS: Seed may be sown in the spring as soon as the ground can be worked and any time thereafter up to the first of August. If seed is sown in the cold of early spring it will help a great deal to plant the carrots on the south side of a windbreak or to place a board on edge along the row in a way that will catch the direct heat of the sun but prevent the west and north winds from reaching and chilling the ground. This will hasten germination, which may otherwise require two weeks, and will shorten by ten days the time required to mature the carrots. Hot-weather plantings require contrary precautions: the seed should not be watered after sowing, so that the surface of the soil will remain rough and loose and act as a protection from the heat, otherwise the seed may not germinate or, having germinated, may burn off. Any finely-divided material scattered over the rows of seed will be added protection against the sun. Gardeners need have no fear that seeds planted in a dry soil will not germinate. If the seed bed has been prepared ahead of time to give the soil a chance to pack and if water or a transplanting solution is poured directly on the seed before it is covered with soil, the seed will germinate quickly without water application to the surface and will give a good stand even in dry periods.

When the seedlings are up, they

should be thinned to 12 plants to the foot of row. The rows should be 15 to 18 inches apart. It is possible to plant carrot seed in a band 2 inches wide if the soil is not too weedy. In this case, the seedlings are thinned to stand an inch apart in each direction. As they begin to attain sufficient size for use, those in the center are removed first, so that the remaining ones will have more room to grow. If carrot seedlings are not thinned, the roots will twist around each other and the carrots will be thin and crooked.

To grow good carrots requires careful treatment. The seed germinates slowly and the seedlings are a long time in becoming established to the point where they can meet competition from weeds. For this reason the seedlings must be weeded when they are quite small. This is made difficult by the fact that the seedlings have a very fine foliage and are easily pulled out when weeds are pulled. If the gardener is careful he can save himself much trouble by following a method which commercial growers often use. They cover the rows of planted seed with an inch of soil to form a small ridge along each row, and about a week after the planting —about the time the seed is just beginning to show a tiny sprout—the ridge is leveled off so that the seed has less than half an inch of soil above it. The process of leveling the ridge will disturb the weed seeds which have germinated—usually the types that give most trouble—and the sprouts will be killed. It is also a good practice to mix early radish seed with the carrot seed, which should be sown thinly in any event. The radish seed will germinate in a few days so that the rows can be seen and

carefully cultivated at the earliest moment. The radishes should be pulled out when they begin to crowd the carrots, but they are usually mature and ready for use before they interfere with the carrot seedlings.

Three plantings during the spring and early summer will assure carrots for the entire season. The last plantings can be harvested as bushel carrots for storage.

DISEASES AND INSECTS: If the soil has been properly limed, there are no diseases of carrots that need concern the small gardener. If the location of the row is shifted so that carrots are grown in the same place only one year out of five, there is little danger of the soil's becoming infested with any soil-borne diseases. The carrot rust fly lays eggs at the base of the leaves. When the eggs hatch out the larvae work into the crowns of the roots. This makes the root worthless for food and causes the older leaves to show a brown rusty appearance. The rust fly is particularly bad on carrots up to June first. If no carrots are planted until after that date there will be no trouble from this pest. One method of control is to cover the seedlings with cheesecloth or mosquito netting. Or crude, flaky naphthalene may be scattered among seedlings to act as a repellent to the flies.

GENERAL RECOMMENDATIONS: Carrots for storage should be dug before the ground freezes, and the tops cut off to within a half inch of the crown. The good firm roots which are free of worms may be stored in a cool place by covering with dry sand, or placed in a storage cellar and covered with paper. They should have some protection if the air is dry. Carrots for animals should be stored in pits and covered.

It must be kept in mind that anything that injures the fine taproot of the seedling will cause the carrot to branch, so that the mature carrot will have two to four points. Though these may be just as good for eating, they are difficult to clean and prepare for the table. There is so much waste to preparing poorly shaped carrots that a person might better buy the highest quality even at double the price. If carrots are to be grown in the garden, they should be well cared for, because poorly formed carrots are no asset. They may not be worth pulling.

Carrots should be grown in every garden unless they can be bought regularly at the local store. They are not as perishable as some of the other vegetables and will preserve their nutritive value even under rather adverse conditions. If they can be kept from wilting, they will maintain their palatability. Carrots shipped from the West Coast to New York arrive in almost as good condition as when they are pulled, because they are packed in ice. Any of our root vegetables are a storage organ by means of which the variety is carried over from one year to the next. The carrot produces the storage root the first year and the seed stalk the second year. The roots contain some inhibitory material which tends to keep their store of starches and sugars from breaking down for at least two months. Thus, there has not been a need to can carrots or preserve them by other methods, as is the case with asparagus, spinach, and other highly perishable products. Some carrots are canned, but they go to special areas where the fresh carrots cannot be shipped.

Casaba
See under Melons: Honeydew

Cassabanana

DESCRIPTION: Cassabanana (*Sicana odorifera*), sometimes called CURUBA, is a member of the cucumber family. It is a fast-growing tropical vine that can be grown in a long season by starting the plants indoors. Sup-

posedly, this plant is a native of South America and can be grown in our southern states. The flowers are as large as the cucumber, yellow in color, and the plants have large leaves. The fruits are long and cylindrical and orange-yellow in color. They have a strong, fragrant, aromatic odor and are edible, although generally grown as a curiosity.

TYPES AND VARIETIES: None available at the present time.

SOIL AND CLIMATIC REQUIREMENTS: Long season with comparatively warm weather and dry air. The soil should be well-drained sandy loam, with a good supply of lime.

CULTURAL DIRECTIONS: The seed should be sown in four-inch flower pots a month before it is intended to set them in the garden soil. They should be watered with a transplanting solution before they are to be set in the garden, and the roots should not be disturbed in transplanting. In localities where no more than 120 days of warm weather can be depended on, the plants should be set on the south side of a building, where they will be protected from cold winds and the vines can be provided with wire or string for climbing.

INSECTS AND DISEASES: The main insect trouble will be the red spider, which is a rather difficult pest to control. If, on occasion, the vines can be thoroughly syringed on the undersides of the leaves, the pest can be checked. The main disease will be mildew, usually due to poor circulation of air.

GENERAL SUGGESTIONS: This is an interesting plant for the oddity garden, having at the same time some value as food and ornament. Seeds may be obtained by inquiring at the Florida Experiment Station at Gainesville, Florida.

Cauliflower

DESCRIPTION: Cauliflower (*Brassica oleracea, var. botrytis*), a member of the cabbage family, is prized for its broad, curd-like, white or purple flower-heads of closely packed buds. The head is produced on a short stalk, after the plant has made a rosette of leaves with some elongation of the stem. The leaves are long and slender very much like the Calabrese broccoli (see Broccoli), which the plant resembles.

TYPES AND VARIETIES: There are two general types, the white short-

season type and the purple long-season type, often referred to as cauliflower broccoli. Among the early varieties of white cauliflower may be

mentioned the Snowball, of which one selection which matures in 82 days is available, and the Dwarf Erfurt. Late white varieties are Dry Weather and Vietches Autumn Giant, which require 95 and 130 days to mature. The cauliflower broccoli, of which St. Valentine is one variety, requires 150 days to mature. There are other local varieties, mainly of the white-headed types, for the purple varieties are not popular and will not be found listed by seedsmen.

SOIL AND CLIMATIC REQUIREMENTS: Cauliflower requires an even more fertile soil than cabbage—a soil well supplied with nutrients, organic matter, and lime. The soil should have an ample supply of moisture and, if it dries out, should be thoroughly soaked to keep the plants growing rapidly. It is easy to stunt cauliflower and poor cauliflower is not worth bothering with. Climatic requirements are very exacting. Cauliflower requires a cool, moist climate. It is not as hardy as cabbage but will withstand considerable freezing in the fall when the heads are maturing. In the spring, a bad frost may cause the plants to head prematurely and stop growing. If this happens, the plants should be pulled out.

CULTURAL DIRECTIONS: Cauliflower plants should be started in late February by sowing the seed in a four-inch pot and transplanting them when two inches high to individual pots, so that they can be transferred to the garden soil with as little disturbance to the roots as possible. While the plants are growing in the pots, they should be watered with a transplanting solution. The plants should be set in the garden, as soon as all danger of frost is past. A quart of transplanting solution should be poured around the ball of pot soil before the garden soil is firmed around the roots. Weeds should be carefully hoed away from the plants without disturbing the roots more than necessary. Disturbing the roots in weeding will cause an uneven growth and make the heads fuzzy in appearance. A number of other abnormalities may be caused in cauliflower if the proper conditions of growth are not maintained. An insufficient supply of nitrogen may cause spoilage of the plant by producing immature heading; any indication of the plant to form a flower-bud early should be the signal to pull it out. Deformity of the leaves before the heads are formed is often caused by a lack of lime or an acid soil; the soil should be kept sweet. Alternate drying and watering will cause the heads to open up and become ricey in appearance. The incidence of small leaves among the curds is due to the unevenness of the growing condi-

tions. Mulching the plants early, so as to maintain a fairly uniform temperature and moisture condition around the roots, will result in perfect heads.

When the heads are full grown, or nearly so, the outer leaves should be pulled up over the top, so that the heads are shaded from the sun. This will bleach the heads to snowy white —a quality highly desired in cauliflower. Or the heads may be shaded with cheesecloth or with paper, but the green leaves should not be shaded in the process. It requires from a week, in the summertime, to three weeks, in the fall, properly to bleach the heads. It may be a good thing, in the garden, to start shading when the heads are half grown, so that they may be used over a longer period. The heads, once matured, do not last long, when the temperatures are high. In the fall, however, the crop grows much slower as the heads are forming and so can be harvested over a period of a month. During the harvest season, cauliflower will resist rather severe freezes. Cauliflower can be stored for a month in a temperature around 35 degrees. Some growers have found that the plants could be successfully stored for several months after the fall growing season, if the roots were lifted with the plants and set in a loose soil in easily accessible pits. A similar idea has proved successful in salvaging plants which fail to head in the garden before the onset of cold weather. By removing the plants with a spadeful of garden soil surrounding the roots of each, setting them close together in a cold frame, soaking the ground around the roots with water, and covering the frame with glass during low temperatures, the gardener may keep the plants growing until he reaps a reward of good-sized heads.

People who complain about growing cauliflower in hot weather will find that any good mulching material with a good soaking of water will make it possible to grow the plants all summer. Successive plantings of the early variety will ensure a continuous crop of cauliflower throughout the whole season; some people, however, seem to think the crop is seasonal and do not care for it until the weather gets cool in the fall.

In the warmer climates the cauliflower-broccoli varieties, which are more resistant to the hot, dry weather, are better suited. They require 150 days to mature, which brings the heading stage well into the cool season. They make a very large plant and a large head.

Cauliflower plants make a heavy growth and should be spaced wider than cabbage (which see) for the fall crop. The early short-season varieties are spaced the same as cabbage.

DISEASES AND INSECTS: Insect pests are the same as for cabbage (which see) and should be controlled in a similar manner. Since they do most of their damage to the leaves before the heads form, it is important to keep the leaves cleaned off during that stage of growth. Aphids, especially, should be cleaned out before heads are formed, because if they once get into the well-knit flower heads, it is impossible to get rid of them.

Besides the diseases mentioned under cabbage, a condition caused by boron deficiency should be mentioned. The heads sometimes show brown spots in the white curd. This is caused by the depth of the stem-

tissue which supplies the curd with water and is due to a lack of boron in the soil. If only chemical plant foods which contain no boron are used, this disease is much more likely to occur than if manure is used as a source of fertilizer. A half teaspoon of borax dissolved in 12 quarts of water and sprinkled around the plants will prevent the disease from recurring.

SPECIAL RECOMMENDATIONS: Unless the soil in the garden is naturally deep and fertile, it may be difficult to grow cauliflower satisfactorily. Filled-in soil is not so good, because it is apt to be quite acid to a considerable depth and difficult to correct with lime. It can, of course, be corrected by digging a trench 2 feet wide and 2 feet deep, sprinkling the bottom of this trench with lime and superphosphate at the rate of one pound of pulverized magnesium limestone and a quarter-pound of superphosphate to five running feet, spading this into the soil and covering it to a depth of one foot with the removed soil, applying and mixing a similar amount of limestone and superphosphate with this foot of covering soil, and finally returning and treating the remainder of the soil in similar fashion, except that only half the former quantity of limestone should be mixed into the surface layer of soil. This makes an excellent place to set cauliflower.

Cayenne Pepper
See Peppers

Celeriac
DESCRIPTION: Celeriac (*Apium graveolens, Linn., var. rapaceum*),

though closely related to celery, has an enlarged root-crown instead of the celery's thickened leafstalks. It is used somewhat as the turnip is, although the flavor is celery-like, and is greatly

prized for soups. The thickened root may also be used for salads. This vegetable is grown more widely in Europe than in America, but has probably been in cultivation as long as celery.

The seed is sown in the hotbed or greenhouse very early in the spring, so that plants can be transplanted to the garden as soon as the ground is warm enough to be worked. The seed is slow to germinate but can be planted in the open for a late crop. When the plants are three to four inches tall, they may be transplanted. They should be set with a transplanting solution 6 to 8 inches apart in rows 2 feet apart. The soil should be fertile, well-limed, and heavier than for most vegetable crops. Celeriac

grows better in the deep loam soils which have a good capacity for water but at the same time are well drained. The plants do not need as much attention as celery, since bleaching is not necessary. As the root starts to enlarge, the crown may be helped to better development and higher quality by removing the fine roots and the soil attached to them. Many lateral roots close to the top of crown tend to make the fleshy part coarse and irregular. When freezing weather occurs, the plants may be lifted and stored in pits with protection over the top, or they may be stored in moist sand in the basement where the temperature is low. Because it is much easier to grow, it has a place in the small garden where celery cannot be grown.

Celery

DESCRIPTION: Celery (*Apium graveolens*), occasionally called Ache and Smallage by Europeans, is grown for its edible leafstalks, which are fleshy and tender and have a nut-like flavor when blanched. Although the green, unblanched celery has a slightly bitter flavor, it is becoming more popular every year. Much of the selection of the cultivated varieties probably was made during the 15th century from a wild, bitter, south European plant once used as a medicine and as an herb for flavoring purposes. In its wild state, celery is a marsh plant with hollow stalks, but the cultivated varieties have been developed for the firmness of the leafstalks. It is one of the most important salad plants grown in the United States, and most of it is eaten raw.

TYPES AND VARIETIES: Celery varieties are grouped into two types, the yellow and the green. The yellow or self-blanching type is represented by Golden or White Plume, which matures in 112 to 115 days, and by Easy

Blanching, which matures in 125 days. The green type is represented by Golden Crisp and Giant Pascal which mature late, requiring 135 days. The easy-blanching types require about a week to turn white, while the Giant Pascal type may require more than a week.

SOIL AND CLIMATIC REQUIREMENTS: Celery is a cool-weather crop which can withstand considerable frost. Sometimes it is not harvested until the surface of the ground has actually frozen. It can be grown in practically all parts of the United States during some part of the year. In the southern states, it is grown during the winter as a spring crop; in the northern states, during the summer as a fall crop.

Celery grows particularly well on muck or marsh lands that have been drained and aerated. Most of the celery produced in the United States is grown on this kind of soil. The soil should be well limed and contain an abundant supply of such nutrients as phosphoric acid and potash. Magnesium-deficiency is quite common on old muck soils which have not been artificially supplied with magnesium limestone, although they usually supply enough nitrogen, particularly when properly drained and limed. The water table should be at least three feet below the surface. Although many people have the idea that celery will not grow on upland soils, some of our best celery comes from such soils. Black mineral soils are often used to grow celery, but too often these are not properly limed, are liable to be poorly drained, and afford a poor medium for root growth. Celery will grow on almost any soil if sufficient water is available; irrigation has been installed on many of the mineral soils for the purpose of growing celery. Except on very sandy soils, it is possible to grow celery without irrigation if there is a good distribution of rainfall and the soil supports a deep root growth. Pulverized limestone should be used freely, deep in the soil. The same type of soil treatment is needed as for cauliflower and asparagus (which see). Celery soil should have a good liberal supply of organic matter; well-rotted manure is one of the best sources of plant nutrients. If the home gardener has a nicely textured soil that grows other plants readily, he should feel free to grow celery.

On the sandy soils it would be highly advantageous to place a mulch between the plants.

CULTURAL DIRECTIONS: For a spring crop, celery seed of an early variety should be sown in a four-inch pot about the middle of February. A pinch of seed will grow all the plants that are needed in the garden. The seed is slow to germinate and the seedlings grow slowly. When the seedlings are three inches high they are ready to be transplanted into the garden soil. For real early celery, the seedlings can be transplanted at the start of spring into coldframes where, if properly spaced, they may be grown to maturity. The plants should be spaced eight inches from center to center in each direction. They should be kept weeded, and protected only when there is danger of freezing. The foliage should not be wet any more than is absolutely necessary; all watering should be applied directly to the ground—never to the plants themselves. Celery stalks may be used as soon as they are big enough to make it worth while; alternate plants should be taken out first. Plants grown in coldframes need no blanching, as they are close enough to shade each other.

When the plants are set in the garden, they are spaced eight inches apart in the row and the rows should be at least two feet apart. It is better to set the seedlings out when a little undersize than to let them get so large that the taproot has formed. If the taproot is broken in transplanting, the crop will not be good. The seedlings should be set with a starter solution and be given two or three feedings of liquid fertilizer at two-week intervals. The plants should be

kept free of weeds and the soil gradually pulled up around the plants with a hoe. When the plants are full grown, they should be blanched by placing a four-inch drain tile around

Celery Bleaching Tube

each. This can be accomplished by sticking the hand through the tile and grabbing the foliage into a bundle, so that the tile will slip down over the plant. Other devices may be used, such as placing boards on edge along each side of the row and securing them about four inches apart with stakes; or a tough paper can be tied with string around the plant so as to form roughly a four-inch cylinder. The loose part of the leaves should stick above the top regardless of the type of blancher used. The blanching will be accomplished in a week.

The fall-celery seed should be sown about the middle of May in a temporary short row in the garden. If very dry, it may be necessary to soak the rows to hasten the germination. Seeds should be kept away from the plants by pulling an inch-high ridge of soil over the top of the row and, when a crop of weeds begins to show there, carefully leveling the ridge enough to destroy the weeds but not deep enough to disturb the then-germinating celery seed; a half-inch of soil should remain over the celery seed. A piece of burlap placed over the row will keep down some but not all weeds; those which germinate must be pulled out. Give the seedlings a side-dressing of liquid fertilizer when they are about two inches tall. In two weeks the seedings should be transplanted to the permanent row and, in this case, should be set 10 inches apart in the rows at least 2 and preferably 3 feet apart. Celery should be planted where it will get good circulation of air and full sunshine. This will prevent the plants from becoming blighted. The plants should be set with a starter solution and given at least three side-dressings during the growing season. Keep the plants free from weeds.

INSECTS AND DISEASES: There are a number of diseases that cause trouble with celery, but the home gardener cannot afford to do much about them. An early blight, often caused by magnesium-deficiency and retarded growth, affects the leaves and causes them to die. The only practical thing the small grower can do is to make sure that there is plenty of magnesium and calcium in the soils and that the plants are watered enough to be kept growing rapidly. In a large planting, growers spray the foliage every week with a copper spray, such as a 5–5–50 Bordeaux mixture, or dust them weekly with a 20–80 copper-lime dust. Insects are not serious, but any leaf-eating caterpillars should be picked off. If the gardener will carefully spade under or burn all plant refuse left in the garden in the fall, there will be much less trouble with pests.

GENERAL RECOMMENDATIONS: Celery should be grown as late as possible and stored for winter use. A good storage method for early winter is to set the plants with their roots in trenches in such a manner that they are closely packed with leaves up and roots in moist soil. This will serve also to blanch the celery. The trench should be protected against freezing with a covering of glass or straw. Late winter celery can be stored in a cool cellar by setting the stalks with their roots in boxes deep enough to enclose the whole stem and with enough soil about the roots to keep the celery from wilting. A small storage-cellar built out-of-doors with a small south door and a dirt roof high enough to leave three feet of air above the celery leaves makes a good place to store celery where it will be accessible most of the winter. The roots should be dug into the floor soil and limestone sprinkled freely over the floor to keep the roots in good condition. The celery will be blanched by the time it is to be used.

Celery Cabbage
See Chinese Cabbage

Celtuce
DESCRIPTION: Celtuce (probably *Lactuca sativa, var. asparagina*) is one of the newer members of the vegetable-salad plants now being offered by seedsmen and was introduced in 1938 from western China. It resembles the early growth of the seedstalk of leaf lettuce, except that it does not have the same milky juice. In the early stages, the leaves are eaten as a leaf lettuce, but when the stems are a foot or more in height, they themselves are cut off, peeled, and eaten either raw or cooked. It is highly prized in its native state.

SOIL AND CLIMATIC REQUIREMENTS:
Although the plant will grow at comparatively high temperatures, it matures in 90 days and produces the

best quality in cool weather. It will grow on most any soil that will grow lettuce, doing particularly well on the loams or sandy loam soils that are well supplied with moisture and contain an appreciable quantity of liming material.

CULTURAL DIRECTIONS: The seed is planted in rows as soon as the ground can be worked in the spring, and the plants are thinned to two inches apart in the rows. When there is sufficient leaf-growth for use as leaf lettuce, the plants are thinned to stand 8 or 10 inches apart in the row. They should be cut for their stems as soon as the stems are three-fourths of an inch to an inch in diameter. They should be chilled after the leaves are removed. Insects and diseases probably will give very little trouble.

Chard

DESCRIPTION: Chard (*Beta vulgaris, var. cicla*), commonly known as SWISS CHARD and mistakenly called SEA-KALE BEET, is the beet of the ancients, described by Aristotle, 350 B.C., and is probably progenitor of the common beet. The wild form is found in the Canary Islands, whole Mediterranean region, and east to southern Asia. Chard is grown generally in the United States for its particularly large leaves, which have thickened midribs, both tender and palatable. The hard and woody roots are not edible.

SOIL AND CLIMATIC REQUIREMENTS:
These are temperate-zone plants that will withstand rather severe winters. The soil requirements are similar to those of the beet—a good loam, well-

drained, well-limed, and containing an abundance of plant nutrients. The use of manure is desirable for this plant.

CULTURAL DIRECTIONS: The seed may be sown at any time up to the first of July. The plants are thinned to 10 inches in the row and the rows should be 18 inches to 2 feet apart. The seed can be sown later in the summer, but the growth will not be big enough for use until the following season.

GENERAL RECOMMENDATIONS: Many people like the chards better than they do spinach, for the leaves are heavier and much easier to prepare for the table. There is less sand to contend with. The flavor is rather mild. A few plants will produce enough for the table. By keeping the flowerstalk picked off, the plants will continue to produce new leaves during their second year.

Chayote

DESCRIPTION: Chayote (*Sechium edule*) is a perennial vine grown in the southern states and tropical America for its edible fruits and tubers. It is a very old vegetable and was grown by the Aztecs. Sometimes referred to as CHUCHU, CHRISTOPHINE, or VEGETABLE PEAR, it belongs to the gourd family and can be grown as an annual where the growing season is no shorter than 135 days. The pear-shaped fruit is three to five inches long and contains a large round seed about one-third the size of the fruit itself. The fruit, usually green in color, is delicious for salads. Where the plant can be grown as a perennial, tubers are produced which are farinaceous in nature and delicious

when cooked. Even the seeds can be boiled and fried in slices in butter.

SOIL AND CLIMATIC REQUIREMENTS: Although a tropical plant, it can be grown in temperate climates if given protection and early forcing. It grows well in sandy loam soils having an appreciable amount of organic matter and lime. It does fairly well in soil that is not too abundantly supplied with water. In temperate regions it should not be too heavily supplied with nitrogen, for that will make the plant too late to mature its fruit. A good supply of potash and phosphorous is beneficial.

CULTURAL DIRECTIONS: Plant the whole seed in a 6- or 8-inch pot in a sandy soil in February and keep in a warm place until the plant is up. Use a glazed pot or a pot wrapped with paper, so that the soil may be kept moistened. The plants make a vigorous vine growth and, when planted in the garden, should be spaced 6 to 8 feet apart each way. It is better to grow the plant on the south side of a building, where it will be protected from cold winds.

INSECTS AND DISEASES: During the first few years of garden cultivation, there will probably be little trouble from insects. Mildews may cause some trouble, but an occasional light dusting with fine sulphur will keep them in check.

GENERAL RECOMMENDATIONS: This is one of those plants for the hobbyist to consider. It has many uses as a delightful food. Although the tubers are not so desirable as the fruit, they may be grown even in temperate regions by growing the plant in a five-gallon tub which may be moved during the winter to a cool basement where the plant may be kept alive in its dormant condition for a second year's growth. Before the tub is moved indoors, the vines may be cut off after they are well matured in the fall before they freeze. More people should get interested in plants of this kind, as there is much satisfaction to be gained from growing plants in localities where they are not particularly adapted. This is particularly true of plants which have so many uses as chayote, for gardeners may get some reward with their fun, without having to think exclusively about weeding and hoeing and fighting insects. The neophyte should not begin a garden without being informed that it is hard work; unless there is much enthusiasm and real interest, it should not be attempted. But with something like chayote to create a little additional interest, weed-pulling will be a great deal easier.

Cherry Pepper

See Peppers

Chervil

DESCRIPTION: There are two chervils, the annual and the biennial. The salad chervil (*Anthriscus cerefolium*) is the annual and is grown for its foliage, and in some sections of Europe was used as a pot herb. It is a native of the Caucasus, southern Russia, and western Asia. It has a parsley-type of foliage and the plant grows about 18 inches tall. The leaves are used for flavoring soups and meat dishes. The parsnip-rooted chervil (*Chaerophyllum tuberosum*) is a biennial. It makes a rosette of leaves and fleshy taproot the first year and

produces seed the second year. The roots are used very much like carrots. They resemble the carrot in shape and are brownish in color, while the

flesh is yellow. The foliage is somewhat coarser than the salad chervil's. Both plants are highly esteemed by Europeans.

TYPES AND VARIETIES: A number of varieties of both chervils are grown in Europe, but in America the chervils are grown as species-types rather than for particular varieties.

SOIL AND CLIMATIC REQUIREMENTS: Chervils are very hardy and will grow in a wide range of climatic conditions. The salad chervil grows best on a loamy soil that is well drained and well supplied with lime and nutrients. The parsnip-rooted type grows better on the sandy loam soils that are well supplied with lime and potash. It does well where hardwood ashes are mixed with the soil.

CULTURAL DIRECTIONS: Salad chervil seed is sown in rows 20 inches apart and the seedlings are thinned to 3 inches apart in the row. The parsnip-rooted type is grown very much like carrots (which see), except that the seed is planted in the fall in moist soil, where it remains until the following spring before it germinates. The seed is not allowed to dry out after it is harvested, or the seed coat will get so hard that it is difficult to soften it again. Hard seed should be scratched or, better, mixed with sand in a can and kept moist in a warm place for a month or two before it is to be planted in the spring. After the seed germinates, it takes about 120 days before the roots are ready to be used. Like parsnips, their flavor is improved by leaving them in the ground until freezing temperatures occur. They may be dug any time, but are usually dug in the late fall and stored in a cool cellar, not unlike carrots or other root crops. The flavor of the root is much more palatable than the parsnip's and may be recommended as a substitute for potatoes. However, the roots are rather small and the yield does not compare with potatoes unless the gardener is willing to plant the seed in rows about a foot apart and do the considerable amount of hand weeding which this occasions.

INSECTS AND DISEASES: Diseases are not serious if the soil is properly drained and well limed. Insects may cause some trouble, for there are worms that eat the foliage and maggots that get into the roots. The worms can be controlled by dusting with a rotenone dust.

GENERAL RECOMMENDATIONS: The plant is worth trying in the garden. If it needs more plant nutrients than the soil affords, the plants can be side-dressed with liquid fertilizer. The salad chervil plants do not do so well in hot weather and should be

grown either as an early crop or a late-season crop; they are quite hardy and will resist a certain amount of freezing. Seed is available from some of the seed-houses which specialize in herbs.

Chick-Pea

DESCRIPTION: Chick-pea or Egyptian pea (*Cicer arietinum*) belongs to the pea family and is grown for its dried seeds both in Europe and the United States. It is a native of the Orient and has been in cultivation probably from before the Christian Era. The plant is a bushy type with hairy stems and leaves. The seeds, which differ among the varieties in size and color, are eaten roasted or in soups, or ground into a fine meal. Even the juice is used for vinegar and for a beverage. The seeds are shaped like a ram's head. They are grown principally in Mexico and the Southwest. The flavor is very good.

TYPES AND VARIETIES: There are large- and small-seeded types, while the varieties differ in the color of the seed, varying through intermediate shades from white to red and black.

SOIL AND CLIMATIC REQUIREMENTS: They will mature in less than 100 days and require sandy loam soils that are well drained and not too fertile. As a matter of fact, they will grow on rather poor soils with a minimum of moisture but, like most plants, will produce a higher yield on slightly more fertile soils that have more moisture.

CULTURAL DIRECTIONS: The seed is sown in rows 2 feet apart and the plants are thinned to 3 inches in the row. They may be watered with a starter solution but should not be side-dressed, for they need little nutrient. The seed is allowed to mature before harvesting and is then separated from the vines by means of a flail or anything that will break up the pods.

INSECTS AND DISEASES: Pests will give very little trouble. If bean beetles happen to get on the vines, treatment should follow that for beans (which see).

Chicory

DESCRIPTION: Chicory (*Cichorium intybus*), also called SUCCORY or WITLOOF, and often ENDIVE or FRENCH ENDIVE, is grown for its tender though somewhat bitter salad leaves by forcing the roots, and for its roots,

which are dried and ground into a powder as an adulterant for coffee. It probably originated in the Orient but is generally grown in Europe as witloof and as *barbe de capuchin*. It is the same plant that grows wild along roadsides in the temperate regions. It is a perennial plant, growing a rosette of leaves and a big fleshy root the first year, and sending up a tall much-branched seedstalk, covered with solitary, axillary, compound flowers of attractive deep blue color, the second year.

TYPES AND VARIETIES: A number of large-rooted varieties have been selected, but they differ very little from the wild form. Most of our seed in this country has come from France, but some is being produced in the United States. The varieties are still far from uniform, due to constant cross-fertilization with wild chicory.

CLIMATIC AND SOIL REQUIREMENTS: Chicory is very hardy and lives through severe winters. Its soil requirements are not too exacting, although it does better on the well-drained soils that have considerable lime and organic matter. Although the plants will crowd out other weeds in waste places, larger and better roots are produced where the soil is in a fair degree of cultivated fertility. If the seed can be germinated in the sandy soils, the plants probably would grow good roots with a side-dressing of liquid fertilizer.

CULTURAL DIRECTIONS: The seed is sown in the open ground about the first of August in rows 2 feet apart. The seedlings are thinned to 3 inches apart in the row. If the seed is sown too early, the roots get too large and the tops are apt to be much branched. As the root develops, dormant buds are formed on the crown, but the central bud, formed on roots of from

¾ to 1 inch in diameter, is all that is necessary. If the secondary buds are permitted to form, as they will if the root has time to grow thicker than an inch, they as well as the central bud will produce when the root is forced, and a branched, loosely knit head will result—not nearly so desirable as a single head, except for the small gardener who is forcing only a few for his own use. If the plants grow intermittently, due to alternating wet and dry weather, the roots will have more of secondary buds than if grown quickly and evenly, as where irrigation is available. The plants should be kept free of weeds until the large rosettes of leaves are formed, after which the ground is sufficiently shaded to prevent weed seeds from germinating.

The roots are usually dug before the ground freezes, and are then thrown into compact piles and covered with sufficient straw or soil to prevent successive thawing and freezing. Freezing does not hurt the roots in the soil, but if they are frozen in the open and then thawed and frozen again, the buds will be killed or weakened. The roots should be thoroughly chilled before they are forced. This chilling seems to break the rest period and the buds will start to grow much more quickly and make a more uniform growth.

Witloof is forced by packing the roots as close together as possible in an upright position in a bench or a box. Sand or sandy soil is packed around the roots. The crowns should all be on the same level. Then about six inches of fine sand is placed on top of the crowns and the whole thing stored in a warm cellar and kept moist. A temperature of 60 degrees Fahrenheit is ideal for forcing. At lower temperatures the buds will start much more slowly and there will be greater possibility of decay starting in on some of the roots. From three to five weeks are needed to force the roots. The sprout will be a folded mass of leaves in a compact conical-shaped head, an inch or so in diameter, and the color will be a creamy yellow with white veins. The leaves are separated to serve in salads. As soon as the sprouts reach the light above the soil, they turn green and will open; they should therefore be harvested when about six inches long.

Witloof can also be produced in the garden in the spring by following these directions: Six inches of soil is placed over the rows of chicory roots in the late fall after the plants have become dormant; after remaining there all winter, the buds start to grow under the surface early in the spring, and remain in a compact head until they reach the open, where the leaves begin to spread and turn green. Since they will then grow very rapidly, they must be harvested in a day or two. This method is therefore not so satisfactory for home use, as people who like witloof want it for a regular diet through the winter. This is accomplished by having a forcing bed in the cellar and making plantings every two or three days or at weekly intervals. A dozen roots set in at a time will supply the average family with a good-sized serving.

BARBE DE CAPUCHIN is forced in somewhat the same way, except that the roots are not covered with more than a half inch of soil. They are forced in the dark, so that the leaves will remain white; they do not form a compact head anyway. The flavor is very much the same, but not quite so fresh as witloof. It is possible to produce *barbe de capuchin* after a crop of witloof has been harvested, simply by packing the roots after the heads have been removed and placing the boxes in the dark. The quantity will not be so large but the flavor will be good.

INSECTS AND DISEASES: There are no serious chicory pests. Insects do not bother the plants much and diseases of the roots occur only if they have been frozen and thawed too much. It is a good idea to keep the sand fresh either by replacing it every year with new or by sunning the old sand out of doors for several months each year till it is thoroughly dry. Weekly turning of the sand during this process will help.

Some ingenious person will one day devise a way to force the roots in moist chambers without any soil or sand, and thus eliminate completely the danger of decay from soil-borne diseases.

GENERAL RECOMMENDATIONS: Most of the difficulty in forcing witloof comes from the growing conditions of the roots. Where they can be grown under irrigation, there will be less trouble than where they are grown during a season of wet and dry weather. It is not necessary to have a root over an inch in diameter. For this reason it is not necessary to plant the seed until late summer in the sections where 140 days of growing weather are available. If the roots are grown with too little nitrogen or other nutrients, they may be so high in carbohydrate material that they will not force satisfactorily. Such roots usually have leaves which

turn yellow prematurely and are small. The leaves should be of good size and dark green until frost.

Most growers plant seed and thin the seedlings. But if the seed is sown in a two-inch band, so that the seed is distributed over a larger area, the seedlings will not have to be thinned, unless the plants become so thick as to interfere with each other. Forcing chicory is a good side line for the hobbyist who has enough ground to grow the roots. The price is usually good and the work can be done evenings. The biggest problem is to provide the space and the benches in a dark place. A root cellar would be a good place.

Chili Pepper
See Peppers

Chinese Cabbage

DESCRIPTION: Chinese cabbage (*Brassica Chinensis* and *Brassica pekinensis*) has also been called Celery Cabbage but it is really a species more nearly related to the mus-

tards than to cabbage. The leaves, much thinner than those of cabbage, are folded together into a conical head more or less open at the top. The color of the foliage is light or yellowish green, while the prominent veins are white to light green. Chinese cabbage is one of the oldest vegetable crops, having been generally grown in China before the Christian Era. The suggestion has been made that it is the progenitor of the long-headed cabbage, with its open heads.

TYPES AND VARIETIES: The best known varieties are Pak-choi, Wongbok, and Chi-hi-hi. Other varieties are Chosen, Shantung, Chokurei, Kinshu, and Che-foo. There is some confusion between the two species, as the varietal differences may not be true species differences.

SOIL AND CLIMATIC REQUIREMENTS: Chinese cabbage is a cool-weather plant, maturing in about 75 days. In hot weather it runs to seed very quickly. It is grown either as an early- or late-season crop. It requires a very fertile soil that is well drained and well supplied with organic matter and lime. It needs a good supply of quickly available nitrogen and a supply of moisture that will keep the plants growing rapidly.

CULTURAL DIRECTIONS: The seed can be sown indoors in early March and the plants set in the garden as soon as the ground can be cultivated. They should be set with a starter solution and should be given a side-dressing of liquid fertilizer about 2 weeks afterwards. Seed for the fall crop is sown out-of-doors in the latter part of July and should be planted with starter solution to hasten germination. The plants should be thinned to 6 inches in the row.

Chinese Lantern

See Tomato

Chinese-Watermelon

DESCRIPTION: Chinese-watermelon (Benincasa hispida) belongs to the gourd family and has a trailing vine with light-green foliage, resembling the squash or pumpkin vine. The flowers are yellow and contain a large amount of wax which is often collected for candles. It is a tropical plant—native of eastern China and the East Indies—much prized for its large, egg-shaped, white or pale-green fruit. The fruit, from eight inches to two feet in length and one-third that in width, is eaten raw for its high, palatable flavor. It has good keeping qualities.

TYPES AND VARIETIES: There are two types grown: the short, almost round type, common in China; and the long slender type, grown in India. The round type is grown in Europe and, experimentally, in the United States. It requires 120 days of growing weather. No definite varieties have been established.

SOIL AND CLIMATIC REQUIREMENTS: The Chinese-watermelon is a warm-climate plant, but can be grown in the temperate zone where the growing season is long enough. In shorter seasons, it is necessary to start the seed indoors, so that the plants can mature in the garden in two months or so. The soil should be sandy, well drained, and well supplied with lime. Too much manure or nitrogen in the soil will make the vines so late that they will not mature their fruits in the ordinary season. Too much fertility will cause the plants to produce a large number of flowers, but they will not set fruit.

CULTURAL DIRECTIONS: It may be a good plan to grow the plants in pots until they have three or four true leaves. In this way the plants can be protected against the cucumber beetles and squash bugs before they are set in the garden. The plants should be spaced as for squash (which see).

Chito Melon

See Melons

Chives

DESCRIPTION: Chives (*Allium schoenoprasum*), a perennial of the North Temperate Zone, with miniature onion-like leaves and tiny bulbs, is

used for the mild onion-flavor of its leaves in such cooked dishes as omelettes and stews. It produces purple flowers in mass, rather attractive for borders.

TYPES AND VARIETIES: No definite varieties are known.

SOIL AND CLIMATIC REQUIREMENTS: It is definitely a cool-weather plant and is hardy in severe winters. It requires a good loam soil, or a sandy loam soil that is well supplied with organic matter and plant nutrients.

The soil should be well drained and well supplied with lime. Moisture is quite important.

CULTURAL REQUIREMENTS: The plants do not produce seed readily, and therefore it is necessary to propagate the plants by divisions from the old plants. The plants are divided into pieces containing two or three bulbs, which are set in rows 2 feet apart and 6 to 8 inches apart in the rows. In a good season, each plant will make a clump 8 to 10 inches across. During the fall, the plants can be lifted and put in 8- or 10-inch pots which can be kept in the kitchen where they will grow for several months and can be used fresh in cooking.

INSECTS AND DISEASES: There are no diseases of importance. Thrips may cause some trouble in dry weather by spoiling the leaves. They can be controlled by sprinkling flaky naphthalene around the plants. Keeping the plants watered will discourage the thrips.

GENERAL RECOMMENDATIONS: A few clumps of chives probably will supply the family needs. However, the plants should be divided at least every three years, as the younger plants are cleaner and much better for cutting. They can be used for border plants in flower beds and need not be planted in the vegetable garden.

Christophine

See Chayote

Chuchu

See Chayote

Chufa

DESCRIPTION: Chufa (*Cyperus esculentus*) is a southern perennial plant, with tremendous possibilities as a food plant. It is sometimes called EARTH ALMOND and ZULU NUT. The plant is grass- or reed-like in appearance and grows to a height of three

feet. It grows wild along the Delaware River and through the South. The tubers are about an inch in length and are very hard. Not unlike the tubers of the Jerusalem artichoke, they were considered a delicacy and were served as desserts more than 2,000 years before the Christian Era. Today they are eaten roasted, raw, or cooked.

SOIL AND CLIMATIC REQUIREMENTS: The plants grow wild in the north central states and in the southern states. They can be grown as an annual in the more northern climates, but the tubers will not live through the winters. They do not produce flowers in the North. The plants grow best in a sandy loam soil that is well supplied with organic matter and contains an appreciable amount of lime. The soil should have a fair amount of nutrient but not so much nitrogen that the plants will grow too

late. Any plant that produces tubers can be given too much nitrogen.

GENERAL RECOMMENDATIONS: This is a very interesting plant for the hobbyist. There is much that can be be done in the selection of varieties and in the development of new varieties grown from seed. The crop is grown by planting the tubers in rows. The plants need twenty inches of space.

Cicely

See Sweet Cicely

Cinnamon Vine

See Yams

Citron

DESCRIPTION: Citron (*Citrullus vulgaris, var. citroides*), a member of the watermelon family, is eaten only in candied form and preserves—never raw. It is, however, not the candied citron of commerce (*Citrus medica*). The trailing vine of citron is almost as vigorous as the watermelon's, which it resembles. Its round fruit of light to dark mottled green, has a hard shell, eight inches in diameter, and firm white flesh. (For the commonly called preserving melon or white gourd of India, *see* Chinese-watermelon.)

TYPES AND VARIETIES: There are no great number of varieties. Colorado preserving citron is a common variety. *Citrus medica* is a tree fruit.

SOIL AND CLIMATIC REQUIREMENTS: The Citron can be grown in any locality where the growing season is over 90 days long. It does best in warm but not hot climates. The best soil is a well-drained sandy loam that will not dry out too much during dry spells. The soil should be well limed and not too well supplied with nitrogen.

CULTURAL DIRECTIONS: The seed is sown in the spring as soon as all danger of frost is past, in hills with 3 or 4 seeds to the hill. The hills are 4 by 6 feet apart.

INSECTS AND DISEASES: A common disease is the mildew, which is bad during wet, cool, cloudy weather, particularly on heavy soils. That is why it is important to plant the seed on well-drained soil where the plants will not be in shade. The cucumber beetle is the worst insect pest. The plants should be well protected with a sprinkling of lime during the early stages of growth. If rotenone dust is used, it must be applied as soon as the first true leaves are formed.

Civet Bean
See Lima Bean

Collards

DESCRIPTION: Collards (*Brassica oleracea, var. acephala*) are really a

tall-growing form of Kale (which see), although the name is also

loosely applied to cabbage seedlings grown as greens and therefore pulled before the heads are formed. Where cabbage is successful, true collards are not popular. They are generally grown in the southern states as a source of greens and as such are highly nutritious—even more so than the heading cabbage, because its leaves are all green.

TYPES AND VARIETIES: Any variety of *B. oleracea, var. capita* may be sown for use in its pre-heading stage, particularly in regions of high temperature where cabbage tends to produce a mass of large leaves rather than heads. In the northern states, however, young cabbage is not generally grown as "collards" because the cabbage plants form heads too readily. The standard variety of the true collards is the Georgia collard.

SOIL AND CLIMATIC REQUIREMENTS: High temperatures are desirable. They require a well-drained and well-limed soil, with ample moisture. The soil should be well supplied with organic matter and enough nitrogen to make the plants grow tall and vigorous. A side-dressing of liquid fertilizer will help to keep the plants growing rapidly.

CULTURAL DIRECTIONS: In the South, the seed is sown in late winter or as soon as the ground can be worked, and are later set 3 by 4 feet apart and cultivated like cabbage (which see). If cabbage seedlings are to be used as collards, the plants are thinned to one for every 2 inches in the row, and it is a good plan to stagger them in a wide row so that they will grow much taller than when they are grown with too much space around them.

INSECTS AND DISEASES: Diseases are not a serious contender but cabbage worms cause as much trouble as they do on cabbage. They should be controlled with rotenone dust as on cabbage.

GENERAL RECOMMENDATIONS: In the North, collards are not generally grown because most people prefer cabbage. However, there is no reason why enough cabbage seed should not be planted so that after the required number of seedlings have been removed for the cabbage bed, the remainder may be left to grow for use as greens.

Cone Pepper
See Peppers

Corn: Popcorn

DESCRIPTION: Popcorn (*Zea mays, var. everta*) is characterized by its very small ears and tiny kernels, with their beaks of corneous endosperm. The stalks are very short but in floral characteristics are the same as those of sweet or field corns.

TYPES AND VARIETIES: Some varieties have sharply pointed kernels, others, round kernels. The dwarf type is represented by the Tom Thumb variety which grows about 20 inches tall and produces 2-inch ears with shallow, smooth, round, golden kernels. Although often grown for ornament, it does make good popping corn. White Rice is a large commercial variety that has ears 7 to 8 inches long and long, white, pointed kernels. The stalks grow to 6 feet. White Pearl is a commercial variety with slightly smaller ears of round, smooth, white kernels. Popcorn va-

rieties require about 110 days to mature.

SOIL AND CLIMATIC REQUIREMENTS: Popcorn grows best in the temperate regions where the air is fairly dry. The Mississippi Valley is the home of popcorn. The soil should be a good loam or sandy loam that is well drained and fairly well limed. Good yields are obtained with smaller quantities of plant nutrients than are required for sweet corn.

CULTURAL DIRECTIONS: The seed is sown in rows, with plants spaced 4 inches apart for the dwarf varieties and 8 or 10 inches apart for the larger varieties. The rows should be 2 to 3 feet apart. The seed is slow to germinate and is usually sown as soon as the ground can be worked. It is planted 1 to 3 inches deep, depending on the amout of sand in the soil. It should be kept free of weeds and will make the best popping corn if the season is bright and comparatively dry. It should be well dried out before it is harvested and should be stored in a dry place where an abundance of air can circulate through it. When thoroughly dried, it is shelled and sacked for storage, preferably in a cold dry room. Popcorn should not be kiln- or heat-dried, or it will not pop well. Immature corn does not pop well, because the popping requires that the corneous endosperm be hard and rigid enough to confine the steam formed from minute droplets of moisture within the heated kernels until explosive pressures have been generated. Field dent corn will not pop because the endosperm has too much give to permit the steam to build up sufficient pressure. Flint field corn will pop to a certain extent, but it makes a small ball which is tough. The harder the endosperm and the greater its proportion of corneous matter, the more violent will be the explosion when it finally pops and the larger and lighter the popped kernel will be. Popcorn should not be stored in a warm kitchen. Popcorn is much better some years than others.

INSECTS AND DISEASES: The main pest of popcorn is the corn borer, for the control of which see *Corn: Sweet Corn*. Root-rots often cause trouble, but they may be eliminated by good aeration and liming of the soil.

GENERAL RECOMMENDATIONS: Popcorn is a good specialty crop, since it can be grown for ornament as well as profit upon a small piece of ground. A wide variety of colors, shapes, and sizes may be obtained for ornamental purposes from seed produced by crossing Black Mexican sweet corn with a yellow variety of popcorn. The returns per acre may be anywhere from 25 to 50 dollars, although the returns from ornamental varieties may be much higher, depending on the locality and how they are sold. Popcorn is a crop for inexpensive land and cheap labor.

Corn: Sweet Corn

DESCRIPTION: The common sweet corn (*Zea mays, var. saccharata*) was probably developed by breeding and selection from the common field corn (*Z. mays, var. rugosa*). It is a cereal and belongs to the grass family. Although field corn is an ancient type that was in cultivation by the Indians in tropical America probably before the 8th century, sweet corn is of recent origin, having been first cultivated about 1800. The plant grows 4 to 8 feet tall with no branches but produces tillers or stools from the crown which grow to half the height of the original stem. The pistillate or female flowers are arranged in rows on the ear about half way up the stalk, and the staminate flowers grow on a branched raceme at the stalk's tip. In order to get seed produced, the pollen which is shed from the staminate flowers must fall on the silk which is produced on the ears. The pollen is carried by the wind, which accounts for the fact that if more than one kind of corn is grown in a garden the resulting seed will not produce the same kind of corn as that on which it grew. Many gardeners pull off the silks and wonder why the ears have no kernels on them.

It takes about 48 hours from the time the pollen drops on the silk until the flower is fertilized and the kernel starts to grow. If insects eat the silks as they are sent out from the leaf-wrapped ears or if rain makes the pollen sticky so that it fails to be released from the tassels, pollination cannot occur and the seeds will not develop. Each silk is attached to an embryo kernel on the cob and each one must have a pollen grain drop on it in order for the kernel to develop. Very often a rainy day is responsible for a long bare tip on an ear of sweet corn. All varieties of corn whether field, pop, or sweet corn will cross with each other. They must be grown at least forty yards from each other to prevent mixtures from taking place.

TYPES AND VARIETIES: There is only one type of sweet corn, but a number of varieties, which may have yellow, white, or black kernels. During the last few years, many new hybrid varieties have been developed, but the hybrids must be re-developed every year, because their seed, if planted, instead of "breeding true," will break up into their constituent varieties or strains. It requires special care to develop seed that will grow hybrids, and for this reason it costs more.

GOLDEN BANTAM CORN

However, hybrids have several advantages: they are more productive and more resistant to the bacterial wilt which sometimes kills half or more of a planting from a true variety.

Golden Bantam is still considered to be the highest quality corn grown. It is the standard with which all other ·varieties are compared. However, most varieties are very tasty if they can be picked from the stalks a few minutes before they are to be cooked. The quality of sweet ·corn, due to its delicately balanced sugars, does not last over a couple of hours after the ear is picked. Corn on the market which is a day old has lost this fine quality, especially so if the weather is warm. Icing or chilling corn before it is taken to market is a

big help in maintaining good quality. If corn is picked a considerable time before it is to be used, it should be placed in the icebox immediately. For these reasons, any variety can be good or bad, depending on how it is cared for after it is removed from the stalks. The following varieties are worthy of trial in the garden:

WHITE VARIETIES: The Mayflower, Burlington County White, Early Minnesota, White Cob Cory, Red Cob Cory, and Growers Selections are early varieties with small 6- to 7-inch ears, having 8 rows of kernels. They require 65 to 73 days to mature.

Medium to late varieties are the Crosby, Kendels Early Giant, Stowells Evergreen, Country Gentleman, Stowells Evergreen Hybrid, and Howling Mob, which have ears from 7 to 10 inches long, 12 to 20 rows of kernels to the ear. They require from 75 to 90 days to mature.

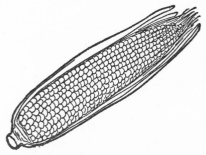

COUNTRY GENTLEMAN CORN

YELLOW VARIETIES: These are the most popular and have slightly better flavor than most of the white varieties. There are also many hybrid varieties available for those who find difficulty in growing sweet corn because of the bacterial wilt.

Early hybrids are the Spancross, the Marcross, and the Ioana (for dry sections); Golden Sunshine and other early true varieties are susceptible to bacterial wilt in certain sections. These varieties are all small-eared, being 5 to 7 inches long, with 8 to 12 rows of kernels to the ear, and require from 60 to 70 days to mature.

Medium to late varieties are the Whipcross, Golden Cross Bantam, and Top Cross Bantam hybrids, and the Golden Bantam, Whipples Yellow, Bantam Evergreen, and Golden Colonel true varieties. These are medium- to large-eared, with 10 to 20 rows of kernels to the ear, and require 80 to 90 days to mature.

BLACK VARIETY: The only black variety is the Black Mexican, which has very good quality, large ears, 7 to 8 inches long, with 8 to 10 rows of kernels to the ear. It requires 85 days to mature. In the milk stage the kernels are almost white, but they soon become purplish in color, which many people object to.

Many other varieties as good as those mentioned are available in local communities. Of the above varieties, the Golden Bantam and the Black Mexican are first and second choice for the home garden where bacterial wilt is not a serious pest. Golden Cross Bantam should be grown in wilt-infested ground. Some of the late varieties are not so susceptible.

SOIL AND CLIMATIC REQUIREMENTS: In spite of the fact that tropical America is the home of corn, its development has reached its greatest peak in the North Temperate Zone. The yield is much greater in the temperate North, where the seed must be cured in the fall and sown in tilled ground in the spring, although there are sweet-corn varieties

that will mature in rather cool climates due to many years of selection and adaptation. The soil requirements are not very exacting, except that a good supply of nutrients must be available in the soil to get the maximum yield. Any well-drained loamy soil that has a good supply of lime will grow sweet corn. Even rather heavy soils will grow good crops of the late varieties. Early sweet corn is grown in the loamy sands and sandy loams. If rainfall is well distributed, sufficient fertilizer can be applied to grow a very good crop. A dry year means poor yields.

CULTURAL DIRECTIONS: Sweet corn of one variety should be planted as soon as the soil can be worked into a good seed bed and weekly planting made thereafter, so that corn can be harvested from the first of August until the first frost in the fall. Corn will not stand frost. The plantings should be made in not less than two adjacent parallel rows, and kernels should be spaced so that the stalks will stand 8 inches apart in the row. The rows of small early varieties can be planted 2 feet apart but rows of the Bantams and later varieties should not be closer than 30 inches. The kernels are planted in holes or furrows 2 inches deep in the sandy types of soil, and a quarter-pint of starter solution should be poured over the seed before it is covered with soil. Weeds snould be killed before they are 2 inches tall. If weeds are allowed to get over a foot tall, they should be cut off at the ground rather than pulled, so as not to disturb the corn roots. Anything that disturbs the roots of the plants will reduce the yield of ears. It is best to hoe as shallow as possible. The plants should have one good side-dressing of liquid fertilizer between the time the seedlings come up and before they become 8 inches tall. After that, the fertilizer probably will do very little good. The ears are harvested by breaking the ears off the stalks and not removing the husks until it is time to put them in the kettle. Corn should not be over-cooked. A few minutes in boiling water is sufficient.

INSECTS AND DISEASES: The only disease that causes any trouble is the bacterial wilt, and the only control is to grow the wilt-resistant varieties. There are a number of insects that cause considerable trouble in some sections. The worst offender is the corn ear worm. The moth lays its eggs on the silks as they grow out, and in five days these eggs hatch into small worms which immediately feed on the silks and work their way into the tip of the ear. They do not eat much of the ear—only enough to spoil its appearance, but if they work their way down between the kernel rows, they may ruin the whole ear. Of the several control measures which have been recommended, the most practical for the home gardener is to go through the plants every four days and clip off with a scissors all the silks that have been out more than a day. The ears will be pollinated by this time and the eggs will drop off with the severed silks. This is not a serious job and only takes a few minutes. A person can do this while he is resting from hoeing or weeding another part of the garden. Japanese beetles, when present, also cause considerable damage. The only good control is to pick them off every evening after it is cool enough to make them sluggish. They will do much damage in the tassels and on the silks when corn is in the process of shedding pollen. They do very little harm on the leaves. A good practice is to snap the stalk over a dishpan; most of the beetles will drop into the pan and can be killed in kerosene or some other oil.

The European Corn Borer is also a bad pest in some sections. The moths lay their eggs on the axils of the leaves, where the small worms hatch and burrow into the stems. If they get into the stem near the tassel, the tassel will break over and the worm can be seen in the stalk. A rotenone spray directed into the axils of the leaves will kill the worms but it is a hopeless task to get all of them, as they would have to be sprayed every day to catch them as soon as they hatch. Borers working in the stem will prevent the plant from growing properly. They also bore into the cob, but do very little damage to the kernels. By keeping all weeds and dead plants cleaned up and burned, the borers will not have a chance to live over the winter. Since the moths fly considerable distances, however, the neighbors must all join in the crusade of clean culture for the method to be really effective. Borers live in many different kinds of plants, including many flowering plants—chrysanthemums, for instance, where they are difficult to control.

GENERAL RECOMMENDATIONS: There is always a question whether corn should be suckered. If the small offshoots are removed from the plant before they get over 4 inches tall, it may be beneficial, but generally the yield will be better if the offshoots are permitted to remain, even though they do not produce ears.

Corn Salad

DESCRIPTION: Corn salad (*Valerianella locusta*, var. *olitoria*) somewhat resembles the smooth-leaved spinach. It is an annual and makes a rosette of leaves which may be used, like lettuce, in salad or, like spinach,

cooked. It grows quickly and may be grown either as an early or a late-season crop or even as a mild-winter crop, for it is quite hardy. The leaves have little taste and so are usually mixed with more flavorous salad plants.

TYPES AND VARIETIES: Large Round Leaf is a variety that is offered.

SOIL AND CLIMATIC REQUIREMENTS: Corn salad grows best in temperate regions where the nights are cool. It will not stand hot weather and for this reason is grown in the cool part of the season. The soil should be well drained and supplied with an abundance of lime. A good loam soil is preferable and, if it contains considerable organic matter, it probably will not require much fertilizer. Corn salad is a good crop to plant before beans.

CULTURAL DIRECTIONS: Sow the seed as soon as possible in the spring and thin to 4 or 6 inches in the row, in rows 16 to 18 inches apart. Cut off the leaves before the seedstalk is formed.

INSECTS AND DISEASES: Aphids may cause some difficulty in the fall crop, but diseases are not bothersome if the ground has been properly prepared. Occasionally worms eat the leaves but they are easy to control with a rotenone dust.

GENERAL RECOMMENDATIONS: This is a mild salad plant which can be used in place of less-relished salad plants or to give variety to the salad dishes. It is very often mixed with stronger-tasting plants such as mustard, peppergrass, or water cress.

Cowpea

Cowpea (*Vigna sinensis*) is a bean which is generally used as cattle feed and as a soil-building plant but in some sections also as food for humans. It probably came from southern Asia in the Mediterranean region, where it may have been introduced from China. Because it belongs to the group of edible beans, it is included here in the interest of completeness. The cowpea is a bushy plant, but may tend to produce vines. It has foliage similar to bush beans. The seeds, small, spotted, and grayish-brown, are produced in long slender pods, edible when tender. The seed is eaten in both the green and dry shell stages in certain sections of the South. The plant does particularly well in high temperatures and grows well in poor soil with less lime-content than is required by many of the other bean varieties. For human food, the seed is sown in drills 2 feet apart with the plants 2 to 3 inches apart in the row. An ounce of seed will plant a 50-foot row.

Cress: Peppergrass, Winter Cress

DESCRIPTION: Cress is the common name for a number of herbs of the mustard family used as salads or garnishes because of their pleasantly pungent flavors. PEPPERGRASS or garden cress (*Lepidium sativum*) is an Asiatic annual, widely used in Europe, easily grown from quickly germinating seeds, which produce a most attractive salad or garnish within three or four weeks. WINTER CRESS (*Barbarea vernapraecox*) is a hardy European biennial which survives severe winters and may be used in spring before the flower stem develops or, if spring-planted, by midsummer. Indian cress (*Tropaeolum majus*) is the common Nasturtium (which see). *See also* Water Cress.

VARIETIES: The two varieties most commonly listed by seedsmen are Fine Curled (a peppergrass) and Upland (a winter cress).

SOIL AND CLIMATIC REQUIREMENTS: The cresses do best in temperate climates and are used in early or late season rather than through the hot weather when they become strong-flavored and run to seed. They do particularly well on very fertile loam soils that are well drained and have an appreciable amount of lime. A well-manured soil is to be desired.

CULTURAL DIRECTIONS: Cress is very easily grown because the seed germinates quickly and the plants grow so rapidly that weeds have little chance to interfere. Peppergrass seed is sown thickly in narrow drills 10 or 12 inches apart and several cuttings may be made if the stems are not too closely cut. Or successive plantings

may be made to insure a steady supply of auxiliary salad-flavoring leaves. Winter cress should be sown in earliest spring or, as a biennial, in the fall.

INSECTS AND DISEASES: The worst pest of the cress plants are flea beetles which come early in the season and take advantage of the plants' early growth. A copper spray such as Bordeaux is a repellent and not harmful to humans.

Cress, Water
See Water Cress

Crickshaw Lima
See Jack Bean

Cucumber

DESCRIPTION: Cucumber (*Cucumis sativus*) is an annual plant with large leaves on a trailing vine that may grow ten or more feet in a season. The plant grows wild in the East Indies and has been cultivated for

3000 years. The vines and fruits have a fine hairy surface, greatly accentuated in dry weather. There are two types of flowers, the male or staminate flowers which contain the pollen, and the female or pistillate flowers which contain the ovary or embryo pickle. The male flowers

live only a day or two and the pollen is short-lived. Bees, preferably honeybees, are necessary to carry the pollen from the male to the pistillate flowers before the small pickle will start to grow. When cucumbers are grown in the greenhouse it is necessary to install a hive of bees unless the operator is willing to take the time to pollinate the flowers by hand. In order to do this, a fresh male flower is picked off and the yellow petals removed so that the tiny center part can be gently rubbed on the center part of the female or pistillate flower. This pollinating must be done in the early morning, because the pollen will not germinate after midday. At room temperatures, the flowers begin to open shortly after midnight and should be pollinated as soon as possible thereafter in order to get well-shaped fruit. There are usually about ten male flowers to every female flower. In the garden, the presence of bees in the flowers in early morning is an indication that nectar is being secreted. Toward noon the bees no longer work the flowers. The female flowers may be pollinated for three or four days, but the fruits will be wasp-shaped if not pollinated the first day. This accounts for many deformed fruits which are referred to as nubbins and wasp types.

Cucumbers vary considerably in size and shape. The fruits, when immature, are red, green, or white and turn orange or dark yellow as they ripen. They are usually used when immature.

TYPES AND VARIETIES: Cucumber varieties may conveniently be grouped according to the color of the immature fruit and according to their size and uses, whether of the short pickling type or the long slicing type, as follows:

GREEN SHORT PICKLING TYPES: Fruits are 4 to 5 inches long when mature or ripe. Pickles are white- or black-spined, warty, and less than 2 inches long when used for pickles. They are not good for slicing, as they turn light green and ripen in a short time when picked. They require 55 days to mature. Mincu, Chicago Pickling, Everbearing, and Early Green Cluster are the principal varieties. Larger pickling varieties, with fruits 5 to 7 inches long when mature, are represented by Green Prolific, White Spine, and Granite State.

GREEN LONG SLICING TYPE: The white- or black-spine varieties, with fruits 8 to 12 inches long when mature, include: Early Fortune, which develops light green stripes as it matures; Black Diamond, which is a dark green fruit and one of the best; Arlington White Spine; and Delcrow, which is a smooth, long, slender, dark green variety.

GREEN LONG ENGLISH TYPE: The fruits, 15 to 36 inches long, are grown in greenhouses—not in open ground. They are dark to light green, smooth, and either cylindrical or slightly tapering in shape. They will develop without being pollinated; when they are pollinated, the tip end becomes bulbous, as the seeds develop only in the tip. Representative varieties are Telegraph, Convent, Sion House, and Duke of Edinburgh.

GREEN RUSSIAN TYPE: The cucumber is 10 to 12 inches long, green, and smooth, with a dense coating of fine hair. Despite its name, this type is probably nothing more than a segregation from the common wild cucumber. Cross-pollination tends to keep the fruits of most cucumbers in a variety rather uniform in shape and size; even seeds derived from self-pollinated plants may produce fruits which vary tremendously in size, shape and color. The Russian type is probably a selection from one of those. It is not a popular type, although the flavor is as good as of those more commonly grown.

WHITE-FRUITED TYPE: This is a type commonly grown in Europe but is not popular in this country. The vines are exactly the same as those of other cucumbers, but the immature fruits are white in color and vary greatly in length and shape. They are creamy in color when mature. Some are smooth, some are netted like the muskmelon, and some are densely covered with fine hairs. They cross readily with the other types but, being recessive, come to light only by controlled self-pollination. It is an interesting type for breeding purposes. White Wonder is a common variety.

ORANGE-FRUITED TYPE: This is a curiosity and is the result of crossing a white with a green black-spined variety. The immature fruits are a deep orange in color, have black spines, and may vary considerably in size and shape. The vines are the same as in the other varieties.

The presence of black spines on the green varieties tends to give the immature fruits a bronzy-green appearance which to some people is an indication that the fruit is no longer fresh. As a matter of fact, the black-spined varieties may have better flavor than the white-spined types, but when the consumer wants a slicing cucumber she wants it as grass-green as she can get it. Cucumbers soon lose their freshness, so that one cannot be blamed for demanding the best.

The West Indian "wild cucumber" (C. anguria), though a different species from the common cucumber, since the two will not cross-pollinate, should be mentioned here. It is the small globular-fruited West Indian Gherkin, sometimes called Bur Gherkin. The flowers are whitish-yellow and very small. The spiney fruits, approximately an inch in diameter and slightly longer, make very fine pickles. Though very seedy and puffy, they have a fine flavor.

SOIL AND CLIMATIC REQUIREMENTS: Cucumbers are tropical plants, but due to the fact that they mature fruits in 60 days they may be grown in the garden in localities where the summers are warm for at least 90 days. They are very sensitive to frosts. They should not be grown in localities of high humidity and poor circulation of air. In the garden the most exposed areas should be chosen as a preventive against mildews. Cucumbers grow best on the sandy-loam soils that are well drained and well supplied with lime. Manure is an ideal fertilizer and the plants respond to an appreciable amount of water. The pickling varieties are grown in poorer soils than the slicing types, because they are picked when the fruit is just starting to grow, while the slicing cucumbers are allowed to attain practically full size. Sometimes growers will plant the slicing types with the idea of growing them for pickles and allowing any which get too large for pickles to grow to full slicing size. When the fruits of the small pickling varieties get too large, they have to be sold as seconds, for they are unattractive when full-grown. For this reason it is better to plant the slicing types.

CULTURAL DIRECTIONS: Cucumber seed is sown in the open ground as soon as the soil is warm and all danger of frost is past. The seed is sown in hills, 6 or 7 seeds to the hill, and a quart of starter solution is poured over them before the soil is replaced. They should be covered not over an inch deep in sandy soil and not over half an inch deep in loamy soils. The hills should be 4 feet apart in rows 6 feet apart. The plants may be grown over A-shaped trellises, in which case they are spaced a foot apart in the row. They do not grow well on strings and wires because the wind whips the leaves too much. The plants should be given several side-dressings of liquid fertilizer. No fruit should be permitted to ripen on the vines; when plants mature seed, they immediately decline and die. Gardeners make the mistake of leaving poorly shaped fruits on the vines, thinking they will grow into nicely shaped cucumbers. This is a sure means of shortening the producing season of the vines. A fruit that is badly shaped when small, will never improve and should be picked as soon as it is seen. Mulching the plants with hay, straw, or weeds will help greatly to increase the yield of the plants and make for a more uniform growth. This means much higher quality in the fruits. Cucumber roots are shallow and cultivation should be shallow.

INSECTS AND DISEASES: There are many pests of cucumbers and diseases are probably more troublesome than insects. But if the soil is well aerated and contains an appreciable quantity of pulverized magnesium limestone and there is good circulation of air around the plants, diseases will give a minimum of trouble.

Bacterial wilt lives in the stem and is spread by the cucumber beetle as it goes from plant to plant and sucks the juice out of the foliage. The bacteria spread rapidly through the stem, plug up the water lanes, and the plants wilt and die. The only control is to keep the beetles from working by dusting the plants with lime. If any plants show signs of wilt, they should be pulled out immediately and burned.

Anthracnose is a spot-disease that affects the leaves and stems and sometimes the fruit. It spreads rapidly in warm, moist weather; hence, good circulation of air is necessary to keep the vines dry. There is less danger of anthracnose if the plants are trained on an A-shaped trellis.

Mosaic is a virus disease that works in the stem and stunts the growth and deforms the fruits. There are several different forms, some of which will kill the plants, starting at the tips and working toward the base. If the foliage of an infected plant is touched and then a healthy plant is touched, the mosaic will spread. Infected plants should be removed and burned as soon as they are discovered. There is no other control than to keep the sources of infection cleaned out, including the weeds which grow in fence corners and waste places, as weeds sometimes carry the disease.

Downy mildews are serious on many plants and develop during periods of moist weather, particularly when dews are heavy. They cover the leaves with a moldy growth which will gradually dry up the plants. Dusting with a finely divided sulphur is a good control. Most any dust has a tendency to dry the mildew. Good air circulation will prevent it. In greenhouses, where it is customary to install large fans to circulate the air, keeping ventilators closed too long will cause it to develop.

Of the insects, the striped cucumber beetle is the worst offender. The beetle lays eggs at the base of the plants. When the eggs hatch, the small grubs work their way into the roots where they eat the tender tissue. This causes the plants to wilt and, if enough grubs are present, to die. Furthermore, they carry the mosaic and the bacterial wilt. The best control is to dust the foliage as soon as the first true leaves are formed and keep the foliage covered lightly with a rotenone dust or a good dustine lime. Cucumber beetles can also be controlled by covering the plants with mosquito netting fastened to a frame. This is worth while because it means controlling two diseases as well as preventing the damage from the beetles. After the plants are well established and start to run, there is less danger from the beetles. It is better to wait a week or two in the spring before sowing the seed, so that when the seedlings are up they will grow rapidly. The greatest danger from the beetles is during cool weather when the cucumber plants make a slow growth.

Plant lice or aphids often get numerous enough in cool weather to interfere with the growth of the foliage. Nicotine sulphate or Black Leaf 40 sprayed on the foliage will control them. In real dry weather in the warm climates, red spiders will cause considerable irritation to the leaves. Frequent watering during these periods in the early morning hours will discourage them.

GENERAL RECOMMENDATIONS: A few cucumber plants will produce enough fruits for the average family. They can be grown over the compost pile, so that the vines hang down the sides. They do well in any material of this kind which is undergoing decomposition. At the same time, they make a good cover. If a coldframe is available, the vines can be grown in it and kept covered with a screenframe in place of the hotbed sash.

Cucumber-Root

DESCRIPTION: Cucumber root (*Medeola virginica*) gets its name from the fact that the bulbous root has the flavor of a cucumber. It belongs to the lily family and is a perennial, with a stem three feet tall and leaves arranged in two whorls. The upper whorl produces small greenish-yellow flowers which are followed later by dark purple berries. The fleshy roots were a common food of the Indians and considered to have fine flavor. Although a semi-tropical plant, it is adapted to northeastern America.

VARIETIES: None have been developed for cultivation in gardens.

SOIL AND CLIMATIC REQUIREMENTS: It grows in moist soil where the roots are protected from severe winter freezing. It does not live through severe winters in upland mineral soils but grows on the edges of swampy or low-lying land. It is not particularly suitable for the small garden but offers possibilities to the hobbyist who is looking for something that has possibilities of future development.

CULTURAL DIRECTIONS: Cucumberroot should only be grown in suitable soils and therefore has limitations as to distribution. Where conditions are favorable, the roots are used to propagate the plants. Seeds in the berries may be used; they offer possibilities of developing new varieties with special qualifications, but may be rather difficult to germinate. No pests are known.

Curuba

See Cassabanana

Dandelion

DESCRIPTION: The common dandelion (*Taraxacum officinale*), a plant needing no introduction to the Ameri-

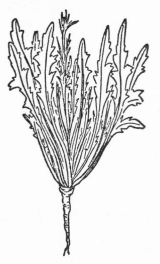

can public, is sometimes grown for greens in market gardens. It is a

stemless, fleshy-rooted herb with a milky juice and sends up yellow flower heads on long, naked, hollow stems. Despite the bitter flavor of the leaves, they are prized in the early spring for greens. Bitter-tasting plants were often considered to have medicinal qualities merely because they were bitter. This probably is a reason for the general idea that dandelion greens are a good spring tonic. If the truth were known, the dandelion leaves, like other green plants, probably have a few extra vitamins in them, which gives some justification for their use for medicinal purposes. Dandelions are of Old-World origin and have been used as a food for centuries, but their cultivation for the purpose is of recent origin. The dried roots were once used as a coffee substitute. The leaves are even blanched for salads by Europeans.

TYPES AND VARIETIES: Due to the variability of the plant and the freedom with which the seeds germinate, it is possible to select hundreds of varieties. Four varieties have been named: Improved Thick Leaf, French Large Leaf, Red Seeded, and American Improved.

SOIL AND CLIMATIC REQUIREMENTS: Judging from the distribution of the dandelion, there is no soil or climate unsuited to it, but the market-gardeners prefer a good, loamy, fertile soil, well supplied with lime and moisture.

CULTURAL DIRECTIONS: Dandelions need not be grown in the small garden, as there are usually enough in the lawn or in the vacant lot. They should be cut off at the ground level before the flowers go to seed. In the garden, the seed is sown thinly in rows 18 inches apart and the plants are thinned to stand five inches apart. The seed should be sown in August. The plants will make a heavy rosette of leaves and live through the winter. They seem to grow at very low temperatures and it is not uncommon to see flowers develop during mild winter weather. As soon as they make a good growth of fresh leaves in the spring, they are ready to be harvested. When grown on fertile soil and given more room, the plants may be tied up so that the inner leaves turn white. They are less bitter this way, but it is a question whether they are as good for food purposes.

INSECTS AND DISEASES: People who spend much time cutting dandelions out of their lawns may wish that pests were numerous. Luckily for the market gardener, none has been observed.

GENERAL RECOMMENDATIONS: Persons interested in killing dandelions in lawns should try fertilizing and liming the lawn to stimulate the grass as much as possible. This means that the grass must be cut often, but the dandelion plants also grow rapidly and will shove their leaves up so that the lawn mower will easily cut them off. Frequent cutting of the tops will starve the roots, and keeping the flowers clipped off will prevent reseeding. A few plants in the lawn can be killed by cutting off the plant and covering the stump with a pinch of the dry fertilizer which is used in liquid fertilizer. The high concentration will kill the roots. Dandelions make seed without pollination of the flowers; the plants have all the

advantages necessary for permanent existence.

Dasheen

DESCRIPTION: Dasheen (*Colocasia esculenta*) is a tropical Asiatic herb, sometimes called TARO, ELEPHANT'S EAR or KALO, grown in the southern United States for its tender sprouts

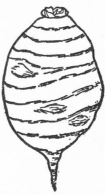

and tubers. The sprouts are the dasheen of commerce, while the tubers are properly called taro. The sprouts are forced in the spring and cut off just as asparagus spears are cut, and marketed. The leaves are very large, being deeply cleft at the base and pointed at the tip, and arise from the stem near the base of the plant. The plant is a perennial, sending up new leaves from the crown every year. The sprouts as they come up and before the leaves unfold are very tender and have a pleasing flavor. The tubers are somewhat similar to Jerusalem artichoke or a long slender white potato and have a flavor not unlike the oyster plant. The plant is grown as an ornamental in greenhouses in the North and is an important food substitute for the potato in the tropical Pacific islands, southern Asia, and northern Africa.

TYPES AND VARIETIES: Many varieties of the plant are grown in its native habitat but in the United States it is restricted to the species. *Colocasia indica* is used for the same purpose, but does not yield as much.

SOIL AND CLIMATIC REQUIREMENTS: It is a tropical plant but may be grown in areas where the soil does not freeze or where the roots may be protected with a mulch to prevent them from being killed. The roots can, of course, be lifted in late fall and planted the following spring. The soil must be a good loam that has an abundance of moisture but at the same time is well drained and supplied with an abundance of magnesium limestone and organic matter. The lighter, drier soils must be mulched to make the plants grow satisfactorily.

CULTURAL DIRECTIONS: The plants are usually grown from the tubers, which may be planted whole, or from cuttings. If they are to be grown for the sprouts, the tubers should be planted whole as soon as the ground warms and all danger of cold nights is past. To obtain the sprouts by forcing, the tubers are planted as closely as possible in sand or sawdust and kept well watered. It is possible to grow a number of roots during the summer and use them for forcing in small quantities during the winter in a warm basement, but the tubers may be lost. If they are forced in the open, the tubers may be left in place, where they will produce plants which will gradually produce another crop of tubers. The plants may be grown from seed by planting in the early fall and transplanting the seedlings the following

spring, as Cannas are propagated from the seed. Plants grown from seed will produce a fair yield of tubers the first year, but not so many as plants grown from tubers. The seedlings or the tubers should be planted 2 feet apart, in rows at least 4 feet apart, and should be set in the ground and covered with a transplanting solution before they are covered with soil. If tubers are used, they should be planted in a furrow 3 inches deep.

INSECTS AND DISEASES: Tubers should be carefully examined for borers and decays before being set in the soil. Any infested tubers should be discarded. Foliage pests are not serious. Any eating worms can be controlled with rotenone dust. Good soil treatment will go a long way in preventing development of diseases.

GENERAL RECOMMENDATIONS: The tubers should have the rind removed completely before they are eaten, in order to avoid its bitter flavor. The sprouts should be chilled as soon as they are cut from the plants.

Dudaim Melon
See Melons

Earth Almond
See Chufa; Peanut

Earth Nut
See Peanut

Eggplant

DESCRIPTION: Eggplant (*Solanum melongena, var. esculentum*) is an annual of a perennial bushy plant which produces very large plum-shaped fruits, dark purple, red, yellow, or white in color. The solitary flowers are star-shaped with purple petals and yellow stamens surrounding the pistil in a kind of beaked structure. The heart-shaped leaves are large and long and covered with fine hairs and spines. The plants were grown in Asia before the Christian Era and were referred to as Jew's Apple and Mad Apple. They were

grown for ornament and later for food and are mentioned in discussions on medicines. They are grown in the United States for their fruits. If not properly prepared, the fruit has an acrid flavor which is not particularly desirable. If the fruit is sliced and then freshened or exposed to air before being fried in a covering of batter, the flavor is very attractive. Most people agree, however, that a few plants in the garden will go a long way. Large numbers of them are grown and shipped to our markets and are appreciated especially by our Asiatic citizenry.

TYPES AND VARIETIES: Varieties differ as to shape, size, and color of the fruits. The varieties commonly grown are the large-fruited types which are round-to-oblong and siightly flattened. The fruits weigh from a pound to five pounds. Black Beauty, Florida Highbush, and New York Improved are all long-season varieties that require 75 to 80 days to mature. Recently the New Hampshire was introduced as an earlier variety which matures in 60 days. It has smaller fruits but is better suited to the northern sections where the other varieties might mature too late.

The Black Pekin is a good variety of very dark color, with a smaller, somewhat cylindrical fruit, slightly tapering toward the base. Many people prefer its fruit, because it is more like a cucumber for slicing purposes. A slice 3 inches in diameter is easier to prepare than one 7 or 8 inches in diameter.

The white varieties are more popular in Europe and people who have grown them in gardens say they are preferable for home use, but there is very little sale for them on the markets. It is another case where the home gardener knows what is good but, in order to sell through a market, must produce something that to him seems inferior.

There are eggplants which produce fruits an inch or so in diameter and a foot or more in length. They are referred to as *S.m., var. serpentinum*. The dwarf types with small, more or less pear-shaped fruits are referred to as *S.m., var. depressum*. The Chinese eggplant is often designated as the scarlet-fruited variety of *S. integrifolium*, sometimes called tomato eggplant. The fruits of red or yellow are often used for ornamental plantings.

SOIL AND CLIMATIC REQUIREMENTS: Eggplant in its native tropics is a perennial; in the temperate zone, an annual. It is very sensitive to cold winds and will not tolerate cold weather, to say nothing of frosts. It does best in hot summer weather. Soil requirements are specific. Eggplants are subject to wilts which supposedly are controlled by acid soils. The plants grow much better, however, on soils that are well supplied with magnesium limestone. Changing the location of the plants every year is a better means of controlling the wilt than with acid soil. Most of the wilts enter the plants in the seedbeds, where special care should be exercised to prevent infections. Virgin soil fertilized with liquid fertilizer should be used as the seedlings need the nutrients. The soils should be good loams or sandy loams that are well drained and are well supplied with nutrients. The plants do not do well on the low-lying soils nor on the very heavy soils.

CULTURAL DIRECTIONS: In order to take advantage of all the hot weather possible, the seed should be sown indoors about the middle of March in soil found where vegetables have not previously been grown. The soil should not be taken from the garden. A mixture of leafmold and sand or moss and sand makes a good medium. The seeds are planted half an inch deep and kept moistened; the flat or pot should be placed in a warm spot. After the seedlings are 2 inches tall they should be spotted about 3 inches apart each way or set in individual 4-inch pots, in the same kind of soil. They should then be watered with a liquid transplanting solution. When the ground is well warmed,

about the twentieth of May or the first of June, the plants should be set in the garden with transplanting solution. By this time the plants should have four or five true leaves. They should be side-dressed at least three times during the growing season. The fruits are picked any time after they have become large enough. But they should be picked green, that is, when they are dark purple. When the fruit ripens, it turns a brownish color and is not very attractive.

INSECTS AND DISEASES: Verticillium wilt is the most troublesome disease affecting eggplants. The organism gets into the stems and plugs up the water-conducting tissue so that the plants wilt and the leaves turn yellow and finally die. Crop rotation in three- or four-year cycles is the only sure means of controlling the disease. Magnesium deficiency accentuates the disease. The bacterial wilt does similar damage, but there is no control for it. A rot that attacks the foliage and the fruit may cause some trouble and be particularly bad in years when the humidity is very high for periods of several days at a time.

Of the insect pests, the flea-beetle does considerable injury when the plants are small, especially when the plants are set out early and don't start to grow immediately. The beetles are very small and black and leave small circular holes in the foliage. They do not stay over two weeks. If the plants can be grown in pots or in a hotbed and not planted too soon in the spring, the beetles will do very little damage. The Colorado potato beetle does considerable damage, particularly if the plants do not start off rapidly after they are set in the open ground. It can be controlled by rotenone dust. The striped hard-shelled beetles do not do much damage, but they lay masses of orange-colored eggs on the underside of the leaves. If there are only a few plants to be examined, the eggs may be seen and destroyed. Otherwise the eggs hatch into soft black grubs which soon turn brownish red in color as they grow. They have a ravenous appetite and will soon eat the foliage. They may be killed by a poisonous dust or spray. The eggplant lace bug does damage occasionally, but it is not serious. The tortoise beetle does considerable damage in the southern states. It eats holes in the leaves and can be controlled by dusting the foliage with a rotenone dust.

GENERAL RECOMMENDATIONS: Eggplant may or may not be a favorite. Enjoyment lies largely in the way it is prepared and how well the acrid flavor has been destroyed. One recommendation is to cut the eggplant into very thin slices, pile them up, and place a flatiron on the top for an hour or two before cooking. This is supposed to get rid of the strong flavor. Some think the slices should be placed in salt water overnight. After the "curing," the slices are coated with batter and bread crumbs and fried. They may be served with maple syrup. A very appetizing dish is prepared by making a casserole of diced eggplant, peppers, onions, and tomato sauce, covered with bread crumbs.

After eggplant is removed from the vines, it will keep for some time without losing its flavor. As a matter of fact, the flavor will probably improve with time by being made more mellow. Exposing the slices to the air will tend to mellow them.

Egyptian Nut

See Peanut

Elephant's Ear

See Dasheen

Endive

DESCRIPTION: Endive (*Cichorium endivia*) is an annual or biennial salad plant belonging to the same group which includes witloof chicory. It forms a heavy rosette of very much curled and cut leaves. It is a native of the East Indies and has been

ESCAROLLE

grown for many years as a salad plant. The second year it produces a seedstalk somewhat similar to wild

BROAD-LEAVED BATAVIA
ENDIVE LETTUCE

chicory. This type of endive is often called ESCAROLLE. In the market, the term endive or French endive generally applies to the witloof chicory (see Chicory).

TYPES AND VARIETIES: There are two types, the narrow- and the broad-leaf. The narrow-leaf type is represented by the Green Curled, White Curled, and Deep Heart varieties, while the broad-leaf type is represented by the Broad-leaved Batavian variety.

SOIL AND CLIMATIC REQUIREMENTS: Endive requires a very fertile loamy soil that is well drained and well limed. The nutritional requirements are fairly high, and an abundance of organic matter to insure a good supply of nutrients is essential. Endive does best in temperate regions and is fairly resistant to frost. It is apt to shoot to seed in hot weather. The plants mature in 60 days.

CULTURAL DIRECTIONS: The seed is sown indoors for the early spring crop. It is sown the first of March in a 4-inch pot for plants for the small garden. As soon as the seedlings are an inch or two high, they should be transplanted to the coldframe or flats and grown in full sunlight at a temperature of 55 degrees F. As soon as the ground can be worked, the plants should be set in the garden in rows 2 feet apart with 10 inches between the plants. They should be set with a starter solution and given a side-dressing 2 or 3 weeks later. They should be kept free of weeds by shallow cultivation. When the plants have made a large compact mass of leaves, the leaves are tied together to cause the center ones to blanch. When they are creamy white, they are ready to be used for salad pur-

poses. The heads may also be blanched by laying a wide board over the tops of the plants, allowing it to rest on the heads. This will exclude the light sufficiently to blanch the center of the heads. For the fall crop, the seed is sown in place in rows sometime during the latter part of July or August. The plants are thinned to stand 8 inches apart in the rows. The plants will grow rapidly and will be ready for blanching by the middle of October; since the blanching process in the fall will be prolonged to two or three weeks because of the colder weather, the heads should be tied up a little earlier than for the spring crop. In the fall, the plants may be covered with a mulch to blanch them.

INSECTS AND DISEASES: There are no serious pests of endive. If the heads are tied up during rainy weather, there may be some difficulty with decay in the center of the head. This is due to the water which is held by the compact leaves. Aphids may cause some trouble on the fall crop, and the plants should be examined for them before the heads begin to form a compact mass. If the aphids get into the folded leaves, it is difficult to kill them. A nicotine spray on a hot day will kill them.

GENERAL RECOMMENDATIONS: Endive can be grown all winter in the South. It can also be grown during cold winters in a coldframe with adequate protection to keep the soil from freezing. A coldframe outside a cellar window on the south side of the house is a good place to grow a few plants for Christmas. The plants can also be lifted in the late fall and placed in shallow boxes near a window in a cool cellar and, if kept moistened, they will grow and blanch themselves. The air around the plants must be kept moistened. This can be done in a very dry cellar by hanging a sack around the box on the side opposite the window. One or two dozen heads can be grown this way with very little trouble.

Escarolle
See Endive

Faba Bean
See Broad Bean

Field Bean
See under Beans

Finocchio

Finocchio (*Foeniculum vulgare, var. dulce*), also called FLORENCE FENNEL or SWEET FENNEL, differs

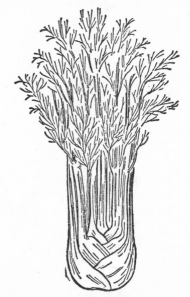

from the common fennel, which is grown as an herb, in having a large bulb-like structure, 3 to 4 inches in diameter, formed by the enlargement of the leaf bases as the plant matures. This "bulb" or "apple," as it is sometimes called, with its combined anise-celery flavor, is cooked as a vegetable. Like celery, it is blanched by pulling the soil up around the base of the leaves about three weeks before it is to be used. The stalks may also be eaten, either cooked or raw.

Finocchio is very palatable and should be grown in every garden. It is a hardy European perennial, but is grown as an annual. Growth is very rapid, so that it may be advisable to make a succession of plantings at two-week intervals. For soil requirements, cultural directions, and pest control, see FENNEL in Part II (Herbs).

Florence Fennel
See Finocchio

French Endive
See Chicory

French Sorrel
See Sorrel

French Spinach
See Orach

Frijoles
See under Beans

Garden Patience
See Sorrel

Garlic

DESCRIPTION: Garlic (*Allium sativum Linn.*) is a hardy perennial plant, probably a native of the Mediterranean region, having been used in ancient times by the Romans. It is grown for its segmented bulbs of very strong onion-like flavor. It produces a seedstalk very similar to the onion. The small sections of the garlic bulb are called cloves, which are enclosed in a thin skin or leaf-base.

SOIL AND CLIMATIC REQUIREMENTS: Garlic is grown to best advantage in warm climates, but it is hardy and will grow well in the temperate regions. In the United States it is grown as an annual. The bulbs do best in good, fertile, well-drained loamy soils. Sandy loam soils will grow good garlic providing there is an ample supply of organic matter. Soils for garlic should be well limed and liberally supplied with moisture during the early season.

CULTURAL DIRECTIONS: Garlic may be grown by sowing the seed early in the spring in the open ground and thinning the seedlings to 2 to 3 inches apart in the rows. The rows may be 12 inches apart. Some plant the seed in a band 2 inches wide, if the ground is not too weedy, for plantings in a band require more hand-weeding than in the single row. The few plants that are needed in the small garden may be obtained by planting the cloves just as onion-sets are planted. The plants should be side-dressed with liquid fertilizer two weeks after they are set in the ground. The cloves develop into good-sized bulbs in 90 days. When the tops are ripe the bulbs are pulled and permitted to dry in the sun. They are usually braided together and hung in a dry place where they will not freeze. One braid a foot long probably will last a family for several years.

INSECTS AND DISEASES: The only serious pest is the onion thrip, which can be controlled by sprinkling naphthalene flakes around the bulbs.

Globe Artichoke
See Artichoke

Goatsbeard
See Salsify

Gold Apple
See Tomato

Golden Thistle
See Scolymus

Goober
See Peanut

Gourds

DESCRIPTION: The name gourd refers, in this country, only to the hard-shell fruited species of *Cucurbitaceae*, although formerly, as in Europe today, it was used also to designate the related pumpkin, squash, cucumber, and melon. Most gourd-plants are vigorous-growing vines which make good covers for unsightly places. The male and female organs are in separate flowers, the female flower carrying the ovary or embryonic fruit. Gourds are not edible when ripe but some may be edible when small.

They vary greatly in size, shape, color, and texture. Most of them are grown only for ornamental purposes. Gourds are tender annuals with trailing vines or climbing tendrils, often planted for summer screens to be trained on trellises or on strings attached to southern porches.

SPECIES AND VARIETIES: Although all of the gourds belong to the Gourd Family (Cucurbitaceae) and have many superficial resemblances which justify their common name, botanically they are less closely related than, for instance, are their cousins the muskmelon and the cucumber. The latter two species belong to a common genus, but the gourds are classified under eight genera, each with one or more gourd-species.

The Mock Orange and Onion-Shape gourds (Cucurbita pepo), are small varieties. The yellow-flowered variety (ovifera) includes the Ap-

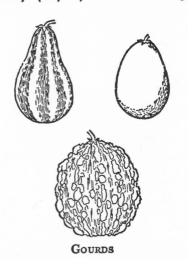

GOURDS

ple, Bicolor, Egg, Orange, Pear, Tashkent, and Turks Turban varieties. The Malabar ground gourd

(Cucurbita ficifolia) of eastern Asia is a related kind.

The Dishcloth or Luffa gourd (Lagenaria leucanthe) is also called Rag gourd because its interior is made up of a meshy network of cellulose strands, sometimes over a foot in length, which may be taken out of the thin papery shell and used as a wash-cloth or as matting. When wet, it is rather soft and slippery—an ideal cloth for bathing. The cellulose is the same as that in cotton and makes a very resistant long-wearing material, and yet people eat the fruit when it is green or immature. The Calabash gourd also belongs to this species. It is the large hard-shelled type, used for making dippers, bowls, pipes, pitchers, and many other useful things. The rind is composed of cellulose and lignin, the constituents of wood in trees. The dried fruits are cut into the desired shape and the inside material is removed. The gourd has a long thin handle. (The true Calabash, however, is not a gourd, but a tropical tree of the Bignonia Family.) Another related variety is called Serpent gourd or Snake cucumber. It grows a fruit that may be a foot to six feet long and one to four inches thick at its largest diameter, though much more slender near the stem.

The Maté or Utensil gourd (Lagenaria leucantha vulgaris) of Paraguay is also often referred to as Hercules Club, Dipper, Bottle Spoon, Powder Horn, or Sugar Trough gourd. It is very similar to the Calabash gourd, except that it is smaller.

The Serpent cucumber (Trichosanthes anguina) has edible fruits which are very long and slender, being less than two inches in diameter.

The Wax or White-fruited gourd (Benincasa hispida) has a long, oblong fruit with a dense coating of fine hairs. It is the Chinese-Watermelon, which see.

The Gooseberry gourd (*Cucumis anguria*) is the wild cucumber of Florida and Texas. It produces a burred fruit the size of a bantam egg or plum. West Indian gherkin is the same thing and is used for pickles when green and before the spines become sharp and hard. The Hedgehog, Ostrich Egg, or Teasel gourd (*Cucumis dipsaceus*) is similar to the Gooseberry gourd except that it is round and much larger.

The Cranberry gourd (*Abobra tenuifolia*) is a small, smooth, scarlet-colored fruit which produces very fragrant flowers, making the plant an ornamental whose rapid vine-growth makes it an excellent cover for unsightly objects. In addition, the plant produces edible tubers somewhat similar to the Dahlia tuber.

The Ivy gourd (*Coccinia cordifolia*) is similar to the Cranberry gourd in color and shape of fruit, but the leaves resemble the English Ivy, being smooth or waxy and therefore very ornamental. It, too, produces an edible tuberous root.

The Bitter gourd (*Citrullus colocynthis*) is a native of North Africa. It has a creeping vine similar to the vine peach, the fruit being the size of an orange, with a pulp made very bitter by its content of Colocynth, a drug which is made from it. The small fruits are used for pickles and for making preserves. The seeds are considered very nutritious and are eaten after the skins are removed. Bitter gourd is not a desirable ornamental plant.

Soil and Climatic Requirements: Gourds are tender plants which may be grown as annuals in any locality where the growing season affords 100 days of good growing weather. They must be grown in full sunlight and do best in seasons that are clear and bright. During seasons of cloudy weather and much rain, gourds may not be a success. Soils for gourds must be well drained, contain considerable organic matter, and supply the plants with abundant water. The sandy loam soils are best for the crop, but heavier soils may be used providing they are not too dense. Heavy clays are to be avoided. Gourds will often do well along the sides of buildings, over compost piles, or along the south side of unsightly fences.

Cultural Directions: Gourds should be started early in the spring, indoors in flats or pots. They germinate quickly and should be sown from the first to the middle of March in a well-drained soil and kept in a warm place until the seedlings are started. Then they should be planted in separate pots and placed where they will get as much sunlight as possible. Porous clay pots are not so good as tin cans with openings in the bottoms. Evaporation of water from clay pots tends to keep the soil too cool for these tropical plants. Do not over-water or over-feed the seedlings. A week before they are to be set in the garden, they should be watered with liquid fertilizer. In the northern states, the plants should be set on the south side of buildings as a protection against cold winds. The plants may be left in the pots until the vines are a foot or more in height, providing the soil is well moistened when they are set in the garden. They should be run up on strings to keep the vines off the ground. If grown flat on the ground, the plants may be grown over racks or an A-shaped trellis. A good mulch is ideal for gourds grown flat on the ground, as it keeps the fruit clean. The best-colored and most shapely gourds are grown where the ripening fruits can hang down from the vines. If fruits ripen while growing on the ground, they become flattened on one side and the color may be faded. Furthermore, the fruits will have much more intensive color if they mature in full sunlight; it is even a good plan to remove a leaf now and then if necessary to give the fruit full sun-exposure. The fruits should stay on the vines until the rinds are hard. They are not ripe until the rind is hard to the fingernail. They will not keep if they have to be picked before they are fully ripened. This is one reason why the fruits should be formed early. If some of the green fruits are to be removed for eating, the more retarded fruits should be chosen. It is true that this will result in fewer fruits being formed, but gourds are usually grown for ornament rather than food. A few good specimens are worth more than many immature ones.

If the soil needs fertility, the plants should be watered with liquid fertilizer once or twice during the growing season. The long growing-vines of gourds should be pinched after a runner has two or three small fruits or one or two large fruits on it. It is not necessary to fertilize the plants if the vines have grown more than six feet. Some of the varieties may grow to 50 feet. They should be chopped or pinched off at 6 feet. If they are growing over a building, however, this is not necessary.

The fruits, when harvested, should be placed in shallow boxes, or the large-fruited types may be placed on shelves, where the temperature is around 70 degrees. They may be stored in the open during warm fall weather but should be protected from frost during cold nights. After three or four weeks of high-temperature storage, they may be placed in a cooler place, such as a cool but not cold cellar. When the rind rings upon being snapped with the finger, the fruits may be shellacked or varnished with a clear varnish. Some may even be painted. Many abnormal shapes may be produced if the gardener will place impediments around the fruits when they are young and before the rind gets hard. This should be carefully done. It is also possible to draw pictures on the green fruits with a pin. The markings from the pin should be very light. As the fruit grows, the rind will heal and will make considerable scar tissue, which will be very conspicuous when the fruits are ripe.

INSECTS AND DISEASES: The most troublesome insect is the cucumber beetle, while the worst disease is mildew. Mildew comes from damp cloudy weather during the latter part of the growing season. This is another reason why the plants should be started in pots early, so that the fruit will be matured before the cool nights begin. Good circulation of air around the plants is a good precaution to take at all times. This requires keeping the plants thinned out to permit free air movement around the leaves.

Directions for controlling the cucumber beetle will be found in the section on Insects and Diseases in the article on Cucumber (which see). Plants which are given a good start before they are set in the field or garden soil will be less susceptible to beetle-injury, because the stems will be hard enough to prevent the small worms or larvae, which want only very tender tissue, from feeding on the roots. The adult beetles will, of course, carry the bacterial wilt to the vines and so should be repelled with a rotenone dust or a sprinkling of lime.

GENERAL RECOMMENDATIONS: Many people grow gourds as a hobby. There is always a sale for the fruits for ornament. The *Cucumis* types are not so desirable as the others for ornamental purposes. *Cucurbita* and *Lagenaria* species are most desirable, although the small scarlet-fruited types may be used for some purposes. The tubers of some of the types may be stored over the winter and planted the following spring. Plants will grow quickly from these and will mature fruits earlier than when grown from seed. The many variations among the fruits of any given species make the culture of gourds an interesting pastime.

Green Beans
See Beans

Green Peppers
See Peppers

Ground Cherry
See Tomato

Ground Nut
See Peanut

Gumbo
See Okra

Haricots
See Beans

Hog Peanut
See Peanut

Honeydew Melon
See under Melons

Horse-Radish

DESCRIPTION: Horse-radish (*Armoracia rusticana*), a member of the mustard family, is prized for its large fleshy roots, which are ground and used as a dressing for meats. It has a very strong, sharp, pungent flavor and it is usually diluted with vinegar. The plant makes a rosette of long leaves, which are two to three inches wide and over a foot long. It has a flower-

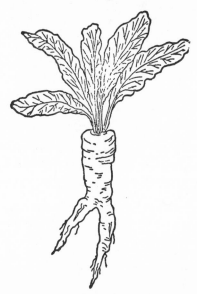

stalk two to three feet tall, with small white flowers. Native to the Mediterranean regions, it has become a weed in many sections of the world. It is not a particularly good plant for the casual gardener, as it will spread and be difficult to get rid of. A large amount of our commercial crop is grown in the Mississippi Valley, particularly in Missouri. Some is grown on the Eastern Seaboard.

SOIL AND CLIMATIC REQUIREMENTS: The plants are hardy in all parts of the United States, but the best quality is grown in the northern states. It does best in the loams and heavier sandy loam soils. The lower-lying soils that are well supplied with organic matter and moisture, if properly limed, are ideal for the crop. Heavy applications of manure are desirable to grow the crop. Many growers depend on organic material as the source of nitrogen and supply potash and phosphoric acid as it is needed by the plants.

CULTURAL DIRECTIONS: Seed does not mature well; therefore the crop is usually grown by setting in the fine roots which are stripped from the large fleshy roots as they are dug for harvest. When the fine roots are removed from the large fleshy roots, the end close to the fleshy root is cut off square, while the tip is cut at a slant. These root cuttings are packed in bunches and stored through the winter by placing in moist sand in the cellar. The cuttings are set 10 inches apart in rows 3 feet apart. The furrows for the rows should be 8 inches deep. The cuttings, usually about 6 or 7 inches long, are set in at a slant, with the square, upper end 3 or 4 inches below the surface.

After the plants are up and have made 3 or 4 inches of growth, the roots are carefully lifted, so that the tip of the cutting is not disturbed, and the fine fibrous roots are stripped from the upper 4 inches. The root and tops are then again laid back in place and covered with soil. This procedure produces a straight, com-

pact root that is best suited for the grinders. Branchy roots are difficult to grind. The plants should be cultivated to control weeds. Either in the late fall or the following early spring, the roots are dug and trimmed and sold, or ground up and placed in quart cans until they are to be used. The roots may also be stored in root cellars or in a cool cellar under the house. People have been known to earn $500.00 from a half acre, by growing the crop as a side line.

INSECTS AND DISEASES: There are no serious pests of horse-radish. The crop should be rotated from place to place, so that it does not grow on the same ground oftener than every four years. The white rust may cause some trouble, but if no plants are allowed to grow wild and the garden is thoroughly cleaned, there should be no difficulty.

GENERAL RECOMMENDATIONS: Gardeners assume that because the plants grow wild, they need not bother to set a few plants for their own use. However, volunteer plants usually grow in grass and the roots are liable to be stringy and very bitter; such horse-radish will not be relished. If it is made from well-grown roots, it is sweet and palatable despite its being hot. For this reason, it should be dug and replanted each year.

Hubbard Squash
See Squash

Hyacinth Bean
The Hyacinth or LABLAB BEAN (*Dolichos lablab*) is a tropical bean grown for its edible pods and seeds. It is occasionally grown in the tem-

perate regions for its long ornamental vines, clothed with very large leaves and purple or white flowers. It grows best on the sandy loam soils that are well supplied with lime, but will grow on poorer soils.

Irish Potato

See Potato

Jack Bean

The Jack bean (*Canavalia ensiformis*), or CRICKSHAW LIMA, is often grown in tropical climates for its tender pods, which are used as snap beans. The plant makes a bushy growth and produces purple flowers and long pods, sometimes a foot long, while the seeds are white in color and similar in size to the smaller-seeded Lima beans. It is an introduction from the southern Asiatic countries and is grown some in the southern states and occasionally—for ornamental purposes—in the northern states. It grows on the poorer soils and requires less lime than some of the other varieties. For cultural directions, *see* Lima Bean.

Jerusalem Artichoke

DESCRIPTION: The Jerusalem artichoke (*Helianthus tuberosus*), although an entirely different type of

plant from the Globe artichoke, resembles it in the flavor of the edible parts. It belongs to the sunflower family, having flowers with yellow ray petals, which make a fine show for a background or for a screen in the garden. The plants grow to a height of six feet or more and have hairy leaves six to eight inches long. The stems usually are not branched. It is a perennial plant and lives over from year to year by means of its tubers, which are edible and have a flavor somewhat resembling the Globe artichoke. This is probably the reason why it is called "artichoke" rather than "potato," which its tubers greatly resemble. It was found growing wild in the central and southern states, supposedly having originated in the Mississippi Valley from the sunflower stock. It was cultivated by the American Indians, who used it both raw and cooked. It was taken to Europe from America and is there highly esteemed as a cooked vegetable after the tubers have been chilled in the soil. It grows in waste places and has become one of the most valuable of the weeds which plague the farmer, who finds it in his corn field. Although it is used more generally as a soil-improving crop and as food for animals, particularly swine, it is of sufficient importance as a food to the subsistence garden to be given careful consideration here.

TYPES AND VARIETIES: There are a number of varieties which differ especially in the color of the tubers. There are white-, purple-, red-, and yellow-skinned varieties, but the flavor is not sufficiently different to be of much concern to the home gardener. Unlike the true sunflower species, it produces no seed and the plants must be propagated from the tubers. The tubers vary in size and shape. There is a Chinese variety (*Stachys affinis*) which has tubers that are longer and more irregular than the short bulgy tuber of the Jerusalem artichoke.

SOIL AND CLIMATIC REQUIREMENTS: The plant is hardy and lives through severe winters by means of its tubers. In the northern climates, the tubers are larger and rounder and much more filled out than in the southern climates where the temperatures are much higher. Also the flavor is slightly better in the northern climates. The plants produce higher yields in the poorer soils than in soils that are too fertile or contain too much nitrogen. They do particularly well in gravelly soils or soils that are open and well drained. For this reason they can be planted in the poorer part of the garden. They will respond to' hardwood ashes but need not be fertilized with any appreciable amount of fertilizer. One side-dressing of liquid fertilizer will usually supply sufficient nutrients. In soils of high organic matter, the plants make a tremendous top growth but are apt to have long slender tubers. If once established they will come up every year because, even though they are dug, there are usually enough tubers left to carry the plants over. A 100-foot row will produce from two to four bushels.

CULTURAL DIRECTIONS: The tubers may be divided and allowed to dry or heal over before they are planted. If they are long and slender, they may be broken in half. Usually the smaller tubers are better suited for planting, as they need not be cut. They are planted 10 inches apart in rows 2½ to 3 feet apart. They are often planted in beds around the compost pile or coldframe in such a way that the plants form a screen with their foli-

age. They should be cultivated and hoed, but they will usually hold their own in competition with weeds and will crowd out weeds, especially where they grow in clumps. They may be harvested in the fall or left in the ground until required or until the ground threatens to freeze too hard to permit digging. If dug early, they should be stored in a cool place, and, if only a bushel is to be stored, they will keep better if covered with dry sand.

INSECTS AND DISEASES: There are no pest problems for this plant—a fact which probably accounts for its growing so freely in large areas under such a wide variety of climatic conditions.

GENERAL RECOMMENDATIONS: This is a plant which should be grown to a much larger extent than it is; it will probably be used more generally as a food plant than it is at the present time. One reason is that the plants will grow on such poor soils that they are among the very few plants which can produce profitable crops on waste land. They contain considerable sugar and insulin, which makes them rather desirable from the standpoint of food. They have tremendous possibilities for the subsistence farmer or gardener who must grow a large part of his food on the soil. Jerusalem artichokes may be grown as pastures for swine. They can be planted in a field and if properly handled can occupy the land for a number of years without requiring much attention. Pigs pasturing on the plants will root up the tubers as their appetites dictate. If the field is pastured in small paddocks, so that the pigs will harvest the tubers rather thoroughly in small areas, they can get practically their entire living from them and there will be enough tubers left to start a new seeding for the following year. An acre will yield as many as 500 bushels. This means considerable feed for pigs during the fall months before the ground freezes. The pigs should not be pastured until after the first of September, because the tubers do not form until the plants have flowered about the middle of August. For winter feed, the tubers can be dug and stored in a pit in the open ground. They are piled up and covered with straw to a depth of 8 or 10 inches. The straw is then held in place with boards or soil. It does not hurt to freeze the tubers as long as they are used as soon as they thaw out.

Kale

DESCRIPTION: Kale (*Brassica oleracea, var. acephala*), a member of the cabbage family, is grown for its leaves

and fleshy midribs. It and the Georgia collard are probably very closely related to the wild cabbage, having been in cultivation for centuries. It is an annual in culture, but produces its seedstalk the second year. The leaves are longer than broad, very curly, and the margins are very much cut and ruffled.

TYPES AND VARIETIES: There are two types of kale: the Scotch, which has a grayish-green colored foliage, and the Siberian, which has a bluish-green color. Both tall and dwarf forms may also be had. The varieties commonly grown are the Dwarf Siberian, the Dwarf Green, the Blue Curled, and the Tall Green. The dwarf varieties are in greatest favor.

SOIL AND CLIMATIC REQUIREMENTS: As one would expect from the variety-names, kale is a hardy winter crop that can be grown practically all winter, if the ground does not freeze. It is our most hardy vegetable crop and matures in 55 to 65 days. It is grown as a very early crop or a late fall crop. For garden purposes, the plants may be grown in late summer and harvested late in the fall or allowed to go through the winter for harvesting as early as over-wintered spinach. Soil that is well drained and that is well supplied with lime and organic matter will grow good kale. The well-drained bottom lands which do not flood in the winter are good for the crop. Kale requires a good supply of nitrogen, phosphorous, and potash.

CULTURAL DIRECTIONS: A heavy application of manure or a good leguminous crop plowed under is good preparation for the crop. In the garden, liquid fertilizer can be used to good advantage. The seed is sown in the open in July or August for the fall crop, allowing 70 days of growing weather. The seed is sown in rows 2 to 3 feet apart and the plants are thinned to stand 12 to 15 inches apart. In the home garden, the thinnings may be cooked for greens. As the plants grow, they should be side-dressed with liquid fertilizer. If the plants are set out early in the spring from seedlings grown indoors, they should be set in with a transplanting solution and side-dressed. The older leaves may be picked off for use, leaving the center leaves to keep the plants growing. Of course, the center leaves are the most tender and it may be desirable to cut off the whole plant, if enough plants are available.

INSECTS AND DISEASES: Kale is attacked by the same pests that are common to cabbage and should be treated the same way. (*See* Cabbage.)

GENERAL RECOMMENDATIONS: Kale is not so good as cabbage, but because it can be grown and be ready to harvest from the garden at a time when cabbage is not available, it is a desirable addition to the kitchen garden. When cabbage is on the market, the price of kale is too low for profit. In localities where it can be harvested during the winter, however, it has possibilities. Because of the nature of the plants, the poundage per acre is low and, although the yield on the basis of volume is very high, it has its limitations as a commercial crop. In cold climates it may be grown during the summer season, but where the season is hot and dry the plants make a very poor food crop.

The plants, if well cared for, make a very nice appearance when growing in a pot and may be worth while from the ornamental point of view. The different colors and the extremely fine-cut, ruffled leaf-margins make it attractive for a table centerpiece.

Kalo
See Dasheen

Kidney Bean
See Beans

Kohlrabi

DESCRIPTION: This plant (*Brassica caulorapa*) is the most interesting of the cabbage family because of the structure of the stem. The leaves are similar to the turnip's, but the stem is enlarged just above the ground to the size and shape of a turnip. The stem is really subtended by the round turnip-like structure. Kohlrabi is not grown to its full size, because if used before the fleshy stem gets too old it has an excellent flavor. If grown rapidly, it is the best-flavored member of the cabbage family, with the exception, possibly, of cauliflower. The

plant seems to be of comparatively recent origin. Kohlrabi is a biennial plant which is grown as an annual in the kitchen garden. The second year it sends up a seedstalk as do other members of the family.

TYPES AND VARIETIES: Kohlrabi comes in white, green, and purple colors. The Vienna variety in any of the three colors, is generally grown.

There is also an early Erfurt variety of similar quality. The White Vienna is probably the most popular.

SOIL AND CLIMATIC REQUIREMENTS: The plant requires about 75 days from sowing to harvest. It is a cool-climate crop and produces its highest quality during cool nights. For this reason, it is usually grown as a fall plant or winter crop in the southern states, but can be grown as a spring crop in the northern states. Where the season does not permit more than 75 days between frosts, it can be grown as a full-season crop. The soil must be well drained and well supplied with lime and organic matter. It will grow on most soils but, like other members of the cabbage family, does best in the loams containing an appreciable amount of water.

CULTURAL DIRECTIONS: The seed is sown in the open ground in rows 18 inches apart, and the plants are thinned to 8 or 10 inches in the row. The seed may be planted as soon as the ground can be worked. When it is desired to set plants, the seed is sown indoors in February in a pot or flat, and spotted to a coldframe as soon as the seedlings are past the cotyledon stage. They should be given two inches of space between plants. A few days before they are to be set in the garden, the ground around the plants should be saturated with a transplanting solution, and another application of the solution should be made when they are transplanted. One feeding after the plants are established will usually carry them through to maturity. The weeds should be kept down with shallow cultivation. Deep cultivation disturbs the roots and may stunt the plants which are very sensi-

tive during the early period of growth. This slowing down causes the formation in the enlarged stems of fibrous tissue which is harmful to the quality.

INSECTS AND DISEASES: Pests of kohlrabi are similar to those found on cabbage and should be controlled in the same manner. (See Cabbage.)

GENERAL RECOMMENDATIONS: Anyone who has not tried this crop should plant a few seeds as a trial and then decide on the quantity to grow. In matters where people's tastes vary so radically experience is the best counselor. Too often, however, one's impression is gained from poorly grown plants which are not representative in quality.

Lablab Bean
See Hyacinth Bean

Leek
DESCRIPTION: The leek is a hardy biennial herb (*Allium porrum*), similar to the onion except that it forms no bulb but grows a three-foot, slender stem with ribbon-flat, rather than hollow, leaf. The leaves originate, however, from a stem-plate as they do on onions. A native of southern Europe, where it has been grown from prehistoric times, it is grown quite extensively in the United States, particularly in the temperate regions. The flowers are produced on the end of the stem in a globular umbel, not bulbous as in the onion. The flavor of leek is much milder than onion. It is used in soup and for a pot herb and, when mixed with a white sauce, is delightful. It may be eaten without ill effects by people who seem to have difficulties with cooked onions.

TYPES AND VARIETIES: London Flag, Broad London, American Flag, and Scotch Flag are listed as varieties, but

they differ only slightly in outward appearance.

SOIL AND CLIMATIC REQUIREMENTS: The plants are grown in localities close to large cities, regardless of the soil and climate. However, the plants require about 130 days to mature and want good growing weather with plenty of sunshine and warmth, but not necessarily hot weather. The soils should be well drained, well supplied with lime and organic matter, and fertilized with manure if possible. They should receive a good supply of water.

CULTURAL DIRECTIONS: The seed is sown early in the spring in rows 20 inches apart, and the plants should be thinned to 3 or 4 to the foot. Soil should be hilled up around the roots to blanch them. The plants may be side-dressed with liquid fertilizer at least three times, if manure is not available.

INSECTS AND DISEASES: Onion thrips are a bad pest in dry weather, but can be controlled by sprinkling naphthalene flakes along the row.

Lettuce

DESCRIPTION: Lettuce (*Lactuca sativa*) is probably our most popular salad plant. It is grown for its large thin leaves, which may be loose green leaves, partially folded heads, or solid heads. The plant is a native of Asia, where it was grown for centuries. It is related to the wild lettuce (*L. scariola*), with which the cultivated lettuce readily crosses. The plant is a rapidly growing annual which forms a seedstalk the same year that the heads are formed. The seedstalk may grow to three feet, with many branches terminating in several small compound flower-heads having yellow flowers.

TYPES AND VARIETIES: There are four types of lettuce, three of which have been grown in this country for many years:

The common HEAD lettuce (*L. sativa, var. capitata*) is grown in greenhouses as well as in different parts of the United States. The butter varieties are represented by Black-Seeded Tennisball, White-Seeded Tennisball, and Big Boston. May King Belmont and Bel-May are greenhouse varieties. The crisp varieties are represented by Hanson, New York, Imperial, Iceberg, and Mignonette. There are many other varieties too numerous to mention here.

The open-head or LOOSE-LEAF type (*L. sativa, var. crispa*) has two varieties. The butter varieties are represented by Earliest Cutting, Golden Heart, and Lancaster. Of the crisp

BOSTON HEAD LETTUCE

varieties Black-Seeded Simpson, White-Seeded Simpson, and Grand Rapids should be mentioned.

The cos or ROMAINE lettuce (*L. sativa, var. longifolia*) forms long heads and is represented by Paris White Cos, Green Cos, Dwarf and Giant White Cos.

ROMAINE LETTUCE

ASPARAGUS lettuce (*L. sativa, var. angustana*) is grown for its long ten-der stalks and is similar to celtuce (which see).

SOIL AND CLIMATIC REQUIREMENTS: Lettuce is a crop that responds to cool nights. As a matter of fact the best head lettuce comes from the mountainous regions of the West, where the days are hot and the nights are cold. Those are the same conditions that grow good head lettuce in greenhouses. Special varieties are used where the crop is to be grown under glass. The smaller types are also used for early-crop coldframe growing in the market gardens of the East. For longer seasons, the larger types are used. Lettuce will grow in any climate that is not too hot. In hot weather the crop shoots to seed without making a head. There are many sections of the United States that will grow good head lettuce if there is a market for it. The north and west slopes of the hills in our northern states are suitable for the crop. However, the soils would have to be built up. In the more southern states, lettuce is not such a good crop, because some years it does not head at all.

Soils for lettuce should be well limed to considerable depths, with an appreciable amount of phosphor-ous in the subsoil. The soil should be well drained and, if manure can be used, it should be used freely and plowed under. Potash should be used sparingly and is not necessary when manure is used. If manure is not available, a good heavy leguminous cover-crop should be plowed under. This is better than to depend on too much nitrogen in the form of salts. Many growers like to use nitrate of soda. However, most of the "tip burn" which farmers complain of is due to these side-dressings of nitrate of soda. The sodium seems to cause the trouble. Ammonium sulphate is a much better source of nitrogen for this crop, but the ground must be well supplied with lime, and preferably magnesium liming material. If the lime is put on just before the crop is to be planted, only pulverized limestone should be used. If it is applied the previous fall and plowed under, it does not make any difference whether limestone or the burned lime is used. It may be plowed under with manure. Superphosphate should be used with manure at the rate of a thousand pounds to the acre.

CULTURAL DIRECTIONS: Lettuce is usually grown from seedlings in order to avoid having it head in hot weather. It requires 75 to 85 days to grow a crop of lettuce, which would bring it into hot July weather if the seed were sown outdoors. For this reason, seed is usually sown in February in hotbeds, or in the fall in coldframes that are protected through the winter, so that the plants are ready to be transplanted in early spring. About three weeks after the February sowing, the plants are set two inches apart in a coldframe, where they are allowed to grow another four weeks before they are transplanted to the field. If the seed is sown in the fall, the plants are held more or less dormant during several months in the winter, during which time they make a fine root growth. In February or March, the covering is taken off and the sun shining through the glass warms the soil and the plants start to grow. They are four to five inches tall when transplanted. If the leaves are too long, an inch or two of the tops can be pinched off as the plants are set in the garden soil.

If the plants can be set with a transplanting solution, they will get a quick start and will need very little more fertilizer. The small gardener does not always have the equipment to handle the plants in this manner, but he can plant the seed in a pot and set it in a sunny window where the temperature is not over 55 degrees, and he can set the small seedlings in flats where he can grow at least 50 plants for transplanting to the garden. A standard flat will hold 80 plants, if set two inches each way. They should be set out-of-doors when the temperature is above 40 degrees and the sun is bright. In localities where the temperature is apt to be high when the plants are heading, it might be advisable to mulch the plants with a finely divided material such as grass clippings. This will keep the temperature of the soil low enough to prevent the heads from shooting to seed too fast. Leaf lettuce is usually sown in the open ground as soon as the ground can be worked. The plants can be used as they are thinned out. Leaf-lettuce plants should have five or six inches between them, while head lettuce should have ten to twelve inches. The New York or Iceberg varieties should be grown for outdoor purposes, while the smaller butter types are grown very early in coldframes. Fall lettuce is sown during the summer and transplanted to the permanent locations, or it can be planted in place, if one is willing to do the necessary hand weeding. Fall lettuce should be side-dressed with liquid fertilizer three weeks after the plants are set with transplanting solution. Head lettuce may be used as leaf lettuce before the heads form, in which case more plants should be set in the row. Head lettuce is quartered for salads, while leaf lettuce is chopped up and eaten with a dressing of some kind. Leaf lettuce usually has more nutritive value, because all the leaves are green. The plants must, of course, be kept free of weeds, but cultivation should be shallow. Not more than an inch of the soil need be loosened around the plants.

DISEASES AND INSECTS: Although there are many diseases and insects that attack lettuce plants, there is nothing the gardener need do about it outside of following good cultural practices. In the seed beds, give the plants all the ventilation they can get. Poor ventilation which keeps the leaves wet a large part of the day will bring on the damping-off diseases. They usually attack the stem near the ground. Water should not be used unless absolutely necessary, and then it should not be sprinkled over the leaves but applied by keeping the end of the hose close to the ground between the plants. Watering in hotbeds and coldframes should be done during the morning of bright days when the plants can be ventilated. Never water on a dull, cloudy day. Such a day is good for transplanting, however. Bottom rot, lettuce drop, gray mold, anthracnose, and mildew are all the result of too much moisture at the wrong time. Good soil-drainage helps to prevent these. Tip burn is due to growing the plants too fast or to bad soil-conditions, such as poor drainage or insufficient lime.

Insects that attack lettuce are not serious pests, except in the fall, when plant aphids may cause some trouble. These must be controlled by the use of nicotine dusts or sprays applied on hot days. Worms that eat the leaves are easily controlled by a rotenone dust, while cutworms are controlled by poison bran mashes. These mashes are scattered around the plants on the ground usually late in the afternoon, as the worms come out at night to do their feeding.

GENERAL RECOMMENDATIONS: Lettuce is one of those crops that has tremendous possibilities for profits when all the governing factors are favorable. First a good head must be grown. The right balance between conditions in the soil and the climate must exist. Moisture and temperature are very important. Then market conditions must be such that the crop can be moved. It is a crop of which a part of an acre may bring in as much money as forty acres of corn. Growers have been known to take in several thousand dollars from a quarter of an acre, but a person must have some breaks on his side to do it every year. Growers like to gamble on the crop and are willing to have several failures in order to reap one profitable harvest. Acres of beautifully headed lettuce have been plowed under because there was no market for the crop, and, again, farmers have received five cents a head for very poorly headed lettuce, because of a paucity of the crop on the market. Lettuce can be worth $3.00 a crate one week and be down to 40 cents the next. The garden is the place to try growing the crop. A few rows or a bed grown several years in succession will soon tell whether a larger area is worth planting. If directions are followed and a number of varieties are compared, the amateur will be able to decide whether he wishes to use his 50- by 100-foot area to grow a crop of lettuce or whether he will stick to a general garden and at least have something to eat. Of the few crops that lend themselves to such part-time farming for profit, lettuce probably has the greatest possibilities. The plantings should be staggered, so that the crop does not have to be harvested all at one time. This may also avoid a total failure due to temporary weather conditions. A crop maturing during a week of hot weather might be a total failure, while a crop the following week might be a huge success. If a person can build up a local market for the crop, the staggered harvest will give him a better chance for success and his labor needs will be spread thinner so that he may not need to hire help. It is worth trying as a side line on a small scale.

Lima Bean

DESCRIPTION: The most common Lima bean (*Phaseolus lunatus*) is the SIEVA or CIVET BEAN of the South and

is considered the progenitor of the Lima bean varieties. It is the true butter bean, generally grown in the South Atlantic States, but occasionally as far north as New England. Its seeds are small, white, brown, or

mottled in color, and grown in little pods containing two or three beans each; the plants are slender pole varieties. Lima beans probably had their origin in tropical South America and are generally grown throughout the warmer sections of the United States. An important addition to our bean varieties, they are used exclusively as green seeds—never as edible pods. They are sometimes cooked with kernels of green corn to make a dish called succotash.

TYPES AND VARIETIES: Unlike the butter beans, the large-seeded dwarf and pole varieties (*Phaseolus lunatus, var. macrocarpus*) are grown from Massachusetts to the South and from the southern states to California; they can even be grown in some sections of the central states. The principal Lima bean varieties are:

DWARF VARIETIES

Large-seeded: Fordhook, Burpees Improved, and Burpees Bush. The seeds are white, three or four to a pod. The plants are bushy.

Small-seeded: Baby Fordhook and Henderson Bush. The Baby Fordhook is fatter than the Henderson Bush but of much higher quality.

POLE VARIETIES

Large-seeded: King of the Garden, Fordhook Pole, and Burpees Improved Giant Podded. The pole Lima is the climbing type.

Small-seeded: Carolina or Sieva (the butter bean) and Florida Speckled Butter.

SOIL AND CLIMATIC REQUIREMENTS: Lima beans require high temperatures to mature properly and should not be planted in cold soil in the spring, as the seed may decay before it germinates. Sandy soils warm up much more quickly in the spring, and for this reason are much safer for Lima beans. However, the large-seeded pole and bush varieties require much more fertility than the light sandy soils afford, and must be supplied with fertilizer if the beans are to continue to produce pods. Lima beans require large amounts of lime in the soil. Calcium and magnesium, the two ingredients in lime, must be in sufficient quantity thoroughly to sweeten the soil, for the seeds will not germinate in acid soil.

CULTURAL DIRECTIONS: The soil should be well prepared for Lima beans, because of the difficulty of germination of the large seeds. If the soil bakes over the seed, the large seed-halves cannot be lifted out of the ground by the young seedling and they may be torn off or prevent the seedling from breaking through the ground. The seed-halves contain a large quantity of stored food on which the plant must live while it is establishing itself. If the seed-halves or cotyledons are torn off ahead of time, the seedling plant starves. A little sand scattered over the top of the ground along the row will keep the soil mellow. Gardeners sometimes make a ridge about four inches high running east and west and will plant Lima bean seed on the south side of the ridge where the sun will beat in and where the cold north and west winds will not have a chance to keep the ground chilled. The beans will germinate quickly and the ground will not bake so hard over the top of the seed. It is a good practice to soak the seed over night before planting,

though not longer than 12 hours nor in water deep enough completely to cover the seed. It is sufficient to place the seed on a blotter or several thicknesses of paper towel in a shallow dish of water covered with newspaper.

Longer soaking will cause the seed coat to break and occasion difficulty in transplanting, as the root or the sprout is very easily broken off. Planting should be done as soon as the ground thoroughly warms and all danger of frost is past.

Lima beans require an abundance of sunlight and should be planted in the sunniest part of the garden. If they are planted in the shade on too fertile soil, they will not set seed pods. They should be planted in rows 2½ feet apart. The large-seeded dwarf varieties should be planted 8 inches apart in the row. They are usually planted 4 inches apart and thinned to 8-inch intervals. Thicker planting will cause a poor set of pods. The plants are a long season crop and make a large bushy plant if given a chance. They should be cleanly hoed or cultivated so that the weeds are well controlled by the time the plants are in bloom. Any disturbance after the small pods are set will cause the plant to drop its pods. It is discouraging to go into the garden a few days after doing a good job of hoeing only to find all the small pods on the ground. The plants should not be disturbed when dew is on the leaves, because of the danger of spreading some of the leaf diseases.

Pole Lima beans are planted around poles spaced 2 feet apart in the row. The rows are set 4 feet apart. Four seeds are planted in a circle around each pole and about 4 inches from the pole. The seedlings are thinned to two for the large-seeded varieties and three for the small-seeded varieties. An ideal support for pole beans is a "tripod" constructed of four 6-foot bamboo stakes, set to form a 2-foot square at the base and tied together at the top. Two seeds should be planted at the foot of each stake and one seedling pulled if both should germinate. The tripods are set 2 feet apart. After the plants are once established, they will hold the tripods in place. Tripods exposed to winds may have to be secured by a wire tied to the legs and anchored in the ground, although it usually takes a very strong wind to blow a tripod over. Pole Lima beans may also be planted in rows and twined up on strings attached to wires strung between two previously set posts or between two conveniently placed buildings.

Large-seeded varieties should be planted an inch to an inch and one-half deep in the sandy soils, and less than an inch in the heavy soils. Small-seeded varieties are planted about half that depth. After the seed is placed, a starter solution should be poured directly on the seed and then covered with soil. If the soil is fertile, this will be all the fertilizer that is needed by the small-seeded bush beans. The large-seeded bush beans, and all pole beans, should be given at least two side-dressings of liquid fertilizer.

There are good and poor Lima-bean years. This is due to a combination of soil and climatic factors. On a fertile soil, if the weather is unusually wet and cloudy, Lima beans will produce a lot of vine growth but no beans. On a poor soil, under the same conditions, they will set a good crop. During a bright sunny season, they need considerable fertility. For this reason, gardeners will find that if they fertilize with liquid fertilizer, which can be applied as weather conditions require, more consistently successful crops will result. In good years Lima beans are not worth over a dollar a bushel and the gardener probably can buy them for less than he can grow them. In bad years, however, beans may be worth five dollars a bushel, and that is usually the time when they taste particularly good.

INSECTS AND DISEASES: Lima bean seed, when planted in cold soil, may become infected with a bacterial disease which causes the cotyledons to decay and so prevents completion of germination. If seed is soaked before it is planted, it should be planted in warm soil, so as to germinate quickly to get ahead of the bacteria. There is also a small manure-carried maggot that occasionally gets into the seed and destroys it. Well-rotted or composted manure probably will not carry the maggots.

Certain disease-like symptoms may be produced by deficiencies in the seed itself, caused by the conditions where the seed was grown. Seed grown on alkali land, which offers an insufficient supply of lime, may produce "blind" seedlings. The growing point between the cotyledons dies and the seedling is said to be bald. It makes the plant at least two weeks late in maturing. The remedy lies in a better selection of seed.

Too much surface moisture fosters a disease that causes the seedling stem to decay at the surface of the soil. The stem tips over and dries up. The disease occurs more often in heavy than in sandy soils. It can be prevented by covering the seed with a little sand.

The Mexican bean beetle is just as bad on Lima beans as it is on snap beans (which see) and can be controlled by the same treatment. It does its damage in a short time and will reduce the set of Lima beans to a much greater extent than on snap beans.

Anthracnose and bacterial blight are leaf and pod diseases that come and go with wet weather. Mildew is bad on the pods during wet weather. However, there are no practical control measures. If the ground is well limed and sufficient phosphorous has been applied, there probably will be very little trouble from these diseases.

GENERAL RECOMMENDATIONS: Lima beans should grow freely and should be fed with liquid fertilizer often enough to keep them growing until the middle of August. If they grow freely up to that time, they probably have sufficient fertilizer to carry them through the growing season. Any tendency of the leaves to turn yellow should be an indication that they need a feeding. The leaves should be a dark green color and should be larger than the leaves on snap beans. The flower stalks should grow freely and the flowers should be produced in abundance. In wet cloudy weather, this will occur with very little additional fertilizer and the plants should not be side-dressed. In bright sunny weather, a feeding every three weeks probably will not be too much. They should not be fertilized from the time they are coming into flower until the pods are well formed. Applying fertilizer during this period may cause the pods to drop off.

Any dusting to kill bean beetles

should be done before the plants begin to produce flowers.

Bush Lima beans should be ready to pick by the fifteenth of July to the first of August. Pole Lima beans should be ready about two weeks later. Large-seeded Lima beans should not be picked until the beans are well formed in the pods, but should be picked before the pods lose their color if they are to be used as green shell beans. No ripe pods should be left on the vines, as this will cause the plant to mature and stop producing flowers. Beans should be picked after the vines are dry for dry shell beans. They should be placed in the shade after they are picked. They need not be chilled immediately, as they are not as perishable as the leafy types of vegetables, but they should be chilled after they have been removed from the pods, unless they are to be cooked at once.

Love Apple
See Tomato

Mammoth Squash
See Squash

Mangels
See Beets

Mango Melon
See Melons

Martynia (Unicorn Plant)

DESCRIPTION: This plant (*Proboscidea jussieui*, formerly *Martynia proboscidea*) is a native of the southwestern states and Mexico. It is grown in gardens for its seed pods, which are used for pickling and as a curiosity because of the long curved proboscis from which the species is named. The plant has a spreading, prostrate type of growth and grows about two feet tall. It is intermediate between a bushy and a short-vine crop. The leaves are large, broad, and lobed and may be either oppositely or alternately placed on the coarse stems. The large, funnel-shaped flowers are produced in short, loose, terminal racemes, with corollas which may be

purple, yellow, or white. The seed-pod, green in color, is large, fleshy, and hairy, and the beak is long and curves inwardly. The flowers have a strong odor.

TYPES AND VARIETIES: Eight related species are known, but this one is the most popular both for ornamental purposes and for pickles. There are no definite varieties listed by northern seedsmen, although the color variations in the flowers and the differently shaped pods suggest that a number of varieties may be known locally.

SOIL AND CLIMATIC REQUIREMENTS: The plants grow in the warmer section of the United States as perennials, but in the northern states they must be grown as annuals, for they are not resistant to freezing weather. The soil must be well drained and fairly light, well supplied with lime and organic matter. The plants

will grow with comparatively small amounts of water.

CULTURAL DIRECTIONS: In the northern states, the plants should be started indoors, where the seed is sown in pots and the seedlings later transplanted to flats, from which they are set in the garden after all danger of frost is over and the soil is thoroughly warm. The plants should be set two feet apart in rows three feet apart. They must be kept free of weeds. The pods for pickling must be picked when they are newly formed and tender.

Melon-Pear (Pepino)

DESCRIPTION: Pepino or melon-pear (*Solanum muricatum*) is a spineless, bushy herb with a rough, branched stem, two to three feet tall. It is a tropical plant and native to Peru. The leaves are long and slender; the flowers, borne in a long, stalked cluster, are usually blue in color; and the yellow, violet-splashed fruit has a yellow flesh and is usually seedless if grown in rich soil. The fruit is egg-shaped, from 4 to 6 inches long, and is aromatic, juicy, and tender—a little like an acid eggplant. It will keep until late winter if placed on a shelf in a cool place.

TYPES AND VARIETIES: It is closely related to the eggplant but is sufficiently different to be worth a trial. No particular varieties are listed.

SOIL AND CLIMATIC REQUIREMENTS: The plants require a soil that is well drained and adequately supplied with lime. The fertility in the temperate regions need not be high, as an appreciable amount of nitrogen added to the soil will make the plant too late to mature its fruits. It is a long-season crop and must be started indoors just as the eggplant and tomato must. It is then set into the field or garden about the same time or a little later than the tomato (which see), as it is very sensitive to cold winds. If the plants are kept slightly on the hard or stunted side of vigorous growth, they will set fruits early and mature a good crop. In general, the plant will grow better in a cool climate rather than in a hot one. Where summers are very hot, the plants should be mulched. In the fall the plants will live through a light frost. They do not set fruits well if the temperature gets above 80 degrees.

Cultural practices are practically the same as for pepper (which see).

Melon: Muskmelon, Cantaloupe, Honeydew Melon, and Others

DESCRIPTION: Melons are an Asiatic or African species (*Cucumis melo*) of long, trailing annuals which belong to the Gourd family. They were in cultivation long before the Christian Era and are even referred to as having been grown by the American Indian during colonial days. Although the wild progenitor of the current melon varieties has not been recognized, it seems probable that one does exist somewhere in the tropics. Today melons are grown in all parts of the world, principally for their large edible fruits, but in some varieties for ornamental purposes. They have small to large yellow flowers, either perfect or bi-sexual, produced singly in the axils of the palmately shaped leaves. The fruits of the several varieties differ in size from the smallness of an egg to a bulk of 20 pounds; in shape from spherical to flat, from

oblong to serpentine; in texture of rind from smooth to warty, densely netted, or deep-ribbed; in color from ivory-white through yellow and light green to grayish-green. The most important of the varieties are the MUSK-MELON, the true CANTALOUPE, and the HONEYDEW MELON—one of the winter melons which include the CASABA. The WATERMELON and the CHINESE-WATERMELON, although they belong to the same family as the melons, are of different genera, and so are treated separately in this book under their own names (which see).

MUSKMELON: The muskmelons (*Cucumis melo, var. culta* or *reticulatus*) which are salmon- or green-fleshed are purchased in our markets indifferently by that name or as cantaloupe. These are not, however, the

true cantaloupe described below, but the soft-rind, netted melons referred to as NUTMEG MELONS. These have both sexes in the same flowers and the fruits may be either large or small. The small-fruited types weigh approximately a pound and a half while the large-fruited types weigh anywhere from two to fifteen pounds. Either may be salmon- or green-fleshed, the green-fleshed supposedly being more delicately flavored. Some of the salmon-fleshed varieties, supposed to have a musky flavor, are:

Benders Surprise	Medium to Large	Oval	85	days	to	mature
Emerald Gem	Small	Oval	75	"	"	"
Hales Best	Medium	Oval	82	"	"	"
Hearts of Gold	Medium	Round	100	"	"	"
Honey Rock	Medium	Round	85	"	"	"
Persian	Large	Round	115	"	"	"
Pride of Wisconsin	Large	Round	90	"	"	"

The green-flesh varieties are: Netted Gem or Rocky Ford, and Extra Early Hackensack, both of which are medium in size and round and require 80 to 90 days to mature.

Several varieties particularly adapted to be grown in coldframes should be mentioned because of their very superior quality. Two of them are: Montreal Improved Nutmeg, and Oka, both of which require 120 days to mature. The forcing melons for greenhouse culture include such varieties as Blenheim Orange, Invincible Scarlet, Sutton's Improved Universal, and Royal Sovereign.

CANTALOUPE: The true cantaloupe (*Cucumis melo, var. cantaloupensis*) should not be confused with the

muskmelons often bought in our markets under the name of cantaloupe. True cantaloupes have simple leaves three to four inches across and covered with a hairy pubescence. The flesh is light green to greenish pink. The flowers may have the sexes divided or together in one flower, as in the netted melon. The fruit is medium-large, light green to yellow, with a very warty hard rind. The name derives from Cantalupo, Italy, where the plant was introduced from Armenia. It is an old variety, long held in high esteem by the Europeans and once grown even in China. It is still grown in the Mediterranean countries, but has not found general cultivation among Americans. It seems to be adapted to high temperatures and comparatively dry soils and, as a long-season crop requiring at least 130 days to mature, deserves a trial in the warmer sections of the United States.

HONEYDEW MELON: The WINTER MELON (*Cucumis melo, var. inodorus*) is so called because its large, mildly scented fruits keep well into the winter. The variety most widely grown in the United States is the honeydew melon, which has a smooth, hard, ivory-white rind, and weighs approximately five pounds. The CASABA, the only other variety of winter melon listed by most seedsmen, has a hard, round, yellow shell, somewhat ridged, and grows to about the same size as the honeydew. Both varieties, with their more or less four-sided heart-shaped leaves, are long-season plants, requiring from 120 to 130 days of good warm weather to mature. They are largely grown in California and the Southwest, from where they come to our city markets. They may be grown in temperate climates if the seedlings are well started in the greenhouse.

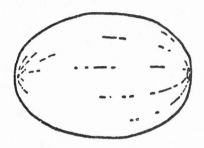

VARIETIES OF LESS IMPORTANCE: The orange or CHITO MELON (*Cucumis melo, var. chito*) is also called MANGO MELON, melon apple, vine peach, garden lemon, and vegetable orange. This melon is used for preserving, but is not palatable raw. It is sometimes grown for ornamental purposes, as the ripe fruits do resemble oranges growing on a vine. The DUDAIM MELON (*Cucumis melo, var. dudaim*), also called pomegranate melon, or Queen Anne's pocket melon, is about the size of a lemon and, though inedible, is cultivated for its fragrant odor. The SNAKE MELON (*Cucumis melo, var. flexuosus*) is sometimes called snake cucumber. The PINEAPPLE MELON (*Cucumis melo, var. saccharinus*) has a very sweet flesh and will keep as a winter melon until Christmas.

SOIL AND CLIMATIC REQUIREMENTS: Melons are high-temperature crops and require from 75 to 130 days of warm growing weather, depending upon the variety being grown. They should be grown in full sun where they will get good circulation of air. The long-season varieties may be grown in temperate regions if they

are given a good indoor start and then placed in a protected spot in the garden, preferably with a southeast exposure, where the damaging cold winds of spring and fall cannot reach them. They require sandy loam soils, properly drained and with sufficient lime and organic matter to give good root growth. They also want a steady supply of moisture, although the soil should be dry enough to be penetrated to considerable depths by the roots. Barnyard manure is a good fertilizer for melons, but it should be well rotted before it is plowed under. However, soil for cantaloupes, especially, should not be too fertile in nitrogen, but should contain a good supply of lime and potash.

CULTURAL DIRECTIONS: In the temperate regions, outdoor melons are necessarily the comparatively short-season varieties. The seed is usually sown out-of-doors in the spring after the soil is warmed and all danger of frost is past. They will benefit by any protection that can be given them, such as transparent caps over the hills, or boards set up on the north and west sides of the plants, or even panes of glass around them, to protect the seedlings against cold winds. The seed may be grown in the greenhouse, but must be grown in pots or veneer bands so that the roots will be disturbed as little as possible when they are transferred to the field. They do not do well if the roots are broken in transplanting. The seed is sown about May 10 to 15, and the fruits should be ready to pick by the latter part of August. The hills are spaced 4 to 6 feet each way, depending on the variety. The later varieties should be given more room. Melons can be grown over trellises, in which case they will require much less space. This is quite helpful for the small garden. Weeds must, of course, be kept under control, and a good mulch before the vines make too much growth will help.

Frame-growing of muskmelons was developed in the Montreal, Canada, section, where late-maturing varieties are grown. These are large melons and their culture is a specialized industry. It is possible for any gardener to grow these melons if he has coldframes or hotbeds. In cold sections it is necessary to grow them in hotbeds, while in the mid-central states they may be grown in coldframes. The seed usually is sown in pots or veneer bands in the greenhouse or hotbed early in March. As soon as the seedlings show the first true leaves, they should be placed in the frames in their permanent place. There they are grown under protection of glass as long as the air temperature is below 70 degrees. This generally means until the first of July. In making the hotbed, there are several means of obtaining heat. (See chapter on Greenhouses, Hotbeds, and Coldframes.) One method is to dig trenches over which the hotbeds are to be placed. The soil should be ridged in beds six feet wide with a two-foot-wide trench about 18 inches deep along the ridge. This is filled with fresh manure and then covered with soil. The boards are then set up and three- by six-foot sash are covered over. Two plants can be planted under each sash. The number of sash will depend on the number of melons that are to be grown. As the vines begin to crowd, the frames may be removed. The fruits are protected from the soil with shingles, boards, or flat stones. The frames should be kept open as much as possible to acclimate the vines and give good ventilation to the vines to prevent diseases from getting started. Winter melons and cantaloupes can also be grown by the Montreal process.

Greenhouse culture of melons is similar to the culture of greenhouse cucumbers (which see). The same precautions as to soils are taken as are taken in the garden. There must be good drainage and a good supply of nutrients. The plants are grown on A-shaped trellises with the plants 3 feet apart along the trellis on either side. The trellis is 6 feet apart at the base. The fruits must be supported by nets to keep them from falling off when they are almost ripe.

DISEASES AND INSECTS: There are a number of insects and diseases that cause considerable trouble in the field as well as in the frames. If melons can be started in pots and set out in the garden when they have made considerable growth, it will reduce insect-injury to a certain extent, as the cucumber beetle which causes most of the trouble does its greatest damage when the plants are small and are making a very slow growth. The cucumber beetle works on the growing tips and after eating the foliage and stinging it, lays its eggs on the stems near the ground. The eggs hatch and the larvae make their way to the roots, where they burrow through the roots and cause the plants to wilt and die. The beetles also carry the bacterial wilt and spread it from one plant to the other. The gardener will find that it is worth while to cover the plants with a screen or transparent cellulose acetate until the beetles are through their life cycle, or dust the foliage with a rotenone dust. If a few cucumbers are planted along the fence to draw the beetles as the melon plants are treated, the infected cucumbers may be pulled as soon as the melons have been freed, and cucumber plants and beetles can be destroyed together. The melon louse or aphid is a bad pest some years. It attacks the growing tips, and can be controlled with a nicotine dust or spray. Mildew is probably the most troublesome disease and becomes serious during cold nights and wet weather. It will ruin the foliage and should be controlled with a dusting of sulphur. Poor air-circulation may be a serious handicap in controlling the disease.

Monks Rhubarb

See Sorrel

Moth Bean

See Beans

Mountain Spinach

See Orach

Mushrooms

DESCRIPTION: The term mushroom refers to a large number of different species and varieties of fleshy fungi, many of which may be used for food.

Mushrooms are a lower form of plant-life than green plants, in that all their food must be in the organic form; they must live on other decaying plant-life. Green plants can get their food by manufacturing it in their leaves from carbon dioxide gas, water, nutrients from the soil, and sunshine. Mushrooms cannot do this and so must depend on the green plants to make this food for them, and then they cannot use it unless it is in the process of decay. Thus, mushrooms are grown on manure and plant-refuse which is being broken down into its component parts. This lower form of life produces fine strands of mycelium throughout decaying vegetable matter and these send up fruiting bodies which we call toadstools or mushrooms. These fruiting bodies may have a conical head on top of a short stem. They may be from a quarter-inch in diameter to six or more inches in diameter. As the fruiting body matures, the rounded head opens like a parasol and exposes gills, which shed a brown powder of spores or, we may say, the seeds of the mushrooms. The cultivated mushrooms, however, are not grown from this so-called seed, but from organic materials which are filled with pieces of the mycelium. Anyone who has seen bread mold, with its fine strands, will know what the mushroom mycelium or "roots" look like. Toadstools include many mushrooms, some of which are edible, while others are very poisonous. People in wandering through meadows will come in contact with many more mushrooms which are edible than those which are poisonous. The few which are very deadly are usually the bold types which are very conspicuous, but chances should not be taken with mushrooms unless one is sure that they are edible. There are some which are very unpalatable but which are harmless, while others which have a very agreeable taste may be poisonous. Mushrooms may be found growing in lawns in isolated clumps, in meadows and cultivated fields, in wooded areas, on rotten logs, on wood piles stored for winter use, under buildings, on compost piles, and in caves. They grow in the highlands as well as in lowlands and probably no summer day goes by that a person does not walk in the vicinity of a mushroom, usually of an edible kind. When it comes to growing mushrooms artificially, only one species (*Agaricus campestris*) is commonly considered; this is the species most likely to be grown by the amateur.

SPECIES AND VARIETIES: A few of the more important types of edible mushrooms which may be cultivated are listed here:

Field Mushroom (*Agaricus campestris*) has a straight stem from the point of departure from the mycelium to the cap. The smooth cap may be white or ivory to the shade of brown; the gills are different shades of pink; the spores are black. Field mushrooms always have a ring of filamentous tissue midway up the stem. The very small types are called Alaska mushrooms and are listed under Snow White and Silver King. The large brown types are "Bohemia" mushrooms, with no particular varieties listed. "Columbia" often refers to the cream-colored types belonging to this species.

Horse Mushroom (*Agaricus arvensis*) is a larger type than the above, otherwise very similar, except that it has two rings on the stem. It has a similar flavor, and some of the dark mushrooms which are cultivated may belong to this species.

Almond-Flavored M u s h r o o m (*Agaricus fabaceus*) is, as its name indicates, a type having a very characteristic almond flavor or odor. It is characterized by a persistent veil and is found in cultivated ground, often in greenhouse soils which have been made from composted manure, plant-refuse, and soil. The lower surface of the veil is covered with frosty scales. It requires a higher temperature than the other species and does not yield quite as well as the field mushroom.

Small Midget Mushroom (*Agaricus silvicola*) is found growing in wooded areas and is the smallest of the *Agaricus* types. It sends up its fruiting bodies during the heat of the summer and requires at least ten degrees more temperature than the others.

Shaggy-Mane or Horsetail Mushroom (*Coprinus comatus*) is an edible type that has a very unattractive appearance; when it is ready to pick, it looks like a closed parasol with a very rough, shaggy exterior. The cap never opens out like a toadstool and it soon disintegrates into a black slimy mass which is full of spores. It often grows as a weed in beds of field mushroom. It grows six inches tall on a long slender stem with a slight enlargement at its base.

Ink-Cap Mushroom (*Coprinus atramentarius*) is a smaller edition of the Horsetail and usually occurs in clusters, also as a weed in mushroom beds. The baby mushroom of this group (*Coprinus micaceus*) is found in large masses around decayed stumps and logs, usually in the shade of trees.

Parasol Mushroom (*Lepiota procera*) is a tall-growing, slender-stemmed type, with a rough cap and white spores, often found growing on lawns and in meadows. The plants are very conspicuous, growing to a height of 10 inches. The cap is reddish-brown and the scales are a darker color. The stem has a slight bulge at its base and a ring up near the cap.

Edible Boletus (*Boletus edulis*) is a large, fleshy mushroom with a short, very thick stem showing no ring and a smooth cap of a grayish-red or brownish-red color. The cap is 4 to 6 inches across and the stem 2 to 6 inches long. The spore-bearing surface on the underside of the cap is porous instead of having gills.

The Coral Mushroom (*Clavaria aurea*) is, as its name implies, a mass of coral-like branches densely grouped on a central stem. They are white or buff to orange. They are found in wooded places in the autumn and are all edible.

The Small Puffball (*Lycoperdon craniforme*), a white ball-like structure found in meadows and on lawns during midsummer, is attached to the ground by a mass of fine mycelium. When the flesh is white they are edible, but they soon develop spores and the whole inside becomes a mass of black powder. The outside then turns dark-brown. The Giant Puffball (*Lycoperdon giganteum* or *Calvatia gigantea*) is found in meadows and around logs and stumps. It may grow to two feet in diameter.

The Morel (*Morchella esculenta*) is an excellent mushroom with an oblong head resembling the sponge, except that the pores are very regular and of equal size. This one also is found growing around rotting tree stumps and logs in wooded areas. Many attempts have been made to cultivate the Morel, but all attempts have failed.

The Truffle Mushroom (*Tuber melanosporum*) is often referred to as the Black Truffle of Southern France.

Those mentioned are all edible types which are highly prized in different sections of the country. Of these, the first mentioned is the mushroom of commerce and the one most easily grown. The poisonous mushrooms are not mentioned, because the above description is not given for the purpose of identifying mushrooms but of indicating the diversity of edible types; and these are only a very few of those that are edible. If there is a question whether a given mushroom is poisonous, a good rule to follow is to throw away any mushroom that has a particularly large base, bulbous in shape and with a ragged membrane at the surface of the ground in addition to the regular ring near the cap. Some edible ones will be discarded by this rule, but that is better than taking a chance. The Amanita (*Amanita phalloides*), which grows singly in light woods, seldom in open meadows, is a beautiful mushroom in appearance, very stocky and colored—as a matter of fact, fascinating to look at. This is the killer and should be given a wide berth. It has the vulvox or sheath-remnant at the base, and the ring just below the cap, and the bulbous foot. There is a very colorful fungus which grows from the base of trees, pinkish-red and many-lobed like liver; to look at it one would think, surely it must be poisonous, but it is edible. The dangerous-looking ones are not always the poisonous ones. In case of doubt, have the specimens identified.

SOIL AND CLIMATIC REQUIREMENTS: Cultivated mushrooms grow entirely on manure that has been cured for the purpose, or on any other composted plant-material; the only soil that is used is for casing over the manure to cause the mushrooms to send off fruiting bodies. The climatic requirements are high humidity, with temperatures between 55 and 65 degrees. Higher temperatures are not satisfactory for the production of mushrooms in structures. When mushrooms are produced on the lawn, it is usually following a heavy rain with cool nights, even though the day may be quite warm.

STRUCTURES FOR CULTURE: There are many types of structures in which mushrooms may be grown. Mushrooms are grown in benches in specially constructed buildings, in beds in cellars under buildings, under greenhouse benches, in storage cellars, or in barrels in cellars. Buildings may be of wood, concrete, stone, or tile construction. These structures require special attention because of the problem of getting proper ventilation; if possible they should be located where natural air-drainage is good—not where air pockets may exist. Many arguments arise as to whether one type is better than another. This depends on whether the building is below ground or entirely above ground. The best location for a mushroom house is on the side of a hill, so that the basement may be entered from ground level on one side and the second floor may be entered from ground level on the opposite side. This makes good circulation of air possible. The basement is then built of stone or cement, while the upper structure is of wood-frame construction with air spaces in the walls. The buildings should be long and narrow, twenty feet wide, with a ceiling that follows the roof line of the gables. Ventilating structures are then placed along the peek or ridge of the roof.

The incoming air should drop down between two tiers of beds, so that the warm air may rise along the outer walls. This permits warm and cold air to mix.

Cellars and caves are difficult to ventilate properly, and the cellar humidity may be so low that the beds will dry out excessively and the mushrooms may harden and crack and be small. Caves, on the contrary, may be so moist that the mushrooms will be excessively large and diseases may become a menace. This usually is due to the fact that the heat is not distributed properly in cellars. The temperature in caves is often too low because no heating system is installed.

HEAT AND VENTILATION: The location of pipes and the type of heating system has much to do with the proper ventilation of the house. The ideal heating system is one in which the heating pipes are located on each side of the house on the outside wall. This prevents dead air pockets from forming on the surface of the beds by causing the air to move toward the ceiling where it is mixed with the incoming cold air from the peak and is carried down in the center of the house to flow out across the tops of the beds. The movement of air must be sufficient to carry away any moisture that might form on the mushrooms, and the excess moisture from the soil immediately after the beds have been watered. Excessive drafts across the beds will form brown-colored mushrooms which stop growing or which will crack, giving the surface of the mushroom a checkered appearance. Cold air coming into the house tends to dry them out, because it takes up moisture as it becomes warm. Ventilation is extremely important and may mean the difference between a three-pound and a half-pound yield per square foot. Good ventilation is the only practical control for diseases which tend to overrun the beds.

The material in the walls of the building will make some difference in the effectiveness of a ventilation system. Growers claim that a building of wood construction is easier to ventilate than a stone or brick structure. The wooden walls permit a certain amount of moisture to escape as well as a certain amount of fresh air to seep in. The ventilation tends to become automatic. Dry air outside tends to draw moist air out, which in turn causes dry air to move in. There are fewer drafts or air currents in a wood structure, as the walls tend to stay warm. Wood is a better insulator than stone or brick. Cold travels through stone and brick and causes the air to cool on the inside surface, so that the air moves down rather than up along the walls. Wooden structures breathe more. When the air inside is wet, the wood takes up moisture, while if the air becomes too dry, the wood gives off moisture. This tends to equalize conditions even in an underground house much more than is possible with stone or brick. Even a wood lining on a stone structure helps to promote better air conditions.

HUMIDITY AND TEMPERATURE: The amount of moisture in the air tends to determine the size of the mushroom. The higher the humidity, the larger the growth. Most growers have a rule-of-thumb method of determining the moisture in the house. They feel the soil and if it powders readily, they take it that the humidity is too low and close down the cold-air inlets and apply water. If they see drops of moisture on mushrooms, parts of the house, or benches, they take it that the air is over-moist and proceed to dry the house out. Some growers have tried determining the percentage of moisture in the air with accurate mechanical devices, but the difficulty is that the optimum percentage varies with other growing conditions which cannot be accurately determined, so they usually fall back on their sixth sense to make the proper adjustment anyway. A good grower can tell when he steps into the mushroom cellar whether the air has the right feel. Cellars under houses with the ordinary system of heating are usually too dry. They are poorly ventilated and the benches dry out too rapidly. The best mushrooms grown in cellars are bedded in barrels. Caves usually have no heating system, therefore very little movement of air, and consequently yield seldom over one pound to a square foot. An installation of electric fans to keep the air moving around the beds will help.

Temperatures are changed with the stage of growth of the crop. When manure is first placed in the house, it may send the temperature up to 130 or 140 degrees, and a week later the mercury will have dropped to around 75 or 80 degrees. The beds are then spawned and kept at a temperature of about 65 degrees for two or three weeks or until the crop begins to break through the manure. The bed is then covered with a casing soil, and the temperature is dropped slowly to 60 degrees, and a little later, as the crop approaches the harvest stage, to 55 degrees. Temperatures below 50 degrees are not profitable, as the mushrooms grow too slowly. If the crop comes in definite flushes, the temperature can be raised to 60 degrees for three days, after which it should be dropped again to 55 degrees or thereabouts. A few degrees higher will not be serious, but too high a temperature will cause the mushrooms to open up too rapidly and make it difficult to keep them harvested. Mushrooms grown at lower temperatures tend to be firmer and will ship better. Since summer temperatures are usually higher than the maximum for good growth, it is practically impossible to grow mushrooms during the summer months except in underground structures where the temperature can be maintained below 60 degrees. Growers have tried air-conditioning, but there are many details to be studied before returns commensurate with cost of installation can be assured. A practical means of controlling temperatures is by drawing air through the house from below, through pipes which are buried in the ground.

PREPARING MANURE: The old standard material for growing mushrooms is horse manure. It should have a good amount of straw in it. Mixed barnyard manure may be used, providing it does not contain more than 25 percent of other than horse manure unless a considerable amount of wheat straw is mixed with it. Manure from cavalry camps is good, providing it is from horses. Manure from mules is not very satisfactory and should be mixed with a horse manure comparatively free of straw.

Synthetic manure may be made for growing mushrooms, but it is not so easy to make as to compost horse manure. There is much work to be done in developing a good synthetic manure. The following mixtures are two of several which have been recommended as having possibilities.

PENN STATE FORMULA:
One ton of wheat straw. (May contain some oat straw.)
Six bushels of wheat scattered through the straw after it has been soaked with water.
Twenty pounds of urea scattered through the straw after it has started to heat.
This material is put together at the first turning. The temperature should rise to 140 degrees in the center of the pile. The material should be thoroughly packed by tromping, so as to keep it heating. In a week, it should be watered, turned by forking, and again packed. This is done three times more, before the mixture is placed in the house.

NEW JERSEY FORMULA:
One ton of mixed straw, wheat, and oats.
Six hundred pounds of a succulent material such as green grass, or any green material that contains considerable water, are mixed with the straw and grain and water is added as necessary.
Four to five hundred pounds of clover hay may be added to the straw and the whole thing soaked down.
Twenty pounds of pulverized limestone should be added to the mixture at about the second or third turning.

Other combinations are also being used by some growers in place of the manure. The requirements for synthetic manure are the mixture of a fibrous material, such as straw, with a succulent green material that contains an appreciable amount of nitrogen, such as green hay which is about to come into flower or head out. Mushrooms must have organic plant food from which to get their energy. There are many combinations that will probably give good results if mixed in right proportions. Rotted sawdust mixed with some good nitrogen source, such as cottonseed meal, and a little limestone would probably grow mushrooms. Synthetic manure offers considerable opportunity to the amateur for experimentation.

Manure may be put through the curing process directly as it comes fresh from the stable, or it may be stored in long ricks, preferably under cover, during the summer before it is composted. If the manure is stored outside, it should be covered with eight or ten inches of soil. When the manure is cured, the soil is mixed in with it. Stored manure will be partially cured when composting starts and will cure in three weeks, while fresh manure may require four weeks. Adding 25 percent by volume of soil to fresh manure will make it possible to put it into the house with no further curing beyond these three or four weeks of composting.

COMPOSTING MANURE: Manure is composted to get rid of excessive amounts of ammonia and to break down the fiber in the straw. Much of the protein in the manure is broken down to ammonia. This goes off as a gas or, if a little soil is mixed with the manure, into the soil by absorption. The manure should be forked over about every five or seven days, until the straw is easily broken between the fingers. The manure should be thoroughly broken in forking it over, so that it is thoroughly aired. If it gets too dry, water should be sprinkled on it. Piles should be long and narrow, not over 6 feet wide and 6 feet high. If it is stored in ricks 12 feet wide, as is common, it should be divided at the first forking into two piles, each 6 feet wide. Synthetic manure may not have to be turned so often until after it is partly broken down, because there is so much chance for air to get in without forking. Enough water should be added to prevent the manure from burning or fire-fanging, but it is better to have the manure a little too dry than to have it too wet. When it is almost cured, the piles should be covered in case of a heavy rain to prevent the manure from becoming too wet. When it is ready to go into the beds, the manure should be wet enough so that a drop or two of moisture can be squeezed out of a handful by twisting it between the hands. The manure should have a sweet smell— not a decaying odor.

BUILDING BEDS IN THE MUSHROOM HOUSE: Beds are built about 6 inches deep and not over 6 feet wide. They are built one over the other and far enough apart so that a person can reach into the middle of the bed below. The floors of the beds are removable so that, as the manure is brought into the house, the bottom bed may be filled without interference from the floor above and, as each bed is filled, the boards of the next higher bed can be put in place. The tiers of beds must be so placed that it is possible to reach to the middle from either side. In cellars, it may be necessary to make the beds up close to the walls, in which case they should be only 3 feet wide. Trays are used for beds where mushrooms are grown in caves or cellars. These trays are usually 3 by 4 feet or 4 by 6 feet, and the manure is packed in them before they are put in place. When the trays are filled and before they are carried to the growing rooms they are stored in a warm room in close quarters to go through a heating process. They are usually spawned and are ready for the casing soil before they are placed in the growing rooms.

FILLING THE BEDS: When the manure is composted sufficiently, it is placed in the beds and carefully packed around the edges and corners so as to eliminate air pockets. If the soil is wet it should not be packed. If in good condition, it is packed down with a packer made from a two-inch plank, 12 inches long and with a handle that will reach to the center of the bed. The manure should be on a level with the side boards. When the beds are all filled, the room is closed tight and the walks lightly sprinkled with water. The manure will heat and the temperature will go up to 140 degrees. At this heat, the houses are usually fumigated with cyanide gas to kill all insects which will have come out of the manure. When the manure cools to a temperature of 75 degrees, the house is opened up and the manure 's ready to be spawned. The spawn will be killed if the manure is warmer than 75 degrees. It requires about six days to go through this heating and cooling stage.

SPAWNING THE BEDS: There are a number of different kinds of spawn which may be used. The desirable types are bottle spawns. Brick spawn should not be used. Bottle spawn is made either with manure, grain, or sliced tobacco stems. The spawn is placed in the manure to start the crop. Three 40-ounce bottles are enough to spawn 100 square feet of bed. Manure spawn comes in bottles and the glass must be broken in order to get the spawn out. The spawn is broken up into pieces the size of a walnut and a piece is planted every 8 inches either way and in a hole extending about an inch below the top of the manure. A stick with sheet-iron teeth is made to reach across the bed for opening the holes. Grain spawn or tobacco spawn is sown across the beds in rows 8 inches apart. The grain is sown thinly and a bottle will go about twice as far as a bottle of manure spawn. Tobacco spawn is sown even more thinly. The spawn is permitted to grow through the manure at a temperature of 65 degrees for about three weeks. When the spawn is well grown through, the manure is ready to be cased. If the spawn does not grow, either the spawn is weak or the manure is too wet.

The composition of the casing soil has much to do with the successful culture of mushrooms. The soil should be a loam with considerable organic matter in it, to which enough pulverized limestone has been added to neutralize all traces of acidity. This soil is usually prepared a year before it is to be used. It is thoroughly limed and a green-manure crop is grown on it and plowed under. This should be repeated as often as possible before the soil is taken up for casing the manure. If the manure is dry, it should be slightly sprinkled before the soil is placed. The soil should be screened through a coarse screen to get rid of all stones and coarse plant-refuse. A coating of this soil approximately an inch thick is then placed over the manure. The soil-case is packed and then moistened—but not enough to soak through to the manure.

Some growers sterilize their casing-soil if there is any danger of contamination by diseases or insects. Their procedure is to lay tile end to end in rows a foot apart on a platform, pile the soil about a foot deep over the tile, cover the whole thing with a tarpaulin, and run live steam into the tile from a portable steam boiler until the soil is heated above 140 degrees. It is then allowed to cool for a couple of days. If soil is hauled a half-mile or more to the plant, there probably is no need to sterilize it. The soil should not be dumped near the houses nor carried in old baskets that have lain around the buildings, for this will subject it to contamination by disease-spores which are bound to be present around the buildings.

After the casing soil is put on, the beds are usually left alone for two weeks to give the spawn a chance to grow through the casing soil. By that time the soil will usually have dried out enough to warrant a good sprinkling—but not enough to drain through to the manure. A moist soil-casing will itself maintain sufficient moisture in the manure. The temperature at this time should be below 60 degrees. If the outdoor temperature is higher than that, it is a good idea to open the houses at night and close them tightly during the day to keep the warm air out. Three weeks

after spawning, the mushrooms should be ready to pick. Only those mushrooms that are ready to break their veil just below the cap should be picked. These may be small or large. Mushrooms the size of a marble may be ready to pick. The amateur will have to learn to recognize this condition by watching them until some break. Only experience will tell him when a mushroom is ready to pick. They should not be left until they flatten out and show the gills. They are edible at this stage, but not wanted on the market. Most growers like to have the beds "come in flushes," as it reduces the cost of harvesting, although some prefer to have them come regularly. To bring them in flushes, so that all the mushrooms of a given growth are ready to be picked at one time, they should be heavily watered if the soil is dry or powdery. If the mushrooms tend to come a few at a time, they must be lightly watered every few days. It usually requires five days between flushes.

If the fine spawn tends to grow over the surface of the casing soil, it is a sign that there is too much moisture in the soil and the air. If mushrooms tend to form under instead of on the casing soil, it is an indication that the soil is too dry. If the manure gets too dry the spawn will gradually form large strands and become dormant. If the manure is too wet the spawn will die out. Manure should feel moist—not wet when the finger is placed in it.

HARVESTING THE CROP: Mushrooms are picked by slightly twisting them. If in clusters, the center ones should be picked first, so that the small ones around the outside are not loosened from their roots. Small mushrooms will turn brown if they are disturbed before they are ready to be picked. Market mushrooms should be carefully picked, trimmed, and immediately placed in the boxes in which they are to be marketed. This requires the minimum amount of handling. If mushrooms are handled after they have been picked, they tend to turn brown in spots. Dumping the mushrooms on a sorting table and grading them is not a good practice. It is better to grade them as they are trimmed. All loose particles, trimmings, and diseased mushrooms should be burned.

LIFE OF THE BEDS: Two crops can be grown if the first crop is started by the first of September. This means that the manure must be started on the curing process about the middle of August. The beds will be filled by the end of the first week in September, can be spawned at the end of the second week, and will be ready for casing by the end of September. Mushrooms can be harvested the second or third week in October. Beds will usually produce six or seven flushes which means that the crop will be finished by the latter part of December. At this time another lot of manure should be ready to go in, so that the second crop will be picked from the latter part of February to the first of May or the early part of June. Curing manure in December is difficult and requires that the compost piles be protected from cold winds. Low temperatures will prevent the manure from heating properly and may make it necessary to prolong the curing period by several weeks.

COST OF PRODUCTION AND PROFITS: Two pounds of mushrooms on a square foot is a good yield, although growers occasionally harvest three. This means that an area 6 feet wide and 100 feet long will yield 1,200 pounds. At 20 cents a pound this amounts to $240.00. A house 20 by 50 feet with six beds would yield 1,800 pounds or, if it contains 12 beds, 3,600 pounds. The cost of growing the crop is around 20 to 25 cents a square foot. In other words, a person must have more beds or work the crop as a side line if it is to pay. Many people have the idea that they can buy ten dollars worth of spawn and live on easy street.

DISEASES AND INSECTS: Pests are controlled by proper cultural practices. Carelessness about leaving diseased mushrooms around the premises or failure to clean up the boards and walls between crops usually means trouble. As was previously stated, mushroom flies and other insects are cleaned out by bringing the heat of the house up to 140 degrees immediately after the manure is placed in the beds and, as the heat reaches its peak, closing the house for several days with cyanogas sprinkled along the walks. Any insect that causes trouble after this must be dealt with while the crop is in, which means special recommendations from an entomologist.

Diseases are controlled by sulphur fumigation of the houses between crops and after the manure has been taken from the beds. Everything in the house is thoroughly moistened and the sulphur is placed in pans or in iron kettles away from any wood and burned at the rate of two pounds to the thousand cubic feet. The houses are kept closed for several days before the fumigant is aired out. A less effective method is thoroughly to spray formaldehyde at the rate of a gallon to 100 gallons of water all over everything. Sterilization of the casing-soil before it is brought in helps some growers feel assured that they are not introducing diseases and insects. The manure should be kept free from old mushroom manure and other refuse between fillings. Spent mushroom soil should be hauled to the field away from the buildings and spread out to prevent insects from breeding. The mushroom maggot is the larva of a small fly that gets into the mushroom as it starts to grow. They spoil the mushroom. These flies live in manure and are brought into the houses with it. Springtails eat the spawn and may ruin a house during the first few weeks.

GENERAL RECOMMENDATIONS: Every year people want information on how to grow mushrooms. They have an idea that they can grow a large number of mushrooms in the basement. This is difficult, as is seen from the previous discussion. Manure is messy to handle and the problem of flies and insects is something that just cannot be coped with there, because it is impossible to fumigate. However, the amateur can have considerable fun with the synthetic mixtures which do not harbor all the bugs and diseases that are common to manure. These composts can be made in small piles and placed in barrels. The work can all be done outside and the barrel brought into the cellar when it is time to spawn the compost. If flies or insects cause trouble the barrels can be fumigated by closing the end.

Anyone contemplating the culture of mushrooms on a large scale should first try to get experience in a mushroom-growing establishment, even if he has to work for nothing for three months. That will be cheaper than to make a failure of a crop of his own. In the cellar, the amateur would not lose much if he did have a crop-failure in a barrel or two. For home use, a half dozen wooden barrels would give a good start and furnish mushrooms for the table at weekly intervals.

Muskmelon

See under Melon

Mustard

DESCRIPTION: The mustards, comprising a number of plants of the genus *Brassica*, are grown and sold

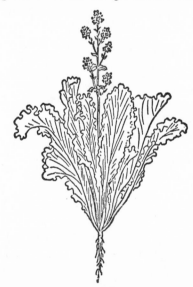

for potherbs in many sections of the country. They are long, broad-leaved annuals, whose leaves are used for cooking and whose seeds are used for condiments. The plants send up seedstalks, sometimes to tremendous heights, with small yellow flowers and long cylindrical pods.

TYPES AND VARIETIES: The white mustard (*Brassica alba*) whose leaves are used for potherbs, is a native of Asia. The Chinese mustard (*Brassica juncea*) is a native of South Asia. In southern Russia, the seed-oil is used as a substitute for olive oil. The Japanese mustard (*Brassica Japonica*) is grown to some extent in the South, for its large plume-like leaves. The black mustard (*Brassica nigra*), a native of Egypt, is grown in the southwestern part of the United States. In the home garden, it is grown for its leaves; commercially, for its seeds, which are the source of the mustard of commerce. Varieties of mustard commonly grown are Florida Broad Leaf, Large Smooth-Leaved, Southern Giant Curled, and Tender Green or Mustard Spinach. Of the black mustards should be mentioned Black Mustard of Sicily and the Large Black-Seeded varieties.

SOIL AND CLIMATIC REQUIREMENTS: The plants are a short-season crop which will mature within 30 to 45 days. The crop does best for salad purposes if sown on heavy loam-soils that are well drained and well supplied with nutrients and water. The plants grow rapidly and should have nutrients quickly available.

CULTURAL DIRECTIONS: For the spring crop, the seed is sown in rows in the open ground as soon as it can be worked; the plants are thinned as they are used for the table. As soon as hot weather occurs, the plant goes to seed quickly and should be pulled before it produces flowers, as it may become a weed. For the fall crop,

plantings should be made in August —not later or aphids may ruin the crop.

Myrrh
See Sweet Cicely

Navy Bean
See Beans

New Zealand Spinach

DESCRIPTION: A prostrate, much-branched, fleshy plant (*Tetragonia expansa*) whose small succulent leaves and tender branch-tips are used as salad and greens in sections where high temperatures prevent the growing of spinach. Despite its name,

the plant is in no way related to the common spinach. It is much more useful than spinach, because it can be grown all summer in heats which spinach cannot stand, because its open growth collects much less sand and can be washed more easily, and because it is much more easily grown and gives repeated cuttings all summer. Although native to New Zealand and Australia, the plant is generally grown in the United States.

TYPES AND VARIETIES: There are several varieties which differ in the size and smoothness of the leaves but are usually listed in the seed catalogues simply as New Zealand spinach.

SOIL AND CLIMATIC REQUIREMENTS:
Soil requirements are not very specific for this crop. A good, well-drained loam soil which holds water fairly well and has large quantities of lime seems desirable. Although the plants will grow well under high temperatures, they will also grow well in temperate climates, as the plants make a rapid growth. Once planted, they will occupy the ground the whole season.

CULTURAL DIRECTIONS: Seed may be sown early either in the open ground or indoors for seedlings to set out as soon as the soil warms in the spring. The plants are set in rows, preferably from pots or veneer bands to save disturbing the roots. They should be spaced 2 to 3 feet apart in the rows and 3 to 4 feet apart between the rows. They must be cultivated to control weeds—but with a hoe, so as not to disturb the roots. The tender tips of the branches may be snipped off as desired if the clippings are not made too close. The plants are easily killed by frost in the fall. There are no serious pests to consider.

Nutmeg Melon
See Melons: Muskmelon

Okra
DESCRIPTION: Okra (*Hibiscus esculentus*), sometimes called GUMBO, is a tall, handsome, tropical annual from the Nile Valley, with a much-branched coarse stem that grows to a height of three feet and produces large-petaled flowers and long, slender, pointed seed pods. The pods are picked green and cooked to make a gumbo or mucilaginous body for thickening certain dishes. They are

also cut up for soups. The ripe seeds have been used as a substitute for coffee. In the United States, the plant is better adapted to the southern states than to the cooler sections of the country.

TYPES AND VARIETIES: There are large and dwarf varieties and the dwarf seem to be in greater favor because their pods ripen earlier. There are three general types which are again divided into different varieties according to the length of the pods. Such varieties as Tall and Dwarf Green, Lady Finger, and White Velvet are listed.

SOIL AND CLIMATIC REQUIREMENTS:
Okra is a semi-hardy plant, very sensitive to cold winds. It requires 65 to 75 days to get edible pods. The southern states are particularly suited to this crop. There it is possible to

get pods from two or three sowings yearly. In the North, the plants should be grown on the sheltered side of buildings or windbreaks. They need a fertile, well-drained, limed soil.

CULTURAL DIRECTIONS: In the North, the seeds should be started in pots so that the plants may be transplanted to the garden without disturbing the roots too much. They do not transplant well. The seed may be started in hotbeds or coldframes and left there to mature. In the South, the seed is sown in the open ground as soon as all danger of frost is past, in rows three feet apart and with 12 to 18 inches between the plants. The dwarf varieties require less space than the large ones. The plants should be kept free from weeds, and the pods should be picked off when green and chilled or cooked immediately; otherwise they get tough. No pods should be allowed to ripen their seed, or the plants will stop producing, become senile, and die.

The ground should be limed, and, if manure is available, it should be plowed under when the ground is plowed. The plants should be set with a starter solution, and should be given two side-dressings of liquid fertilizer, once when about a foot high and again when the pods have started. No pest seriously troubles okra.

GENERAL RECOMMENDATIONS: Okra is definitely a garden plant, because the pods retain their tenderness only a short time after they are picked and can best be appreciated, therefore, only by the homegrower. They should be picked every day and used as soon as possible. Even though they are not to be used, they should be picked. Okra can be preserved for use in soups during the winter either by canning or by drying. If the pods are split and strung together, they will dry for easy storage until used.

Anyone who has not used or tried this vegetable should do so. Some people like it very much, while others may have to become accustomed to its flavor. Four or five plants in the garden will produce enough for the average family.

The last pods formed should be left for seed. Where winters are not too severe, the plants will live through, especially if they are given a small amount of protection with some mulching material. Even in the North, they can be carried through if the ground can be prevented from freezing.

Onion

DESCRIPTION: The onion (*Allium cepa*) is a hardy biennial of the lily

family, grown for its immature stems, which are sold as green or bunch onions, and its ripe, firm bulbs. These bulbs come in various shapes and colors and with different degrees of pungency. The onion contains much sugar and varying amounts of mustard oil. The bulb is closely packed leaf-bases and the long, slender, tubular blades are fleshy and dark green. The flower-stalk is tubular and fleshy and produces a globular head of very small greenish-white flowers, or the seed-stalk may have, in place of the flowers, clusters of small onions which may be used as seed for new plants. The plants grow to a height of three feet when in blossom.

SPECIES AND VARIETIES: The common garden onion is a native of Persia and is grown throughout the United States either from seed or sets. Its principal varieties are:

White Varieties: Southport White Globe, White Sweet Spanish (round), Crystal White Wax (flat), Earliest White Queen (small and round), and White Portugal (very large, flat, and medium-late).

Yellow Varieties: Southport Yellow Globe, Utah Sweet Spanish, Early Yellow Globe, Yellow Bermuda, Yellow Globe Danvers, Ebenezer or Japanese (flattened globe-shape), Yellow Danvers (flat), and Sweet Bermuda (flat).

Red to Brown Varieties: Southport Red Globe, Red Weathersfield, and Prizetaker. Red Italian Tripoli is a flat type that is perhaps less known.

The Tree Onion (Allium canadense), a native of North America, grows wild in some sections of northeastern United States and Canada. It produces bulblets at the top. It is listed only as the Tree or Egyptian Onion, without varieties.

Ciboul or Welsh Onion (Allium fistulosum), sometimes called two-bladed onion, is a native of Siberia. It forms a slight swelling at the base of the leaves and does not form large onions. It is grown for its leaves, which are used in salads. The small, flat, brownish-green bulbs are often used in pickling. It is very hardy and keeps well in storage and some think it is the progenitor of the garden onion. It is propagated from seed.

Shallot (Allium ascalonicum) is a native of western Asia. The bulbs are compound and separated into cloves similar to but much milder than those of garlic. These cloves are used in salads and for all sorts of cookery and flavoring. They make excellent pickles. The plant is propagated by planting the cloves.

The Multiplier Onion is probably a variety of the common onion differing only in the manner in which the bulb develops. Instead of a single growing center, the bulb has three or four, and each one of these, if separated and planted, will make as many more. Examination of garden onions in the field will show some of these types, but probably not the true multiplier. They may be propagated from seed, although the plants are very shy seeders.

The Wild Onion (Allium cernuum) is a native of North America, very hardy and a bad weed. It has a very strong flavor and produces small bulbs which are edible. It also produces seed. It is difficult to eradicate, as it comes up very early in the spring and, unless the bulbs are dug up, the early growth will store sufficient plant food to live through the winter. Unmolested, the plants make large clumps of bulbs, which, on cultivation, are scattered and remain dormant for the following year.

SOIL AND CLIMATIC REQUIREMENTS OF THE GARDEN ONION: The early varieties will grow well from outdoor, spring-sown seed in sections where there are 100 to 120 days of growing weather or from sets or greenhouse seedlings in much shorter seasons. The later and larger varieties require a longer growing-season with higher temperatures, and must be propagated by means of seedlings or, in some cases, sets. The large Bermuda and Sweet Spanish types are grown in the southern states.

Soils for onions vary from the light, sandy loams for the culture of early onions from sets, to the muck soils for seed- and seedling-onions. Muck soils have been known to produce from seedling culture over 1,500 bushels of onions per acre. Yields from sets on the sandy soils do not run that high. Any soil must be well drained but must supply an abundance of water. The sandy soils should be well supplied with organic matter and lime. Onions like a sweet soil.

CULTURAL DIRECTIONS: One method of growing onions is to buy "sets," which are really little pickling onions, and plant them as early as the ground can be worked. After the ground has been prepared, the sets are spaced 2 inches apart in rows 2 feet apart. These will produce onions by the first-to-middle of August. Where severe freezing does not occur, the sets may be planted during the winter or even in the fall for very early green onions. Sets for planting should be sorted into two lots, those that are less than five-eighths of an inch in diameter and those that are more than that. The larger sets will produce seedstalks and bad-sized onions with big necks and difficult to cure when harvested. If the seedstalk is pulled out of the onion when it is not over 6 inches tall, the mature onion will have a normal neck and a large-sized bulb. If the seedstalk is permitted to grow until the seed cluster begins to form, the base will be too large for its removal to do any good. The small sets, however, will produce a larger yield and the individual onions will be larger. Weeds must be kept out of the onions, as they draw heavily on the moisture. The bulbs should be watered with a transplanting solution when they are set in the ground and should be given a side-dressing of liquid fertilizer when they are six inches high.

In light, sandy soils that are well drained and have a liberal quantity of lime, the sets are planted to their full depth, so that just the tip sticks above ground. On heavier soil, about one half of the upper part of the set is exposed. If the bulb is set too deep, it will decay before it grows. A pint to a quart of sets will serve the average family. Sets may be grown in the garden. The seed is sown early in the spring in a row two to four inches wide, thickly enough so that the onions will be crowded. The seedlings are not given any fertilizer. When the majority of the seedlings are beginning to turn yellow, about the latter part of July or thereabouts, they are loosened by pulling or by cutting under the bulbs with a hoe, and raked out in a small windrow so that they have a chance to dry. When thoroughly dry, they are gathered and sorted and any bulbs that approach or exceed an inch in diameter are used for pickling onions. The small ones are then kept in a dry airy place in slatted or wire-bottom trays, where they are cured. They should not be allowed to freeze during the winter.

Top or multiplier onions may also

be grown, and the bulblets or parts of the large multiplier onions may be used in place of sets. Onions of this type are usually grown on uplands and with irrigation if it is available. In wet seasons or unless the season is excessively dry, irrigation is not necessary. This is particularly true if the soil is in good tilth.

Onion culture on the muck soils involves the sowing of seed. The seed is sown thickly in rows 14 to 18 inches apart and the seedlings are thinned to stand two inches apart. As they grow, they crowd each other so that the row may be the width of two onions. For real large, fancy onions, they should be thinned to three inches apart. The cost of keeping out weeds is tremendous on new ground. Side-dressings of a liquid fertilizer low in nitrogen, such as a 3-12-15 mixture dissolved in water at the rate of 50 pounds to 200 gallons, are applied when the seedlings are three to four inches tall. Ten pounds of copper to the 200 gallons of water will improve the color of the bulbs.

The culture of the large late-maturing varieties, whether they are grown in the temperate regions or in the South, is entirely a case of transplanting seedlings. The seed is sown in hotbeds or greenhouses six weeks before transplanting to the field. The seedlings are then set in rows as soon as the ground can be worked in the spring. Light frosts usually do not hurt them. Considerable labor is needed to transplant them, as a large number of seedlings per acre is required. In the home garden, this is not much of a job. The seedlings should be ready to be set as soon as the ground can be cultivated. The seedlings are set three to four inches apart. The cost of transplanting is

offset by the cost of thinning, so that the seed and seedling cultures are about equally costly. Some growers and gardeners can plant more thinly and remove some of the onions for green-bunch onions, thus thinning and harvesting a crop at the same time. This is ideal for the home garden. The commercial growers usually grow their green bunch onions in separate fields, however, as the cost of harvesting is then much less. When onions are disturbed by removing some for bunch onions, they are slightly checked in their growth and are liable to mature before they are full grown.

INSECTS AND DISEASES: There are a number of pests of the onion which may give considerable trouble. The onion smut disease is probably the worst offender. It is more severe in the temperate regions than in the warmer sections in the South. The smut organism apparently does not develop as well at the higher temperatures. The common control now is to apply a formaldehyde solution along the row with the seed. Onion mildew sometimes causes some trouble by attacking and killing the leaves. Its development depends on moisture conditions, and there is not much that can be done except to keep all dead or dying plants from spreading spores to healthy plants.

Of the insects that cause trouble, the onion thrips are probably the worst, but can be easily controlled by scattering naphthalene flakes along the rows around the plants. This repels the thrips but does not kill them. Thrips are bad in dry weather but give very little trouble in wet ground. In the garden, it is a simple matter to sprinkle the ground around the plants often enough to keep the ground from drying out.

The onion maggot is the larva of a fly which is slightly smaller than a housefly. The eggs are laid at the base of the leaves where they hatch and the small larvae, about a third of an inch long, work into the stem and the bulb. They kill the leaves and by working into the bulb cause it to decay.

GENERAL RECOMMENDATIONS: The price of onion sets may be anywhere from two to six dollars a bushel. The person who wants a little side line as a hobby can grow from a half acre to an acre of sets with very little expense and have a good income for his spare time. By having the ground in good condition a good yield can be obtained. The sets must be stored in an airy, drying place until freezing weather, when they have to be stored in a place where they will not freeze. They must be stored in shallow trays while they are being cured, but may be stored, to save space, in bags after they are cured. The trays may be stored outdoors with a cover over the top.

Orach

DESCRIPTION: Orach (*Atriplex hortensis*), often called FRENCH or MOUNTAIN SPINACH, is an annual that grows to a height of three feet and has a very succulent, branched stem with inconspicuous flowers and long, slender, soft-textured leaves, for which the plant is sometimes called Butter Leaves. The plants are native to the Mediterranean countries and are usually found wild in saline soils, especially those near salt marshes or desert country. They are used as a potherb or as a substitute for spinach.

TYPES AND VARIETIES: There are a number of species, but only the *hortensis* is much used. It has three varieties which differ in the color of the foliage.

SOIL AND CLIMATIC REQUIREMENTS: The plants serve their purpose best in temperate climates. They have a short growing season. They do best in soils that are well limed and well drained.

CULTURAL DIRECTIONS: The seed is sown in the spring as soon as the soil can be worked. Plantings are made every two weeks. The seed is planted in rows 18 to 20 inches apart and the plants are blocked out to 10 inches apart in the row. The plants are used as soon as the young leaves are formed, so that if they are thinned as they are used, there is no need to thin them otherwise. When the weather gets hot, the plants shoot to seed quickly and new plantings should be made. The old plants are then pulled out. The culture of orach is very much like spinach (which see). This is a good plant to use as a variety with spinach and other potherbs.

INSECTS AND DISEASES: There are no serious pests of this plant. If occasionally some have leaf miners, they should be thrown out, as there is no control for them.

Oyster Plant

See Salsify

Parsley

DESCRIPTION: The parsley plant (*Petroselinum hortense*) is an Old World herb that is grown in practically every home·garden and is extensively grown in market gardens. It is a biennial that produces a bunch of finely divided and curly leaves the first year, highly valued for their

CURLY PARSLEY

aromatic-flavoring properties. The leaves have the characteristic of neutralizing the pungent flavor of onion. The second year the seedstalk is sent up and produces a flat head of numerous small white flowers.

TYPES AND VARIETIES: There are a number of types and varieties of parsley. The plain-leaved parsley is not so common as the curled-leaf

(*Petroselinum hortense, var. crispum*). The celery-leaved or Neapolitan is not generally grown in the United States. The fern-leaved vari-

ROOT PARSLEY (HAMBURG)

ety (*filiunum*) is occasionally grown, while the Hamburg or turnip-rooted parsley variety (*radicosum*) is grown in market gardens near large cities. The following varieties are listed by seedsmen: Extra Curled Dwarf, Paramount, Plain Dark Green, and Hamburg, of which there are several selections.

SOIL AND CLIMATIC REQUIREMENTS: Parsley will grow in all parts of the United States and under a wide range of temperatures. In the temperate regions, it is usually grown as an annual and will produce several crops. The early crop will require about 90 days to mature while the second crop will be ready 30 days later. In the garden, the older leaves are removed as they are wanted and new leaves continue to be formed. In market gardens, the whole plant is removed at one time, and the plants will make a second crop and sometimes a third. Soil requirements are not very exacting except that the plants will yield better on the heavier loam soils that are well supplied with moisture. Soils for the Hamburg parsley should be deep and sandy in texture as this variety is grown for its *root*, which is excellent in soups. The soil should, of course, be well drained and contain a liberal supply of organic matter. It should be well sweetened with pulverized limestone.

CULTURAL DIRECTIONS: The seed of parsley germinates slowly and weeds are apt to crowd out the seedlings. The seed can be sown in the greenhouse and the seedlings transplanted to the garden—a satisfactory procedure for the home garden. The seed can be sown in rows 15 inches apart and a small ridge of soil an inch high is placed over the seed. In ten days the ridge is leveled down to soil level. This kills the weeds that have germinated and the parsley seedlings will be ready to come through with little interference. This may be a dangerous practice, however, if the ridge is not removed soon enough. A stake should be placed at the end of the row carrying the date of planting, so that not more than ten days will elapse. The seedlings should be thinned to 6 inches in the row. The Hamburg parsley is thinned to 4 inches in the row.

Because of the hardiness of the plant, parsley may be grown in protected places during the greater part of the winter. It can be grown in frames, with a little protection, during freezing weather. Parsley should be dug from the garden in the fall and placed in six-inch pots to be used as a kitchen plant. It should be placed in a south window in a deep

saucer and watered from the bottom. By removing the older leaves for cooking, the plants will always be attractive and have a fresh, green appearance. When parsley is marketed, the leaves are picked and bunched together, making a bouquet of curly green leaves.

INSECTS AND DISEASES: There are no serious pests of this crop. A borer sometimes gets into the seedstalks, but this only does damage in seed fields. The celery worm sometimes eats the young foliage but may be controlled by dusting the plants with a rotenone dust.

GENERAL RECOMMENDATIONS: Parsley should be kept growing with side-dressings of liquid fertilizer. The seedstalks should be kept down the second year, to keep the base leaves growing. The leaves may be dried and kept in jars for flavoring purposes.

Parsnip

DESCRIPTION: The parsnip (*Pastinaca sativa*), is a vegetable for the special palate, as its flavor does not attract people generally. The plant is grown for its long, slender, cream-colored root. It is a biennial and produces a much-branched seedstalk with the greenish-white, small, inconspicuous flowers arranged in a flat-topped head. The leaves are long and much divided. Parsnip is a native of Europe and of ancient culture.

TYPES AND VARIETIES: There are a few varieties listed by seed houses but the Hollow Crown is still good. Guernsey, Long Smooth White, and Short Thick are others that might be mentioned.

SOIL AND CLIMATIC REQUIREMENTS:
A deep rich soil that is well drained
and thoroughly aerated and sweetened with lime is essential to grow
this crop successfully. The sandy-

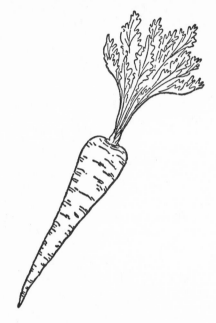

loam types are desired. The heavy
soils are too dense to grow long roots.
A subsoil plow should be run through
the soil under the rows, if the subsoil
tends to be dense. The plants are
very hardy and are usually left in the
ground all winter. Parsnips require
around 100 to 130 days to mature.

CULTURAL DIRECTIONS: Sow the seed
as soon as the ground can be worked.
The seeds are slow to germinate and
a ridge should be left over the seed
and removed within ten days to destroy the germinating weeds. The
plants are thinned to three inches
apart in the row. Weeds should be
controlled to keep the plants growing rapidly. The roots are left in the
ground until the tops are frozen. The
flavor of the roots is much improved
by freezing and, in the garden, it is
better to leave them in the soil until
they are to be used. As a matter of
fact, some people say they are not
good unless they have been frozen.
They need not be stored during the
winter. They should be used in the
spring before growth starts, as the
roots soon become bitter. Commercial plantings may have to be dug
in late fall if the ground freezes
solid during the winter. There are no
serious pests of this crop. Do not
make too large plantings of this plant
in the kitchen garden unless you have
already tried it.

Pattypan Squash
See Pumpkin

Pea Bean
See Beans

Peanut
DESCRIPTION: The peanut (*Arachis
hypogaea*), a product of tropical

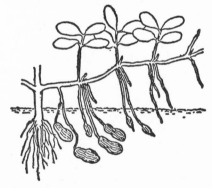

America, also called EARTH NUT,
EARTH ALMOND, GOOBER, GROUND
NUT, and PINDAR, is grown for its
nuts, which have become an integral
part of American life. No baseball

game is complete without its peanut venders. The oil from the nuts is used as a substitute for olive oil. The plants are also used as hay in the southern states. It has become a field crop, but is sometimes grown in vegetable gardens. The peanut is an annual, herbaceous, sprawly plant with a much-branched stem. The leaves are compound, with long, narrow leaflets. The flowers are produced in twos and threes in the axils of the leaves, the staminate flowers resembling yellow sweet peas. After the inconspicuous female flowers open, the plant directs the ovaries toward the ground, where they bury themselves, and the seeds are formed underground.

TYPES AND VARIETIES: There are two varieties listed. The Virginia Jumbo is a large podded sort, with two or three seeds to the pod, and has a very vigorous growth which is much used for forage purposes. The Spanish variety is a dwarf sort, with smaller peanuts, which are very sweet. The HOG PEANUT (Amphicarpa monoica or pitcheri) is often a pestiferous weed and of small horticultural interest.

SOIL AND CLIMATIC REQUIREMENTS: Peanuts are a poor-soil crop and will grow on any sandy loam or loamy sand that has an appreciable amount of organic matter and that is sweetened with magnesium limestone. They also need some phosphorous and potassium but little if any additional nitrogen, because they are capable of taking nitrogen from the air and using it in their growth. Applying nitrogen to the plant will cause it to make such a succulent growth that it will make a light set of

nuts and the plants will be very late. The plant should be grown as a soil-improving crop. Peanuts are a tropical plant and should be grown in warm climates. They can be grown in localities where 120 growing days are available. In the temperate regions, they should be grown in southern exposures where there is protection from north and west winds, and preferably on the sandy soils, because such soils warm quickly in the spring.

CULTURAL DIRECTIONS: The seed is planted about the time that maple leaves are the size of squirrels' ears. The seeds should be carefully removed from pods and planted a foot apart in rows about 3 feet apart. If the seed can be sown in pots, so that the seedling can be transplanted without disturbing the roots, the season can be lengthened by a month or more, thus making it possible to grow a really good crop in the garden. However, the peanut does not transplant well, because of the long taproot. The seed should not be planted too deep. An inch or slightly more is sufficient. Weeds should be kept away from the plants without disturbing the roots. After the flowers have buried themselves in the soil, the ground should not be disturbed. They do not bury themselves in soil that is baked on the surface. A mulch of loose material around the plants is helpful in keeping the growing nuts close to the surface of the ground. The plants are left in the soil until frost, when the nuts should be dug. Under a mulch, it is a simple matter to pull the plants up and remove the peanuts. They will lift out rather easily. Otherwise, it may be necessary to dig them with a fork.

They are then dried and packed in bags. If the home-garden crop is roasted in an oven for home use, the nuts should be watched carefully to keep them from burning. This is a good plant to play with in the garden, but the average person can probably buy peanuts more cheaply than he can grow them.

INSECTS AND DISEASES: Pests will not give much trouble in the home garden. In commercial plantings, they should be brought to the attention of Government agencies. Where they have not been grown in the past, there are not apt to be any problems.

Peas

DESCRIPTION: The garden pea (*Pisum sativum, var. arvense*) is a variety of the field pea. It is a trailing plant with oblong leaves and purple and white flowers. The fruit is a pod containing from four to ten seeds. The seeds may be smooth or wrinkled and green or cream colored. The va-

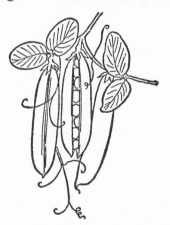

rieties that are grown in the garden are sweeter than field peas and, in some cases, even the pods are eaten. The field peas usually have a narrow and somewhat cylindrical pod, while the garden varieties have broad pods which are somewhat flattened. Peas are one of the most important vegetables from the standpoint of canning, ranking next to sweet corn in importance. It is one of the oldest vegetables in cultivation, having been grown in its native Egypt long before the Christian Era. As a green vegetable, however, it is not so important as snap beans.

TYPES AND VARIETIES: Of the smooth-seeded varieties, the Alaska probably ranks first, particularly for canning purposes. It is wilt-resistant and very early, maturing in 55 days. The seed is small and the pods are about 2½ inches long. The vines grow to 3 feet. Of the wrinkled varieties, there are many which may be recommended. Among the dwarf varieties should be mentioned American Wonder and Notts Excelsior, both having short, heavily productive vines. Laxtonian or Blue Bantam has long, green pods 4 inches or more in length. Gradus, Thomas Laxton, and Little Marvel are semi-dwarf varieties with long, flattened pods. These are the good garden varieties.

The tall-growing or mid-season sorts, such as Alderman, Telephone, Dwarf Telephone, and Perfection, require around 75 days to mature and make vines 4 feet tall with pods 4 to 5½ inches long. Improved Stratagem and Large White Marrowfat are late vigorous-growing varieties that require 80 or more days to mature. Melting Sugar and the wilt-resistant Dwarf Gray Sugar are grown for their edible pods. They produce tall vines, with medium to long pods, and mature in 70 to 75 days.

SOIL AND CLIMATIC REQUIREMENTS: Peas produce best in temperate regions where the summer temperature is not too hot. They are fairly hardy and will withstand slight frosts. They should be grown on good sandy-loam soils, although they will grow in a wide variety of soil conditions. They prefer well-drained soil that is sweetened with lime and that contains an appreciable amount of organic matter.

CULTURAL DIRECTIONS: Peas are sown as soon as the soil can be worked. In the garden, it is preferable to grow them in rows 2 to 3 feet apart or in closely placed alternate rows to form double rows which should be separated by three feet. For the garden, it is possible to soak the seeds in water and allow them to show tiny sprouts before planting them in the soil. Seeds should not be placed in deep water, but should be spread out one pea deep with enough water to cover only half of the seed. Careful planning is necessary, because a lot of seed may be spoiled unless it is planted as soon as it is ready.

If the seed is sown in furrows, a transplanting solution should be poured over it before the soil is placed on it. This will make the seed germinate about five days earlier and will supply enough nutrients so that the plants need not be fertilized further. If peas have not been grown on the soil before, it is advisable to inoculate the seeds, that is, to coat them with a bacterial mixture which helps them to get their nitrogen from the air. Peas do not need much fertilizer.

The vines should be supported by brush to keep them off the ground. Or they can be supported on trellises. If two rows are planted together, they do not need so much support. The dwarf varieties do not need support.

INSECTS AND DISEASES: The insects and diseases that affect peas are not serious. They are usually due to poor cultural practices. Root rot causes considerable damage, but it is usually due to a lack of lime in the soil. Too much fertilizer too close to the roots seems to weaken the plants so that they are more susceptible to the root-rot organisms. Mildew sometimes causes trouble in wet weather, but there is no practical control for it except to keep the plants off the ground, so the air can move around the plants freely and keep the foliage dry. Spots sometimes appear on the pods. These are due to organisms growing in the moisture on the pods. They can be controlled by good air circulation.

Pea aphids are bad pests in cool weather. They get on the growing tips of the plant and on the under sides of the smaller leaves. On young plants, they will ruin the crop. On older plants, they may do very little damage. A nicotine sulphate spray will control the aphids. If the plants get an early start and make a rapid growth, there is less danger of bad infestations on the early varieties. The late varieties are usually more vulnerable. The pea weevil does some damage by burrowing into the seeds in the pods. The eggs are laid on the pods and, as they hatch, the larvae work into the seed and may remain there until the following season. Cleanliness will help to keep this pest in check.

Rabbits will do much damage to peas in the garden. There is no practical way to keep them away except to have a dog close by. Starlings and blackbirds probably will do more damage, because they work in flocks. They usually do not disturb the peas until the day before you wish to pick them. They seem to have an uncanny way of timing the harvest. A dog near the peas will keep them away. Starlings will take the entire crop if they have a chance.

GENERAL RECOMMENDATIONS: Peas are picked by hand for home use or for the market. For the canning industry, they are mowed off and taken to vineries where they are threshed. This is the main expense of growing peas. Two or three pickings are usually made. The dwarf varieties usually set heavy and can be almost cleaned off in one picking. They are pulled out by the roots and the pods are stripped off. The pods should be picked as soon as they are filled and before they start to harden. When the seeds start to harden, they soon lose their flavor. The pods usually turn a light green when they are ready to be picked. If they are picked too soon, the yield will be reduced. The large-podded garden varieties suffer less in quality with age than do the small-podded varieties. When peas are picked, they should be left in the pods until they are to be cooked. They will stay fresh much longer. It is also a good idea to chill them, when they are picked for home use. This tends to preserve the sugars in the seed. Field peas are sometimes used for the table. They are fine if they are picked early enough —before the pods turn light green and the seeds gain full size. Field peas naturally have less sugar in them and, as soon as the pea is full size, the sugar is converted to starch.

Several plantings of the dwarf varieties are probably better for the home garden than one planting of early, medium, and late varieties. Peas need not have a special area in the garden devoted to their culture. They should be planted according to a plan, so that they will be between two late-growing crops, such as tomatoes and egg plants. Or, if the peas are located among the tomatoes, the emptied vines can be pulled and left on the ground to help mulch the tomatoes. Or the peas may even be planted between summer squash and sweet corn.

Pepino

See Melon-Pear

Peppergrass

See Cress

Peppers

DESCRIPTION: The garden pepper (*Capsicum frutescens,* formerly *annuum*) is one of our most popular vegetable plants. The plants are bushy annuals, and the stems are much branched. The leaves are long

PEPPER

and taper toward either end. The flowers, with grayish-purple petals, are borne singly in the axiles of the leaves. Both sexes are contained in the same flowers. The fruits, when ripe, may be yellow, red, or a very dark purple, and may vary in size from small to long and slender or large and blocky.

TYPES AND VARIETIES: The following varieties of garden pepper, including both sweet and hot peppers, are commonly recognized:

SWEET PEPPERS (*var. grossum*), sometimes called the bell type, are the ones most commonly grown in the home garden. These may be either long and tapering or blocky with deep side-grooves folded in to form a blunt tip. Although red or yellow when ripe, they are often picked while immature for use as GREEN PEPPERS in salads or for stuffing. Seedsmen list Ruby King, Sweet Yellow, World Beater (including Rutgers mosaic-resistant), California Wonder, Oshkosh, and, for cooler seasons, Waltham Beauty.

CHERRY PEPPERS (*var. cerasiforme*) are erect or bending, red, yellow, or purple, round, from a half inch to an inch thick, and very pungent. Red Cherry and Yellow Cherry are the common listings.

CONE PEPPERS (*var. conoides*) are erect, small, linear, and pointed, about an inch and a half long.

The TABASCO or RED CLUSTER PEPPERS (*var. fasciculatum*) include the Small Red Chili and the Orange-Red Cluster. They are erect, slender, and about three inches long. The four-inch Cayenne and the two-inch Red Chili are sometimes classified as a different variety (*acuminatum*).

CAYENNE and CHILE PEPPERS (*var. longum*) are pendent, slender, and tapering, growing to a foot in length. These are very hot and are ground into a powder for use as a condiment.

Listed varieties are Long Red and Yellow, Ivory Tusk, and Black Nubian.

CAYENNE PEPPER

PIMIENTO PEPPERS is a name sometimes applied to a number of the garden varieties called the perfection group. These are semi-conical, three or four inches long, thick, and relatively mild. Principal varieties listed are Grant and Spanish. They have no relation to the tropical American aromatic tree (*Pimiento officinalis*) called allspice.

The BLACK and WHITE PEPPER of commerce has no relation to the garden peppers, being made from the berries of a tropical shrub (*Piper nigrum*).

SOIL AND CLIMATIC REQUIREMENTS: Peppers are sandy-soil crops. They yield better on the well-drained sandy loams that are sweetened with lime. On the heavier soils they are liable to produce a very luxuriant foliage with a light set of fruit. On poorly drained soils, the fruit will be poorly formed. The shape of the fruits are easily changed by abnormal soil conditions, particularly poor aeration. Peppers should have their fertilizer plowed under. Abrupt fluctuations are not conducive to a good crop of peppers. The soil must be well supplied with magnesium and phosphorus. Temperatures put definite limits upon the varieties that can be grown in a given locality. Varieties that are particularly adapted to the New England states are not suited to the southern states. California Wonder and World Beater are suited to high temperatures. They do not set fruit well in New England except in rare seasons. A cloudy, wet season is not conducive to the production of good peppers. Most peppers mature in 60 to 80 days. They are very sensitive to frost and cold winds and do particularly well in hot summer temperatures.

CULTURAL DIRECTIONS: The seed is sown in hotbeds about ten weeks before the seedlings are to be set in the garden soil. They will then fruit in two to two and one-half months. When the plants are 2 inches tall, they are transplanted to flats and spotted 2 inches apart. They should be 5 to 6 inches tall when they are set in the field. The plants should be watered with a transplanting solution about five days before they are set in the garden soil. Then they should be set 2 feet apart in rows 3 feet apart, with another application of the same solution. The plants should be given two side-dressings of liquid fertilizer during the fruiting season. Salad peppers are usually picked when full grown but still green, although red fruits are also used occasionally. However, when they are picked for seed, the fruits must be ripe.

The hot peppers are picked when ripe. They are then either dried and ground or pickled. The fruits should be cut off, as the plants are not rooted too firmly and pulling on the fruits will disturb the roots. Just before frost approaches, all the green

fruits should be picked off, placed in hampers, and stored in a cool but not cold cellar. They will keep for three months or more. Ripe peppers are often preserved with a salt brine for winter use. When they are used, they are freshened by soaking in water. Some people like peppers as a steady diet, but in the kitchen garden five or six plants probably will provide enough.

INSECTS AND DISEASES: The best control for diseases is good culture. If the soil is lacking in magnesium, the leaves become spotted and drop off and the fruits become sunburned. In this condition, they are easily affected by the fruit-rotting fungi. Having the soil well supplied with a pulverized magnesium-limestone is good insurance against some of these difficulties and experiments have shown that the yield of fruit may be doubled. The mosaic virus sometimes does considerable damage to the plants by stunting them, so that they do not set fruit. The prevalence of mosaic seems to be increased where the plants are grown on soils that have too little lime or that are too dense to permit good aeration around the roots. Sweet-potato growers who use large quantities of potash and keep the soil acid to prevent tuber diseases invariably have poor pepper yields when peppers are grown as a rotation crop, and their peppers usually show disease symptoms. Peppers should, however, be grown on different soil each year, whenever possible. Insects are no particular problem, although occasionally the plants become infested with aphids which migrate from the spinach, the potato vines, or the tomato plants. Nicotine sulphate will kill them.

Pimiento Pepper

See Peppers

Pindar

See Peanut

Pineapple Melon

See Melons

Popcorn

See Corn: Popcorn

Potato

DESCRIPTION: The white or Irish potato (*Solanum tuberosum*) is one of the most popular vegetables grown in America. It is a native of the highlands of Chile and Argentina, where it grows wild. It was cultivated by the Incas. The plants make a growth of three feet, the branches sprawly,

the stems winged, and the compound leaves having small oval leaflets with a hairy surface. The flowers are bisexed and borne in clusters, each flower consisting of a five-pointed corolla and calyx with a white to purple color. The seed ball, if present, is small and round. The tubers are borne on the end of short stems underground. The colors vary from white to red, and the shapes from long and slender to round. (*See also* SWEET POTATO.)

TYPES AND VARIETIES: Potatoes may be grouped into early and late varieties. There are many varieties available, and certain ones seem particularly adapted to certain localities. They may be sorted into eight or ten groups according to color and shape of the tubers and time of maturity.

Among the early varieties may be mentioned the Bliss Triumph, which is a red, round potato, generally grown in the Gulf states for early market in the North, and maturing in 70 days; the Irish Cobbler, a round, white, rather rough potato, which is grown along the Eastern Seaboard on the heavier soils; the Rose varieties, represented by the Early and Late Rose, Manistee, and many others, which are longer than wide and somewhat flattened, with pink skin and flesh, in many cases suited to the lighter soils, and largely grown in the northeastern states; and the Early Ohio, a very early, oblong, pink-skinned potato grown in the north central states.

There are other varieties, beside the Late Rose mentioned above, which take longer to mature. The Burbank, a medium-late potato, is grown on the Pacific Coast and particularly in the inter-mountain irrigated sections. It is a long, cylindrical, and slightly flattened type, considered the baking potato *par excellence*. Green Mountain is an oblong, flattened, white, medium-late type, generally grown throughout the north tier of states and southern Canada. Carmen and Gold Coin are other varieties of this type. These potatoes require fertile, heavy soils. The Rural is one of the older types, round and flattened, shorter and somewhat later than the Green Mountain and not so popular. Rural New Yorker, Million Dollar, and Rural Russet are similar varieties and are grown in the same areas that grow the Green

Mountain. The Pearl variety is grown in the Far West. The tubers are round to heart-shaped and flattened, with dull white or brownish color. Peachblow is the South Atlantic type. It is represented by several varieties which are round and slightly flattened or oblong, with creamy white to pink skins.

Of the newer varieties, the Chippewa should be mentioned as the sandy-soil potato. It is round and slightly flattened. It is rather watery and a poor keeper, but is desired for the potato-chip industry. Some claim the flavor is fine and some claim it is not mealy enough. It is a high yielder and growers have reported 600 bushels to the acre on light, sandy loams. It is slightly later than the Cobbler. Katahdin is another variety in the late group which has considerable merit. It is a fine keeper, has fine flavor, and is very attractive. There are a number of other recently introduced varieties which are recommended for the heavier soils.

For the gardener, there are several oddities that are listed by some seed houses. They have no commercial importance. There is a Lady Finger variety, for instance, that produces a long, slender tuber about an inch in diameter and two to three inches long, supposed to be a salad potato.

SOIL AND CLIMATIC REQUIREMENTS: Potatoes are being grown on practically all the soil types. The Aroostook County, Maine, potato industry is located on a loam soil that is rather rocky. The crop is late on such soil. In the Atlantic States and the Coastal Plain, the soils are sandy to heavy-sandy loams and even silt loams. The North Central States grow potatoes on sands, loams, and muck soils. A good soil is one that is very fertile, well drained and well aerated, in which the subsoil is not too dense. The soil should have a good supply of organic matter, but should be quite acid. On sweet soil, the tubers are affected by ground diseases, so that growers who wish to sell their crop try to keep their soils rather acid. In the kitchen garden, this is of little consequence and no distinction with respect to lime is made between the potato and other crops. If a good supply of organic matter is maintained, the incidence of ground diseases will not be serious enough to spoil potatoes for peeling. A small amount of lime increases the yield of potatoes.

The climate has a great influence on the eating quality of the potato. The Burbank potato is considered the ideal for baking, if it is grown in the West under irrigation. It is very mealy and of high quality. The bright days, abundance of sunshine, and cool nights seem to be responsible for this high quality, and tremendous yields have been reported. Potatoes from Wisconsin, Maine, New York, and Minnesota are more mealy than potatoes grown farther south, where the nights are warmer. The storage of starch, which is associated with high quality by people who like mealy potatoes, apparently is facilitated by cool nights. For people who prefer the watery potato, the mealy character may not be desirable.

The potato is considered a temperate climate crop, although some varieties are being developed which are well suited to the warmer climates. The Chippewa seems to do better at higher temperatures than some of the other varieties. It also responds to moisture. In fact, any soil, to be well suited to potatoes, must be capable of supplying adequate water to the plants. Potatoes will root deeply, if given a chance, and the subsoil should be of a friable or loose texture to encourage deep rooting. Deep-rooted plants will get much of their moisture in dry weather from the deeper levels.

CULTURAL REQUIREMENTS: Potatoes are planted by cutting tubers in sections and planting the sections 14 to 18 inches apart in rows which are 3 feet apart. Potato tubers have dormant buds, called eyes, and in cutting the tubers for planting, the cuts should be made in such a manner that each section has at least one eye. Potatoes ordinarily do not make seed. Some varieties, in some localities, will set seed in the ovaries of the flowers, and the seed ball or fruit resembles a small green tomato. This seed, if permitted to mature and dry out, will germinate and produce potato plants, but the tubers will not be characteristic of the variety on which the seed was produced. The new varieties are obtained by planting this seed and selecting the plants for certain characteristics. The first year, the tubers are small, but the second-year tubers, grown from sections of the first-year tubers, are larger. Occasionally, growers will use the small unsalable tubers for their planting. These are usually not very satisfactory. A better practice is to plant potatoes late in the season and harvest them after frost in the fall; such tubers will be small and are planted without being cut the following spring. In the heavier soils, the potatoes are planted shallow, while, in the sandy soils, they are planted three inches below the surface.

It is a good practice, in growing the commercial crop, to plant seed grown in areas certified by a Government Inspector as being free of all diseases that may be carried in the tubers. Seed is usually grown in the colder climates and used for three or four years before it is replaced by new seed. Much of the seed planted in the southern states is grown in the northern part of the country.

The commercial crop is grown with commercial fertilizer and in rotation with grain and hay crops. Planting potatoes on the same field, year after year, may produce fair yields, but it soon becomes unprofitable. Sooner or later, growers realize that the sure way to profitable yields is to rotate the crops so that an appreciable amount of organic matter is maintained. The fertilizer is usually placed in two-inch bands, three inches from, and about as deep as, the seed. Another method is to plow under the fertilizer at the rate of a ton of 5–10–10 to the acre. Cow manure is used on dairy farms. Horse manure should not be used unless it has been composted for a year before being applied or unless it has first been applied to another crop. It tends to cause scab on the tubers.

In the kitchen garden, potatoes are fertilized somewhat differently, and higher yields may be secured, because more lime is used. Scab on the tubers for peeling does not interfere with their eating quality, but they are not so good for baking. The tubers should be planted in good soil about the first of April or as soon as the ground can be worked, and the seed-pieces should be covered with a pint of transplanting solution before the soil is covered over them. The soil should be hilled up slightly above the seed, so that germinating weeds may be killed by leveling the hill down with a rake. This raking should be continued even after the potato sprouts appear above the ground. If carefully done, it will not disturb the sprouts. They should not be broken off, however. When the sprouts are up two or three inches, they should be given a good side-dressing of liquid fertilizer, and if any mulching material is available in localities where the day temperatures approach 80 degrees or higher, it should be placed around the plants. A 2-inch layer is satisfactory. Where a mulch can be placed around the plants, the seed should be planted alternately in a 6-inch double row, 12 inches apart in each row. A second side-dressing of liquid fertilizer should be given about the time the plants are coming into flower. A 50-foot row will produce anywhere from 1 to 3 bushels of tubers. In the kitchen garden, only the early varieties are grown, and, unless the garden has some size, it is better to use the space for something else. In the subsistence garden, potatoes make a good crop. If the garden, has an appreciable area, so that potatoes can be grown for storage, it is advisable to grow also some of the late varieties.

INSECTS AND DISEASES: Of the leaf diseases, the late blight is probably the worst offender. It is controlled by weekly sprayings with Bordeaux mixture. Tuber scurf, which looks like particles of black dirt on old tubers, may prevent the sprouts from growing. It is controlled by soaking the seed in corrosive sublimate solution. The common disfiguring scab is controlled by keeping the soil acid. Scab hurts the sale of potatoes. There are other diseases, such as wilts, leaf roll, and mosaics, which are controlled by proper seed-selection.

Of the insects, the Colorado potato beetle is the worst offender. It must be controlled by spraying with a poison or by dusting with a rotenone dust. The flea beetle and leaf hopper are controlled by spraying with Bordeaux mixture, as for blight. Potato aphids are controlled by sprays of Black Leaf 40. White grubs and wire worms may cause considerable damage to the tubers if they are not dug as soon as mature, especially late in the fall.

GENERAL RECOMMENDATIONS:·If potatoes are to be used immediately, they may be dug soon after the flowers have disappeared, but the yield will, of course, be low. As the plants mature, the crop increases very rapidly if moisture and temperature are satisfactory. When tubers are dug too green, the skins peel off and cooking produces a wet rather than a mealy potato. The flavor, however, is excellent. Whoever has not tasted new small potatoes and peas, direct from the garden, with a white sauce over them, has a surprising treat in store for him. If tubers are to be stored, they should be left in the field until the vines are completely dead. If the vines are killed by frost, or for some other reason the tubers do not mature, they may shrink considerably in storage. The best storage potatoes are those that are dug in cool weather when the soil is dry. Potatoes dug in hot weather are easily scalded and will not keep in storage. When the tubers are dug, they should be placed in slatted crates and piled up so that air can circulate around them. The temperature should be as close to 38 degrees as possible. If kept too warm they will sweat. This is one objection to placing them in bins, unless they can be cooled rather quickly. In the home-storage cellar, a few slatted crates are very satisfactory.

Prairie Bean

See Beans

Preserving Melon

See Chinese-Watermelon

Pumpkin

DESCRIPTION: Pumpkins fall into two groups: one (*Cucurbita pepo*), includes the common summer and autumn pumpkins and the bush pumpkins, and the other (*Cucurbita moschata*), embraces the winter crookneck or crushaw pumpkins. That

PUMPKIN

pumpkins are closely related to their cousins the squashes (*Cucurbita maxima*) is well illustrated by the fact that many pumpkins, such as the PATTYPAN and SUMMER SQUASH, are commonly called squashes. The difference in foliage and fruit characters of the two species of pumpkins as contrasted with the squashes should be clearly noted. Pumpkins have coarse, harsh, large, deeply lobed or entire leaves on bushy or trailing vines. The flowers are borne singly in the axils

of the leaves on long stalks and are either staminate (male) or pistillate (female). The flowers are large and funnel-shaped, with orange-yellow petals. The fruits vary tremendously in size, shape, and color. The seeds are flat and oblong, with a gentle taper toward either end. Pumpkins are native to Tropical America, as is the squash (which see).

TYPES AND VARIETIES: Pumpkin varieties may be conveniently grouped under eight types,* as follows:

CONNECTICUT FIELD PUMPKIN GROUP (*pepo*). Running vines with fruits of various sizes. Connecticut Field is a large, orange pumpkin with slight ribbing. May weigh over 50 pounds. Sugar pumpkin is golden-yellow or brownish-yellow and flattened, and weighs only 4 or 5 pounds. Pie pumpkin is usually orange-yellow but several pounds larger than the Sugar. Fort Berthold is similar to Sugar but weighs only half as much. Golden Oblong, almost twice as long as broad, is golden-orange and weighs 7 to 8 pounds. Mammoth Tours, which is the king of the pumpkins for size, is twice as long as broad, mottled green, orange and yellow, and weighs as much as 100 pounds in some localities. Omaha is oblong and pointed toward the stem end, orange in color, and weighs 4 pounds. Sandwich Island is oblong, about twice as long as broad, tapering toward stem end, and prominently grooved, with brownish-

*We are indebted for this classification to the studies of Castetter and Erwin of the Iowa Agricultural Experiment Station, reported in *Bulletin 244*, and to the studies of Erwin and Haber of that station, published in *Bulletin 263*, of the Iowa Agricultural Experiment Station.

yellow color. And small varieties are excellent for pies, mostly for summer and early winter use.

FORDHOOK GROUP (*pepo*).. Mostly runner types, this group includes such varieties as: Delicata, oblong, 2 to 3 pounds, orange- and green-striped; Fordhook and Fordhook Bush, alike except for size of foliage-growth, with oblong fruit slightly grooved and tapering toward stem, about 4 inches in diameter, and cream to lemon-yellow in color; Panama, with lemon-colored, bell-shaped fruit, deeply grooved at the large end and weighing 1 to 2 pounds; Perfect Gem, spherical in shape but flattened at both ends, and straw-colored; Table Queen, slightly elongated and pointed at the blossom end, dark green in color, and weighing 2 pounds; and Winter Nut, a cream-colored fruit of nutty flavor, shaped like an apple with grooves radiating from the depressed stem end, and weighing 4 pounds. These varieties are all summer and fall types, ideal for baking. The flavor is best soon after removal from the vines.

PATTYPAN GROUP (*pepo*). Bush types. The Early White and Yellow

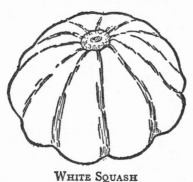

WHITE SQUASH

Bush Scallop, Long Island White Bush Scallop, Mammoth White Bush

Scallop, and Golden Custard are similar in shape but vary in color and size as the names indicate. Sizes range from 8 to 14 inches in diameter. This group is used almost entirely when the fruits are still very immature, when the skin can be easily broken with the fingernail. They are not used when ripe, generally speaking.

CROOKNECK GROUP (*pepo*). Bush types. Fruits have a crookneck at the stem end. They are white or yellow in color and have a warted skin when

CROOKNECK SQUASH

ripe. They are used as summer squash and are picked when the rind is soft. The White and Yellow Crookneck and the Strickler are the older varieties. To these should be added the Connecticut Straightneck, which has a straight stem and a smoother skin, yellow in color; also the Giant Summer Crookneck, which is larger.

VEGETABLE MARROW GROUP (*pepo*). Bush and vine types. The Cocozelle and the Vining Cocozelle are similar in fruit characters, with fruits 3 times as long as broad, cylindrical in shape, dark-green with light-green to yellow stripes, and weighing 5 pounds. Long White Marrow is slightly smaller than the Running White Vegetable Marrow, which is about the same size and shape of the Cocozelle. Both are lemon-yellow to white in color.

ZUCCHINI Bush is very similar to Cocozelle, but the green fruits have a lighter gray mottled effect. These are summer varieties which are used when they are very small and tender, not after ripening.

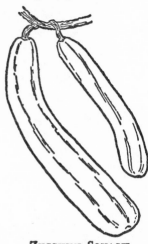

ZUCCHINI SQUASH

CHEESE GROUP (*moschata*). Running plants. Calhoun is a small cheese pumpkin of creamy-buff color and weighing 5 to 6 pounds. The Large Cheese, similar in shape and color to the Calhoun, weighs 10 pounds. French Cocoanut, slightly elongated and tapering toward the ends, is creamy buff in color and weighs 15 pounds. Quaker Pie is pear-shaped, deep buff in color, and weighs 9 to 10 pounds. These are all varieties that are suitable for canning and for stock feed and will keep fairly well.

CUSHAW GROUP (*moschata*). Plants of the running type. These all have slightly to extremely crooked stem ends, with a much larger bulbous blossom end. Japanese Pie is pear-shaped with a fairly straight neck; the skin is dark green with lighter green stripes. Mammoth Golden Cushaw has a dull-gold color and a pronounced crook at the stem end; it weighs 12 pounds. Small Golden Cushaw is very similar, but smaller, weighing 7 pounds. The White Cushaw has less of a crook at the stem end and is white in color. The Striped Cushaw is similar in shape but has netted green stripes. Both White and Striped Cushaws weigh about 12 pounds. The Tennessee Sweet Potato is more pear- or bell-shaped and weighs 15 pounds. It is white in color or may have light green stripings. These are used for canning and are good winter-keepers, if carefully handled when placed in storage.

MORE RECENT TYPES OR INTRODUCTIONS:

Yankee Hybrid, probably belonging to the crookneck group, is very prolific and early but will not come true to name; it is fine for the kitchen garden, but the seed cannot be saved.

Vegetable Spaghetti is a white-skinned, cylindrical fruit, 10 inches long and 5 inches thick, with a runner-type plant. The fruit is cooked whole, and, when it is cooked, the meat is stringy like spaghetti but has the flavor of squash. It is a good keeper and will last until spring.

There are other varieties listed by seed houses which should be tried out to determine their characteristics. Big Tom is Connecticut Field, Boston Pie and Small Sugar are Sugar, Cymlin is Early White Bush Scallop, English Cream Marrow is Fordhook, French Tours is Mammoth, Italian and Green Bush Marrow are Cocozelle, Jonathan is White Cushaw, Kentucky Field is Large Cheese, Mammoth Yellow Bush Scallop is Golden Custard, Pattypan is Early White Bush Scallop, Sugar Pie is Sugar Pumpkin, Sweet Cheese is Large Cheese, and Winter Luxury and Winter Queen are Pie Pumpkin.

SOIL AND CLIMATIC REQUIREMENTS: The best soils for pumpkins are the sandy loams or loams that are well drained and well aerated and which have a good supply of organic matter or have been supplied with well-rotted manure in the vicinity of the hills. The soils should be capable of supplying adequate moisture. The bush types of pumpkins which are popularly referred to as summer squash will produce fruits in 50 to 55 days. The runner types require a longer period. Although they are sensitive or tropical annuals, they can be grown in temperate regions with comparatively short growing seasons. They do need some hot weather. The runner types and the Cushaws require around 120 days to mature.

CULTURAL DIRECTIONS: The bush types of pumpkins, or SUMMER SQUASH as they are popularly known, should be planted in hills 3 by 4 feet apart. Eight or ten seeds should be sown in a circle a foot in diameter to form each hill. When the seedlings are up, the hills are thinned to three or four plants. The runner types should be planted in hills 4 feet apart in the rows, and the rows spaced 5 or 6 feet apart. In the small garden, the summer squash should be planted between the hills of corn and, as soon as the corn is picked, the stalks should be broken down to give the squash a chance to develop in full sunlight. The small sugar pumpkin should be planted with a few of the other varieties. They will then take over the ground as the corn matures.

INSECTS AND DISEASES: There are a number of bad pests which are common to both pumpkins and squash. The diseases, which usually are not serious, are the mildew, bacterial wilt, and anthracnose. Mildew and anthracnose are the result of moist, cloudy weather and poor air circulation. The bacterial wilt is carried by the cucumber beetle. Repelling the beetle, as soon as the seedlings are up, with lime or rotenone dust will control the wilt. Of the insects, the squash bug and the squash vine-borer are the hardest to control. The squash vine-borers enter the vines near the ground. They should be removed with a pen knife, if they are seen in time. Also, cover the base of the vines with soil to encourage rooting at the nodes. Keep everything clean by destroying old vines. The squash bug is controlled by placing small pieces of flat board near the plants and every evening lifting the boards and killing the bugs. After a few days, they will be destroyed.

GENERAL RECOMMENDATIONS: The best way to find out about squashes or pumpkins is to try out a few different ones each year. A few hills will be sufficient, as they are usually quite prolific and one specimen makes a meal for five people.

Purslane

DESCRIPTION: Purslane (*Portulaca olerocea*) is a very common weed on moist sandy soils, but there are garden varieties which have been developed by French gardeners for salad purposes. These varieties are more popular in Europe than in this country. The plant has fleshy, watery stems and leaves which are the size of squirrels' ears. The plant grows flat on the ground unless crowded. It produces very small, white to pinkish flowers. The improved varieties have large leaves and tend to grow more upright than the wild forms. The flavor is mild and faintly acid. It makes a good addition to a mixed green salad because of its succulence.

TYPES AND VARIETIES: The common annual forms include such varieties as Green purslane, Golden purslane, and Golden Large-Leaf purslane. A perennial commonly known as CUBAN WINTER PURSLANE (*Claytonia perfoliata*) grows upright, with the leaves cup-shaped on a long petiole which comes from the crown. The plant is bushy and is used for salad purposes. Although it is a perennial, it will not live through severe winters.

SOIL AND CLIMATIC CONDITIONS: Purslane grows best on light sandy soils that are well drained and contain appreciable quantities of lime. It grows best in temperate regions. It is killed by the first frost.

CULTURAL PRACTICES: The seed may be sown in rows as soon as the ground can be worked, and the plants are later thinned to stand 6 inches apart in the row. They require very little fertilizer. Any fairly good soil will grow the crop. It may be used as soon as the plants have produced sufficient size. They should be removed as soon as they begin to flower, so that they will not self-seed, because the plants can become troublesome as a weed.

Radish

DESCRIPTION: The garden radish (*Raphanus sativus*) is one of the easiest vegetables to grow and is probably grown in more gardens than any other vegetable. It is a native of Asia and has been in cultivation for centuries, having been highly prized by the Pharaohs of Egypt and by the Greeks. During the days of minimum sunlight, the plant produces a rosette of leaves and a thick, very tender taproot of various dimensions and colors, and as the days become longer, it sends out a tall branching seedstalk with small purplish white flowers. Radish seed sown in late summer produces good radishes which do not make a seedstalk until the following spring. (*See also* Horseradish.)

TYPES AND VARIETIES: The spring radishes comprise the quick-growing sorts, also used for forcing in the greenhouse, and may be classified into the following types and varieties:

Roots flat or oblate: Early Breakfast; White.

Roots round: Scarlet Turnip (white-tipped); Sparkler; Comet (scarlet).

RADISHES (ROUND)

Roots oblong: French Breakfast (scarlet, white-tipped); Ne Plus Ultra.

Roots half long: Half Long Scarlet.
Roots long: White Icicle; Long Scarlet Short Top; Cincinnati Mark.

RADISHES (LONG WHITE)

Summer varieties which require 10 to 20 days longer than the spring radishes to mature are:

White Strassburg, which has a long, slender, pointed root.
White Vienna or Lady Finger, more cylindrical in shape.
Stuttgart or Chartier, oval and white in color; also a long variety.
Long Scarlet Short Top: Long Cardinal.

Winter varieties, which require about 60 days to mature and are planted in late summer for winter storage, are grouped as follows:

Roots oblong: Chinese Mammoth, White Chinese, or Chinese White Winter.
Roots round: Round Black Spanish; Sakurajima (very large).
Roots long: Long Black Spanish.

SOIL AND CLIMATIC REQUIREMENTS: Radishes may be grown on most any kind of a soil that is fertile, well drained, and moderately supplied with lime. The soil should warm up rapidly to insure a rapid growth.

Slowly grown radishes are hot and woody. Grown in too high a temperature, they become pithy and of very poor quality. For this reason, the seed should be sown as early as the ground can be stirred, so that the roots will be formed in cool soil. Too much nitrogen in the soil will tend to make them large and pithy. They grow best in cool temperatures and, when grown in the greenhouse, the temperatures are usually held down to 45 degrees to get as solid a root as possible. The early varieties will develop in 20 to 30 days. The summer varieties will require around 45 days, while the fall or winter varieties will require approximately 60 days.

CULTURAL DIRECTIONS: The seed is sown in drills which are a foot apart. Or, if the seed is sown in with early beets or carrots, they answer a double purpose: they germinate quickly and will mark the row for cultivation of the slower-germinating beets or carrots before the quicker-germinating weeds can get a head start. They should be pulled as soon as the roots are a half inch in diameter, as they rapidly become too large after reaching this stage. The summer varieties are planted a little later. These are usually the long, slender varieties and will develop satisfactorily at slightly higher temperatures. The fall varieties are planted in late summer, usually about the middle to the last week in August. They will have time to form a good-sized root which will be crisp and tender and will store well for winter use. They should be given about 2 to 3 inches space in the row and the rows should be 16 inches apart.

The plants must be kept free of weeds and should be watered when the soil gets too dry, as the roots become fibrous if the soil is too dry. Radish roots go down 18 inches to 2 feet if they have the opportunity, which emphasizes the need for deep tillage. The roots are very tender and fragile and salt-concentration will kill them. They should be grown on soil that has not been fertilized too heavily with commercial fertilizer. The late varieties should be given a side-dressing of liquid fertilizer when the seedlings are three inches high.

Forcing radishes is a good side line for the man who is equipped with some sort of a forcing structure. The culture of radishes in hotbeds or heated coldframes, or in greenhouses, is a gamble at which the stakes are high if prices are good but at which the loss is not great if the prices are not good. The cost of growing radishes in the greenhouse is not great, because the crop will grow at a temperature that requires heat only during short periods in sections where winters are mild. The temperature may be maintained at between 45 and 50 degrees, after the seed has germinated. The crop can be harvested thirty days after the seed has germinated. The seed is sown in drills 6 inches apart across the beds. No other attention is needed until the radishes are harvested, except perhaps to water the beds. Very little fertilizer is needed if the soil is being used for other crops. Furthermore, the crop is grown during the months when other crops cannot be satisfactorily grown. Radish and lettuce are grown during the cold winter months and tomatoes or cucumbers are grown during the brighter warmer weather. The man who has a small lean-to greenhouse or a plant house can grow radishes without any outside heat, if he can keep the place from freezing on cold nights. The sun's rays during the day will warm the place sufficiently to grow radishes all through the winter in areas where the temperature does not get below 20 degrees. During zero weather, additional heat is needed. Radishes can be grown satisfactorily in pure sand culture by watering three or four times with a nutrient solution.

The gardener who has a small lean-to greenhouse can arrange several shallow three-foot beds 4 to 6 inches deep, one above the other, on the north side of the house, so that the sun can reach to the back of the bench. Three or four benches can be arranged at two-foot vertical intervals, thereby saving much ground area, because of the complete utilization of space on the north side. Radishes can also be grown in coldframes placed just outside a basement window so that heat from the cellar will keep the plants from freezing. During the heat of the day or when the sun shines, much heat will be captured if the coldframe is insulated. There is also a possibility of using a solar heater to heat water in an insulated tank, which can be drawn on to heat the coldframe when the sun is not shining. Fortunately, on cloudy days the temperature usually is not as low as it is on bright days.

Radishes can be grown in the kitchen window, if it is facing south, if a special structure is provided in the form of a window box. This usually results in a sand culture procedure, in order to get away from too much dirt in the kitchen. Radishes can even be grown in six-inch glazed pots in south windows. This can be done in basement windows where the temperature is below 60 degrees.

INSECTS AND DISEASES: There are very few pests that bother the radish plant. The main ones are plant lice, which can be controlled with a spray of nicotine sulphate or Black Leaf 40; flea beetles, which do not bother enough to warrant spraying them; and the cabbage root maggot, which is bothersome in some localities but for which there is no practical cure except to keep the plants screened from the flies. These controls are necessary only out-of-doors. Pests are usually bad only on the early varieties. The late varieties have very few troubles and are usually not sprayed.

GENERAL RECOMMENDATIONS: If radishes are to be sold, they must be harvested when they are of a size so that bunches of 6 to 12 can be made of a single-sized root. They do not make a good appearance if they vary much in size in the bunch.

Red Pepper

See Peppers

Rhubarb

DESCRIPTION: The common garden rhubarb or PIEPLANT (*Rheum rhaponticum*), a native of Southern Siberia, is a perennial, herbaceous plant which is grown for its fleshy petioles, commonly referred to as stalks. The leaves are very large and somewhat heart-shaped and the petioles are two to six feet tall, depending on where the plant is grown. The leafstalks, used for making sauce and pies, are harvested early in the summer, before the seedstalk is sent up. The flowers are borne in a cluster on the tall stem and are greenish white in color. The crown of the plant is a rhizome with many-branched, large, fleshy roots.

TYPES AND VARIETIES: There are a number of species resembling rhubarb and differing mainly in the size of the leafstalks or in the color. Many of these are edible. Some seem to have purgative properties. In one form (*Rumex abyssinicus*), the leaves are eaten as spinach and the plants are called SPINACH-RHUBARB. They all seem to cross with each other and when the seed is sown from any plant the seedlings may resemble any of the different species. Considerable study is needed to establish the authenticity of the species status.

SOIL AND CLIMATIC REQUIREMENTS: Rhubarb is grown on the sandy loam soils that are well drained and well supplied with organic matter. They should be well limed and contain a good supply of plant nutrients. The plant is very hardy and can be grown in most of the temperate regions. In the hot climates the leafstalks are apt to be small and spindling. It needs cold winters to produce large leafstalks.

CULTURAL DIRECTIONS: The subsoil should be loosened up to considerable depths to give the roots a chance thoroughly to penetrate the subsoil to obtain the necessary water supply.

Rhubarb can be grown from seed, but this practice requires considerable judgment in making selections, as the seedlings will vary considerably in color and size of roots and leafstalks. The plants produce seed as a result of cross-pollination and any seed produced by this method will not resemble exactly the parent plants. For the gardener, this is a satisfactory, though slower, method of obtaining good roots. He may be able to make a selection which suits him much better than if he takes an established variety. The commercial grower makes his plantings by dividing up the roots from an old field. The divisions are made so that each one will have a single bud on the crown, and a root. This is done in the early spring before growth takes place. The roots are divided by breaking rather than by cutting the crowns to pieces. Cutting is liable to spread any fungous rots that may be present in the crowns. The root divisions are set in the ground so that the bud is just below the surface of the soil. They should be placed three feet apart each way. In commercial plantings, the practice is to apply several forks of good, composted manure over the plants in the fall and this is left all winter. In the spring if there is any appreciable amount left, it is scraped off and left between the plants. Where manure is available, 20 tons to the acre are applied the first year and plowed under

before the roots are set in the field. The second year the manure is spread broadcast between the plants. Commercial fertilizer may be broadcast and plowed under or broadcast between the plants and mixed with the soil when the plants are cultivated.

Three or four good plants in the garden are usually enough for the average family. One plant should be dug up each year to divide for new plantings, while the others are used for sauce and pies. Rhubarb plants will remain in the same location for four or five years, but grass may get so bad that it will crowd them. Rhubarb must have clean culture to grow well. If a little lime and fertilizer or manure can be applied around the plants and the ground forked or spaded over around them, they can be left for four or five years, although they are better if they are divided every third year. Early in the spring before growth starts, a box open at both ends and 15 to 20 inches high should be placed around the plants. An opening a foot in diameter is sufficient. This will cause the leafstalks to grow much more rapidly, because of the protection from cold winds, and cause them to grow taller. Anything that can be set around the crowns will serve the purpose. It may make a difference of a week or more in earliness of maturity.

Rhubarb can be forced in the basement in the winter time. The procedure is to dig up roots two or more years old in the fall when the ground is loose. They are then thrown on a pile without protection to be frozen at the first hard frost. They are then packed in sand in boxes or benches, deep enough to accommodate the length of the roots. They are placed as close as possible, and the sand is filtered in around them so that moisture can be applied to force the roots. If they are grown in the dark, the leafstalks will grow to a height of three or more feet without expanding their leaves to any appreciable degree. The darkness will also make the stalks dark red in color, which is desirable from the market standpoint. Commercial growers use lean-to sheds which are equipped with a heating system. The roots are stored in these sheds after they have been frozen and allowed to remain there with the sand or soil packed around them until it is desired to force them. Then the heat is turned on and water is applied in sufficient quantity thoroughly to wet the sand around the soil and the soil under the roots. Such forcing can only be done in localities where freezing weather occurs, unless one is willing to place the roots in cold storage for freezing before they are forced. Rhubarb does not force well if it is not chilled. It has a natural rest period, just as most bulbs do, and it takes a certain length of time before the buds become active. Chilling them causes the rest period to be broken and makes possible the rapid growth of all the buds at the same time. This, of course, is important where the crop must be harvested all at one time. The roots should not be chilled much below the freezing point. Dropping the temperature too rapidly and too far, more than five degrees below the freezing point, may kill the tissue, under which conditions they will not force. If they are in the soil when chilled, there is less danger of this injury to the tissue. This makes a good side line for a part-time job and can be carried on in conjunction with the forcing of chicory (which see),

for they can both be carried at a temperature of 60 degrees.

INSECTS AND DISEASES: There are no serious insect pests, but several crown rots may cause some trouble in old plants. Cuttings should not be taken from diseased plants and new plants should not be set where diseased plants have been.

GENERAL RECOMMENDATIONS: Rhubarb can be forced in the coldframes early in the spring. The roots are dug early, if possible, or the previous fall and immediately placed in the coldframe with soil around them. The hotbed sash is not put in place until it is desired to force the roots. Then it is put in place and heat is captured from the sunshine. It is well to insulate the sides of the coldframe with manure, to help hold in the heat. The coldframes can be built up slightly to increase the height of the stalks. These will, of course, have large green leaves, because they are grown in the light. However, this is not objectionable. As a matter of fact, the stalks will be more nutritious than when forced in the dark. Any seed stems that are formed should be picked out as soon as they make their appearance, unless a crop of seed is wanted.

Rice Bean

See Beans

Rutabaga

DESCRIPTION: The rutabaga (*Brassica napobrassica*) is similar to the turnip, except that it has a much denser flesh and is usually a better root for storage. The leaves are smooth and greenish blue in color. The plant is a biennial, but the gardener is only interested in the root which is produced the first year. The second year brings forth a much-

branched seedstalk, which produces masses of small purplish flowers and, therefrom, seed pods containing numerous, small, round, brown seeds. Rutabaga is a native of Northern Europe and is therefore sometimes called SWEDISH TURNIP.

TYPES AND VARIETIES: There are two types of rutabaga, the white- and yellow-fleshed. The varieties are Purple Top Yellow, Golden Neckless, and White-Fleshed Neckless. The golden-yellow varieties are generally preferred. An early white-fleshed variety is Sweet Perfection.

SOIL AND CLIMATIC REQUIREMENTS: Rutabagas do well on any of the heavier soils, such as the loams and heavier sandy loams. They will make a good crop on the lighter soils if supplied with sufficient nutrients. Whatever the soil, it must be well drained and well supplied with organic matter. A good supply of lime to keep the soil sweet is essential. The crop does its best in the cooler temperate regions. It develops its greatest degree of quality where the night temperatures are cool.

CULTURAL DIRECTIONS: The seed is sown in the latter part of July or early August in rows and thinned to stand 4 to 6 inches apart. The rows should be spaced about 3 feet apart for field culture or 2 feet apart in the garden. The seedlings should be given several side-dressings of liquid fertilizer. It takes about 100 days to mature the roots. They will withstand considerable frost in the fall and are usually left in the field until the first killing frost. In mild winters, they may not be dug until after Thanksgiving.

Rutabagas are not suited to hot weather and, for this reason, should not be planted in the spring. If planted early, they make a slower growth, as the stem continues to elongate, and the result is a long neck with a small root on the bottom. In hot climates, the roots are small and fibrous. Too much nitrogen and a late, hot fall are not conducive to good rutabagas. It is better to grow them for a shorter period in the fall, even though the fleshy root may be smaller. In short-season sections, where the growing season is only 100 days long, they are sown in the late spring. They produce large yields of roots in cool sections on limestone soils, and many growers in the sections where new land is being cleared often sow the seed broadcast after the ground is plowed for the first time. Such ground cannot be cultivated because of the roots from stumps. Rutabagas will grow to a size of five or six pounds with excellent quality, although the smaller size is more desired. Any soil that is low in nitrogen but well supplied with phosphorus, potash, and lime will usually grow exceptionally large yields.

INSECTS AND DISEASES: There are no serious diseases of the rutabaga. On soils improperly limed and overly fertilized with chemicals, the roots may be of poor quality because of the deficiency of boron. Ten pounds of borax to the acre will prevent this. Plant aphids sometimes cause some trouble in the fall by covering the leaves and making them messy to handle. However, they are usually not sprayed, although this can be done if proper equipment is available. Nicotine does not kill the aphids in cool weather unless special methods are resorted to, to vaporize it.

GENERAL RECOMMENDATIONS: Rutabagas make a good crop to store in the winter, as the roots will keep without much care until spring. They will keep at the same temperatures as potatoes (which see).

Salsify (Oyster Plant)

DESCRIPTION: OYSTER PLANT (*Tragopogon porrifolius*), also called SAL-

SIFY and VEGETABLE OYSTER, gets its name from the fact that its fleshy

root has an oyster-like flavor. It is commonly grown in gardens for its roots and stems. It is a hardy biennial. The first year, it makes a rosette of long, slender leaves and establishes a long, slender, white root similar to the parsnip's but not as large in diameter. The second year, it sends up a much-branched seedstalk with purplish flowers. A native of the Mediterranean countries, probably coming from the Nile Valley, it has been in cultivation for many years.

RELATED SPECIES AND VARIETIES: GOATSBEARD, the common name of the genus, is also used more narrowly to refer to a species (*T. pratensis*), which was once extensively cultivated until salsify displaced it. Another related species (*T. crocifolius*) also has an edible root. A common variety of salsify is Sandwich Island Mammoth. (*See also* Scolymus; Scorgonera.)

SOIL AND CLIMATIC REQUIREMENTS: Salsify is hardy in temperate regions and will grow where there are at least 120 growing days. Although it is a biennial, the plant is grown as an annual or a winter annual. It requires a fertile, well-drained soil that is well supplied with lime and nutrients. Several side-dressings of liquid fertilizer should be given to keep the plants growing during the long growing season. A deep, sandy loam-soil is ideal because of the length of the taproot.

CULTURAL DIRECTIONS: The seed should be sown in the early spring as soon as the ground can be worked, in rows 20 inches apart. The plants are thinned to stand 4 or 5 inches apart and are cultivated the same as any other crop. The roots can be used as soon as they are large enough, but their quality improves after cold weather sets in. The roots may be dug late and stored in moist sand in a cold cellar, although stored roots are not so good as those used directly from the garden. Those that remain in the ground after freezing can be dug in the spring before growth starts, or they may be left in the ground to produce green shoots which may be cut off as they come up and used as asparagus.

Scallop Squash
See Pumpkin

Scarlet Runner Bean
See under Beans

Scolymus

DESCRIPTION: Scolymus, GOLDEN THISTLE, or SPANISH OYSTER PLANT (*Scolymus hispanicus*), is a biennial plant which is used very much the same as is salsify. The white roots are long and slender and the leaves are long, narrow, prickly, and ragged. The plants yield more than salsify, but the flavor of the roots is weaker, more or less intermediate between salsify and parsnip. The stem is tall and branched, with golden-yellow compound flowers on a branched terminal stem. It is a native of the Mediterranean region.

SOIL AND CLIMATIC REQUIREMENTS: The plants make their best yields in fertile, well-drained, well-limed loam soils. They are grown as annuals, as the roots are usually the only portion of the plant used, although the second-year leaves can be used in place of Cardoon (which see). The rosette of first-year leaves are spiny and difficult to handle. The plants

require about 120 days to make roots a foot in length and an inch in diameter.

CULTURAL DIRECTIONS: The seed is sown in early spring in rows 20 inches apart, and the plants are thinned to stand 4 inches apart in the row. They should be side-dressed with liquid fertilizer. The roots are harvested in the fall or the following spring. They may be dug and stored, if the ground freezes so hard that they cannot be dug through the winter. There are no serious pests.

GENERAL RECOMMENDATIONS: If salsify and parsnips are on your list as desirable vegetables for the garden, this may be a good addition. If they are not appreciated, then this vegetable probably would not be desirable.

Scorzonera

SCORZONERA *hispanica*, variously called BLACK OYSTER PLANT, BLACK

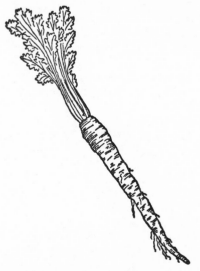

SALSIFY, and VIPERS GRASS, is a perennial plant similar to salsify (oyster

plant), but the leaves are broader and the flowers are yellow. The long and fleshy root has a black epidermis with white flesh. The stems grow to a height of two feet and bear the flowers in solitary heads at the terminals of their many branches. The plant was used at one time as protection against snake bites. The roots are used like common salsify (which see). Scorzonera is a native of Central Europe but has been introduced by seedsmen into this country. No special varieties listed. (*See also Scolymus*).

It is particularly important that the soil be of good tilth and that the subsoil be sufficiently well drained to prevent poor aeration during heavy rains. The soils must be well supplied with lime and organic matter and be free of any sticky material. A good supply of organic matter is essential. The plant is fairly hardy but as the roots are dug at the end of the first year, it is usually grown as an annual. It requires 100 to 120 days to produce a good root. For cultural directions, *see* Salsify.

This plant 'deserves more attention than it has received; anyone who likes salsify will like this vegetable even better. It may still be difficult to obtain seed from American seedsmen.

Scurvy Grass

See Sea-Kale

Sea-Kale

DESCRIPTION: The common sea-kale (*Crambe maritima*) is a large-leafed perennial which forms a rosette of leaves the first year and sends up young stalks in the spring which are cut when tender and used for food similar to asparagus. This is often called SCURVY GRASS, but should not be confused with the true plant of that name (*Cochlearia officinalis*), so called because of its anti-scorbutic properties. The latter is a plant of

the Arctic regions, resembling water cress more than sea-kale, and is not so well known. Sea-kale has become popular among gardeners in America, although it is a native of the Mediterranean seashore regions. It is usually bleached before it is cut for food.

TYPES AND VARIETIES: No particular varieties of this species are listed, but there is a related species (*C. orientalis*), grown as a substitute for horseradish, while the TARTAR BREADFRUIT (*C. tartarica*), a plant not common in this country, is highly prized by Europeans for its large, sweet, white roots, as well as for its tender shoots in the spring.

SOIL AND CLIMATIC REQUIREMENTS: Sea-kale produces its crop early in the spring when there are few other vegetables, and it is adapted to culture in the north temperate regions. In some localities, it may be necessary to protect the crowns during the winter. The soil should be a good, well-drained, fertile loam or sandy loam that is thoroughly sweetened with limestone. The soil should be capable of supplying an abundance of water for large yields and long-lived beds. The subsoil should be prepared similarly to that recommended for asparagus (which see).

CULTURAL DIRECTIONS: The plants may be propagated by seeds or by cuttings. Seeds should be sown in a sandy loam soil at a depth of one inch. These plants will require about a year to develop to a good-sized plant, a culture similar to asparagus being necessary. If they are to be planted in the permanent positions the first year, the seedlings, when four to six inches high, should be planted three feet apart and the space between planted to beans or similar quick-growing crops. The plants may be propagated by cuttings after a few plants are established. The cuttings are made from the roots, similar to the culture of horse-radish (which see). The cuttings should be 4 or 5 inches long, and are set in the spring as soon as the ground can be cultivated. The plants should be well fertilized with a heavy application of liquid fertilizer each year. The second year, the plants may be large enough so that the shoots can be cut for a few weeks, but the heavy harvest should be left until the second spring after setting the plants. Before the winter weather sets in, the plants should be cleaned of all old leaves and the crown covered over with manure, if it is available; if not, with a good compost material, or, as a last resort, with leaves or straw. The spring that cuttings are started, the plants should be covered with flower pots which have

a hole in the bottom or with any other container that will exclude much of the light, so that the sprouts will not turn green. Sometimes loose soils are hilled up over the plants so that the stalks have to grow through six inches of soil. They are then cut near the crown with a long-bladed knife. If the color is permitted to develop, the sprouts become slightly bitter, but they will contain many more vitamins than the blanched sprouts, and gardeners should try them both ways. Asparagus was all blanched at one time, but the green stalk was found to be so much better that white is no longer popular. The same might be true of this plant.

GENERAL RECOMMENDATIONS: This is a good plant to try out, and, although seed is difficult to get, there are seedsmen who have it. The shoots should be cut when 4 or 5 inches high and the cutting season may be extended to six weeks. It is a good plant to put in with the other perennials, for variety.

Sea-Kale Beet
See Chard

Sieva Bean
See Lima Bean

Skirret
DESCRIPTION: Skirret (*Sium sisarum*) is a hardy East Asian perennial, grown as an annual for its numerous fleshy roots, which are produced somewhat like sweet potatoes but about the size of a man's finger. They are very tender, with a pleasant, sweet taste, and are used somewhat in the same manner as salsify (which see). The first year, a rosette of finely divided leaves are produced, while

the second year there is a much-branched stem with umbels of small

white flowers. The roots are produced in clusters. They are cylindrical in shape, but have one objection: the core becomes fibrous and must be removed when they are prepared for the table. They must be grown rapidly to make them especially palatable. No particular varieties are listed.

SOIL AND CLIMATIC REQUIREMENTS: The plants require a rich soil that is freely supplied with organic matter and well sweetened with lime. It should be capable of supplying abundant water to the plants. The plants are very hardy and will live over from year to year, similar to the Jerusalem artichoke (which see).

CULTURAL DIRECTIONS: The plants are usually grown as annuals by sowing seed either early in the spring or late the previous fall. They will make a good crop the first year. The seed may be sown early indoors, and the seedlings are then transplanted to the permanent locations in rows 2 feet apart and 10 inches apart in the row. This procedure will greatly in-crease the yield. The roots, if left in the ground, will produce seedstalks. The roots may be planted in beds and, as the plants are produced, they can be taken off and rooted. It is a question whether this is worth while, except to maintain a variety which will come true to type. There is a chance to do some good breeding work with this plant.

Smallage
See Celery

Snake Melon
See Melons

Snap Bean
See Beans

Sorrel

DESCRIPTION: Common Sorrel (*Rumex acetosa*), sometimes called SOUR GRASS, is a large, acid, thick-leafed potherb, also prized as a salad plant. It is a perennial which sends up tender leaves early in the spring, when most garden plants are still dormant

or just making a start in growth. The first year, a rosette of leaves is made, and the second year, a 2- to 3-foot seedstalk is sent out, with inconspicuous flowers producing small triangular-shaped brown seeds.

TYPES AND VARIETIES: There are a number of species that may be called Sorrel. SPINACH DOCK (*Rumex patientia*) is the earliest of the group. It is also called GARDEN PATIENCE or MONKS RHUBARB. Like the common sorrel, it is a native of southern Europe. Garden sorrel (*Rumex scutatus*) has very acid leaves. FRENCH SORREL (*Rumex montanus*) is in very high esteem among the northern Europeans and has a milder flavor than the previous species. There are ten or more other species of this genus, including Sour Dock, which are used in a similar manner but have some characteristics which make them less desirable than the particular species mentioned. Large-leaved French is a good variety.

SOIL AND CLIMATIC REQUIREMENTS: These plants have a wide adaptability to soil conditions and will grow on comparatively poor soils, providing they are well drained and have a good supply of lime in them. They will, however, respond to higher levels of fertility. They are all hardy and will grow throughout the temperate regions, maturing in 60 days. In fact, they are so hardy that in some places some of the members are considered noxious weeds, having escaped from cultivation.

CULTURAL DIRECTIONS: The seed may be sown in rows two feet apart and thinned to six inches in the row. If planted early, they will produce a good crop of leaves the first year. They can also be sown in late summer for a crop the following spring. Sour grass is available in our markets during a large part of the season.

Sour Dock
See Sorrel

Sour Grass
See Sorrel

Soybean

The soybean (*Soja max* or *Glycine max*), introduced from China in 1804 but comparatively unknown until recent times, probably has more divergent uses than any other plant grown—cotton possibly excepted. Soybeans are of many varieties. The seeds, in yellows, browns, black, and

all combinations of these, are slightly larger than the Navy bean. The plant grows to two feet tall, usually bushy but occasionally twining, and produces small, inconspicuous, white-to-pink flowers and pods which contain from four to seven seeds. It requires a well-limed soil but will grow with a minimum amount of fertilizer. It is particularly adapted to the well-drained sandy soils, and can be grown in practically all parts of the United States. It has been used largely as a stock-food and green manure crop. Lately it has gained much prominence in the manufacture of oil and plastics. In China, it was fully as important a food as rice, but it was not used as food in this country until the development of the sweet varieties, which are much more palatable to the human taste. At the present time, the green beans are canned the same as peas and are sold roasted in place of salted nuts. It is probable that as many uses will be found for the soybean in this country as the Chinese have put it to for many years.

Spanish Oyster Plant

See Scolymus; Scorzonera

Spinach

DESCRIPTION: Spinach (*Spinacia oleracea*) is one of our most important vegetables and makes up a large percentage of the bulk of vegetable produce marketed every year. It is a fleshy-leafed annual that forms a heavy rosette of broad, crinkly, tender leaves, very high in vitamin-content. During hot weather, the plants send

up flowering stalks with long pointed leaves which bear inconspicuous male or female flowers. The male flowers are borne in clusters on a spike, while the female flowers are borne in clusters in the axils of the leaves. The percentage of male plants is usually larger than the number of female

plants in any field-lot of seedlings. Spinach originally came from Asia and eastern Europe but is now grown in practically every corner of the world.

TYPES AND VARIETIES: There are two types of spinach, the smooth-seeded and the prickly-seeded, but there are a large number of varieties, some of which are better adapted to certain localities than others. Some of the varieties listed are:

GIANT THICK LEAF: Leaves are thick, long, and spreading, making very large plants. Grows rapidly.

BLOOMSDALE SAVOY: Dark-green leaves are thick and crinkly. An excellent variety.

BLIGHT-RESISTANT VIRGINIA SAVOY: Similar to above.

VICTORIA: Leaves are round, high in quality, but not too vigorous.

OLD DOMINION: Leaves are thick and crinkly, particularly suited for planting in the fall and harvesting the following spring.

PRICKLY-SEEDED or WINTER SPINACH: Makes a large plant of round leaves. Does well in mild winter weather.

Other good varieties are King of Denmark, Juliana (which is slightly later), and Summer Savoy.

SOIL AND CLIMATIC REQUIREMENTS: Spinach is definitely a cold- or cool-season crop which goes to seed quickly in hot weather. It is therefore an early-spring or late-summer plant. It is harvested all winter where the weather is mild, as in the southern states, and it is possible to buy spinach practically the year around. The crop can be grown on any good soil and even on some of the lighter soils, if proper fertilization is given.

The early crop does best on the sandy loam soils, while the early summer crop is better suited to the silt loams. It is also grown on the black muck soils, where it is less gritty than when grown on the fine sandy loam soils. The main objection to the sandy soils is the amount of grit that is lodged in the folds of the leaves. Anyone who has eaten spinach and has sharpened his teeth on fine grit can be sure that the crop is coming from the sandy loam soils of the Eastern Seaboard. Regardless of the kind of soil, spinach does best if abundantly supplied with liming materials, preferably magnesium lime. If magnesium is deficient in the soil, spinach will blister in bright sunlight. If there is insufficient lime in the soil, spinach goes to pieces in wet rainy weather. The plants are very sensitive to poor aeration in the soil. In the heavier soils, it is almost impossible to grow spinach, because it is impossible from a practical standpoint to get on enough liming material. An application of three or four tons of pulverized limestone a year for three years per acre may be necessary on some of the heavy soils before a real crop can be grown, but such soils, when once thoroughly supplied with lime, will produce tremendous yields. Soils should be practically sweet or neutral. The crop not only is very sensitive to toxic materials that are released in acid soils, but also has a high lime-requirement in itself. On the lighter soils, much less lime is needed but those soils do not produce the yields that are possible on the heavy soils. Spinach is considered a heavy feeder, and for this reason 1,000 to 1,500 pounds of 5–10–5 fertilizer to the acre are needed. This fertilizer should be broadcast and plowed under.

Spinach is a deep-rooting plant but has a very sensitive root system and is easily burned by poor conditions in the subsoil. For this reason, it is a crop that will do much better on the limestone soils. On the naturally acid soils, it is advisable to plow under limestone for several years to get the subsoil in as good condition as the surface soil. On problem soils, it may be necessary to plow deep and run a subsoil plow in the bottom of the furrow, with a special attachment placed on the plow-beam to run the limestone in as the plowing is being done. This does a fine job of opening the soil and promoting better crop-growth by improving drainage and aeration. If spinach tends to be yellow, it should be side-dressed with a little nitrogen, but usually, if the soil is in good condition and properly limed, it will be impossible to improve the crop sufficiently to pay for the side-dressing.

CULTURAL DIRECTIONS: Spinach seed is sown in the open ground as soon as the ground can be worked; some growers even prepare the ground in the fall and sow the seed after the soil is frozen. Or, it may be sown early enough in the fall so that the plants will make an inch of growth before the soil freezes. The plants require 40 to 50 days to mature. Virginia Savoy for the early crop, followed by King of Denmark, would give a succession-crop planting that would make the plants available for a month. A later planting of Summer Savoy or New Zealand Spinach would prolong the season if that were desirable.

When the seedlings are an inch tall, they should be thinned to stand 6 inches apart in the row, unless it is desired to use the plants before they are full grown, in which case they may be thinned to 3 inches apart and every other plant removed when they are half grown. In small plantings in the garden, this can be easily done. The rows should be a foot apart. In the garden, it is not necessary to fertilize with more than one side-dressing of liquid fertilizer when the plants are 2 inches high.

In weedy ground, a small mound of soil an inch high is placed over the seeded row when the seed is sown, and in five days the soil is leveled over the row to kill the large number of weed seedlings which are just beginning to grow. That is the easiest time to kill weeds. A shove hoe or a wheel hoe is a good tool to run up and down the rows a few times as the seedlings are growing.

INSECTS AND DISEASES: The development of blight-resistant varieties has done much to eliminate the hazards of growing the crop, although most of the difficulty with spinach is due to improper preparation of the soil. Spinach aphids are a serious pest in the fall crop and may do considerable damage. They get on the underside of the curly leaves and are very difficult to kill. A three-percent nicotine in lime dust is very effective in controlling the aphids. However, the dusting should be done before the plants get so large that control becomes difficult. Beet-leaf miner is a bad pest in early spinach, and is controlled as for beets (which see).

GENERAL RECOMMENDATIONS: A ten-foot row of spinach in successive plantings will be enough for the average family. It is better to have a number of different plants for pot-

herbs than to depend on a single species or variety. Spinach plants are cut off at the ground and the whole plant used. Even the seedstalks can be used if they have not gone to the flower stage.

Spinach Dock
See Sorrel

Spinach-Rhubarb
See Rhubarb

Squash

DESCRIPTION: Squashes (*Cucurbita maxima*) have strong runner vines with cylindrical stems and kidney- or heart-shaped leaves of various sizes. The leaves are soft and less harsh and spiny than those of the pumpkins. The flowers are borne singly in the axils of the leaves and consist of staminate (male) and pistillate (female) types, funnel-shaped and orange to yellow in color. The male flowers are somewhat smaller, much more numerous, and a week earlier than the female flowers. The fruits are of various shapes and sizes and the colors vary from orange through yellow to green, with stripes. The squash is probably a native of tropical America. (*See also* Pumpkins.)

TYPES AND VARIETIES: The various varieties of squash may be grouped into four general types. As commonly used, the term "squash" includes many of the types and varieties listed under pumpkins, but by botanical classification the SUMMER SQUASH, for instance, is a pumpkin. At the end of our discussion of squash, we mention in a miscellaneous group varieties commonly called "squashes" which are discussed under PUMPKIN in this book because botanically they are pumpkins. The following four important groups are true squashes (*Cucurbita maxima*), having fleshy flower stems:

BANANA GROUP: Fruits elongated and tapering slightly toward either end. They are not so popular and do not keep so well as the other groups, but some are very palatable. BANANA SQUASH averages 15 inches long and 6 inches wide and is greenish gray in color. PLYMOUTH ROCK is similar but its greenish-gray color is flecked with lighter shades. WINNEBAGO is similar to Banana but is smaller, weighing around eleven pounds, and has a dark-green color, but the skin is lightly warted. MAMMOTH WHALE is the big member of the banana group, averaging 30 by 8 inches in size and weighing 18 pounds; it is olive green with lighter stripes. GILMORE is 15 by 7 inches, salmon-colored, splotched with bluish-green. ALLIGATOR is cylindrical and slightly pointed, 25 by 8 inches, 18 pounds in weight, dark green, and smooth but slightly irregular. This variety is a good keeper and is the best of the group. All the others are late fall varieties.

HUBBARD GROUP: The chief group grown in the United States. Its fruits which are generally ovoid in shape are always pointed at the flower end. The stem end is tapered but has a heavy shoulder. GREEN HUBBARD is dark green, with dirty-white stripes toward the blossom end, and weighs about 13 pounds. BLUE HUBBARD is similar but greenish blue in color. CHICAGO WARTED HUBBARD is slightly larger, weighing 15 pounds, and more warted than Green Hubbard. GOLDEN HUBBARD weighs 9 pounds, is an orange-red color with cream-colored stripes toward the blossom end, and is several weeks earlier than the

Green Hubbard. The KITCHENETTE weighs 5 pounds and is dark green and glossy; though not a heavy yielder, it is of good quality and of a

HUBBARD SQUASH

size more suitable for the kitchen garden. ARIKARA is 12 by 9 inches and weighs 8 pounds; it is smooth, light salmon striped with bluish-gray, early, prolific, and a good keeper. AUTUMNAL MARROW is like the Green Hubbard except that the stem and blossom ends are straight instead of curved and the skin is light orange and pocked; it is about 9 inches thick and half again as long and weighs 8 pounds. PROLIFIC MARROW is an inch shorter but weighs 7 pounds more; it is lemon-shaped, orange-red, and slightly warted. DELICIOUS is top-shaped, 8 by 12 inches in size, weighing 8 pounds; it is smooth, dark green in color, with light stripes toward the blossom end. GOLDEN DELICIOUS is similar, but golden yellow in color. MARBLEHEAD is lemon-shaped, 9 by 12 inches in size and weighs 8 pounds; it is bluish gray and bumpy, somewhat similar to Blue Hubbard. SIBLEY is more pointed toward the tip, smooth, slate gray, and 8 by 12 inches in size. IRONCLAD is a 16-pound squash, 15 by 12 inches, pointed at the blossom end, smooth, and silvery gray with lighter stripes toward the blossom end.

TURBAN GROUP: Turban-shaped fruits with a button at the blossom end. These are all good keepers except the AMERICAN TURBAN, a short, cylindrical fruit, flattened at both ends; turban-shaped with a distinct button at the tip; 7 by 10 inches in size and weighing 8 pounds. The skin is deep lemon-yellow and rough. This is the poorest of the group; not a good keeper. ESSEX HYBRID is similar in shape, 6 by 9 inches in size, and weighs 10 pounds; it is yellow to orange and sometimes splashed with green. BAY STATE is a 7-pound squash, sized 7 by 10 inches, similar in shape but with a slate gray color and smooth skin. WARREN is extremely warty, orange-red in color, 8 by 10 inches in size, and weighs 15 pounds. VICTOR has the characteristic shape except for the button on the blossom end. It is an 8-pound squash, 6 by 9 inches in size, and orange-red in color.

MAMMOTH GROUP: These are the large squashes and may weigh 100 pounds or more. They are often confused with the large pumpkins. They are generally used for stock feed or canning, as they are too large for kitchen use. ATLAS is somewhat egg-shaped and grooved, 20 by 13 inches, and weighs 35 pounds; the skin is reddish yellow, smooth, and glossy. ESTAMPES (Etampes) is short and cylindrical, flattened at both ends, 10 inches broad and 18 long, weighing about 30 pounds; the skin is reddish orange with the grooves of lighter color, rough, and bumpy. GENUINE MAMMOTH is a 60-pound squash, a foot and a half by two feet in size,

nearly spherical, with the blossom end pointed or somewhat flattened; it may be prominently grooved; the skin is dull salmon-yellow. MAMMOTH CHILI is similar in shape, being 16 by 12 inches in size but may weigh over 100 pounds. The skin is smooth and mottled orange and yellow with lighter stripes.

MISCELLANEOUS GROUP: We must mention here those important types which are pumpkins according to their botanical characteristics but in the markets are referred to as varieties of SUMMER SQUASH. See PUMPKIN for descriptions of the following varieties: White- and yellow-fruited PATTYPAN, SUMMER and GIANT CROOKNECK, VEGETABLE MARROW, BUSH MARROW CUSHAW varieties, and the ZUCCHINI types. The small acorn type is also included here although it is a fall or early winter type.

SOIL AND CLIMATIC REQUIREMENTS: Squashes produce the biggest yields on well-drained and well-aerated soils that contain some sand but considerable organic matter. They need a liberal supply of moisture. The soil should be well supplied with lime and have a good level of fertility. The plants require at least 120 days of good growing weather. They are tropical annuals but can be grown in temperate climates if the growing season is long enough. The plants are all frost-sensitive.

CULTURAL DIRECTIONS: The soil must be well prepared and in good tilth before the seed is sown. It should be loose and friable, so that the ground does not bake over the seed when it is planted. The seeds are planted in hills 4 to 6 feet apart in rows at least 6 feet apart. Some of the large-fruited varieties should have 8 feet between the rows. Liberal applications of manure mixed with the soil under the hills is good assurance of good vine growth and good yields, although it is possible to get vines too vigorous. With hills so far apart, it is practical to prepare the soil by digging 2- by 3-feet pits 2 feet deep and mixing the removed soil with lime and superphosphate at the rate of a big handful of each to a hill. The nitrogen and potash can be applied as a liquid fertilizer later. This mixture of soil may be replaced and 5 or 6 seeds planted in each place. As soon as the vines begin to run, it is no longer possible to cultivate, so that the weeds must be brought under control early. In some sections, it may be advisable to start the seedlings in a hotbed or a greenhouse and have them ready to set in the field when the soil is warm and there is no longer danger of frost. If the seedlings are grown in veneer bands, they can be transplanted with little disturbance to the roots. The soil should be soaked with transplanting solution before the plants are set in the garden. Treat insects and diseases as for pumpkins (which see).

GENERAL RECOMMENDATIONS: In the small garden, it is not practical to grow the winter varieties of squash, as they take a considerable amount of space. If a fence corner is available that would otherwise be wasted, a few hills can be planted. Squash should be harvested before frost hits the vines. They should be stored where a temperature of 70 degrees can be maintained for several weeks. Then they are placed in permanent storage and should not be piled more than two deep. To keep well, only

squash that have a rind hard enough to resist denting by a thumbnail should be placed in storage. They should be carefully handled, as bruised fruits will decay. Well-ripened fruits, carefully handled and properly cured, will last until the following May, if stored in a well-ventilated storage cellar where the temperature is not over 50 degrees. For garden purposes, the small- to medium-sized varieties should be grown, as large squash which are too big for a meal are apt to dry out before they are used, and much waste results. When fruits are properly ripened, they must be chopped with an ax, because the rind is so hard. When growing several varieties of squash, the gardener should not save the seed, unless the varieties can be grown by themselves at least a quarter of a mile apart. Squash will cross with pumpkins of one species (*Cucurbita moschata*) but not with those of the other (*Cucurbita pepo*). Of course, if the gardener wants some fun, there is no reason why he should not save seed from crossed varieties and see what he gets. If he uses the proper technique, he can develop new varieties which are always in demand. Seedsmen are always looking for something new that is really good. If squashes are not grown in the home garden, they should be bought in the fall and stored.

Strawberry

DESCRIPTION: The garden strawberry (*Fragaria virginiana*) is probably more generally grown than any other plant in the kitchen garden. Anyone who plants a garden also plants strawberries—a fact which warrants the inclusion of strawberries in a book on vegetables. The strawberry is a perennial, herbaceous plant that produces a rosette of leaves, with stolons or runners. The three-part leaves are borne on a long petiole from the base of the plant. The flowers are borne on a noded, branched stem, which comes from the base of the leaves. In some varieties, the male and female organs may be in the same flower; in others, they may be in separate flowers. All the newer varieties are of the former kind, so that it is not necessary to plant two varieties to have fruit set.

TYPES AND VARIETIES: Most varieties listed are those which produce fruit from the middle of May to the middle of July, depending on the locality. The everbearing or perpetual varieties (*Fragaria vesca*) ripen their fruit through the summer and late into the fall. They will produce berries until snow flies, but for several reasons have been more of a curiosity than a regular garden entity. People seem to want strawberries before the Fourth of July and do not care much about them in the fall, when so many other fruits are available. The following varieties are only a few of the many that have been developed for the American gardener. No attempt will be made even to approach completeness. The following are given merely as suggestions to the kitchen gardener:

PATHFINDER is a recent introduction by the New Jersey Experiment Station under the guidance of Professor J. H. Clark. It is a round, pink berry that is early, prolific, mild and richly flavored, making a rapid growth. It has proved to be an excellent berry for the kitchen garden in localities where temperatures are not too high

during the picking season. It is too perishable for shipping from warm sections. Two hundred and fifty plants have been known to yield enough in excess of home requirements to bring $100.00 on the market. Some of the berries attain a good two inches in diameter. But they must be picked every morning in order to reach the consumer in as fresh a condition as the grower demands for his own table. The berries are very highly marketable.

PREMIER is a good market berry for the northern states and seems to be very hardy. It is an early variety. The berry is red, medium to large, and heart-shaped. HOWARD 17 is the same as Premier.

CATSKILL is a fine berry for mid-season, being a companion berry to Premier. The berries are large and light red in color. They are of good flavor and firm enough for shipping.

FAIRFAX is a high-quality berry that has a fine red color which turns dark on aging. It is the early berry in the southern states, though two weeks later than Pathfinder in the North. It is medium to large and somewhat irregular in shape. The quality is very good, but it does not compare in yield with the Pathfinder.

DORSET is somewhat similar to Fairfax, but is more particular in its climatic requirements. It is a slightly longer berry, almost as good in color, but does not yield like Pathfinder.

BLAKEMORE is a shipping berry. The berries are rather long and pointed, rather dark in color, and quite tart. It is a better canning berry than a berry for the kitchen garden.

MAYTIME has just been released from the United States Department of Agriculture. It is a very early berry for the southern states, but has not had much of a trial in the northern states. STARBRIGHT is another government introduction and is a mid-season berry for the southern states. SENATOR DUNLAP is one of the oldest varieties and is still being grown in the middlewestern states. NORTH STAR is a new one.

BIG JOE is a late, dark-red berry, rather particular in its climatic requirements, of fair quality, and a good southern variety. MISSIONARY is also a southern berry, as are FAIRMORE and DAYBREAK. The latter is a garden variety that is quite early. CHESAPEAKE does not yield enough, although it has been planted for many years. Like REDSTAR, it is a late berry.

Two good northern berries are ABERDEEN and DRESDEN. Aberdeen is a good variety for heavy soils in the northern states. Dresden produces very large yields, but it is too sour for garden purposes.

Among the everbearing varieties, the following should be mentioned: Mastodon, Gem, Green Mountain, Champion, Gemzata, and Wayzata.

SOIL AND CLIMATIC REQUIREMENTS: Strawberries respond to careful cultural practices. Soils should be well drained and supplied with sufficient lime to eliminate all but slight acidity. At one time it was thought that berries did best on very acid soils. This has been disproven. Sandy soils may be fairly acid, but the heavy soils should be sufficiently limed to bring the reaction close to the neutral point. The soil should be well supplied with organic matter to get best results. A ten-ton application of manure to the acre, plowed under, will assure sufficient plant food to carry the crop. It is particularly important

that the soil supply an abundance of water, without being poorly aerated. The soils should not supply too much nitrogen. Many a good variety has been condemned because the soil was too fertile for the variety. Some varieties will do much better on very fertile soils, while others will do much better on a soil low in nitrogen. Dorset and Fairfax are easily over-fertilized with nitrogen. They make large vines and will be shy on yield. A planting of Pathfinder on a piece of ground which had a graduated nitrogen-fertility from very high at one end of the row to very low at the other produced the biggest yields of uniformly large berries on the middle two-thirds of the field. On the high-nitrogen ground, the plants were vigorous and dark green, but the berries were soft and flavorless and the yield was less than a quarter of the average for the crop. At the poor-soil end, the vines were very scant but they were loaded with an exceptionally large number of berries, which, though they ripened small, were the sweetest and firmest of all. No variety should be judged unless it has been grown under high- and low-nitrogen conditions in each particular climatic environment.

CULTURAL DIRECTIONS: If a new bed is set out as soon as good plants can be dug in the spring, the plants will get the advantage of cool weather and moisture, and the soil will settle before dry weather begins. Plants set after the picking season is over may not do any more than establish themselves, unless the season is particularly favorable in rainfall. A variety that makes a lot of vine growth should be given plenty of room. There is nothing that will reduce yields more than crowded plants. Most gardeners plant too many plants in a small place. One of the biggest yields per plant ever observed were from plants that were set three feet apart in rows that were six feet apart. This made a row three feet wide, with plenty of room between for a walk, and the runners had plenty of room. If the plants are planted late, they need not be grown so close together. It requires around 5000 plants to plant an acre, leaving two by four feet between plants—a fine distance for most varieties.

Runner plants should. be used. for setting the new beds if they are available; otherwise, sections should be taken from the younger plants that make a clump. In exceptionally dry weather, strawberries do not make runners but produce plants from the old crowns. In digging these, only those plants that have good roots should be taken for the new plantings, and they should be separated to single plants. As the runners start out from the plants, the vines are kept ten to twelve inches apart. They should be moved eight or ten inches each way as they are being hoed. This will space them so that they will make their maximum growth and produce the maximum number of berries.

Strawberries should be given plenty of water. They will practically double their yield by a thorough soaking. Water should be applied abundantly and only once or twice during the picking season, rather than by frequent light sprinklings. Light sprinklings do no good and may actually damage the fruits. The yields from fairly fertile soils will probably not be increased with applications of fertilizer. On lighter soil, however, the plants may respond to a side-dressing of liquid fertilizer after they have become well established.

Strawberries should be mulched. Any straw or hay or cut-up cornstalks make a good material to spread over the plants during the winter to prevent them from starting too early in the spring. The ground around the plants should be covered with a light mulch to protect the berries from sand or mud in case of wind or rain. If the plants are kept clean up to the first of August, crabgrass may then be allowed to grow up around the plants, particularly if the vines are fairly vigorous; the crabgrass dies down after the first frost and makes a light mulch which tends to check the soft growth sufficiently so that the plants will set a heavy crop the following spring. This may sound like a lazy man's method and might get one into trouble, but it should be done with an understanding of what the vine growth means in terms of fruit. In some cases, annual weeds will do more good than harm.

In order to get early fruit, the plants should be protected from north and west winds. This may mean a difference of two weeks. There is one precaution, however, that must be taken: protection against a severe frost at the time the flowers are in bloom. Cold-injury at that time will cause the formation of mummies— stunted fruits that do not grow.

The berries should be picked as soon as they are ripe. This will keep the small berries growing. Leaving berries on the plants to get overly ripe tends to slow down the growth of the green fruit. Keeping all the ripe berries picked, including the small ones which may not seem worth picking, will keep the plants bearing longer.

Strawberry plants can be lifted in the fall, after the growing season is over, and placed indoors in six-inch pots, where they may be brought into bearing rather as an oddity than as a profitable venture. Forcing strawberries is no longer a profitable practice, since berries are being frozen for the consumer. If one wishes to have a little fun and grow them indoors, they can be placed in a cool window, where they will blossom and set fruit.

INSECTS AND DISEASES: The Pathfinder variety is immune to serious diseases. The red stele disease is bad on susceptible varieties. It gets into the crowns and kills the plants. Insects are not a serious menace during the fruiting season, although the Japanese beetle does considerable damage to the foliage during the summer months when the plants are making their most rapid growth. The strawberry weevil causes a little trouble occasionally, but there is nothing that can be done about it.

GENERAL RECOMMENDATIONS: If a person really wishes to specialize in garden strawberries, he has several opportunities. The plants may be lifted and placed in coldframes late in the fall. The plants should be lifted with a spade so that enough soil is transferred to disturb the roots as little as possible. They are placed eight or ten inches apart each way and watered. The plants are covered with a light mulch and left during the winter. About the first to the 20th of February the mulch should be taken off and the sash placed over the plants. The sun will gradually warm up the soil and start growth. The plants must be covered for protection against freezing during the

cold nights. The sash should be lifted on warm days.

In the garden, unmulched plants will produce two weeks before those that are held back by a mulch. A few of the late berries should be planted to end up the season with, and if one wants still more berries, a variety of the perpetuals can be planted for late fall. For the garden, the delicate, poor-shipping berries are best. For the market, the good-shippers which can be thrown across the room and still be marketable are recommended. They do not have much flavor, but people seem to want them, because there are a large number sold. People who have never grown berries in the garden probably have never tasted a real strawberry. Many a good local business has been established by taking the pains to grow something really good for the consumer who appreciates good things.

Strawberry Tomato
See Tomato

String Bean
See Beans

Succory
See Chicory

Sugar Beets
See Beets

Summer Squash
See Pumpkin

Sunflower

DESCRIPTION: Although the sunflower (*Helianthus annuus*) is not strictly a kitchen vegetable, it is such a common sight in the kitchen garden that it seems advisable to include it among the other garden plants. It is a tall-growing annual with a very coarse stem and hairy, lance-shaped leaves. The stem is a single stalk topped by the flower, which is a disc of many seeds outlined by yellow ray petals. It gets its name from the resemblance to the sun and the habit of its heads to turn with the sun while growing. The plant is grown for the large seeds which are used for parrot and chicken feed. They are edible and palatable and were once used roasted as a substitute for coffee. The young flowers, when small, were also eaten, just as the bud of the globe artichoke is eaten, and were relished by some of the early American settlers. The plant is a native of western America and probably Mexico. The yield of seed per acre exceeds 50 bushels. The seeds are sometimes used as a source of oil; a bushel of seed will produce a gallon of oil and the pressed cake is used as stock feed. The plant has possibilities as a source of paper, and the fine fibers of the stem may be used as a substitute for silk. The plants make a good green-manure crop, because of the large yield, and they have been used as silo fodder for cattle. For this purpose, they are grown close together so that the stalks do not grow so large. The heads of specimen plants will grow to a width of two feet, if given plenty of room. The heads are hung in the chicken coop for hens to jump up to in order to get the seeds, giving them some exercise.

TYPES AND VARIETIES: Mammoth Russian is one variety that is listed, though there is a question whether this may not be the *Helianthus giganteus* of the eastern United States. The ornamental sunflowers may be smaller varieties of a species (*H. annuus* or *H. doronicoides*) which is closely related to the Jerusalem artichoke (*H. tuberosus*), a hardy perennial. The perennial sunflower varieties include Soleil D'or and Miss Mellish.

SOILS AND CLIMATIC REQUIREMENTS: The plants are grown as annuals and require 100 to 120 days to mature. They are sensitive to frost and leaves are easily killed. Soils should be well drained, sandy loam to loam, or even a heavier if well aerated. The plants tend to be somewhat later on the heavier soils. The soil should be fertile and well supplied with lime.

CULTURAL DIRECTIONS: In the garden, the plants should be planted in full sun in corners of the garden where they will not shade other plants. They can be used to advantage to serve as stalks for pole beans if the beans are planted at the bases of the sunflowers after they are well above ground. The sunflower stem will grow to a height of 8 to 12 feet. The beans and the stalks should be side-dressed with liquid fertilizer several times during the rapid growth of the plants. Sunflowers can also be planted close together in rows to serve as a very effective screen on the north side of the garden. By liberal feeding, the plants will grow to a tremendous size. Ordinarily the plants are allowed to stand a foot to two apart in rows. If more than one row is planted, they should be given more space. These are interesting plants for youngsters, as they can be planted in designs and used to outline inclosures for outdoor houses.

INSECTS AND DISEASES: There are no troublesome pests of this plant. If any bugs or worms should give trouble by eating the foliage, they may be controlled by dusting with a rotenone dust. Mildew is the result of wet weather and can be controlled by dusting with a fine sulphur.

Sweet Fennel

See Finocchio

Sweet Pepper

See Peppers

Sweet Potato

DESCRIPTION: The Sweet Potato (*Impomoea batatas*) belongs to the morning glory family, having the much-branched trailing vines and white, characteristically funnel-shaped flowers. Its fleshy root-tubers are highly nutritious and much desired by a large portion of the people of the world. The sweet potato is the most popular food-plant of the tropical countries and ranks seventh in importance among our own commercial food-plants. It is a native of tropical America and is probably the oldest of the cultivated vegetable crops which originated in America. It has many uses as a food plant.

TYPES AND VARIETIES: There are two main types of sweet potato: those which are mealy when cooked and are usually called sweet potatoes, and those which are wet when cooked and are popularly miscalled yams (which see). Vineless, Gold Skin, Yellow Jersey, and Red Skin are representative dry-fleshed types, while the Nancy Hall is a good variety for a wet potato. A more detailed classification of the varieties follows:*

*This classification is based upon H. C. Thompson and J. H. Beattie, *Bulletin 1021*, the United States Department of Agriculture, 1922.

A. LEAVES DEEPLY LOBED OR PARTED:
 a. Leaves with deep purple stain at base of leaf blade:
  Ticotea group: Ticotea and Koali Sandwich. These varieties are not particularly important.
 b. Leaves without purple stain at base of leaf blade:
  Belmont group:
  1. Vines long, creeping.
   Varieties: Belmont, Eclipse Sugar Yam, Yellow Yam, White Sealy, Georgia (Old Time Yam), and Pumpkin Yam.
  2. Vines very short and bushy.
   Varieties: Gros Grandia, Bunch Candy Yam (also referred to as Bunch Yam), Vineless, Prolific, and Gold Coin.
B. LEAVES NOT DEEPLY LOBED OR PARTED:
 a. Leaves with purple stain at base of leaf blade:
  1. Stems purple or greenish with a decided tinge of purple.
   Varieties:
    a. Roots light yellow to russet yellow and ribbed to smooth; flesh white to yellow: Pierson (Arkansas Beauty, California Golden, Early General Grant, Golden Skin, and Duttons Beauty), Yellow Strasburg (Adams and Extra Early Golden), Yellow Spanish (Bronzed Spanish) Triumph.
    b. Roots light yellow, tinged more or less with rose or deep rose; strongly ribbed or veined to

smooth and regu-
lar: Red Bermuda
(Cuba Yam, Pore-
land, Yellow Red),
Red Brazil or Red
Brazilian, Porto
Rico (Golden
Beauty, Key West
Yam), and Creola.

c. Roots dark red to
purple, regular and
not so constricted;
the flesh is white
tinged with purple
beneath the skin
and at the center:
Red Spanish (Black
Spanish), Purple
Yam ("Nigger
Choker"), and Da-
homey.

2. Stems green, leaves entirely
to slightly shouldered.

a. Roots white: Shang-
hai (Early Golden)
and Minnet Yam.

3. Stems green, leaves toothed
with six to ten low,
marginal teeth, roots
salmon or yellow tinged
with salmon.

a. Florida (Arizona
Prolific, Provi-
dence), General
Grant Vineless, and
Nancy Hall. Nancy
Hall is the most im-
portant variety in
the South.

b. Leaves without purple stain at
the base of the leaf blade:
1, Stems purple.

a. White Yam and
Southern Queen
(Hayman, Califor-
nia Yam, Arkansas
Hybrid, Brazilian,
Cuban, Common
Yam, Johnsons Ba-
hama, Archers
Hybrid, Hamburg,
Caroline Lee, Cull-

man Cream, Ca-
tawba White, Ca-
tawba Yellow, and
Ballinger Pride).

2. Stems green, medium to
large; roots fusiform,
yellow tinged with sal-
mon having light yellow
veins.

a. Pumpkin Yam
(Early Yellow and
Spanish Yam),
Norton, Dooley,
and White Gilke.

3. Stems green, slender; roots
russet-yellow or red,
ovoid to fusiform; tex-
ture mealy.

a. Roots red: Red
Jersey (Connelly's
Early Red, Early
Red Carolina, Red
Nansemond, Van
Nest Red) and
Japan Brown.

b. Roots russet-yel-
low:

1. Stems short and
bushy: Vineland
Bush, Georgia
Buck, Vineless
Bunch Nanes-
mond.

2. Stems long, me-
dium to large:
Phillipili and Big
Stem Jersey
(Florida and Im-
proved Big Stem;
Maryland Gold-
en probably be-
longs here).

3. Stems slender:
Yellow Jersey
and Goldskin.
The following
probably are Yel-
low Jersey: Up
Rivers, Cedar-
ville, McCoy's
Sweets, Red
Nose, Nanes-

mond, Early Nanesmond, Yellow Nanesmond, Early Carolina, Big Leaf, and Early Yellow Jersey.

The many other varieties which have been introduced since this classification was established will all fit under one or another of the groups.

SOIL AND CLIMATIC REQUIREMENTS: Sweet potatoes are tropical plants that are very sensitive to cold weather and light frosts. They are grown as annuals, and cultural practices must be so timed that a good crop is assured during the prevailing growing season. It must be kept in mind that the tubers never do mature in the true sense. This accounts for the fact that growers have such difficulties in keeping the tubers in storage. The shrinkage ranges from 10 to 60 percent. This is largely due to the fact that growers have not fitted their cultural practices to their growing season. As annuals, sweet potatoes can be grown over a wide range of climatic conditions. In central Wisconsin, for instance, usually regarded as having a very unfavorable climate, sweet-potato crops have been made to yield better than the average yield in one of the regular sweet-potato states. The secret is in the treatment of the soil.

The sweet potato is a poor-soil crop and will give a good account of itself on soils that are too poor to grow anything else. On the other hand, bigger yields will be obtained if some improvements in the soil are made. The plants will withstand dry weather providing the soil is open to a considerable depth, so that the roots can penetrate sufficiently deep to make contact with water in the lower soil levels. This is contrary to the prevailing opinion that chunky potatoes cannot be grown in soil that has an open subsoil. The shape of the sweet potato is determined by physiological factors which have no connection with hardpans and plow soles. It is true that by stunting the growth of the roots a chunkier potato can be produced, but it is at the expense of yield. Big yields of sweet potato cannot be grown on soils that have a hard subsoil. To make the culture of sweet potatoes a profitable venture, large yields are necessary, and this is possible only where the plants are able to make a normal growth. The nutrients, particularly nitrogen, are responsible for the shape of the tubers. The amount of nitrogen also plays an important part in the earliness or lateness of the crop's maturity. However, this is modified by the amount and distribution of rainfall. An abundance of nitrogen during a year of excessive rainfall may make the plants so late in maturing that the tubers will all be long and slender instead of chunky. If those same plants were given another month to grow, the tubers would thicken and make a very large, chunky potato. During a dry year, on the other hand, when the plants cannot make full use of the nitrogen in the soil, they probably will produce a good crop of chunky potatoes no matter how much nitrogen is applied. Since a deficiency of potassium will prevent the roots from thickening into a crop of chunky potatoes, because the roots fail to grow in diameter, it has been argued by many growers that amounts of potassium in excess of the actual needs of the plants will increase the yield of tubers. This has been investigated under controlled conditions and, actually, it has decreased the yields. Soils should be well drained and aerated for sweet potatoes. The soils should be acid or sour, not because the plants grow better on acid soils as such, but because the acidity prevents the development of certain ground diseases which mar the surface of the tubers and make them unmarketable. The addition of 300 pounds of pulverized limestone to a fair soil, at just below plow-depth and directly under the row of plants, has increased the yield from 240 to 485 bushels. However, the same application to a heavily nitrogenous soil might actually decrease the yield, because the limestone stimulates the vine growth so much that the set of tubers may be light. Many growers do not realize that excessive vine growth and high yields do not go together. It is so often the case that a field on one side of the road, which has made such a poor vine-growth that one-third of the soil surface is exposed, will yield 300 bushels, while the field across the road where the vines are vigorous and heavily cover the soil may yield only 125 bushels. These are differences of nitrogen availability and reflect the kinds and amounts of fertilizer applied. Good growers use a 2–8–10 or 3–8–10 mixture on the poorer soils or a 3–12–15 mixture on the better soils, at the rate of 800 to 1200 pounds to the acre. It is applied broadcast and plowed under before the crop is planted.

CULTURAL DIRECTIONS: The first important step in the production of high yields is the production of good plants. Plants are grown from over-wintered tubers selected in the field from individual hills at digging time the previous fall. They are selected for freedom from exterior diseases and internal rot. The stem is split and any discoloration of the stem tissue is a signal to discard the hill. The tubers are stored in baskets in warm, airy storage-cellars.

For large plantings, the tubers are bedded in coldframes and hotbeds. The tubers are placed on a 2-inch layer of soil covering 8 or 10 inches of horse manure or other heating equipment. The tubers are placed horizontally as close together as possible without touching. Enough soil should then be placed over the tubers so that 2 inches of soil will be above them. They are then watered and kept warm, but not hot, until the plants are well through the ground. They are covered with sash or salt hay to protect the plants during cold weather, and carefully ventilated to keep them from burning during hot days. They are usually bedded about a month before they are to be planted in the field.

When all danger of frost is past and the soil is thoroughly warm, the plants are pulled off the tubers, sorted into large, medium, and small, and planted in order of size, the largest first. If there are more plants than necessary, the smallest ones are discarded, for small plants are not conducive to high yields. The plants are set 15 inches apart in the rows 2½ to 3 feet apart. With large plants, the distances should be 2 feet in the row and 3 feet between the rows. This will require about 7,200 plants to an acre. The plants should be set with a starter solution as they are planted. If the grower is equipped to apply liquid fertilizer, dry fertilizer need not be applied when the ground is prepared for the crop. Where dry fertilizer has not been used, the plants should be side-dressed with an application of liquid about two weeks after the planting and a second application three or four weeks after the first. The applications are made just at the edge of the foliage and in a furrow, so that the liquid makes contact with the moist soil. One hundred pounds of a 6–24–24 mixture is applied to an acre in 200 to 300 gallons of water. If the grower has no machine equipped for applying the liquid, it is a simple matter to apply it in a half-inch stream as the plants are being cultivated.

When the plants are growing fairly vigorously, the yield of tubers doubles every two weeks from the 1st to the 30th of September. From then on it increases, but at a lessening rate. In other words, the longer the crop can be left in the ground, the greater the yield will be. However, the harvesting of the crop is a hand proposition. The tubers are lifted with a plow and must be picked from the vines by hand. This is a slow job, so many growers decide to start the harvesting early in order to get them dug by the first frost, probably early in October. Machinery for harvesting has not been successful, as the crop bruises easily and, because of the high sugar-content of the tuber, decay-producing organisms spoil a large number of tubers. Even hand-picked tubers must be laid—not thrown—into the hampers. If the tubers are sold from the field, this precaution is not so necessary, but if they are to be stored, great care must be taken not to scrape off the skin and especially not to bruise them.

When the tubers are stored, they must go through a special storing temperature. They are placed in the storage houses and kept at a temperature of 75 degrees for two weeks. This helps to heal over the broken places in the skins. Then the temperature is dropped and the remainder of the storage is carried on at 40 to 45 degrees. In wet harvesting seasons, the tubers are liable to shrink badly in storage. In dry harvesting seasons, when the tubers have been well matured, shrinkage will be less than 10 percent. Growers feel that the price must be 35 cents a bushel higher over the harvest-season price to pay for storing. If the price is more than this, there is a profit in storing, providing the shrinkage is normal.

Sweet potatoes in the kitchen garden involve some difficulties, unless the garden is big enough to accommodate the running vines. There are other solutions of the vine-space problem, however. Sweet potatoes can be grown in box-troughs a foot deep, 6 to 8 inches wide, and as long as available space will permit. These boxes must be provided with good drainage by providing a false bottom and an opening in the end to permit the water to run out. They can be placed 4 to 6 feet above the ground on the south side of a building, and the vines can be draped down over their sides. These vines are attractive and may be worked into a decorative scheme so that, in addition to producing some tubers, they also serve the purpose of a screen. It is not impossible for sweet potatoes to be grown in boxes placed on the roof of a porch, in such a manner that the vines will grow down over the edge of the roof. They will grow to a length of 8 or 10 feet. This is worth trying. It will be necessary, of course, to water them, as the boxes will dry out.

Anything that injures the vines of the sweet potato plant will reduce the yield. This is due to the fact that extensive vines are produced as a result of an abundance of nitrogen in the soil. In order to balance the nitrogen-effect, the plant must manufacture sugar and starch to fill out the tubers. The more leaves, the better. If the leaves are cut off, the manufacture of starch is reduced, and the tubers do not fill out properly. Vines root at the nodes as they fill in the space between the rows. The general practice is to move the vines from one side to the other to permit the plants to be cultivated. This loosens the vines from the soil. This practice may reduce the yield if the purpose of cultivation is merely to keep the soil loose. If weeds are heavy, however, and there is danger of crowding the vines, the weeds may do more damage than would be done by moving the vines. If the vines are too vigorous, there may be an advantage in loosening them from the soil, thereby reducing the amount of nitrogen taken into the plant. Stunted vines, on the other hand, may need the extra nitrogen, and there is a good possibility that the yields would be decreased if they were moved.

INSECTS AND DISEASES: Insects do not cause much trouble in the culture of the crop. The sweet-potato gold bug occasionally causes some damage in spots by eating the foliage, particularly early in the season when the plants are first set out. A rotenone dust will control them to a certain extent.

The sweet-potato weevil causes considerable trouble in certain sections of the South. The adults feed on the leaves and lay eggs on the stems near the ground. These eggs hatch and the larvae feed on the developing tubers. A program of hygiene and arsenical sprays has been developed to keep this insect under control.

Wire worms do considerable damage to the tubers during certain seasons, particularly if the harvest season is especially dry. No control measures have been worked out for the wire worm.

Diseases are much more common and troublesome. Field and storage diseases take a heavy toll in years when wet, cloudy weather prevails. That is why, when tubers are bedded, they are usually dipped in a solution made with one or another of the organic mercury compounds. Stem rot makes its appearance early in the season. It is especially bad where the plants are stunted for some reason or other. Growers who use the old practice of placing the fertilizer along the row under the plants usually experience from 10 to 25 percent mortality due to the presence of stem rot. It lives in the soil and infects the plants when their resistance is low, due to fertilizer injury. This disease is controlled by carefully selecting the tubers for seed and using new soil in the plant-growing beds.

Black rot produces blackened areas on the tubers and may gradually cause the whole tuber to decay. It continues to develop in storage. Use clean seed and rotate the fields where the crop is grown. Foot rot causes similar decay of the tubers. Soil stain or scurf is a brown discoloration of the skin of the tuber, but is not so serious as some of the others. Root rot causes considerable trouble in the South.

Soft rot, ring rot, dry rot, Java black rot, charcoal rot, and others are troublesome storage diseases that develop if conditions are favorable. Their control is good storage conditions. When the tubers are being graded and packed in hampers, they are put through a dip containing 20 pounds of borax to 100 gallons of water. This protects the tubers while they are being sold. When potatoes are being taken out of storage they have gone through their rest period and chemical changes are taking place which are particularly favorable to the development of the decay-organisms. The slightest amount of bruising of the skin of the tuber makes an entry place for the spores. Potatoes taken from storage may decay in a week if they are not treated. Borax is very toxic to any form of plant life and protects the bruised places against the spores.

Sweet-potato pox is a serious tuber disease in the field and makes the tubers unsightly and unsalable. This disease develops in soils that have a very low acidity or that are very low in organic matter. This is one of the main reasons why sweet potatoes must be grown on acid soils or without lime. There is no objection, naturally, to having lime in the subsoil, as long as it does not get mixed with the surface soil where the tubers develop.

GENERAL RECOMMENDATIONS: The sweet potato is an interesting crop in that it is probably as nutritious as any crop that we use for food and the possibilities of increasing yields are unlimited. (See the chapter on "Growing Vegetables with Fertilizer in Water" for an account of the achievements of that method.) A person who wishes to get his mind off his troubles might try growing an acre to see what he can do. This might be a good pastime for the person who sits at an office desk most of the day. Of course, he might harvest only 75 bushels. Crop production of any kind is a gamble. The production of high yields is an achievement which should give one as much satisfaction as a new car.

Swiss Chard
See Chard

Tabasco Pepper
See Peppers

Tapioca
See Arrowroot in Part II (Herbs)

Taro
See Dasheen

Tartar Breadfruit
See Sea-Kale

Tepary Bean
See under Beans

Tomato

DESCRIPTION: Perhaps the most popular and most widely grown vegetable is the garden tomato (*Lycopersicon esculentum*). It is grown in most parts of the world and a tremendous quantity is canned for world-wide distribution. It is a native of tropical America and the fruit, formerly referred to as the GOLD APPLE and the LOVE APPLE, was once considered poison. The plants are succulent annuals, much-branched, with compound leaves having many leaflets, and small, perfect, yellow-petaled flowers produced in clusters of from three to a dozen or more in long racemes. The fruits may be as small as a currant or as large as a small

pumpkin, and the shapes include the berry, pear, plum, heart, apple, and the large flat fruits that weigh over two pounds. The colors include the white, yellow, pink, and red varieties.

TYPES AND VARIETIES: Because of the importance of the tomato the types and varieties are given in detail, the large-fruited varieties first:

From the standpoint of the kitchen garden, where it is desired to have a good red garden tomato of high quality both for canning and for table use, of attractive appearance, and of a type that ripens from the center to the outside, there probably is no better variety grown than the Rutgers. There probably has never been another variety developed that has gained such wide popularity among growers over such a wide area in so short a time. The Rutgers tomato was developed by Professor Lyman G. Schermerhorn of the Vege-

table Department at Rutgers University. Because of the deep-red color of the pulp, it makes an ideal juice tomato. It is wilt-resistant. Three and four fruits make a pound, although occasionally the fruits are much larger. Much credit is due the man who first recognized the sterling qualities of this tomato. Unfortunately for the small gardener, the seed for this variety is not put up in small packets, and if he asks for the plants he probably will get something else, so that the home-grower, who should benefit most from this variety, does not get it. He should write direct to the seed house to get it.

Other varieties of the common tomato (*Lycopersicon esculentum, var. commune*) are:

MARGLOBE, a good red variety, but one which does not ripen well late in the season. It is mild and about as large as Rutgers. It requires 75 days to mature from the time the plants are set in the garden.

PRITCHARD, slightly smaller, but a good market tomato, smooth and prolific, requires a very fertile soil and matures in 70 days.

BONNY BEST is a fine tomato for the temperate regions, where it produces a heavy crop. It requires a very fertile soil in the areas where the summers are apt to be hot and dry. On poor soil, the variety loses its foliage and exposes the fruit to the sun. John Bear and Chalks Early Jewel are similar to Bonny Best. All require around 65 days to mature.

STONE is a large, red, slightly flattened fruit, one of the older varieties. It is a late variety, requiring 81 days to mature.

Of the early 60-day varieties, Earliana and Penn State are large-fruited; Bounty and Victor are small-fruited; and Globe is a large-fruited pink variety, also used for forcing. GREATER BALTIMORE is a late, midwestern, large, red-fruited variety used for canning. Indiana Baltimore and Early Baltimore are selections from the older variety. GROTHEN'S GLOBE and BREAK O'DAY are somewhat alike in that they have a medium-sized, round, red fruit and mature in 65 to 68 days.

MATCHLESS, OXHEART, BEEFSTEAK, and PONDEROSA are commonly grown in gardens, although Matchless has also been extensively grown as a market tomato. They have large, meaty fruits, red or pink in color. Oxheart is deeper than broad, while the other three are flattened. Ponderosa is pink in color.

TANGERINE and GOLDEN QUEEN are large-fruited, golden-yellow varieties, grown in some sections as specialties. There is also a large white-fruited variety, grown largely as a curiosity. STOKESDALE and VALIENT are medium-sized, red-fruited varieties of recent introduction for market purposes.

Of the forcing varieties, the MICHIGAN STATE FORCING is probably outstanding. It is a large, red-fruited variety that is very smooth and prolific. MARHIO is a pink-fruited variety, having a fruit similar to the Globe varieties. WALTHAM FORCING is a medium-sized, red-fruited variety that is prolific and sets fruit well during the winter. COMET is a slightly smaller fruit, but very prolific. There are several other English varieties which may be grown, but they are too small for our local markets.

The potato-leaf tomato (*var. grandifolium*), like most of the common varieties, is large-fruited. The foli-

age is much coarser than the common varieties, resembling a potato plant rather than a tomato. Although large-fruited and red in color, it has no particular merit over our other varieties, in most localities. A native Brazilian tomato (*Lycopersicon humboldtii*) is a smaller-fruited type than the common tomato and much more roughened. The flavor is good, but it is only grown as a curiosity.

SMALL-FRUITED TOMATOES. The common tomato also gives us some of the small-fruited varieties so desirable for individual salads and for preserving that every home garden should have a few plants. The plum tomatoes, for instance, of which the San Marzano is a popular variety, are smaller than a hen's egg, and somewhat oblong in shape. They have a mealy, bright-scarlet, non-juicy fruit, used for making tomato paste. Then there is a goose-egg tomato, which is a large plum, but juicy and either red or pink in color. The pear tomato (*Lycopersicon esculentum, var. pyriforme*) is smaller than a plum tomato but is shaped like a pear with a small neck. The red and yellow pears are good varieties. The cherry tomato (*var. cerasiforme*) has fruits the size of a sweet cherry, in yellow and red colors, which are used for preserves and are canned whole.

The current tomato (*Lycopersicon pimpinellifolium*) is the smallest of all the varieties. The foliage is finely divided and the small red fruits are borne on racemes which may contain twenty or more fruits. This tomato grows wild in South America. It is important from the standpoint of plant-breeding, because of its resistant qualities to certain leaf-mold diseases. Dr. L. J. Alexander of the

Ohio Experiment Station has crossed this with the large-fruited varieties to develop a large-fruited hybrid which is resistant to leaf mold. This has been a great help to greenhouse growers who have seen their crops reduced by this disease.

The husk tomato (*Physalis pubescens*), also called GROUND CHERRY and STRAWBERRY TOMATO, is a native of North America. It is found growing wild and is also cultivated in gardens. It is a small, yellow, cherry-like fruit enclosed in a membranous husk. The fruits are mild and of good flavor and are highly prized by some people. There are a number of similar varieties, ascribed to other species, which are found in the tropics as well as in temperate regions, and all are referred to as ground cherries or strawberry tomatoes. For example, the CHINESE LANTERN or WINTER CHERRY (*Physalis alkekengi*) of Europe and the Orient is often grown in gardens because of its fine flavor.

Many other kinds of tomatoes and new varieties have been introduced during the past ten years as particularly suited to certain localities.

SOIL AND CLIMATIC REQUIREMENTS: Tomatoes grow best on the sandy-loam types of soils. They are very sensitive to poor drainage and poor aeration. Soils that tend to accumulate water after heavy rains in ponds or in which the water does not readily move down to the subsoil are not suited for tomatoes. The subsoils should be open and well aerated. They must also be well supplied with lime to considerable depths to encourage deep rooting of the plants. Under such conditions, a high yield can be expected. The tomato is a tropical plant grown in temperate regions as an annual; for this reason, varieties should be chosen for their adaptation to the particular locality. The early varieties require 60 days from the time plants are set in the field to mature. The midseason varieties require 70 to 75 days, while the late varieties require around 80 days or more. The plants must be started in warm temperatures, as the plants are very sensitive to frost. There are tomato varieties available for practically every section of the United States.

CULTURAL DIRECTIONS: The seed is sown in flats about the first to the middle of March. The plants are grown at a temperature of 60 degrees or higher and are ready to be spotted to other flats around the first to the middle of April. They are spotted two inches each way and are permitted to grow until the first to the middle of May, or until all danger of frost is past. Then they are set in the field. They should be set with a transplanting solution, or in ground which was saturated with a transplanting solution about five days before.

The soil should be well prepared to make a good seed bed, and sufficient lime should be applied to thoroughly sweeten the soil. On limestone soils this is not so necessary. If manure or chemical fertilizer is used, it should be plowed under with the liming material. Chemical fertilizer, if used, should be applied at the rate of 1200 pounds of 5-10-5 to the acre, or about 30 pounds to a thousand square feet. A more economical method is to use only liquid fertilizer. Two side-dressings of 20 pounds of 13-26-13 or its equivalent dissolved in 50 gallons of water and applied about the time the plants are well established and again when the first cluster of fruit is full grown will usually be sufficient, although in the small garden it may be necessary to put on another application later in the season.

The early varieties are set 2 feet apart in the row, and the rows are 3 feet apart. The midseason varieties should be set 3 by 4 feet apart, and some of the rapid-growing sorts should be set 4 by 5 or 4 by 6 feet apart if the growing season is particularly long. If tomatoes are too crowded, they will not set fruit heavily. There is no reason why tomatoes should not produce from 15 to 25 pounds of fruit per plant. If the plants are crowded, they may produce only a third of that amount. A mulch of any sort of plant refuse, two inches deep and completely covering the ground, may double the yield and save a tremendous amount of hoeing and weeding. The mulch should be put on as soon as the plants are well established and before the weeds get too much of a start. The ground should be clean before the material is put on.

Growing tomatoes on stakes is a specialized type of culture which should be used in the garden. The plants are trimmed to a single stem, just as they are in the greenhouse, and tied to strings which are supported by wires carried by posts set every 15 to 20 feet, or the plants may be tied to single stakes as pole beans are. The poles may be set in, 2 feet apart each way, and tied together at the top to form tripods. A single plant is trained to each post. This saves much space in the garden and greatly increases the yield per square foot. Growers who use this method usually figure on 50

tons to the acre. The plants are fastened to the stakes with soft twine or pieces of rag, loose enough to prevent the bark on the stems from being cut. The plants should be pruned by pinching out the small shoots when they are not over two inches long. Tomato plants grown by this method should be given a good feeding of liquid fertilizer every two weeks to keep the vines vigorous. The fruit will size up much better and, if grown rapidly, will be of a higher quality. Rutgers, Marglobe, or Michigan State Forcing are good varieties in the southern states. In the northern states, the Bonny Best or Stokesdale may be more satisfactory.

Growing Rutgers tomatoes is an art the perfection of which is worth striving for. The Rutgers variety is a free-growing variety which responds quickly to cultural changes. It produces vine even though it is loaded with fruit and grows particularly well on soils of low fertility. A small amount of fertilizer will give this variety much more of a push in the spring than it will give to some of the other varieties. Utilizing these considerations, a technique has been worked out which makes it possible to grow Rutgers as an early-fruiting variety which will carry through to the first frost in the fall. Growers who have used the following procedure have found Rutgers a very satisfactory variety. The seedlings are started early in the greenhouse but grown with practically no nitrogen or only enough to maintain a slow, steady, not too succulent growth. They are grown to the flowering stage in the pots, and then soaked with a transplanting solution for a few days before they are set in the garden. Care must be taken in removing the plants from the pots not to disturb the roots; they should never be removed while the soil in the pot is dry. The plants are then set slant-wise in the ground so that they will not be broken off by the wind. Such plants soon take hold and the cluster of flowers will set fruit. They should not be given any other fertilizer, particularly nitrogen, until the fruits are of good size. From then on, the plants should be fertilized freely. Large growers who have learned this relation of nitrogen to the growth of the plants have been able to lengthen the picking season and greatly increased their yields. In the cooler sections of the country, the tendency is to feed the variety too heavily with nitrogen, so that the fruits do not ripen until late and then are likely to be excessively large and correspondingly soft. Mulching the plants with straw is a big help in preventing the fruits from decaying.

The culture of tomatoes in the greenhouse is not so different from the culture on stakes in the field. The plants are started as for the field, except that they are spotted to four-inch pots when two inches tall. For the fall crop, they should be ready to set in the soil by the first of August, while the plants for the spring crop should be ready by the first of February. The plants are set in the ground beds in double rows. The rows of each pair are a foot apart and the double rows are three feet apart. The plants are set two feet apart in the row to alternate with the plants in the companion row. Plants for the fall crop should be forced along to get as much growth as possible before dark weather begins in November. The plants should be bearing ripe fruit by the second week in September. Beginning with the third cluster of fruit, it may be necessary, if bad weather prevents pollination, to treat the flowers artificially in order to keep the fruits growing.

The spring crop is a little different to handle, as the poor growing weather comes at the beginning of the growing season rather than at the end. The plants should not be forced and should be grown as dry as possible to keep them from becoming too succulent. Even after they are set in the bed, they should be given only enough water to keep them from wilting. The soil should be well supplied with pulverized magnesium limestone. Superphosphate should be worked into the soil if a test shows it to be low in phosphoric acid. Nitrogen should be withheld until the plants show a tendency to turn a light-green or a yellowish-green. They should have a good green color at all times. After the fruit on the first three clusters is set (they may have to be sprayed with the solution mentioned above to insure the fruit setting), the plants may be forced slowly by giving them more water. If the plants get too succulent, the fruits will rot on the stem end. This is called blossom-end rot and is the bane of the careless grower. It should be kept in mind that the big deficiency in the winter is sunlight and everything possible should be done to conserve the sun's energy which does reach the plants. Keeping the plants dry, reducing the nitrogen around the roots, keeping the night temperature low, never above 60 degrees—all tend to augment the effect of the weak sunlight during the winter months. As the sun gets brighter, the plants can be forced more and more.

INSECTS AND DISEASES: Three or four pests may cause the grower considerable difficulty under certain conditions. Of the diseases, the fusarium and the bacterial wilt are probably the worst offenders. The fusarium is first evidenced by wilting of the mature plant and the curling in, yellowing, and dying of the leaves. If the stem is cut, the cambium or the line between the bark and the wood of the stem will be brown. The fungus prevents water from ascending in the stem. The fungus lives in the soil for several years, and the control measures are to rotate the tomato fields once in four years or to grow such varieties as Rutgers and Marglobe which are wilt-resistant. Bacterial wilt is carried by seed, and is spread from plant to plant by nematodes in the soil and by insects. The stem becomes black, and a yellow, sticky, slimy sap is seen when the stem is cut. Treating the seed is a good precaution and crop rotation is helpful.

Collar rot is bad some years. This is a rot that affects the stem about at the soil line. Before the plants are set the stems should be examined for black spots; if the plants are set deep enough for such spots to be covered, the rot will not have serious effect. Otherwise, it will kill the plants. It often occurs on plants which are kept moist at fairly high temperatures for an appreciable period. It sometimes develops in the field but is more common in the greenhouse, where the plants are more apt to be kept too moist. Beside the control measures mentioned, the best remedy probably is to discard the diseased plants.

Blossom-end rot is a physiological disease which occurs under certain growing conditions. It is always associated with succulent plants which are low in starch and which have a very high water requirement. In the greenhouse it occurs on the first few clusters of the spring crop if the plants have been forced too fast with too much water. In the field, it is serious during years when the weather is cloudy and rainy while the plants are making their first fruits. Such weather, followed by a period of bright, drying weather, may cause the whole planting to show the black area on the blossom end. Infected fruits should be picked off as soon as they are seen. Too much fertilizer under the plants or too much nitrogen early in the life of the crop will cause the plants to make such a rapid growth that they do not store up enough starch to give them substance. The roots cannot supply the water fast enough to make up for that lost through the leaves, so the plants start to draw it from the fruits. This causes a disturbance in the fruit which kills the cells. Applying fertilizer in liquid form is a good control measure.

Blight diseases occasionally cause some trouble, but most cases of so-called blight may be corrected with magnesium sulphate applied at the rate of 100 pounds to the acre. Most growers mistakenly call anything blight that causes the older leaves to turn yellow and die. Mosaic-like symptoms on the foliage are quite common on non-limestone soils. Particularly if plants have been grown rapidly on such soils will the symptoms be severe—sometimes severe enough to kill the plants. As the foliage hardens later in the season, however, light symptoms will disappear.

Streak disease is a virus type of disease which will kill the plants. The leaves and areas on the stems will die out in long, irregular patches. It seems to be most severe on plants which are extremely soft. It is carried by workers who are in the habit of handling cigarettes while they work. The smoke itself does little damage; it would seem rather that the virus is contained in the tobacco and is carried on the smoker's hands and clothes to the tomato plants as they are being set or pruned. The best method of control is to keep smokers from touching the plants.

Dropping of flowers by free-growing varieties of tomatoes may be serious during continued spells of cloudy weather. At such periods, the plants are apt to have too little sugar, so that the pollen is sterile and the fruit will not grow. A serious infestation of thrips may cause some flowers to drop off, but this does not happen frequently. Or cold spells when the first clusters are forming, particularly if the temperatures remain below 40 degrees for a series of days, may prevent the pollen from germinating and cause the stigmas on the pistils to lose their receptivity. Spraying the flower clusters with the solution suggested for greenhouse tomatoes will cause many seedless fruits to develop.

Of the insects, the Colorado potato beetle is a bad pest early in the season when the plants are first set out, particularly if the plants do not start growing immediately. Anything that stunts the plants also encourages the potato bug to multiply. On rapidly growing plants, they usually give very little trouble. It can be controlled with rotenone dust. Flea beetles may cause some trouble when the plants are still in the cold frames.

They may be repelled with a Bordeaux spray.

Cutworms sometimes give considerable trouble in fields that were in sod the previous season. They may be controlled with poison bait. This is spread around the plants late in the day, as the worms come out of the ground at night to feed. The tomato hornworm is also a bad actor. It grows to be over two inches in length and a half inch in diameter and will eat up a plant in a few days. The worms can be picked off or killed by spraying with a rotenone spray. The tomato fruit worm is a serious pest, as it is so difficult to control once it gets into the fruit. It is the same pest that works on the corn ear and the cotton bolls. It prefers the corn silk and it is advisable to plant corn somewhere in the vicinity to attract the moths to lay their eggs there, so that they may be cut off and destroyed.

Plant aphids sometimes cause considerable trouble in cold seasons. The aphids disappear in real hot weather. Occasionally, it is advisable to spray the field with a nicotine sulphate spray to kill them. Experienced growers, however, usually watch the weather closely before they resort to spraying.

GENERAL RECOMMENDATIONS: The cost of growing tomatoes varies with the locality. It costs less to grow canning tomatoes than it does to grow market tomatoes. However, the yields are usually better from market tomatoes, because they are picked before they are fully ripe and very few are lost, while canning tomatoes must be picked when fully ripe and two or three tons must be left in the field unless they are picked every other day. Market tomatoes must be packed in containers, which add to the cost of the crop. The cost of growing tomatoes is in the neighborhood of $100.00 per acre, whether the yield is good or not. Therefore, the more tomatoes that can be grown on an acre, the less the cost per ton. Cannery prices, generally provided by contract, are usually found to be more satisfactory than the price of market tomatoes. Some years, growers will receive as much as $1000.00 an acre from early market tomatoes in the metropolitan areas. Other years, the returns may barely cover costs. In order to make money by growing tomatoes, it is necessary to compensate for the fluctuation in prices by getting consistently large yields. The man who grows less than five tons of tomatoes per acre has lost before he ever starts to harvest the crop. Growers who have built up a special producer-to-consumer business, either through direct delivery or through roadside stands, have usually done very well with the crop.

Tomatoes should be the main crop in the kitchen garden, regardless of its size, because they are a good subsitute for fruit in the diet. They are used fresh, either ripe or green, or canned either whole or pulp, or can be used for making juice. They are a valuable crop for the subsistence garden.

Turban Squash
See Squash

Turnip

DESCRIPTION: The turnip (*Brassica rapa*) is a native of northeastern Europe. Turnips and rutabagas are closely related. When planted in the garden in the spring, it is an annual

that sends up a tall, much-branched flowering stalk with pale-lavender flowers and long, slender, cylindrical, pointed pods. When the seed is planted late in the season, it is a winter annual, as it does not send up the seedstalk until the following spring.

TYPES AND VARIETIES: Turnips come in round, flat, or top shapes, and one variety is actually cylindrical in shape. Regardless of the variety, all turnips have the same flavor if grown under the same conditions. A few of the varieties listed include: Extra Early Purple Top, Golden Ball, Large White and Yellow Globe, Snowball, White Egg, Yellow Aberdeen, and Early White Flat Dutch. Cowhorn is the large cylindrical type, often grown for cattle feed. Seven Top and Shogoin Foliage are grown for their tops rather than their roots.

SOIL AND CLIMATIC REQUIREMENTS: Turnips must be grown rapidly to be good for the table. They must be grown on good soil that is well supplied with lime, organic matter, and a fair supply of fertilizer, although they may be grown in practically any place that will support a garden. They are a short-season crop. The best quality is grown during cool weather.

CULTURAL DIRECTIONS: Turnips should not be permitted to get too large; the small ones are palatable and tender, but the larger they get the more fibrous and strong they become. Otherwise, they are grown in the same manner as the rutabaga (which see). Turnip pests are not serious.

Udo

DESCRIPTION: The common garden Udo (*Aralia cordata*) is a perennial vegetable which was introduced from Japan, where it has been grown for centuries. Several varieties have been developed in Japan, but no separate listings are made by seedsmen in this country. It is a vigorous-growing plant with tremendously large leaves and long flowerstalks. The plant produces a large number of stalks early in the spring; these are cut and used very much as is asparagus. The yield is about the same as asparagus.

SOIL AND CLIMATIC REQUIREMENTS: The plant is hardy in the temperate regions and in our southern states, but the quality probably is better in the cooler regions. The tops die down each fall, just as asparagus does, and the crowns may be mulched to give them some protection against alternate freezing and thawing. The plant requires a very deep, fertile soil, well supplied with organic matter and lime. The soil should be well drained and yet should not dry out exces-

sively. A heavy, sandy loam or a loam are best suited.

CULTURAL DIRECTIONS: The seed should be sown indoors in pots in February at a depth of about a quarter-inch. When all danger from frost is past, the plants are set in the garden, 3 to 4 feet apart each way. They should be grown one year before they are used for food. The young spring shoots are blanched as they grow by hilling up the soil around them to a height of 6 inches. Or they may be blanched by setting a drain tile over the emerging stalks, or a deep flower pot, or anything that will keep most of the light away from the shoots. The shoots should be kept in the dark, as they become bitter when they get green. When they are prepared for the table, they must be cooked in salt water for ten minutes to remove a turpentine flavor which they have. The flowerstalks should be kept pinched off unless seed is wanted. Two or three Udo plants should be tried out before a full crop is planted, as the average person will either enjoy this plant very much or not at all.

Unicorn Plant
See Martynia

Vegetable Oyster
See Salsify

Vegetable Pear
See Chayote

Vegetable Spaghetti
See Pumpkin

Velvet Bean

The Velvet bean (*Stizolobium deeringianum*) is an introduction from southern Asia and is grown some in the southern states. It is grown rather for ornamental purposes than for food. Its fast-growing, long, twining vines may attain a length of more than 20 feet in a single season. It produces large clusters of purple flowers and small pods which have two to four small globular seeds. It is adapted to the same conditions that characterize the cowpea (which see).

Vipers Grass

See Scorzonera

Water Cress

DESCRIPTION: Water Cress (*Nasturtium officinale*) carries its small, round, pungent leaves on long petioles from a much-branched stem that sprawls over the bottom of clear,

shallow streams or in wet, shady places. It is a perennial of the North Temperate Zone, and will live as long as the water does not freeze solid. It is similar to the mustard leaf in pungency, and sweeter than highland cress, very much in demand as a salad plant. The tender stems as well as the leaves are used.

TYPES AND VARIETIES: There is only one variety. *Cardamine rotundifolia*, often called water cress, is more bit-ter and therefore less desirable. (*See also* Cress.)

SOIL AND CLIMATIC REQUIREMENTS: This is one crop that has no specific soil requirement, but has a limited field for outdoor culture. It must be grown in running water or in wet, shady places. It is also grown in greenhouses, where it is partially shaded in a good loam soil that is well supplied with water. It is a lime-loving plant and does well in running water that carries considerable calcium. As long as the plant is covered with fresh water, there is no danger of winterkilling; it will stand near-freezing temperatures.

CULTURAL DIRECTIONS: The plants may be grown in pools, shallow ditches, or canals especially constructed. These may be 20 feet wide, having a very gradual slope of a few inches to the 100 feet. In steeply sloping ground, it is advisable to make successive pools at different levels, so that each drains into the next lower one. Two inches of a rich compost is placed at the bottom of the water and the crop is planted. Either seed or rooted cuttings are used to start the beds, although the cuttings will save some time. Seed may be sown in soil which is kept moist until the seedlings are big enough to transplant. The seedlings can be easily lifted when the soil is moist and set in the permanent beds. The water should be just deep enough to cover the leaves. Cuttings are simply stuck in the soil, where they will root in a short time. When once established a bed will last almost indefinitely, unless it gets hot enough to weaken and kill the plants. It is a cool-season plant and usually takes a full year before the plants are ready to be harvested. Since the leaves become bitter when the seed-stalks form, they should be grown rapidly and harvested often enough to keep the seedstalks from forming. At harvest time, the water is lowered so that the leaves can be picked without reaching into the water. In frosty weather, the water should cover the foliage.

In the greenhouse, water cress is grown in partial shade and, if the heating pipes do not interfere, it may be grown under the bench. The drip from the benches above will usually keep the soil sufficiently moist and the humidity high enough for the plants to make a very satisfactory growth.

Diseases and insects do not seriously trouble this crop.

GENERAL RECOMMENDATIONS: For sale, the stem tips and leaves are packed in bunches about six inches long and of varying diameters. The leaves should not be allowed to get warm or wilt too badly. They should be iced when they are to be shipped any distance. There are times when the price is exceptionally good, and a good income is made from a small area. It is a good side line for the person who has the facilities for growing it. A small stream through the trees is an ideal place to grow it, and it is not unattractive to have growing in a stream.

Watermelon

DESCRIPTION: The garden watermelon (*Citrullus vulgaris*) is a native of tropical Africa and is grown extensively in the warmer climates of the United States. It can, however, be grown in the temperate regions where

130 to 140 days of growing weather prevail. There are several small-fruited varieties developed especially

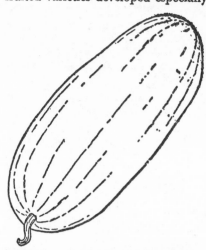

for the northern states. The plant is a trailing vine with deeply lobed, medium-sized leaves and yellow flowers which are borne in the axils of the leaves. The fruit ranges in size from a large grapefruit to a large field pumpkin, while the shape is anything from oval to cylindrical. The color is light or dark green, with gray-green stripes running lengthwise in some varieties.

TYPES AND VARIETIES: Although there are many different types, the following varieties are representative:

Stone Mountain is the watermelon most of us know. It is a large, oval, grayish-green melon with deep-crimson flesh and white seeds and matures in 88 days.

Harris' Earliest, also called Coles Early, is medium-sized, nearly round, dark-green striped with lighter green, and pink-fleshed. It matures in 84 days.

Early Northern Sweet has small,

round fruits, dark green with faint lighter green striping, and bright pink flesh. They require 78 days to mature.

Luscious Golden Sweet is medium-large, longer than broad, with a golden-yellow flesh and dark-green rind. It requires 83 days to mature.

Tom Watson, an exceptionally large, dark-green melon with deep-crimson flesh and brown seeds, which requires 95 days to mature, is a favorite in the South.

Kleckley's Sweets are medium-sized, long, oval-shaped melons, with a bluish-green color, dark-red flesh, and white seeds, requiring 85 days to mature.

Dixie Queen is medium to large, light-green with dark-green longitudinal stripes, and shaped like Stone Mountain. The flesh is deep-red with small white seeds. It matures in 90 days.

There are many other varieties that might be mentioned. The small ones are for the North, while the old standards are the southern varieties that have been in cultivation for many years. The following should be tried in the home garden in addition to the above-mentioned varieties: Halbert Honey, long and slender, of excellent quality, and maturing in 87 days; Early Kansas, round, medium to large, with reddish seeds, and maturing in 85 days; and three varieties of Klondikes, which differ slightly in size, in color of seeds (brown or black), and in color of rind (either clear or striped).

SOIL AND CLIMATIC REQUIREMENTS: The watermelon grows best and sets most fruit on a sandy loam-soil in the northern states, but also on loams in the longer-season regions. The soil must be well drained and should not be too fertile from the standpoint of nitrogen, as this will grow a luxuriant vine with very few fruits. The plant is not particular about the lime-content of the soil. The yield of melons is in direct proportion to the number of growing days in the season. The shorter the season the smaller the tonnage.

CULTURAL DIRECTIONS: In the short-season locality, the seeds may be planted in veneer bands or pots indoors and the plants set into the garden when the soil has warmed. Cold soils and cold winds are not conducive to good watermelons. Sandy soils are warm soils. In a long season, the plants can be grown from seed sown directly in the garden, in hills which should be placed 4 by 4 or 4 by 6 feet apart for the small varieties and as much as 10 by 10 feet apart for the large varieties. Eight or ten seeds are planted in each hill and the seedlings are thinned to three or four after they are well established. Well-decomposed manure should be placed under the hills in preparing the soil for the plants. Liquid fertilizer can be used to side-dress the plants when manure is not available. Weeds should be kept down until the plants cover the ground.

INSECTS AND DISEASES: Practically the same diseases and insects that attack other melons (which see) are apt to be present on the watermelon, and the same controls apply.

GENERAL RECOMMENDATIONS: It usually is not very practical to grow watermelons in the kitchen garden unless there is sufficient room for them to spread. The plants must be grown flat on the ground, because of the weight of the fruit. Cucumbers may be grown on trellises, as the vines will hold the fruit, but this is not possible with fruits which weigh anywhere from 10 to 50 pounds. With some care in handling the vines, they can be trained along one side of the garden, but it is usually more practical to buy the melons.

People often wonder how to tell when a melon is ripe. On most of the varieties, the skin or rind gets very hard when the fruit is ripe. If the melon is snapped with the finger it will ring. If there is only a thud, it is still green. Don't use the finger nail to puncture the rind, as it will make an opening for diseases to get started. If the rind is gently rapped with a lead pencil, it will ring hollow instead of with a dead thud. A little experience will soon enable one to tell the ripe ones 100 percent of the time.

Melons can be stored in a cool cellar if they are thoroughly ripened and are not bruised when they are placed in storage. They should not be frosted. On the farm, firm, green melons are sometimes piled in the hay barn and covered with hay where they ripen sufficiently to make it worth the trouble.

Wax Bean
See Beans

West Indian Gherkin
See Cucumber; Gourds

White Potato
See Potato

Winter Cherry
See Tomato

Winter Cress
See Cress

Winter Melons
See Melons: Honeydew

Witloof
See Chicory

Yams

DESCRIPTION: Yams are tropical plants comprising the genus *Dioscerea*, not to be confused with the soft sweet potatoes (*Ipomoea batatas*) popularly referred to as yams.

True yams are seldom grown in even our southern states, and then almost only in Florida. They all have trailing vines resembling the larger-leafed sweet potatoes. The yam tuber is an important food of the natives of the tropics, where some of the species are represented by as many as fifty different varieties. There are a large number of species listed as having definitely different characteristics. They may be found to be rather more closely related, however, upon closer inspection.

The Birch-Rind Yam (*Dioscerea aculeata*) is a native of southeastern Asia. It is rather large but of good flavor. The White Yam (*Dioscerea alata*) is cultivated throughout the tropics and is one of the best. The AIR POTATO (*Dioscerea bulbifera*) is more of a curiosity but it is used for food. It produces tubers the size of Brazil nuts in the axils of the leaves.

They are edible. In some places the roots are also eaten. The Chinese Yam or CINNAMON VINE (*Dioscerea divaricata*) is a native of the Philippines but is found cultivated generally throughout the tropics. Being a very deep-rooted plant, the tubers are difficult to dig, so that the plant is grown more for ornament than for food. One small yam (*Dioscerea fasciculata*) which is highly esteemed by the Filipinos, has tubers the size, shape, and color of kidney potatoes, and probably resembles the mealiness of white potatoes more than any other yam. The Tivolo Yam (*Dioscerea nummularia*) is a large cylindrical-shaped tuber which has a very good flavor. Another yam (*Dioscerea triloba*) is probably the smallest of all the species, but it is very desirable as a food.

Within the climatic limits set by their tender tropical characteristics, yams may be grown by following the cultural directions prescribed for the Sweet Potato (which see).

Yard-Long Bean
See Asparagus Bean

Zucchini Squash
See Pumpkin

Zulu Nut
See Chufa

PART II

The Encyclopedia of Herbs

The Encyclopedia of Herbs

Absinthe

DESCRIPTION: Absinthe (*Artemesia absinthium*) is a shrubby, aromatic plant, sometimes called WORMWOOD, with silky, white, segmented leaves. The name also refers to the highly intoxicating green alcoholic liquor made from its leaves. Although there

are some variations within the species, they have not been segregated into varieties. For a related species, see Tarragon.

SOIL REQUIREMENTS: These plants grow in very poor soil and the amount of aromatic oil contained does not increase with soil fertility. They do best on a well-drained or even gravelly soil that has been well supplied with liming materials.

TIME FOR PLANTING AND GROWTH: They may be grown by sowing the seed in pots and transplanting the seedlings at intervals of 12 inches in rows two feet apart. The plants will bloom from August to September and should be harvested when coming into bloom in order to obtain the maximum amount of aromatic oil from the leaves. If grown for ornamental purposes, they may be harvested immediately after they have passed their prime as a flowering plant.

DISEASES AND INSECTS: Any insects that feed on the leaves can be controlled by the rotenone or pyrethrum dusts. Diseases are not serious unless the plants are grown in too fertile a soil.

GENERAL SUGGESTIONS: Much can be done with the various species related to Absinthe by the hobbyist who does not value his time so highly that he must be reimbursed. It requires patience to develop plants, for instance, that have a much higher condiment value. When once developed, a good character can be maintained by propagating the plants by cuttings, as they live over from year to year.

Aegopodium

Aegopodium podagraria, often called BISHOPS-WEED or GOUTWEED, is a perennial herb whose parsley-like leaves are used for seasoning. It is a fast-growing weedy plant, which becomes quite bushy and may reach to a height of 18 inches. It produces umbels of white or yellow flowers and, being bushy, makes a good ground cover, particularly since it grows well in shady places. The plant produces rootstocks by which it spreads over the ground rapidly.

There is one variety (*variegatum*), which has white-margined leaves and is attractive as a border plant.

Aegopodium grows well in a somewhat fertile, well-drained soil, but needs moisture for rapid growth where used as a ground cover. When intended for flavoring, it is better if grown in poorer soil where it will get more sunshine. The plants can be grown from seed by planting early in the spring, but rootstocks, if obtainable, are much more satisfactory to start a new planting. No pests are known. The leaves are ready for harvesting when full grown.

Agrimony

Agrimony (*Agrimonia eupatoria*), a member of the Rose Family, grows two to three feet tall and has clusters of small yellow flowers. The plants are grown for their leaves, which have an aromatic, astringent quality, often used by Europeans in making a tonic tea. The plants will grow on most any soil that is well drained and contains sufficient lime. They are best propagated from rootstocks.

Anise

DESCRIPTION: Anise (*Pimpinella anisum*) was introduced from the Mediterranean countries, where it is still grown on a large scale for the seed. Its cultivation is recorded previous to the Christian Era and it probably had its origin in Asia Minor,

although the plant has not been found growing wild in any of the localities where it thrives. The Greeks and Egyptians, who used the seed,

as we do, for flavoring wines and seasoning foods, also grew the plant as a potherb and considered the leaves to be excellent in raw salads. In the United States the seed is popular as a condiment and is used as a source of Oil of Anise, an aromatic, volatile oil of agreeable odor and warm sweetish taste, once widely used as a medicine for stomach and kidney disorders of babies.

TYPES AND VARIETIES: There is some difference in the shape of seeds available through trade channels, but as far as is known no attempt has been made to subdivide the species into definite varieties.

SOIL REQUIREMENTS: Anise requires a fairly fertile soil, a fact which probably accounts for the absence of wild Anise from uncultivated ground where it would have to compete with other plants. It will grow in any good garden soil that is well drained and contains an appreciable amount of organic matter. The soil should be well limed for best results.

CULTURAL REQUIREMENTS: The seed may be sown early in flats for transplanting or sown in the open ground in the warmer sections of the country. When sown in the open, the seed should be mixed with radish seed and as soon as the weather is warm, sown thinly in rows at least 2 feet apart in a well-pulverized soil. The seed is slow in germinating, but the radish seed will indicate the location of the rows, so that the ground on either side of them can be carefully cultivated to prevent weeds from encroaching on the tender seedlings. When the small seedlings are well started, the radish seedlings should be pulled and the Anise seedlings thinned to stand 8 inches apart. The plants grow to a height of 2 feet and will mature seed in approximately 75 days.

DISEASES AND INSECTS: There are no specific problems from the pest standpoint. If the plants are grown in full sunshine on a well-drained soil and the location of the plants changed in the garden from year to year, diseases will not cause any trouble. There may occasionally be some insects, but the leaf-eating pests can be controlled by dusting with rotenone and the juice-sucking pests by nicotine dust.

GENERAL SUGGESTIONS: Anise is grown in gardens belonging to Southern Europeans because they have been accustomed to the flavor and they are familiar with its culture. By the uninitiated, it deserves a trial. A small packet of seed will go a long way in supplying sufficient plants for the small garden. If a small pinch of seed is planted in the end of the row, the novice will have no trouble in recognizing the seedlings as they come up, and will not mistake them for weeds. When the plants are mature—past flowering—and the seed seems well matured, the heads should be removed and placed in paper bags, which must be left open until the heads are thoroughly dried out. The seed can then be rubbed out and any that falls out of its own accord during the drying process can be salvaged. The leaves are usable at any time.

Arrowroot

DESCRIPTION: Arrowroot (*Maranta arundinacea*) is a tropical American

plant which produces rootstocks, rich in a finely divided starch, and the source of the arrowroot and TAPIOCA of commerce. It makes fine puddings, considered a delicacy and supposedly very easy to digest. The wild plant was prized by the Indians as a food plant. Its rhizomes, source of its fine farina starch, enable the plant to live from year to year. The plants grow from two to six feet tall, with leaves a foot long and three inches wide. The plants produce small white solitary flowers. The flowers produce berries the size of currants. The rhizomes may be a foot long and one-half to three-quarters of an inch in diameter. They are white and covered with large paper-white scales. The roots are dug and used when a year old.

TYPES AND VARIETIES: The type grown in Bermuda is considered slightly superior to the others. *Maranta indica* is considered a variety of *Maranta arundinacea* rather than a separate species, but is not so well flavored. Arrowroot of an inferior grade is also obtained from *Calathea allouia* and *Clinogyne dichotoma.*

SOIL AND CLIMATIC REQUIREMENTS: Arrowroot is a plant of tropical areas or regions where the soil does not freeze. In more temperate regions it may be grown with adequate protection against cold winds and winter. It is very susceptible to frost. Any good sandy loam soil of fairly high fertility, if well drained and supplied with an appreciable amount of lime, will grow the plants. Organic rather than nitrogenous salts should be supplied. Too much active nitrogen will reduce the amount of starch in the rhizomes and therefore the yield per acre.

CULTURAL DIRECTIONS: The plants are propagated from root cuttings. The cuttings are planted in rows 3 to 4 feet apart and 18 inches to 2 feet apart in the row. The roots should be set 3 to 4 inches deep, with transplanting solution. Weeds are controlled by shallow cultivation. In heavy soils the plants are liable to grow spindly and leafy. Best root development requires good soil aeration. The roots may be dug in twelve months, when a good yield may be expected, or they may be left in the ground longer. The plants may be grown from seed, but the variety may vary considerably. When grown from seeds, several years are necessary to get an appreciable yield of roots. When ready to harvest, the roots or rhizomes are lifted to the surface with a special plow. They are then collected and are ready to be prepared for the table. They must be carefully peeled to get all the rind off the rhizome. This rind contains a very bitter drug which would spoil the flavor of the other parts of the roots. The peeled roots are crushed or rasped and the starch is washed out from the fibrous part. The starch must not be allowed to stand long, as fermentation will set in soon after it is removed. Thorough heating will prevent souring. The starch is then ready to be used for puddings or other dishes.

INSECTS AND DISEASES: There are a few pests which may prove troublesome. Mildew on the leaves may be controlled with dusting sulphur. Rots which may occur in the rhizomes can be controlled only by treating the roots with an organic mercury dip as they are planted. Foliage-eating worms can be controlled with the rotenone dusts.

Balm: Lemon Balm

DESCRIPTION: Lemon Balm (*Melissa officinalis*) is a sweet, aromatic, perennial herb, grown in many gardens for its foliage, which is used in seasonings, in compounding liquors and perfumes, and formerly, for medicinal purposes, in Balm tea. The plant grows two feet tall and produces small, unornamental flowers in

August. The leaves have a decided lemon odor and flavor. It is a native of southern Europe and probably was introduced into this country from England. It was often grown in Europe as a source of nectar for honey bees.

VARIETIES AND RELATED SPECIES: There is only one variety of Lemon Balm. Other and less common species are: Bee Balm (*Monarda didyma*), Moldavian Balm (*Dracocephalum moldavicum*), Horse-Balm (which see), Canary Balm (*Cedronella triphylla*), and Molucca Balm (*Molucella laevis*). The Bastard Balm (*Melittis melissophyllum*) is a very beautiful plant and, when dried, has a delightful fragrance, which it retains for some time.

SOIL AND CLIMATIC REQUIREMENTS: This group of plants will grow on a wide variety of soils but does not require the fertility needed by some plants. As a matter of fact, the content of aromatic oil is higher and the odor more intense if the plants are grown on a poor soil and in full sunlight. They grow well in the cooler climates.

CULTURAL REQUIREMENTS: The seed of the Lemon Balm may be sown indoors early in the spring and later transplanted to the garden soil, 8 to 10 inches apart. Pieces of roots from established plants may be set in to start the new bed. When the plants are in bloom, they may be cut off and dried in paper bags. The fresh leaves may be used at any time. There are no insects or diseases to cause any trouble.

Basil

DESCRIPTION: Sweet basil (*Ocimum basilicum*) is an annual plant having its origin in the East Indies and having been grown through southern Europe and Asia longer than most herb plants. It was considered harmful by some and a particularly good seasoning plant by others. It is now much used for cooking by Europeans, who sometimes eat the seeds. Generally found in herb gardens in this country, it grows about a foot in height and the leaves have a sweet aromatic flavor.

There is only one variety although the name is often applied to several other species which are bushy or treelike. The name is also applied to several species of *Pycnanthemum* and to *Calamintha clinopodium*. *Calamintha acinos* is often referred to as BASIL THYME and is becoming more popular among southern Europeans in the United States. *Ocimum*

gratissimum is commonly grown in China as basil.

SOIL AND CLIMATIC REQUIREMENTS: The plants grow in warm climates and must be favored with some protection from wind to be grown satisfactorily in the colder parts of the United States. They require a fairly good soil but should not be grown too vigorously if grown for seed. They should not be grown in the shade.

CULTURAL DIRECTIONS: The seed may be sown in the garden as soon as all danger of frost is past. In heavy soil it is a good idea to cover the seed with a small amount of sand to hasten germination. The seedlings should be thinned to 6 inches in the row. They are harvested, if the leaves are wanted, right after they are through blooming. For seed, the plants must be well matured. The plants are hung up in bunches to dry, preferably covered with large paper bags. In a good soil, a second crop of leaves may be produced. There are no insects or diseases to cause any trouble in the garden.

Basil Thyme
See Basil

Bastard Balm
See Balm: Lemon Balm

Bee Balm
See Balm: Lemon Balm

Bergamot Mint
See Mint

Bishops-Weed
See Aegopodium

Borage

DESCRIPTION: Borage (*Borago officinalis*), a coarse, hairy-stemmed trop-

ical plant with racemes of blue flowers, is grown for its aromatic oil, used for flavoring drinks and foods and, at one time, for medicinal purposes. The plant is grown as an annual and attains a height of two feet, with erect, branched stem and elliptical leaves tapering toward the base. The flowers are wheel-shaped, with petals radiating from a cone-shaped hub. At one time, because of its rich blue flowers, Borage was highly esteemed as a flower plant and as a cordial flower supposed to possess exhilarating properties. According to Girard, toward the close of the 16th century, the flowers were put in salads "to make the mind glad" and were "used everywhere for the comfort of the heart, for the driving away of sorrow, and increasing the joy of the mind." The leaves of Borage impart a coolness to the beverages in which they are steeped and was used with wine, water, lemon, and sugar to make "cool tankard." The flowers secrete large quantities of nectar which has made the plant popular among bee men.

TYPES AND VARIETIES: There are no varieties of the species *officinalis*. A related species, *Borago laxiflora*, is a perennial, low-growing plant, raised in rock gardens.

SOIL AND CLIMATIC REQUIREMENTS: Although a native of the Mediterranean countries, it can be grown in cool climates by planting the seed each spring. It grows best on a loamy, well-drained soil that is not strongly acid, and will not do well on the light sandy soils.

CULTURAL DIRECTIONS: The seed is sown in drills early in the spring and the plants are thinned to 8 to 10 inches in the row. The leaves should be used green, before they become too old, to get the largest amount of oil. Borage matures in 80 days.

Burnet

DESCRIPTION: Burnet is the common name for *Poterium sanguisorba* and several species of *Sanguisorba*—hardy perennial herbs with mats of long, compound leaves and a sprawly or rosette type of growth. White, greenish, purple, or crimson spike-flowers

are borne on stems which grow to a height of several feet. The leaves are used in flavoring salads and drinks. It has a flavor somewhat like the cucumber. Although in cultivation since ancient times, it is no longer so popular as formerly.

TYPES AND VARIETIES: The difference in color of flowers suggests the possibility of several varieties but none are listed. *Sanguisorba minor* should not be confused with the *Poterium sanguisorba*, a similar herb, often occurring as a weed in fields of sainfoin, or with its related purely ornamental species.

SOIL AND CLIMATIC REQUIREMENTS: The plant is a temperate-zone type and the leaves are very resistant to cold weather. The soil should be a good loam that is well drained and well supplied with nutrients. A good supply of moisture is essential.

CULTURAL DIRECTIONS: The seed is sown indoors and is transplanted to the garden 8 inches apart in the row. After the plants are established, the mats of leaves cover the ground, so that no weeds interfere with the growth of the plants. The younger leaves are used for flavoring purposes. When once established, the plants may be divided.

GENERAL RECOMMENDATIONS: One or two plants in the family garden will probably give sufficient leaves for flavoring purposes, even if the flavor is particularly desirable. There are other herbs which probably would have wider uses.

Camomile

DESCRIPTION: Camomile (*Anthemis nobilis*) is a perennial herb of the daisy family, having an erect stem with a flattened head of many small yellow-disc and white-ray flowers. The plants are branched and 1 to 2 feet tall. They are grown for the drug camomile, which is used in medicine. Anyone who has not tasted home-made camomile tea has had his education neglected and has missed a real experience of childhood. That in itself is sufficient reason for including this plant in a book of this type. The plants are too bitter to be listed as a salad plant.

TYPES AND VARIETIES: Several different species are carelessly referred

to as camomile, but only *Anthemis nobilis* is listed as the true plant. There are no varieties.

SOIL AND CLIMATIC REQUIREMENTS: The plant is hardy in temperate regions and grows best on a well-manured soil that supplies an abundance of organic matter and moisture. The soil should be well limed but not too sandy.

CULTURAL DIRECTIONS: The seed is sown thinly in rows 2 feet apart, about the latter part of August. The seedlings should be thinned to at least a foot apart and kept free from weeds. The first year, the seedlings will make a small rosette of leaves; the second year, they will send up a seedstalk.

INSECTS AND DISEASES: These are not very serious, as the foliage is too bitter to be attractive to most insects. The Japanese beetle may cause some trouble but can be repelled by a dusting of lime. Diseases are mainly those which live in the stem and for which there is very little control except to change the location of the plants.

Canary Balm

See Balm: Lemon Balm

Caraway

Caraway (*Carum carvi Linn.*) is an annual or biennial aromatic herb, probably of South Asian origin. It is grown for its seeds, which are used to flavor bread, cheese, and cakes. The young shoots and leaves may also be eaten in salads or as flavoring for

other vegetable dishes or meats. Because of the aromatic, volatile oil which it contains, Caraway was once quite generally used to scent liquors, soaps, and perfumes, and at one time oil of caraway was even used for medicinal purposes. The oil was obtained by distilling the steam of a water in which the crushed leaves had been soaked.

Caraway is easily grown from seed. The seed is sown in the open and the plants are thinned to 10 inches apart in rows 2 feet apart. The first year, the plants establish themselves by making a rosette of leaves. During the second year, when the seed stalks are

produced, the seeds should be allowed to mature; then the stalks are cut off, dried for a few days, and hung up in bags with the heads down. Many of the seeds will drop out as the flower heads dry out. The greatest yield of oil is obtained from plants that are grown on the poorer soils where the nitrogen content is not too high. Plants that become too succulent from an abundance of nutrients and water tend to have a low content of aromatic oil. The harder growths also produce seed stalks which set more seed. Wet weather with high humidity is ruinous to abundant seed production, and if high temperatures also occur, particularly when the flowers are setting seed, the flowers will blast and fail to set seed. The best weather for good seed production is bright and sunny, with a low humidity and a temperature not over 80 degrees. During such weather even vigorous plants will set seed abundantly.

Cardamon

Cardamon (*Elettaria cardamomum*) is a perennial, aromatic herb not generally grown in the United States but familiar to many people whose immediate ancestors have come from Europe. Anyone who has ever tasted cookies or pastries flavored with cardamon will never forget them. It is used as a flavoring by Europeans and, when they can get it, by Americans of German extraction.

The plant is grown either from seed or from the iris-like rootstocks. It requires a very fertile soil and grows better in partial shade than in full sun. The plants are very sensitive to cold and will not live through freezing weather. Although they can be grown in pots in northern climates, they require much protection. The climate of southern Florida is suitable.

If the plants are grown from seed, three years development must be allowed before an appreciable crop of seed-pods may be expected; if from rootstocks, the plants may produce pods the first year and certainly the second. Crops can be harvested from the plants for several years. The pods are picked and dried and sold either in compound spices or separately.

The seeds contain an aromatic, pungent spice, somewhat weaker than pepper, with a peculiar flavor very agreeable to some people. The oil of cardamon is recovered by crushing the seeds and distilling from water. Because of its cordial and stimulant properties, the oil is used in medicines to make the flavor more agreeable. Several different species are referred to as a source of cardamon, but their flavor is weak and their oil-content low. Most of the cardamon of commerce comes from the Far East.

Castor-Bean

DESCRIPTION: Castor-Bean (*Ricinus communis*), often referred to as CASTOR OIL PLANT and CHRISTI PALMA, is grown in gardens as an ornament and for its large, flat, grayish-brown seeds —a source of castor oil and other medicinal drugs. The seeds are used to rid the garden of moles by being placed in the burrows. Among the related species which may be grown, *R. communis* seems to be the most popular. The leaves are five-lobed and may grow to be 3 feet in diameter, although they are usually about 20 inches across. The red and brownish veins and stems make the plant rather colorful. In a good location, plants may grow to be 8 or 10 feet tall, with a spread of leaves almost as

wide. The flowers are borne in panicles and are covered with dark-colored spines. Other species have red, brown, or purple flowers. The fruit is a capsule which usually contains three seeds.

SOIL AND CLIMATIC REQUIREMENTS: Castor-bean plants do well on any well-drained loamy soil that is well supplied with moisture and an appreciable quantity of plant nutrients. They will do very well on the heavier soils. They will grow on the sandy soils, but not so large and ornamental. They prefer well-limed soils. They grow as annuals where freezing weather prevails, but become large, non-woody, perennial trees in tropical climates.

CULTURAL DIRECTIONS: The seeds should be planted in pots in early March and kept in a warm place until all danger of frost is past. They may then be set in the garden in a location where they will help to make the vegetable garden more attractive.

INSECT CONTROL: There is some idea that the plants will keep certain insects out of the garden, but this is more rumor than established fact. Nevertheless, insects do not bother the plants. Both plants and seeds contain an alkaloid which is poisonous to animals and humans.

Castor Oil Plant
See Castor-Bean

Catmint

Catmint (*Nepeta cataria*), also known as catnip, is a hardy perennial grown in old-fashioned gardens because cats are so fond of it. It has a strong aromatic odor when the leaves are bruised and carries a volatile oil which attracts cats to it. Cats will claw at the first spring plants in order to bruise the leaves and will then roll in the foliage. As the seed stalks develop cats lose their desire to chew the leaves. The plant grows generally on most any fertile soil and, in many sections of the country, has become a weed because of the heavy, white rootstocks which make it possible for the plants to live through

severely cold winters. It apparently has little use as a flavoring herb and is only grown for the purpose mentioned. Because it has become a weed in many localities, it is no longer used for ornamental purposes. It should be included only in the herb garden. Usually plants can be dug up in fence corners and moved to the garden, or seedlings may be grown and transplanted to their permanent location. They should be grown a foot apart in the row. The plants grow to a height of 3 feet and have whorls of small white flowers on an erect stem. The flowers may have a rose or purplish cast, somewhat like the mint that is

grown in the garden for flavoring beverages.

Catnip

See Catmint

Chamomile

See Camomile

Chives

See in Part I (Vegetables)

Chusti Palma

See Castor-Bean

Clary

DESCRIPTION: Clary or MEADOW CLARY (*Salvia sclarea*) is a biennial plant from the Orient, having blue flowers in racemes upon stems which grow to a height of three feet. The long, pointed leaves are used for seasoning omelettes and meat dishes. Clary is not as commonly used in the United States as is the sage, a related

species (which see). HORMIUM CLARY (*Salvia hormium*) is, another related species grown for similar uses.

TYPES AND VARIETIES: In Europe three varieties are recognized: the broad leaf, the long leaf, and the wrinkled leaf.

SOIL AND CLIMATIC REQUIREMENTS: Like all members of *Salvia*, clary can be grown in temperate regions. It grows wild in certain parts of Pennsylvania as an escape from garden plantings in Colonial days. It grows best in the heavier soils that are well drained.

CULTURAL DIRECTIONS: The seed is sown in the open ground as soon as the ground can be worked, and the plants are thinned out to stand 2 to 3 inches apart. When the plants are 4 to 6 inches apart, alternate plants may be removed. After the roots are cut off, the leaves may be dried and placed in a paper sack for use. They should be dried in an oven at a low heat or by some other type of artificial heat. When quite crisp, they should be rubbed between the hands and placed in a glass jar. They are then ready for cooking purposes.

The plants remaining in the garden should be side-dressed with liquid fertilizer several times through the season. The first year they make a rosette of leaves; the second year, a seedstalk.

DISEASES AND INSECTS: On a good soil there probably will be little trouble from pests. There are no insects that eat the foliage, as far as is known.

GENERAL RECOMMENDATIONS: Although this plant is not as popular as sage, there are many people who like it better. It is worth giving a try.

Coriander

DESCRIPTION: Coriander (*Coriandrum sativum*) is a biennial or perennial herb that is grown for the aromatic oils in its leaves and seeds,

which makes them highly desirable for flavoring of confections and liquors. The young leaves are also used in salads and soups. The plants, resembling parsley, grow to a height

of two feet and are much branched. Native to the Orient, they are grown in southern Europe and have been in cultivation for 2000 years or more.

SOIL AND CLIMATIC REQUIREMENTS: Coriander can be grown as an annual in the northern states, but if the plants do not live through the winter only the rosette leaves will be available. In regions of mild winters, it will live through and produce a seedstalk the second year. If the northern gardener wishes to go to the trouble, he can sow the seed in early fall in flats or pots and grow the seedlings during the winter. Toward spring the plants can be put into a dormant state by drying. The following spring they may be set in the garden to produce seedstalks. Soil requirements are similar to other herbs. They should be grown on comparatively poor soils to get the maximum amount of seed, for fertility beyond what is needed to produce a good plant is not conducive to good seed production.

CULTURAL DIRECTIONS: Where the soil freezes, the plants may be handled as was mentioned above or they may be heavily mulched in late fall and so protected from freezing until late the following spring, when they are uncovered before new growth starts. Most plants of this type will live through the winter if the soil does not freeze and thaw alternately. The seed is harvested by cutting the plants when the heads are ripe and pounding them out on a sheet. The seed is cleaned by allowing it to fall a short distance in a strong wind.

Cress

See in Part I (Vegetables)

Cumin

DESCRIPTION: Cumin (*Cuminum cyminum*), an annual herb resembling parsley, is grown for its leaves and especially its seeds, which are used for flavoring soups and pickles. It is a native of the Mediterranean regions, particularly the upper Nile region, from where it was carried to Arabia, India, and China. It was a very popular herb at least as early as the 13th century. Some say its culture dates back to the pre-Christian era. In Holland it was used to flavor cheese and it has been considered an appetizer. It is not generally grown in the United States except in certain local areas.

SOIL AND CLIMATIC REQUIREMENTS: It matures in 90 days and can therefore be grown in temperate regions. The seeds should mature in warm, dry weather. The soil requirements are not too exacting, although the best development of the plants occurs on the loam soils or good sandy loams that are well drained and well sup-

plied with lime. Any comparatively fertile soil will grow the plants. It must have sufficient moisture to do well.

CULTURAL DIRECTIONS: Sow the seed as soon as the ground can be worked in the spring in rows 16 to 18 inches apart. The plants should be thinned to stand 6 inches apart. They should be given the same care as parsley (which see).

INSECTS AND DISEASES: Pests are not a serious contender providing the soil is well aerated by having it well supplied with limestone. Occasionally green worms feed on the foliage, but these are easily controlled with a rotenone dust.

GENERAL RECOMMENDATIONS: A good plant for the herb garden and an interesting plant for the specialist.

Dill

DESCRIPTION: Dill (*Anethum graveolens*) is an annual whose bitter seeds

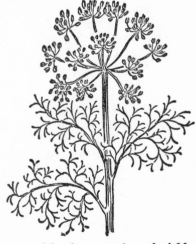

are used in the seasoning of pickles. Large quantities of dill are grown in the United States for the large dill-pickle output. The plant grows three feet tall and produces its flowers in an umbel-head. The foliage is finely divided and the flowers are small and greenish-white.

SOIL AND CLIMATIC REQUIREMENTS: The plants mature in 70 days and can be grown in almost any locality where the growing season is long enough. It does well on a wide variety of soils but produces the largest amount of seed in the lighter, well-drained soils that have an appreciable amount of organic matter and lime. The soils should be copiously supplied with moisture.

CULTURAL DIRECTIONS: The seed is sown in the spring, as soon as the ground warms up, in rows that are at least 3 feet apart, as the plants make a very bushy growth. The plants should be thinned to not less than a foot apart. The young plants are used for flavoring soups and can be thinned out as used for that purpose. The plants are permitted to mature but are sometimes used in pickles before the seed is actually ripe, by placing the whole head in the jar with the pickles. In large pickle crocks, the flowering heads with some of the tender leaves are spread out in layers between the pickles. Commercially, the seed is ripened and used as such.

GENERAL RECOMMENDATIONS: The plants may be cut off a foot from the ground when the seeds are still quite soft and tied up in bunches and hung in a dry place till the seeds may be separated. There are no serious pests.

Fennel

DESCRIPTION: The common fennel (*Foeniculum vulgare*) is a hardy European perennial which is quite generally grown in gardens for its aromatic seeds and tender fragrant leaves, both used for flavoring. The

leaves are very finely divided, giving a very feathery appearance.

The herb Fennel should not be confused with the vegetable variety *dulce*, called Finocchio or Florence Fennel—which is discussed in Part I of this book under FINOCCHIO. The two varieties call for similar garden care however.

SOIL AND CLIMATIC REQUIREMENTS: The plants mature in 60 days when grown from seed. They can be grown in any region where the growing season is long enough. The plants do best in a well-drained loam soil that is well limed and well supplied with organic matter.

CULTURAL DIRECTIONS: The seed is sown early in the spring in rows and the seedlings are thinned to 4 inches apart. The plants should be side-dressed with liquid fertilizer as soon as the seedlings are four or five inches tall. The tops may be used as soon as there are any leaves for flavoring. The bulbous roots should be allowed to get at least 3 inches in diameter before they are to be used.

INSECTS AND DISEASES: Small green worms are sometimes troublesome on the foliage, but these may be easily controlled by dusting with a rotenone dust.

GENERAL RECOMMENDATIONS: This plant should be tried in the garden on a small scale. If desired, successive sowings may be made every two weeks.

Garlic
See in Part I (Vegetables)

Ginger: Wild Ginger

Wild ginger (*Asarum canadense*), sometimes called INDIA GINGER, is grown in the United States for use as a spice, the rootstock having a warm, aromatic flavor very similar to the

imported ginger (*Zingiber officinale*) of commerce. The plant con-

sists of two very large heavily-veined, heart-shaped leaves on long stems. The flower, reddish brown in color, is formed close to the ground at the base of the leaves and is often hidden by the debris of twigs and leaves of the forest floor. The plant is low-growing and is found in moist forests that afford considerable fertility, from New England to North Carolina and Kansas.

Wild ginger should not be confused with *Zingiber officinale* or the other members of the true ginger family, which have never been introduced into the United States. If the ginger from the East is shut off, *Zingiber officinale* may possibly find a place in the near-tropical sections of the United States, but until that development occurs only the wild or India ginger will concern the home gardener.

The plants are grown in moist, well-drained soils that are high in organic matter and that do not freeze. They are adapted to our southern states. The plants are propagated by planting the rootstocks. They offer possibilities for the hobbyist.

Ginseng

DESCRIPTION: "Ginseng" is here used in its limited sense to refer to the *Panax quinquefolium*—a fleshy-rooted perennial found growing wild in moist and shaded woodlands from Maine to the Mississippi Valley and in the southern mountain regions, principally in the hardwood forests. The plant is very slow-growing and sends up a stalk with three five-foliate compound leaves and a terminal flowerstalk. The flowerstalk produces 6 to 15 greenish-yellow, small, star-shaped flowers, followed by as many crimson berries, each containing 1 to 3 wrinkled seeds, the size of small peas. The plant is grown for its thick, spindle-

shaped aromatic root, valued in China as a medicine. The roots may be 1 inch in diameter and 4 inches long.

VARIETIES: There are no definite varieties established. The northern wild form seems to give best results.

SOIL AND CLIMATIC REQUIREMENTS: Almost complete shade is necessary to grow the plants. They prefer the temperate regions and soils that are well supplied with humus and moisture. The soils should be well drained. Plants are usually found growing on the slopes of ravines or on high-level ground.

CULTURAL DIRECTIONS: The seeds are gathered when mature and, before they have a chance to dry, they should be mixed with moist sand or sawdust or leaf-mold and stored in a cool damp place until they are to be planted. The seeds are planted the second spring or the first fall after they are harvested. They will not germinate the first spring. The seedlings grow only about 2 inches during their first year. In their third year, during which they will grow about 8 inches tall, they bear fruit for the first time. A single plant will produce 50 seeds. A pound of the seed contains about 9000 seeds. The seeds should be cracked before they are planted. They should be planted 8 inches apart each way in permanent beds which have been built up to form in-between troughs for draining off the rain water. The ground should not be worked too deeply. The seeds may be sown close together the first year and the roots transplanted to the permanent beds the second year. If the plants are to be grown in the open, it is necessary to build some shade—easily accomplished by nailing laths at half-inch intervals to 2 x 4 pieces placed on posts set in the ground. The laths should run north and south so that the plants are alternately sunned and shaded. The shade should be at least 6 feet from the plants, to permit good circulation of air in order to control diseases. The soils are not fertilized during the growth of the crop, but should be prepared a year ahead by applying some lime, phosphoric acid, and potash or wood ashes. Nitrogen should be used sparingly. Good leaf-mold probably is the best material to use for the purpose. The beds are mulched during the winter with leaves, hay, straw, sawdust, or other non-nitrogenous material. The mulch should be 4 or 5 inches thick in the fall and a 2-inch mulch during the growing season may help to grow better plants. If plantings are made in forests in order to take advantage of the natural shade, the underbrush should be cleared out to allow good circulation of air and the plants set as for open-field plantings. The plants cannot be dug until the 5th or 6th year. The older the roots, usually, the better the quality. They are shaken free of soil and dried in ventilated trays by means of artificial heat.

GENERAL RECOMMENDATIONS: Growing ginseng is not an amateur's job, except on a very small scale. If it is done, it should be tried on a 4- by 10-foot bed. The market for the crop is mostly export, and some years the price has been exceptionally good— probably as lucrative as any cultural enterprise, but it may also be bad. If the crop cannot be sold, it does not hurt it to stay in the ground another year—certainly a redeeming feature.

Glasswort

See Samphire

Gontweed

See Aegopodium

Gypsywort

See Horehound

Herb-of-Grace

See Rue

Hoarhound

See Horehound

Hops

DESCRIPTION: Hop (*Humulus lupulus*) is a perennial vine or climbing plant belonging to the Nettle Family. It is grown in temperate United States and Europe. Wild, it grows over trees and fences and makes a very vigorous, thick growth of leaves. It is cultivated extensively in New York State, Washington, Oregon,

California, and Wisconsin. The plant has rough stems. The female plants produce the flowers which result in fruits, while the male plants produce only the pollen flowers. The leaves

are heart-shaped and 3- to 7-lobed. The female flowers produce the hops of commerce, used in the brewing of beer and ale. The flower is a mass of papery, pale-yellow segments, with the very heavy odor used for the flavoring in beer. The plants are also used for ornamental purposes, because of their rapid growth and interesting female flowers.

TYPES AND VARIETIES: Hop is generally known by the locality in which it is grown, for the locality has much to do with its worth as a flavoring for beer. The differences in flavor among the beers of different countries are in part due to the hop that was used. The northern European countries are noted for hop-growing sections.

SOIL AND CLIMATIC REQUIREMENTS: Hop may be grown on a variety of soils, but it must have a well-drained subsoil to be productive. On the other hand, it must have considerable moisture and does not do well in droughty seasons. The plants yield th.. best hops in the temperate climates, and each locality seems to have a correct soil and climate. Limestone soils are well adapted to the culture of the crop. A good supply of organic matter is essential to maintain a good level of moisture and plant nutrients.

CULTURAL DIRECTIONS: Hop is propagated by cuttings made from the underground stems by which the plants live through the winter. The ground should be prepared by plowing deeply and plowing under a crop of grass or legume. On limed soil, a small amount of phosphoric acid and potash might be necessary. The ground should be tilled to make a fine seed bed. The cuttings are set 2 feet apart. One male plant is set for every 100 female plants, but Europeans grow the female plants by themselves, as they claim the formation of seed in the female flower makes the product too bitter. Weeds are kept down by shallow cultivation. The vines are trained on wire trellises. The flowers are picked by hand and dried, after which they are baled for market. The active ingredient of the hop flowers is an aromatic, yellow resinous material which acts as a preservative. It prevents the lactic-acid bacteria from growing, while permitting the yeast to grow.

INSECTS AND DISEASES: Hop plants are affected by a mildew which covers the leaves and causes a poor quality hops. The mildew is due to poor circulation of air and for this reason varies in intensity with the seasons. It may be held in check by spacing the plants and thinning the leaves or by dusting the foliage with a very finely divided sulphur. Insect pests

include the hop louse or aphid. The insect lives over the winter on plum trees where it feeds until the hop plants are ready. Then they migrate to the plants and live on them until late summer, when they go back to the plum trees. One plum tree in a locality is enough to attract the aphids; proper spraying of the tree with nicotine will go a long way toward control of the aphids and prevention of their migration to the hop. There are numerous other insects which cause trouble by feeding on the foliage. Many of these can be controlled with rotenone dusts.

Horehound

DESCRIPTION: Horehound (*Marrubium vulgare*) is an aromatic perennial herb used for flavoring candies

and lozenges and supposed to have some sedative value for throat afflictions. The plant has a woolly appearance and produces opposing leaves on a square stem, with flower-clusters coming out of the axils of the leaves. The flowers are small and the petals white. The plants grow to a height of two feet and the roundish, ovate leaves have a coarse appearance because of the heavy hairy growth over their surface and on the stems. The plants are native to southern Europe and Asia. One species is grown in the United States and is found wild in waste places.

TYPES AND VARIETIES: Although there are several related species, only white horehound is well adapted to the United States. The others can be grown here if occasion demands. The European black horehound (*Ballota nigra*) is closely related to *Marrubium*. Water horehound (*Lycopus europoeus*) is commonly referred to as GYPSYWORT. Doubtless, both of these have been introduced into the United States, but their whereabouts is known only to plant collectors.

SOIL AND CLIMATIC REQUIREMENTS: The plants grow best on well-drained, gravelly or sandy loam-soils and can withstand dry weather. As a matter of fact, the plants are more aromatic if grown on the poorer and drier soils than on very fertile soils. The white horehound is adapted to the temperate regions and, if once established, will live through severe winters. The species of other genera are more finicky and must have some protection for perennial culture. They may all be grown as annuals where 100 days of growing weather are available.

CULTURAL DIRECTIONS: The seeds are planted in rows in the open ground and thinned to stand 10 inches apart. The leaves are harvested when still young, and dried. Clean leaves, free from insects and diseases, should be selected.

Hormium Clary

See Clary

Horse-Balm

Horse-balm is an aromatic, herbaceous perennial (*Collinsonia canadensis*) belonging to the mint family and found growing naturally in open woods and in moist places. It is a

coarse-growing plant with bold foliage, and produces clusters of small, yellowish flowers. It is native to temperate America. (*See also* Balm.)

Horse-Radish

See in Part I (Vegetables)

Hyssop

DESCRIPTION: Hyssop, an aromatic perennial herb (*Hyssopus officinalis*), grown for culinary and medicinal purposes, is a native of southern Europe or Asia. It has long, narrow leaves and clusters of small white flowers produced on long flowerstalks from the axils of the leaves. The plant grows about 18 inches tall, has a strong odor and pungent, bitter taste. The green parts of the plant

are used with wormwoods in the manufacture of absinthe. It has been used as a flavoring for corn salad plants and the powdered dried flowers are used as flavoring for soups. The flower spikes are cut just as the flowers begin to open, are dried and ground, and used as an expectorant in the treatment for coughs.

CULTURAL DIRECTIONS: The plants grow in cool climates in well-drained, not too fertile soils. They may be propagated by seeds, root cuttings, or by plant division. The soil should be well limed and the seed sown in drills, where the plants are thinned to stand 10 inches apart. If propagated by cuttings, the plants should be placed a foot apart; although the cuttings may be made in the fall, it is better to start them in the spring. The beds should be renewed every

three or four years. Beyond this, the plants should be treated like mints (which see).

India Ginger

See Ginger: Wild Ginger

Indian Cress

See Nasturtium

Japanese Mint

See Mint

Lavender

DESCRIPTION: The common lavender (*Lavandula vera*) has many uses because of its sweet-scented foliage and flowers. This is the narrow-leaved

lavender which grows in the waste places of southern Europe but is extensively cultivated in northern Europe for its oil, as well as in our own northern states. It has a pungent fragrance and a spicy bitter taste. The Oil of Lavender which it contains is used in perfumes. All parts of the plant apparently have some use. The flower spike is used in medicine as a tonic and nerve stimulant, while the dried flowers are used as sachets in wardrobes. The plants send up tall, slender stems with long, narrow leaves placed oppositely on them. The stem ends in a branched flower-stalk, with the small tubular florets bunched around the stem.

TYPES: The narrow-leafed type is most generally used, but there is a broad-leafed sort (*Lavandula spica*) which is tenderer and must be given winter protection.

SOIL AND CLIMATIC REQUIREMENTS: The narrow-leafed type grows in the temperate regions but may kill out in exposed places. The broad-leafed type is grown in warmer regions, where the ground does not freeze. Soils must be well drained and preferably the poorer types, such as the gravels and sands, which are apt to be dry. The soil should be well supplied with lime. Limestone soils are well suited for this plant. Rock gardens or stone outcroppings are good locations. It wants plenty of sunshine and a dry soil. Under these conditions the yield of Oil of Lavender is high. If the plants grow too soft, as with too much water or nitrogen, the yield of oil and nectar is low.

CULTURAL DIRECTIONS: Seed may be sown and, for small garden purposes, will produce plants that grow satisfactorily, but for the hobbyist who wishes to grow the plants as a project, the seed-sown plants will probably be too variable in character and in oil-content to make it a profitable business. He probably would want to select the better plants and propagate

from cuttings or get cuttings instead of the seed. Cuttings taken from one-year-old wood or from the crowns may be put directly into the soil. Scions must be cut so that there are several buds on each and the stem must be planted right side up, so that the roots will form. The plants are fairly easy to propagate as privets are. Many privet hedges are started merely by sticking a foot-long stem-tip in the ground where the plant is wanted, and in a year the plants will be well started. Of course, if the top growth kills off during the winter, it may be necessary to propagate the plants in a protected place during the cold season. The plants should be set 2 feet apart. Growth that is too succulent is more susceptible to winter killing. The new growth usually comes up from the roots. When the plants are in full bloom, the flowers may be picked off and dried. The best stage for harvesting the leaves is after they are full grown but before they have ceased to be active.

INSECTS AND DISEASES: As far as is known these plants have no serious pests. Aphids may cause some trouble by collecting on the growing tips around the flowers during late summer when the weather gets cooler. A nicotine spray will kill them. Diseases are not serious if the plants are grown in their proper environment. If they are grown with too much fertility and water, they may develop some mildew and other diseases.

Lemon Balm

See Balm: Lemon Balm

Lemon Grass

DESCRIPTION: Lemon grass is so named because of its fragrance, which reminds one of lemon oil. There are two species (*Andropogon nardus* and *Andropogon schoenanthus*), both grown as tropical ornamental grasses, three to four feet in height and very beautiful because of their panicles of flowers and attractive foliage. They are ordinarily too coarse for cattle feed, but if the leaves are cut when young, they may be used as food for animals. The fresh leaves are used to make a tonic tea which is supposed to have some beneficial effects in stomach disorders. Lemon grass oil, an extract from the young leaves, is used as a stimulant for rheumatic ailments. It is used principally, however, in perfumery and is often miscalled oil of verbena.

SOIL AND CLIMATIC REQUIREMENTS: They are suited only to sections which are warm enough to prevent the soil from freezing. The grass dies down in the cold weather when frosts occur. The soils must be well drained and highly limed. Sandy loam soils are most satisfactory. They do not have a particularly high fertilizer requirement but they do, however, require considerable moisture.

CULTURAL DIRECTIONS: The seed is sown in rows or broadcast as other grasses are. No special precautions are necessary. When used for ornamental purposes, they are grouped in bunches or in heavy rows. For this purpose, the bunches should be thinned to a foot apart in the row.

GENERAL RECOMMENDATIONS: This plant is mentioned here merely to keep the list of plants used for essential oils fairly complete. It probably has no place in the garden except for ornament and would only interest the amateur collector who might be interested in knowing that it exists.

Lemon Verbena

DESCRIPTION: Lemon verbena (*Lippia citriodora*) is a small perennial shrub with long, slender leaves growing in whorls. It is a native of Chili and is grown out-of-doors in the warmer parts of the United States, but in the North it is grown as a

house plant, in pots or window boxes, for its sweet, lemon-scented, lemon-colored, showy foliage. The flowers are borne in slender spikes. The leaves are used in making perfume and to flavor jellies. They can also be used to make an infusion for a cooling drink.

SOIL AND CLIMATIC REQUIREMENTS: The plant grows well on a soil that is rather fertile, well drained, and having good aeration. A sandy loam-soil, well supplied with organic matter and fairly sweet, is best. It is a tropical plant that can be grown in the garden in the summer, but it must be lifted and kept over the winter indoors in pots.

CULTURAL DIRECTIONS: The plants are propagated by dividing the crowns and transplanting. A good plan is to divide the plants in the spring when they are set in the garden and, in the fall, to lift a few and place in six-inch pots to carry through the winter. In the South, the plants may be left in the ground all winter, and they will make a tremendous growth which is very showy. The leaves have small glands on their undersides, which are the source of the lemon flavor and odor. This is an interesting plant to grow just as a house plant, as it will withstand many of the conditions that many plants will not tolerate. The odor may be rather strong, although it probably is no more intense than the scented geranium. You can smell it upon entering the room, but after you have been in the room for a short time you get accustomed to it.

Lovage

DESCRIPTION: The common lovage (*Levisticum officinale*) is a European

perennial, hardy in the southern states but needing some protection in the temperate regions. It is a coarse-

growing plant that forms a rosette of glossy, dark-green, deeply-lobed compound leaves and sends up a seedstalk to a height of five feet. It has greenish-yellow flowers. The aromatic quality of the leaves has been used as a flavoring in confections. At one time, the leaves and young stems were used as celery. They have a strong sweetish odor and a warm pungent taste. Lovage is included in the herb garden.

TYPES AND VARIETIES: There are two species of another genus which have leaves of similar character: the American lovage (*Ligusticum officinale*) and the Scotch lovage (*Ligusticum scoticum*), a hardy plant which grows from the northern states into Canada.

SOIL AND CLIMATIC REQUIREMENTS: Climatic requirements have been discussed above. The soil should be a deep, well-drained loam that is fertile and amply supplied with moisture from below.

CULTURAL DIRECTIONS: The seed can be sown in drills in the spring and the seedlings thinned to stand 18 inches apart in the rows. They are fairly rugged plants and will meet considerable competition. The American species grows wild as a weed and can be gathered freely from the margins of low-lying land, so that it is superfluous to plant it in the garden. The roots were once chewed in place of tobacco.

Maple Syrup

Maple syrup is, of course, not a garden vegetable, but many people who grow gardens also have a number of sugar maple trees on their grounds and would like to make sugar and syrup if only they knew how. It is easily made, but since there are no publications on the subject readily available, a concise description of method may be useful to a good number of gardeners.

Sugar or syrup can be made from any of the maple trees, namely: Silver, Norway, Swamp, or Sugar Maple. However, more than twice as much syrup can be made from a given account of sap from the sugar or rock maple (*Acer saccharum*) than from any of the others. Since the sap of the others is sweet, however, people sometimes use it to make wine by fermentation.

The trees are tapped early in the spring before the ground thaws by boring a ¾-inch hole into the tree at at 2-foot height from the ground. A 10-inch spigot is made from a piece of pine wood by cutting a groove ¼-inch deep in one side of an inch-square stick. One end is made round and forced into the inch-deep hole in the tree. If the tree is large, two or three spigots may be inserted at different places. A gallon pail is set under the spigot so that the sap will drain into it. As soon as thawing weather commences the sap starts to flow. The sap is collected every day and must be boiled down to the consistency of syrup. This can be determined by the individual taste. The sugar is made by boiling the syrup down to a very thick consistency, whipping it for five or ten minutes, and pouring it into molds to harden.

Sap cannot be collected in localities where there is no alternate freezing and thawing. For this reason most of the maple syrup is made where winters are severe, as in our northern states. But it can be made in other sections where maples seem to grow well.

Marjoram
See Sweet Marjoram

Meadow Clary
See Clary

Melissa Balm
See Balm: Lemon Balm

Mint

DESCRIPTION: The Mints are perennial plants of various species of the genus *Mentha*, which is the characteristic member of the mint family

PEPPERMINT

(*Labiatae*). The plants are grown for the essential oils which are distilled from their leaves. With their inconspicuous flowers and aromatic leaves, the mints deserve a place in the herb garden.

SPECIES AND VARIETIES: The common mint (*M. canadensis*) has erect, square stems with long pointed leaves placed oppositely on the stem. The plants are spread by rootstocks and runners. The small, light-purple flowers are born in circles around the stem. The very aromatic fragrance of the leaves has often misled people to mistake the plant for peppermint. Native to New England, it grows wild in wet places and even in the margins of streams. PEPPERMINT (*M. piperita*) is very similar to the common mint, but its purple flowers are produced in sessile whorls on long spikes. Another difference is that the heads are much branched. Peppermint is in cultivation in the United States and is grown on moist soil. There are two varieties, the white and the black mint. The white mint has green stems and light-green leaves, while the black mint has dark-purple stems and dark-green leaves. The black mint is the most popular in the mint-growing sections of New York, Indiana, and Michigan. SPEARMINT (*M. spicata* or *viridis*) is a na-

SPEARMINT

tive of Europe and Asia, but is grown in the United States for the oils produced in its leaves. The plants grow more erect than peppermint, as do its much-branched spikes of flowers, while the leaves are slightly longer and narrower. It is propagated by stolons. BERGAMOT MINT (*M. citrata*) is a perennial plant that is propagated by stolons and is cultivated for

BERGAMOT MINT

its lemon-flavored oil, used in perfumes. ROUND-LEAFED MINT (*M. rotundifolia*) is also a perennial propagated by stolons, and is sometimes used as a substitute for peppermint. JAPANESE MINT (*M. arvensis, var. piperascens*) is sometimes grown for its oil. (*See also* Pennyroyal.)

SOIL AND CLIMATIC REQUIREMENTS: Mints produce the most oil in temperate climates. They are hardy and once established should remain for some time. The biggest yields of foliage are obtained on the muck soils, those level black-soil areas but recently reclaimed from the swamps. The soil should be well drained and should be fertilized with phosphoric acid and lime if the muck is sour. The plants can, of course, be grown in the garden and the foliage may be used for flavoring purposes in drinks and in cookery. They will do best in the loam soils, but may be grown on the sandy soils if the ground is mulched around them.

CULTURAL DIRECTIONS: Commercial plantings should not be made until all the wild mint has been removed. It produces an inferior oil, and, if any of the roots are left in the ground, they will send up plants as weeds in the peppermint or spearmint beds. The rootstock or stolon cuttings are used to propagate the beds as the plants produce very little seed. The soil should be cleaned of perennial weeds and grasses, as the mints occupy the land for some time. After the rows are once planted, it is difficult to clean out weeds, as the plants soon spread out between the rows, making it impossible to get in with machines to cultivate. The runners are taken from an established plant and are laid end to end in a furrow 4 inches deep in muck soil or 3 inches in regular soil, and the soil is pulled over them and packed down. The rows are 3 feet apart. In the small garden, mint is grown in patches in the fence corner or other unused places. Young plants may be taken from plantings and set out to start new patches. Commercial mint is harvested by cutting the plants in full bloom with a mowing machine, after which the plants are raked together and hauled to local stills where the oil is removed by live steam. The steam and oil is then condensed, and the oil is separated from the water.

INSECTS AND DISEASES: During wet weather, a rust-fungus attacks the older leaves and causes them to drop off. This is serious, as the yield of oil is dependent on the number of leaves harvested. Magnesium deficiency causes the older leaves to turn yellow and drop off. When these difficulties occur, the plants should be cut immediately, as the older leaves will turn yellow rapidly and the loss will be greater as time goes on.

The mint-flea beetle eats small holes in the foliage. In late summer, the beetle lays eggs on the lower stems and the larvae which hatch from the eggs work their way into the roots, where they live during the winter. They do considerable damage to the roots. This causes the plants to wilt and later die. After the crop is cut, the fields are dusted with a poison dust which kills many of the larvae before they do much damage. Cutworms do some damage and, when heavy infestations occur, are killed with bran mashes scattered among the plants. Grasshoppers are also killed by this poisoned bait.

GENERAL RECOMMENDATIONS: In the small garden, a few mint plants will be sufficient as they are used only for their green, fresh leaves. Commercially, it costs around $2.50 a pound to produce, while the selling price is around $3.00 a pound. A distilling plant must be available, the cost of which is anywhere from $1500.00 to $4000.00 and is usually erected by the community to handle the output from a given area. Huge profits from the culture of mint are not made. It is a perennial crop that is on a par with some of the better farm crops in sections where it can be grown. The production of higher-yielding mint plants is something for the hobbyist to undertake as a side line. There is no reason why the oil-content should not be stepped up in plants.

Moldavian Balm
See Balm: Lemon Balm

Molucca Balm
See Balm: Lemon Balm

Mustard
See in Part I (Vegetables)

Nasturtium

DESCRIPTION: The garden nasturtiums (*Tropaeolum majus* and *minus*) are highly ornamental as well as useful as garden herbs. They are native to South America and are grown in practically every flower garden. The petals of the flowers and the leaves are used for flavoring salads and the seed capsules, when still succulent, are used for pickles and capers. As such, they are sometimes called INDIAN CRESS. The dwarf plants have short stems and round, smooth leaves. The climbing plant grows to a height of eight feet in a season. The flowers are solitary, the size of a silver dollar or larger, with yellow and red petals. The seeds are formed in capsules which are found in groups and, occasionally, singly.

TYPES AND VARIETIES: There are dwarf- and tall-growing varieties which differ in size and color. Dwarf Mixed, Tall Mixed, Golden Globe, and Scarlet Gleam are listed as obtainable varieties.

SOIL AND CLIMATIC REQUIREMENTS: The plants are annuals, very sensitive to cold and killed by the lightest frost. They are generally grown in temperate climates. They will grow on any well-prepared soil that is not too rich in nitrogen, but has a good supply of organic matter.

CULTURAL DIRECTIONS: Plant the seed in the open ground as soon as the soil is warm and danger of frost is past. The plants should be spaced 6 to 8 inches apart. The tall-growing varieties should be grown along a fence or strung up on the side of a building in full sunlight. They should be planted as part of the flower garden, because they are one of the best annuals for ornamental purposes.

INSECTS AND DISEASES: Black aphids, a bad pest which gets on the undersides of the leaves, can be controlled with a nicotine sulphate spray.

Old Man

See Southernwood

Parsley

See in Part I (Vegetables)

Pennyroyal

The leaves of pennyroyal (*Mentha pulegium*) have a mint-like flavor which makes them acceptable among the garden herbs used in cooking. It is one of the sweet herbs, much more popular in the past than at present. The plants are supposed to have some properties offensive to mosquitoes and the leaves are supposed to repel them. It is sometimes used as a border plant. The plant grows to a length of three feet, the stems being prostrate. The square stems carry grayish leaves, set oppositely, and lavender flowers produced in whorls in the axils of the leaves.

European pennyroyal is the garden variety and was introduced by way of California from England. It is a native of Southern Asia and is of ancient culture. American pennyroyal (*Hedeoma pulegioides*) is a small-growing annual with purplish flowers, which grows wild in the temperate regions from Quebec to the Mississippi Valley.

Pennyroyal grows in moist soil that is well drained. It grows best in temperate climates, but is not too hardy and will kill out in severe winters. The culture of the plants is the same as for mints (which see).

Peppermint

See Mint

Roselle

DESCRIPTION: Roselle (*Hibiscus sabdariffa*) is a native of tropical Mediterranean countries whose large yellow flowers are used for food purposes as well as for ornament. The petals and flower bracts are the source of considerable fruit acid, which is used for making a cranberry-like jelly. It is also fermented to make a drink. In some countries it is cultivated for its bark and fruits as well as its flowers. The flowers are borne in the axils of the leaves and last for only a day. The red calyces and bracts enlarge and the fruit which develops in a few weeks resembles the cranberry. The bark contains a fiber which is made into roselle hemp. It is an annual plant, related to cotton, okra, and the ornamental hibiscus. It resembles cotton in that it has a coarse-growing, reddish, branched stem, which grows to a height of five feet. The young leaves are entire, while the older leaves are five-lobed. It is grown throughout the tropics and is cultivated to some extent in Florida and Southern California.

TYPES AND VARIETIES: Two varieties are listed, the red and the white, but they probably differ little except in color.

SOIL AND CLIMATIC REQUIREMENTS: Roselle is quite sensitive to frost and is therefore grown principally in tropical regions. The plants can, of course, be grown in temperate regions with protection, but there is a question whether they will set fruit. However, where they do not set fruit, the growing tips of the plants have properties similar to those of the flower parts. There is a possibility of selecting earlier plants, but little has been done along this line.

Roselle will grow on almost any soil that is not too rich in nitrogen. In northern climates, especially, it is advisable to grow the plants on soils that are very low in nitrogen, to make them mature earlier. Even in the southern states, it is advisable to keep the plant from making too vigorous a growth. A well-drained, sandy, loam soil would be desirable. Sufficient lime should be added to make the soil as near neutral as possible. In the garden, this can be done with wood ashes.

CULTURAL DIRECTIONS: The plant makes a deep root system and the soil should be deeply tilled to accommodate it. Seed may be sown indoors, if the season is not long enough to mature the crop in the open. In the southern states, the plants flower during October. Thus, in the northern latitudes, the normal season will not permit complete growth unless the seed or cuttings are started in February or early March and given protection until the middle of May or slightly earlier. The plants should be started in pots, so that they can be set into the garden without disturbing the soil any more than is necessary. The taproot should not be broken, if this can be helped. The plants are set in rows 4 feet apart, and there should be 3 or 4 feet between the plants in the row. They should be set with a transplanting solution and will probably need no further feeding.

INSECTS AND DISEASES: The plants should be started in as dry a soil as possible and, as long as they are in the greenhouse, they should be kept as dry as possible. This will prevent leaf-borne diseases from getting started. There are not many insects that cause much trouble. Plant aphids may cause some trouble. Japanese beetles may eat the foliage. Dusting with any dust will tend to repel them.

GENERAL RECOMMENDATIONS: The fruit is ready to gather when the flower parts have turned red and are plump and crisp. The fruit is snapped off and may amount to eight or ten pounds per plant. It should be used before it wilts. The fruit capsule should be removed before the rest of the flower is used.

Rosemary

DESCRIPTION: Rosemary (*Rosmarinus officinalis*), is a hardy evergreen shrub which is grown for its oil, used in medicine and perfumes, and for its

scented leaves, which are used in cooking. The plants are shrubby, with slender, pointed leaves, the margins of which are turned in toward the center on the underside. Racemes of small blue flowers are produced in the axils of the leaves. In warm climates the plants are used as hedges. The leaves are gathered when mature and are dried, after which they are ground into a fine powder.

TYPES AND VARIETIES: In addition to narrow-leafed, broad-leafed, silver-striped, and gold-striped varieties, there is a variety, *prostratus*, which is a low-growing type, often grown in rock gardens. It grows to a height of 18 inches, while the other varieties may grow to a height of 6 feet.

SOIL AND CLIMATIC REQUIREMENTS: The plants are not hardy where the winters are severe and so must be given winter protection. In the warmer climates they may live for ten years or more. The plants grow best on poor soils. They grow naturally in the Mediterranean regions where the soil is rocky, well drained, and extremely well supplied with lime. They will not live-over in moist soil. On very fertile soils the oil-content of the leaves is extremely low and therefore the fragrance is not sufficiently pronounced to make them useful as an herb.

CULTURAL DIRECTIONS: Plants may be established by buying plants and setting them 18 inches apart in rows 3 feet apart, or by sowing seed and transplanting the seedlings to a nursery row, where they should be planted not over 6 inches apart. When they crowd the rows, they may be thinned to 18 inches. The seed may be sown in the ground when it has become dry and warm enough to promote rapid germination, but it is more desirable to sow the seed in a flower-pot soil in late winter, and transplant the seedlings to the garden in late spring. The seed is very fine and should be sown on the ground surface and covered with ⅛ inch of sand. The pot should be set in a saucer so that it may be watered from the bottom by keeping the saucer filled with water. After the plants are established in the garden, they need very little attention beyond keeping weeds and grass from choking the plants. They need very little fertilizer, but the soil should be well supplied with lime. Wood ashes may be placed around the plants during the winter. If winters are severe, the plants should be protected from north and west winds. Insects are no problem and diseases are not troublesome if the soil is suitable.

Rue

DESCRIPTION: Rue (*Ruta graveolens*), sometimes called HERB-OF-

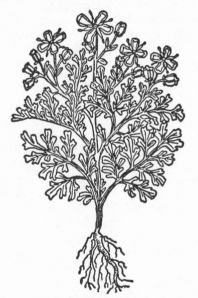

GRACE, is an aromatic, herbaceous, perennial which was at one time much grown in gardens for its flavoring and medicinal properties. The leaves have also been used for salads and pickles. The plants produce a rosette of leaves the first year, at which time they are most useful. The flowerstalk is much branched and quite woody at the base, with pinnately divided compound leaves, while the flowers are produced in terminal corymbs or panicles and are yellowish or greenish in color. It is a native of the Mediterranean countries.

SOIL AND CLIMATIC REQUIREMENTS: It does best on a gravelly type of soil that is well drained and well aerated. It should be well supplied with organic matter and an appreciable amount of lime. In the southern states, it is always hardy, while in the northern states it is half hardy.

CULTURAL DIRECTIONS: The seed should be planted in rows in the spring as soon as the ground can be worked. When the seedlings are well developed, they should be thinned to stand 8 to 10 inches apart. They require clean culture and the leaves may be used at any time that they are large enough to make it worth while. There are no serious pests. Though not as popular as formerly, except with some of the recent European immigrants, rue should be included in the herb garden.

Saffron

DESCRIPTION: Saffron (*Crocus sativus*), a native of Greece and Asia Minor, was generally grown in European gardens for the orange-colored stigmas of the flowers, which were dried as a dye for coloring creams, biscuits, preserves, liquors, and even butter and cheese. It was also used for its medicinal qualities as a diaphoretic in eruptive diseases of chil-

dren. It is used as a dye in many localities, but most of it is imported. It is water soluble or it would be a good dye for cloth. It is a fall-blooming crocus, which has a flower with lavender-white flowers and orange-yellow stigmas. The bulbs are perennial and come up every year, if undisturbed.

SOIL AND CLIMATIC REQUIREMENTS: Any good sandy loam that is not too well supplied with nitrogen or organic matter and that is well drained is suitable for growing the bulbs. The less nitrogen in the soil, the more intense will the dye become, although the yield will be lower. The bulbs are very hardy and will live through winters just as the spring-blooming sorts do.

CULTURAL DIRECTIONS: The bulbs are planted in rows or even broadcast in ground that will not be disturbed. The spring-blooming sorts are usually planted in the lawn, but the fall-blooming kinds cannot be placed there, as the leaves will be cut off in mowing. They can be dug in the spring and stored until August, when they can be planted about 2 inches deep. If left in the ground, year after year, they should be given 4 to 6 inches. If dug every year, they can be placed 2 inches apart. They will make small bulblets by which the plantings can be increased. Any irregularity in the petals should be a warning to discard the bulbs, as a virus disease may be the cause of the abnormality. With the source of saffron shut off, this may be a good side line.

Sage

DESCRIPTION: The garden sage (*Salvia officinalis*) is a perennial garden herb much used in the flavoring of sausages, dressings, and sauces. It is a semi-shrubby, hardy plant that grows in mountainous country on sunny slopes. The whole plant has a very strong aromatic odor and a bitterish, aromatic, slightly astringent taste. It contains an essential oil called Oil of Sage. The plant has small lanceolate

leaves on a branched stem, which produces flowerstalks that have clusters of blue flowers at opposite sides of a raceme. The leaves have a grayish cast with a slight pubescence. It is also an ornamental plant. It is a native of the Mediterranean regions, but is much grown throughout eastern America. It is hardy on the Eastern Coast.

TYPES AND VARIETIES: There are several other plants which are often referred to as sage. MEADOW CLARY (*S. sclarea*), also called clary (which see), was much used in place of the present common species, but it is only found wild. The SAGEBRUSH of Nevada and the Southwest (*Artemisia tridentata*) is often used as sage. BETHLEHEM SAGE (*Pulmonaria saccharata*), JERUSALEM SAGE (*Phlomis fruticosa*), and the crimson, purple, white, and black sages (*Audibertia grandiflora, nivea, polystachya,* and *stachyoides*) are all more or less well known species.

SOIL AND CLIMATIC REQUIREMENTS: For the best yield of oil and seasoning, sage should be grown on a dry soil that is not too fertile but that is well sweetened with lime. The soil should, of course, be well drained. The plants are hardy in the south central states, but in the northern sections should be protected by being placed on the south slopes or south side of buildings. The roots can, of course, be mulched to keep the soil from freezing and thawing too much.

CULTURAL DIRECTIONS: The seed should be started in beds and the seedlings transplanted to the permanent positions, where they are spaced from 14 to 18 inches apart. The young stems and leaves can be used as soon as they are large enough and when there is enough foliage on the

plants so that at least half of it will remain on the plants. After the first year, the plants may be propagated by crown divisions. The plants continue to increase in size from year to year if not disturbed. The plants must be kept free from weeds. After the first year, it may be desirable to side-dress the plants with liquid fertilizer once or twice through the season, so as to keep the foliage fresh and growing freely, but not enough to make it succulent.

When the leaves are picked off they should be dried immediately in an oven at a temperature of about 150 degrees. They should not be scorched. When thoroughly dry, the leaves may be crushed and rubbed between the hands and, when fine enough to use, placed in air-tight containers and stored. Three or four plants are enough for the average family, and the plants should be placed in the perennial border where they are not in the way of garden cultivation.

INSECTS AND DISEASES: Sage does not have any serious pests. The aromatic flavor of the leaves is not to the liking of insects. Diseases sometimes cause trouble, but they are usually controlled by moving the plants from one location to another every three or four years.

GENERAL RECOMMENDATIONS: This is one of the more desirable of the herb plants for the herb or flower garden. It is a plant that grows with very little attention and is suited for the dry or gravelly corner of the garden.

Samphire

DESCRIPTION: Samphire (*Crithmum maritimum*) or SEA FENNEL is a perennial that grows one and one-half feet high in rocky cliffs near the sea, but is also grown in gardens in very

poor soil. It is used in salads and pickles for its piquant, aromatic taste. It is a native of the Mediterranean countries but is grown all through Europe. It is supposed to give salads a pleasant flavor. The foliage resembles parsley.

TYPES AND VARIETIES: There are no particular varieties. GOLDEN SAMPHIRE (*Inula crithmoides*) is another species but is used in a similar manner. MARSH SAMPHIRE or GLASSWORT (*Salicornia herbacea*) is found growing in brackish water in North America and also is used for pickling.

SOIL AND CLIMATIC REQUIREMENTS: Samphire is a poor-soil plant that must be grown in full sunshine. It does best on the sandy loam soils that are quite sweet but do not contain much calcium. It is hardy as long as it is not forced with too much nitrogen. If the plant becomes too succulent it will winterkill rather easily.

CULTURAL DIRECTIONS: This plant is easy to grow and, like sage, should be planted in the poorest, most ex-

posed, gravelly soils in the garden, even doing well in spots where the soil has been filled in with subsoil from a cellar hole, a soil that is often found around new houses. It will, of course, grow on a sandy loam soil, but should not be fertilized. The seed is sown in rows and the seedlings should be thinned to 10 or 12 inches apart in the row. The seed can also be sown in pots and the seedlings transplanted. After the plants are once established, the clumps can be divided. Three or four plants are enough to start with in the small garden.

INSECTS AND DISEASES: There are no particular pests to bother these plants. As with most plants which are not generally grown in any quantity, insects have not become established.

Savory

DESCRIPTION: The common savory (*Satureia hortensis*), also called SUMMER SAVORY, is a native of south Europe. It is an annual with shrubby stems and small pale-lilac or white flowers, the entire foliage having a very fragrant odor. It grows to a height of from six to twelve inches. A very useful culinary herb, it is used either green or dried to flavor soups, dressings, salads, stews, and homemade sausage. Green savory leaves, if crushed and rubbed on bee stings, will take out the pain almost immediately.

WINTER SAVORY (*Satureia montana*), a woody perennial shrub with purple flowers and sharp-pointed leaves, is not so desirable as the common species.

SOIL AND CLIMATIC REQUIREMENTS: The savories are particularly suited to poor soil and gravelly knolls and slopes that are well drained, are well

limed, and exposed to full sunshine. They are quite hardy to cold, although the perennial form, if grown on the rich garden soils where it makes a lush growth, will winterkill.

CULTURAL DIRECTIONS: Because the seeds are so tiny, it is advisable to germinate them in pots where they can be protected from beating rains. The seedlings are transplanted when 2 inches high. The annual seedlings are set 8 inches apart in the row, and the rows need not be more than 18 inches apart. The seedlings should be set out when all danger of frost is over. The perennial seedlings should be transplanted to the garden in rows 18 inches apart and 12 inches apart in the row; these plants can be moved after the first year and may even be divided after a year's growth. No serious pests are known. The leaves, when harvested, may be dried and

rubbed to a fine powder, and stored in an air-tight container.

Sea Fennel

See Samphire

Sorghum

Sorghum (*Sorghum vulgare* or *Holcus sorghum*) is a tall grass with very coarse, long, linear leaves and a tassel or panicle seed-head producing small, oval, pointed, brown or black seeds, which are used as food by people in the South. However, the main purpose of the plant is as a source of sorghum syrup. It is an annual and matures in time so that it can be grown as a source of syrup in the north temperate states. For the gardener who wishes to be self-sufficient, this plant offers a source of sweetening for his other foods. In the southern or tropical sections, sugar cane (*Saccharum officinarum*) is available for the same purpose.

Sorghum is grown from seed, which is sown in rows early in the season and thinned to stand 6 to 8 inches apart in rows 3 feet apart. The plants will grow on any good sandy loam soil that is fairly fertile. The stalks should be grown on soils that are not too fertile, however, in order to get the maximum amount of sugar in the juice. Large vigorous stalks are usually lower in sugar than those which are grown more slowly and which are not over a half-inch in diameter.

The juice is squeezed out of the stalks when they are cut late in the growing season. They should not be permitted to dry out in the sun before they are run through the roller mills. After the juice is squeezed out, it must be heated over a slow fire until it is concentrated to the point where it has the consistency of a dark syrup.

During the slow cooking process, much of the proteins and green coloring matter comes to the surface as a greenish scum. This must be skimmed off from time to time. Sorghum syrup is very nutritious.

Sorrel
See in Part I (Vegetables)

Southernwood

Southernwood or OLD MAN (*Artemesia abrotanum*) is a perennial with gray-green foliage and small greenish-yellow flowers borne in loosely panicled heads. The foliage is sweet-

scented and was at one time much used for flavoring beer. It was also used for its medicinal properties. It is propagated by seeds, by cuttings, or by root divisions. For further culture, *see* Tarragon.

Spearmint
See Mint

Summer Savory
See Savory

Sweet Basil
See Basil

Sweet Cicely

DESCRIPTION: Sweet cicely (*Myrrhis odorata*), sometimes called MYRRH, is a European perennial herb which has a thick root and finely cut fern-like foliage. The flowers are white. The sweet flavor of the root and the foliage is very much like anise. This plant was once very popular in England for use as a potherb but has lost some of its popularity. The leaves were eaten or cooked in soups or stews, as well as being used green in salads. The seeds are also being used for flavoring. It is of ancient culture and has been grown in American gardens.

TYPES AND VARIETIES: A wild form of sweet cicely has been brought into cultivation in American gardens and has become more popular for its sweet roots and foliage than the European type. There are four kinds now being grown in America, all derived from the wild form, some being better adapted to warm climates, the others hardy in temperate regions.

SOIL AND CLIMATIC REQUIREMENTS: The plants grow in temperate climates and in partial shade. The wild form grows in moist wooded sections having partial shade. It will grow in a wide variety of soils but prefers a moist soil that is well supplied with organic matter. A good plant to grow on the shady side of a tree.

CULTURAL DIRECTIONS: The seed is sown in the garden as soon as the soil can be worked in the spring and thinned to 8 inches apart in the row. Or the seed may be sown as soon as it is ripe in the fall and it will live through the winter and come up in the spring. When once established, it will last for years. The leaves are used green and may be picked as needed. The seeds, of course, must be permitted to ripen before they are harvested and stored. The roots are not ready to use until fall and must be dug, of course killing the plant. Seedings can be made to supply roots every year.

Sweet Marjoram

DESCRIPTION: A perennial herb (*Majorana hortensis*, formerly *Origanum majorana*) is grown as an annual under the name of Sweet Marjoram in many gardens, because of its sweet-scented, aromatic leaves and flowers, which are used for seasoning dressings and meat dishes. It is a native of the Mediterranean countries.

It has an erect, branching habit of growth, with grayish-green, oval leaves. Terminal clusters of small white flowers appear in midsummer and produce small, oval, dark-brown seeds. The plant's pleasing odor and warm, bitterish taste is caused by its volatile oil, which is soluble in water.

TYPES AND VARIETIES: A number of varieties which bear separate species-names have the same properties and may be used for the same purpose. The common MARJORAM (*Origanum vulgare*) is naturalized in this country and grows wild along roadsides. Several European species (*Origanum onites, sipyleum, pulchellum,* and *dictamnus*) are little known in this country.

SOIL AND CLIMATIC REQUIREMENTS: These plants will grow on a large variety of soils which are well drained and well supplied with organic matter. The soils should not be too fertile; as a matter of fact, too much nitrogen will produce a highly vegetative growth which will not have so much of the volatile oil as one that grows more slowly. The plants are not hardy in the northern states and must be started every spring. However, if they can be protected by heavy mulches during the winters, they can be carried along as perennials, so long as the soil does not freeze.

CULTURAL DIRECTIONS: The seed is sown in rows in the early spring as soon as all danger of frost is over, and the plants are thinned later to stand 6 inches apart. Cultivation should be shallow. If the plants are transplanted, they should be protected from the sun until they are established. The leaves are harvested when full-grown and are dried in the shade. When dry, they may be placed in jars.

Tansy

DESCRIPTION: The common tansy (*Tanacetum vulgare*) is a strong-scented herbaceous perennial which is used for flavoring culinary dishes. It is native to Asia and Europe but has become a weed in northeastern United States. The annual flowering stems have deeply cut, coarse leaves

and small, yellow flowers borne in corymbs. Extracts from the foliage are used in medical preparations.

TYPES AND VARIETIES: There are some variations in the foliage but the plant grows wild and produces such a profusion of leaves that it is cultivated only in those sections where the plant has not become a weed. Varieties have not been established.

SOIL AND CLIMATIC REQUIREMENTS: The plants are very hardy in the temperate regions. They grow in the fertile loam soils of the creek bottoms and waste places, spreading rapidly in meadows. The plants are no trouble in cultivated ground, however. The soils must be well drained, as the plants will not live in places where the water cannot drain away.

CULTURAL DIRECTIONS: Where the plants do not grow wild, they can be grown in the garden and a half dozen plants will supply the needs of the average family. The seed is sown in a corner in the garden where the ground is not to be spaded. The seed

will probably germinate even in the grass and the plants will establish themselves. If the seeds are not permitted to ripen, the plants will not spread, as they propagate by seed rather than by roots. Insects or diseases will give no trouble.

GENERAL RECOMMENDATIONS: Tansy is not as popular as it was in times past, due to the fact that there are so many other plants that serve the purpose of flavoring foods. However, there are probably some sections where these plants might be a welcome addition to the perennial-herb garden.

Tarragon

Tarragon (*Artemisia dranunculus*) is a European perennial closely related to wormwood or absinthe. The stem tips and leaves, with their fragrant smell and anise-like taste, much favored by French chefs, are used for

flavoring vinegar pickles, etc. The plant has a seedstalk two to three feet tall, with long, slender dark-green leaves and inconspicuous flower heads of small, greenish florets. Oil of Tarragon, obtained from the foliage by distillation, is used to flavor meats and other dishes. About the time the flowers are ready to open, the foliage contains the maximum amount of oil.

The plants are hardy unless grown too rapidly on rich soils; they do best on well-drained soils that contain appreciable amounts of organic matter and lime. Too much nitrogen in the soil produces foliage which is liable to be low in essential oil. Unless the winters have enough snow to keep the ground covered, it may be necessary to cover the plants with a mulch of some sort, so that the ground does not alternately freeze and thaw.

Since the plants seldom produce seed, it is generally necessary as well as easier to plant root cuttings for new plantings. Stem cuttings can also be made early in the spring. The cuttings are planted a foot apart in the poorer soils of the garden. The plants are moved about in the garden every three or four years to prevent the development of any ground diseases that may affect the roots or crowns. However, seed may be bought and pot-sown and the seedlings set in the garden in rows to get a start.

The leaves can be picked from garden plants as soon as they have made a thrifty growth, and dried in a well-ventilated place where the sun does not strike the leaves. They will retain their green color and fragrance and, when thoroughly dry, can be rubbed to a fine powder and placed in an air-tight container for future use. Some people have the idea that they can cut plants and tie them in bunches and hang them in the attic until needed, but such plants lose much of their essential oil and the leaves are of little value as a flavoring material.

Thyme

DESCRIPTION: The ordinary thyme (*Thymus vulgaris*) is a native of Europe and is very widely grown. It is a small, hardy perennial, growing to a height of 10 inches and producing clusters of pale-purple flowers at the ends of the branched stems. It is

used as a culinary herb, as a medicine and, commercially, as the source of the volatile oil Thymol which is used as a deodorant and anesthetic. Thymol is also used as a sterilizing agent in the laboratory and as a dye for the detection of inulin in plant tissue. It probably has more uses than any of the other herbs, besides having ornamental value in the garden.

TYPES AND VARIETIES: There are several varieties: Narrow Leaf, Broad Leaf, and Variegated. The Broad Leaf is most commonly used. Lemon thyme is a related species (*T. serpyllum*), also called Mother-of-Thyme or Creeping Thyme. It has several varieties, but they are largely restricted to certain sections of Europe.

SOIL AND CLIMATIC REQUIREMENTS: Thyme grows best in dry, gravelly soils that are well limed that are not too fertile with respect to nitrogen. They are fairly hardy, especially if not forced too fast.

CULTURAL DIRECTIONS: The plants are started by sowing the seed in pots of soil and transplanting the seedlings to stand 6 inches apart in the row. The plants grow so coarse and woody in a few years that they should be replanted every two or three years. Thyme will live through the winter better if it is grown in masses so that the foliage protects the roots against successive freezing and thawing. The tops should not be cut off after the first of September, as this will cause the plants to send out another lot of new growth and thus deplete the reserve foods in the roots, so that the roots may winterkill. The best time to harvest is just after the plants have come into full bloom. The clippings are dried and stored in air-tight containers.

Water Cress
See in Part I (Vegetables)

Wild Ginger
See Ginger: Wild Ginger

Winter Savory
See Savory

Wormwood
See Absinthe

PART III
The Gardener's Guide

The Gardener's Guide

Gardens for Everybody

As a nation we are all gardeners at heart, and there are as many kinds of gardens as there are types of people. Some plant gardens for financial reasons; others, from the inborn desire to get their hands in the soil; still others do it as a pastime. There is something in a man's soul that finds expression in a garden. I am reminded of the anonymous words:

> I was a wanderer, I was alone;
> I found a plot that I could call my own,
> I planted a seed, I watched it grow into a sturdy plant,
> I was a part of the process of life,
> My loneliness was gone.

A garden may be anything from a patch of ground 10 by 12 feet square to an acre or more. Just where a garden stops and a commercial planting begins is a question. Some people can spend all their time on a few window boxes. Others can care for an acre of ground and have time to spare. Some people like to have the rows absolutely straight; others don't care whether the rows line up or not. Some people can't make a garden without having all the tools that are available, while my neighbor makes a garden on a half-acre of ground and has only a hoe to work with.

The garden usually reflects the effort that the owner can put into it. It is surprising what some people can do with a small amount of ground. I once heard of a vegetable garden that was developed on a Massachusetts rock bluff near the seashore where there was practically no soil except in small depressions and crevices in the rock. The gardener conserved all the plant material he could get, by composting it and spreading it in the rock-depressions. He grew radishes, lettuce, beets, and beans the first year, but most of his efforts were for love, because he harvested so little. After five years, however, when he told me his story, he had grown a remarkable crop of potatoes in one of the patches. The cooling effect of the rocks, in addition to supplying moisture, seemed to suit the potatoes. There is real pleasure in being able to grow a garden against such odds.

Another garden which comes to mind was that of an Italian workman whose house was practically hidden by grapevines trained over an arbor. There was no lawn. Behind the grapevines were a few fruit trees and around these were planted tomatoes and peppers. Small- and large-fruited varieties were in evidence. Along the south side of the house, almost close enough to be picked from the kitchen window, were pole beans, while in the back yard potatoes, onions, carrots, and cabbage filled the entire expanse from house to fence. Every available yard of earth was planted with an eye to use rather than to beauty, but the garden exemplified the thrifty soul of a man whose outlook on life was that of a provider.

People living on farms probably pay less attention to a garden than any other group. Regardless of the landscaping that may be done around the rural home, the vegetable garden is not planted with the idea of beauty. It is usually planted in some out-of-the-way corner of a field where it can be cared for with horse-drawn tools at the same time the main field-crop requires attention. Such gardens are motivated by a desire to have fresh foods after the restricted winter diet. Usually only the easily-grown varieties are included, because the hand work in the rural garden falls to the women of the house, with what help they can inveigle from the youngsters who are not old enough to help in the fields.

The suburban garden is the result of many motives and ideas. It is the garden that is placed in the back yard, carefully screened from view of the house by the annual flower garden, a grape trellis, a hedge, or even the garage. It usually gets the least attention of all, except when, in times of war, it is placed in a prominent place on the front lawn where it must be cared for. Suburban gardens usually fill in the place that is left over after the flower beds have been located. They may be anywhere from a few square feet for salad plants to the large specialty gardens. The most interesting of the suburban gardens are often those developed by businessmen, either as a prosaic method of getting exercise or as a realization of the dreams aroused by an excursion through a seed catalogue. It is in such gardens that some of our best varieties of plants have been developed. Through the keen observation of an earnest amateur many an idea has been born by the chance spotting of something different or very much worth while. It was in a small monastery garden in Brünn, Austria, that the principles of the science of genetics were formulated and established.

Of all the gardens I have known, the one which gave its owner the greatest pride and joy was that of a 13-year-old 4H-Club boy, who was able to report, after his harvest was gathered, that he had given his mother enough table vegetables for her family of five and had sold the surplus at a net profit of $112.76. And he did this on a little less than a quarter of an acre—a plot 65 x 150 feet.

Much has been written about "the Lord's gardens" wherefrom a church was wholly supported by the proceeds of vegetables grown and cared for by the members of the congregation. Such a project has much to commend it—a community working for a common cause in which the young people probably carried the larger portion of the load.

There are, of course, those elaborate vegetable gardens on estates where the head gardener does the planning and the instructions are carried out by one or more assistants. These gardens are well planned, attractive, and well cared for, but they probably reflect very little of the personality of the owner.

The advantages of a garden cannot be numbered and evaluated. There are many.

My garden gives me fresh greens for my table;
My garden gives me roses too,
My garden gives me sweet sanctuary
From care, and builds my hope anew.

The purpose of a vegetable garden, for one thing, is to grow vegetables which may be gathered and served fresh. People have learned by experience that vegetables must be served soon after they are picked in order to give their real flavor. One who has never eaten them within an hour from the time they were removed from the vine has never tasted the real flavor in, for instance, sweet corn, garden peas, summer squash, or asparagus.

Scientific investigations have disclosed a definite chemical basis for the deterioration of vegetable flavors. Rapid decomposition of the delicate sugars and volatile oils with which these flavors are associated results in bitter by-products which make the vegetables unpalatable to one who has eaten them in their pristine freshness. Although the icing of vegetables in transit has helped to preserve their flavor and increase the per capita consumption, the treatment which the retailer gives these shipments in his store often spoils what flavor the product had when it arrived. In many cases we can buy vegetables more cheaply than we can grow them but those of us who have really experienced the quality of certain perishable crops, will, if we cannot buy them with their pristine flavor, grow them at any cost.

The home gardener has also come to appreciate his own garden the more because he knows from personal experience that, in order to sell through the markets, he must often produce inferior showy varieties in preference to the better-flavored ones. Golden Bantam sweet corn, for instance, is first choice of the home gardener, but when he wants to grow corn for sale he must grow a large ear of much inferior quality, because the general public wants a lot for its money. This situation is gradually disappearing, however, as the consumer public begins to realize that good things do not always come in big packages. Nevertheless, the better varieties are still often unobtainable in the markets. We have been fed rubbery strawberries for years now, because that particular variety can be picked, shipped for several thousand miles, and held in the retail store for two weeks and still be sold as strawberries. This is one of the main reasons why people want to grow vegetables in their own gardens. They have learned to recognize quality and are usually disappointed if they try to get it in the open market. And so they establish their own gardens where they can grow the types and varieties that taste best to them.

In those communities where there is little assurance that we can buy vegetables, we will want to grow them for the wide variety of vitamins they contain. With staple foods so highly processed, vegetables are the only form in which we can get these vitamins. Vegetables also contain large quantities of the minerals required by our bodies. How valuable the vegetables which you grow are in this respect will depend on how closely your soils and cultural practices measure up to the standards established by experienced gardeners. The recommendations in this book will help you get the most out of your garden.

Vegetables and Better Health

There is much written about the value of vegetables as food and as a source of minerals and vitamins. In the fresh state, when the plants are tender and growing rapidly, they have their greatest content of vitamins, because vitamins are responsible for the growth of the plant and its ability to transmit life to the seed, tubers, or other structures which are responsible for carrying plant-life through to another growing season. Humans live on plant-storage products and must depend on these for their vitamins. So the time when the plant has stored the most vitamins is also the time when it is most valuable to humans. However, the value of the vegetable as a source of vitamin is also dependent upon proper methods of handling after picking and proper preparation for the table. Much can happen to a vegetable between the vine and the dish. Too often the following lines are true:

> *My vegetables had vitamins*
> *I named them A and B,*
> *And went right down the alphabet*
> *Until I came to G.*

A lady put them in a pot
And boiled them hard and long,
A semblance of their form remains
But, ah! my vitamins are gone.

If people appreciated how perishable these vitamins are, how easily destroyed by heat, how frequently discarded with the water in which the vegetables were cooked, they probably would have fewer aches and pains. In many cases, the juice in which the vegetable was cooked is far more valuable as a food than the part that is served. The best food, of course, is raw food, and green leaves probably have much more vitamin material than the blanched or white leaves. Growers go to considerable expense to bleach celery, but in doing so they are destroying valuable vitamins.

Although the perishable vegetables are good sources of vitamins and minerals, they are also high in water content, so that one must eat comparatively large servings to get as much vitamin as is obtained from some of the more concentrated foods. However, they also contain appreciable quantities of fibrous material and therefore are particularly suitable in diets for those who do no hard manual labor. Where the ditch digger wants potatoes and beans, the office worker gets along better with salads. The type of work done by those for whom you maintain a garden, will have some bearing on the type of vegetables you should grow there.

Of a given vegetable, certain varieties may have a higher content of one of the vitamins, or of minerals, proteins, or energy-producing calories in the form of sugar, starch, fats, and oils. Unfortunately the vitamin-content has not been determined for all vegetable varieties. We do know that some varieties of tomato differ considerably from others, and we may assume with a considerable degree of certainty that the same thing is true of other vegetables, even though they have not been tested. The color of the fruit or vegetable product supposedly is associated with certain vitamins. In general, the freshness of the flavor is associated with the food value of the product broken down in the plant. Anything that breaks down the volatile oils and sugars on which the flavor depends may also detract from the food value of the plant or its parts. Therefore a variety that has a particularly high flavor probably also has a good supply of vitamins.

The foliage or stems which are used for food are usually the most perishable; the fruits, such as the tomato, are slightly less perishable; while the storage organs, such as the seed or the tubers, are fairly stable and can be stored for considerable periods. There are many factors that may detract from the value of a particular vegetable as a source of food for humans.

The kind of soil on which the vegetables are grown affects the food value of their parts. The mineral-content of vegetables is highly important from the standpoint of food for humans. Soils that are low in calcium salts will grow large yields of some vegetables, but such crops will be low in calcium and therefore a poor food for people who have a high calcium-requirement. The same might be said of soils deficient in magnesium or phosphorous. Vegetables grown on mineral-deficient soils probably are also low in vitamins, because there is a relationship between certain minerals and vitamin-content. Many people cannot understand why they must take vitamins in concentrated form when they eat what seems to be a good variety of foods. The only answer, except for people whose vitamin-need is abnormally high, is that the vegetables have lost, or never had, their expected quota of vitamins. I once ran an experiment on Lima beans by purposely keeping calcium from the roots. These plants made a certain amount of growth and produced some seeds which, to all intents and purposes, were normal. But when the seeds were planted, some failed to germinate, and those that did, produced a very abnormal plant. That same seed, if eaten, would not have been the source of calcium in a diet for which Lima beans are ordinarily excellent.

The stage of maturity of the crop will have some effect on its food value. Vegetable plants store up sugars, starches, proteins, oils, fats, fiber, minerals, vitamins and numerous other materials in smaller quantities. As a rule the leaves are rich in many of these products until the plant starts to form blossoms and fruit, when much of this material is dissipated as a source of energy for the growth processes or is transferred to the fruit and the seed. We must remember that vegetables do not make this food for our benefit. We have learned by experience to use plants in various stages of their growth, and to get the most out of them, we must harvest them at the stage when the particular part that we want is the richest in food value.

The manner in which we handle the crop after harvesting it is another factor which affects its food value. If we take leaves, they must be more carefully handled than if we harvest, for instance, the seed. Life processes in leaves and tender parts of the plant go right on after they are removed from the plant, unless we can arrest the process by chilling, heating, or some other form of preservation. The tubers of the sweet potato, on the other hand, represent a form of storage evolved to preserve plant-life through the dormant stage of the life cycle during seasons too cold for leaves to live. Accordingly, they contain certain chemicals which tend to make them inactive except under growing conditions. We take advantage of this fact and store them in our storage plants so that we can use them over long periods after they have been removed from the plant. Anything we can do to arrest the life-processes in the vegetables we harvest will tend to preserve the delicate flavors of the foods that have been stored. Asparagus, fresh peas, sweet corn, and similar tender vegetable material should be chilled or cooked immediately after it is removed from the plant. The fine flavor of these vegetable products is quickly lost, if, after being removed from the plant, they are permitted to lie in the sun or in a hot kitchen for several hours.

When asparagus loses its freshness, it becomes bitter because decomposition-products are accumulated as the proteins begin to break down. People who have never tasted fresh asparagus from the garden know it only by the bitter acids which begin to form several hours after it is cut from the plant. Summer squash is tasteless when it is a day or two from the vine. When picked fresh, it has a delightfully delicate flavor.

So few people have learned the real flavor of fresh vegetables, that many are willing to accept vegetables because they are vegetables. On the other hand, I have seen conscientious people build businesses by delivering vegetables to the consumer garden-fresh, and there are wonderful opportunities for many more to do the same thing. However, it takes time to build up such a trade, because it is necessary to educate people to the real quality in vegetables.

Canned and frozen foods have much of their food value preserved in them. But they are only as good as they were when they were processed. Tomato products have lost very little of their food value in canning. During the winter months, vegetables are shipped from one part of the country to another in refrigerator cars, and many products are delivered in almost as good condition as when they were harvested. Spinach-growers who have to ship their produce long distances put a shovelful of ice in each bushel basket to thoroughly chill the leaves. However, perishable fruits and vegetables, either canned or frozen, are not good unless they are processed within a couple of hours after they are harvested.

A Comparison of the Food Value of Some Important Vegetables

In order to obtain the fullest benefit from the nutritive value of vegetables, it is desirable to know what energy food (protein, carbohydrate, or fat) each important vegetable contains; also what vitamins are present; how good the mineral content is; and what the calorie value is. The table on the two following pages gives this information in convenient form.

A COMPARISON OF THE FOOD VALUE OF
SOME IMPORTANT VEGETABLES

Vegetable	Important Energy Food	Vitamins Present*	Mineral Content	Calorie Value per Serving
Artichokes				
Globe	Protein	B, a, c	Good	75
Jerusalem	Carbohydrate	c, b, a	Fair	105
Asparagus				
Fresh	Protein, sugar	A, C, B	Good	20
Canned	Protein	A, – –	Poor	15
Beans				
Snap	Protein	A, C, b	Good	30
Wax	Protein	C, b, –	Good	30
Lima	Protein, starch and fats	B, a, c	Good	100
Shell	Protein, starch and fats	B, a, c	Fair	120
Beet Root	Protein and carbohydrate	b, a, –	Fair	30
Leaves	Protein	C, – –	Good	15
Broccoli	Protein	A, C, b	Good	45
Brussels Sprouts	Protein	C, a, b	Good	60
Cabbage				
Fresh	Protein and carbohydrate	C, b, a	Good	30
Boiled	Protein and carbohydrate	C, – –	Poor	20
Carrot, Raw	Protein and sugar	A, c, b	Good	50
Cauliflower	Protein	C+, a, b	Fair	50
Celery	Protein	c, a, b	Fair	10
Chard (Swiss)	Protein	A, c, b	Fair	50
Collards	Protein	A, c, b	Good	60
Corn (sweet yellow)	Sugar, protein	A, c, b	Fair	120
Eggplant	Protein and carbohydrate	a, – –	Fair	65
Endive	Protein	A+, c, b	Good	10

226

Vegetable	Important Energy Food	Vitamins Present*	Mineral Content	Calorie Value per Serving
Greens				
Dandelion	Protein	A+, C, b	Good	10
Mustard	Protein	A+, B, c	Good	10
Turnip	Protein	A, c, b	Fair	10
Kale	Protein and carbohydrate	A+, C, B	Good	80
Lettuce				
Leaf	Protein	A, c, b	Fair	10
Head	Protein	trace of c, a, b	Fair	10
Muskmelons	Sugar	trace	Trace	10
Okra	Protein and carbohydrate	a, b, c	Good	20
Onions	Sugar, protein	trace	Fair	25
Parsley	Protein	A+, C+	Good	Neg.
Parsnips	Carbohydrate	c, b, –	Fair	90
Peas (green)	Protein, sugar	A, b, C	Fair	75
Peppers (red or green)	Protein and carbohydrate	A+, C+, b	Fair	20
Potatoes, Sweet	Carbohydrate	A+, b, c	Good	110
White	Carbohydrate and protein	c, trace of a, b	Fair	70
Pumpkin	Carbohydrate and protein	A+, trace of b, c	Fair	25
Rutabaga	Carbohydrate and protein	C, trace of b, a	Fair	30
Spinach	Protein	A+, C, b	Fair	10
Squash				
Hubbard	Carbohydrate	A, trace of c, b	Fair	40
Summer	Carbohydrate	a, trace of c, b	Fair	10
Tomato		A, c, b	Fair	30
Turnip	Carbohydrate	C, trace of b	Fair	36
Water Cress	Protein	A+, C, b	Good	5

*Capital letters mean good supply. + after letter means exceptionally large supply. Small letters mean fair to low amount. Order of letters indicates relative importance of vitamin content. Vitamin B here stands for the entire B-complex, usually found in combination as produced in vegetables.

227

Planning the Garden

I must have herbs, tomatoes bright,
Some carrots, beets, and salad greens,
Fat ears of corn, and Hubbard squash,
And rows of green and yellow beans.

Whether we wish to follow a plan or not, it is a good idea at least for the first year to sit down with a pencil and paper and sketch a garden in the plot that is available. By following directions in the average seed catalogue it is possible to plan out the particular varieties you want and how much of each is needed. Some people want a large variety, while others are satisfied with a few things. Personally, I like to concentrate on those vegetables which are highly perishable and are particularly good when they come from the garden not more than an hour before they are served at the table. This would include such plants as asparagus, rhubarb, lettuce, peas, sweet corn, snap beans, broccoli, celery, endive, summer squash, strawberries, and tomatoes. Next in order should be cabbage, carrots, and beets. Other crops are added as space permits.

The amount of each crop to plant, of course, depends on individual taste. For a family of four I would suggest the following:

ARTICHOKES: Four plants. Set plants after danger of frost.

ASPARAGUS: A hundred feet of row or 50 roots. Set early in the spring.

BROCCOLI: Not more than six plants.

BRUSSELS SPROUTS: Four to six plants. Set as early as possible.

CABBAGE: Six early and six late heads of the common type and six heads of Savoy.

CARROTS, CELERY, AND BEETS: Ten feet of row for all three.

EGGPLANT: One or two plants.

ENDIVE: Twelve plants, if desired.

HERBS OR MINTS: Five feet of each, if desired.

LETTUCE: Twelve plants for head lettuce; ten feet for leaf lettuce.

ONIONS: Ten feet of row for green onions.

PEAS: Fifty or more feet of row. First crop to be planted in the spring.

PEPPERS: Four sweet-pepper plants.

RHUBARB: Six roots. Set early in spring.

SHELL BEANS OR POLE BEANS: Fifty feet of row, or twenty-five hills or poles.

SNAP BEANS: Twenty-five feet of row. Plantings every ten days after danger of frost is past.

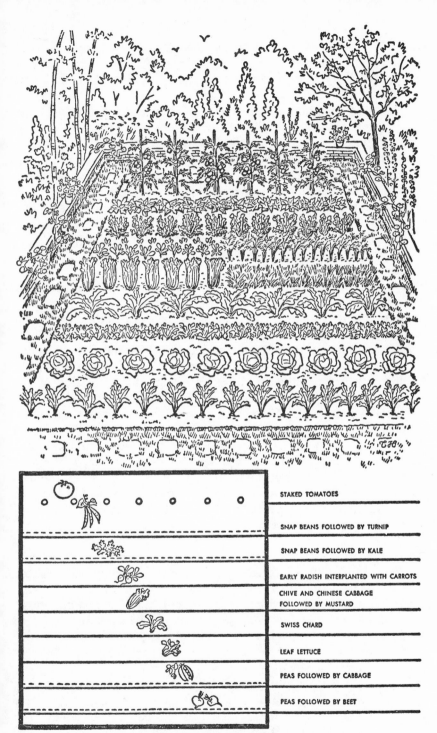

	STAKED TOMATOES
	SNAP BEANS FOLLOWED BY TURNIP
	SNAP BEANS FOLLOWED BY KALE
	EARLY RADISH INTERPLANTED WITH CARROTS
	CHIVE AND CHINESE CABBAGE FOLLOWED BY MUSTARD
	SWISS CHARD
	LEAF LETTUCE
	PEAS FOLLOWED BY CABBAGE
	PEAS FOLLOWED BY BEET

GARDEN PLAN 20′ × 20′

SPINACH: Twenty-five feet or ten feet of Swiss chard or both. These may be planted early.

SQUASHES: Two hills each of the crookneck and the Zucchini summer squashes and two hills of the winter storage squash.

STRAWBERRIES: Twenty-five plants. Set early in spring.

SWEET CORN: Two 25-foot rows side by side. Make successive plantings to fill in space, if possible. It is better to plant corn in two short rows than in one long row, because of pollination.

TOMATOES: One to two hundred feet of row or twenty-five. to fifty plants. Tomatoes are easily canned, and this quantity will provide from 300 to 500 pounds of ripe fruit in addition to green fruit for mince meat and green tomato pickle. Plants are set after all danger of frost is past.

There is a chance to do considerable planning in interplanting these crops. Many of these plants that require two or three feet of space should be planted in the same rows with peas and other crops that will mature early. In this way, a 25- by 50-foot lot will produce a large amount of produce and considerable space will be saved. The perennial plants should be put in a permanent place at one side of the garden. The low-growing plants should be placed on the south side of the garden, so that they are not shaded early in the season.

The following plan is offered as a possibility for a small garden and can be enlarged to suit individual requirements. But the gardener should do his own thinking when it comes to plans, because any plan that might be suggested could represent only one garden, adapted to the tastes of one individual, the particularities of one location, the predilections of a single nationality. An Italian gardener would have an entirely different plan from a Swedish gardener's plan, regardless of how much money he spent on it.

A PLAN FOR A GARDEN 35 FEET WIDE AND FROM 50 TO 100 FEET LONG
The rows run lengthwise of the garden and are reckoned either from the north or west edge, as follows:

FIRST ROW, 3 FEET FROM EDGE: Asparagus; Rhubarb. Set asparagus in a double row two feet wide. Plants should be three feet apart in the row and set to alternate with the plants of the companion row. Enough space should be left to set in six rhubarb plants two feet apart in double rows.

SECOND ROW, 8 FEET FROM EDGE: Beans. A good place for pole beans, if you wish. They will occupy the ground all season. A half row of Kentucky Wonder for snap beans and a half row of King of the Garden for large pole Limas or of Sieva for the small butter beans. I would plant sunflowers for poles and, when up, plant pole beans.

GARDEN PLAN 30' X 40'

If you prefer bush varieties, as I would, because the poles are apt to be too scarce or too costly, I would plant a row of the large-seeded Lima beans.

THIRD ROW, 11 FEET FROM EDGE: Corn; Snap Beans. Plant the corn in hills three feet apart and plant snap beans, Bountiful or Wax, between the hills. Leave eight inches on either side of the hill of corn. However, I would plant only one-third of the row and make successive plantings at ten-day intervals.

FOURTH ROW, 14 FEET FROM EDGE: The same as the third row. Plant at the same time so that two rows of corn will be adjacent and maturing at the same time.

FIFTH ROW, 17 FEET FROM EDGE: Tomatoes. Full row, mostly of Rutgers but with a few early Rutgers-type plants which have been grown in pots and kept hard by light watering, so that they are setting fruit when they are set in the ground. Where the season is cooler, as in the northern states, Bonny Best may be better unless you learn how to handle Rutgers to make it come early. In the real short-growing season, the earliest varieties, such as Victor, Penn State, or Bounty, should be grown.

SIXTH ROW, AT LEAST 21 FEET FROM EDGE: Cabbage. Include some early, medium, and late varieties as well as a few Savoy and, if you like, red varieties. See discussion on cabbage.

SEVENTH ROW, 24 FEET FROM EDGE: Peas; Broccoli. I would plant peas as early as the ground can be worked, in a double row with a foot space between them. When the peas are through the ground, I would set broccoli and Brussels sprouts down the middle between the rows of peas. A few cauliflower plants should be set in this manner, but they must be kept growing to prevent them from maturing too early. Cabbage could also be set in this row. If you like mustard, Swiss chard, or kale, they could be planted between the peas. If any of these crops come off by the first to the middle of August, rutabagas may be planted in the northern states or turnips in the more southern states. In the southern states, collards may be grown in place of the cabbages.

EIGHTH ROW, 28 FEET FROM EDGE: Salads. Ten endive plants, ten lettuce heads, and ten feet of leaf lettuce, five feet of Chinese lettuce, five feet of parsley, and five feet of chives.

NINTH ROW, 30 FEET FROM EDGE: Radish; Beets; Carrots. Mix radish seed with early beets for half of the row and with carrots for the other half of the row.

TENTH ROW, 32 FEET FROM EDGE: Onions; Beets. The onion sets should be followed by late beets. Part of this and the ninth row

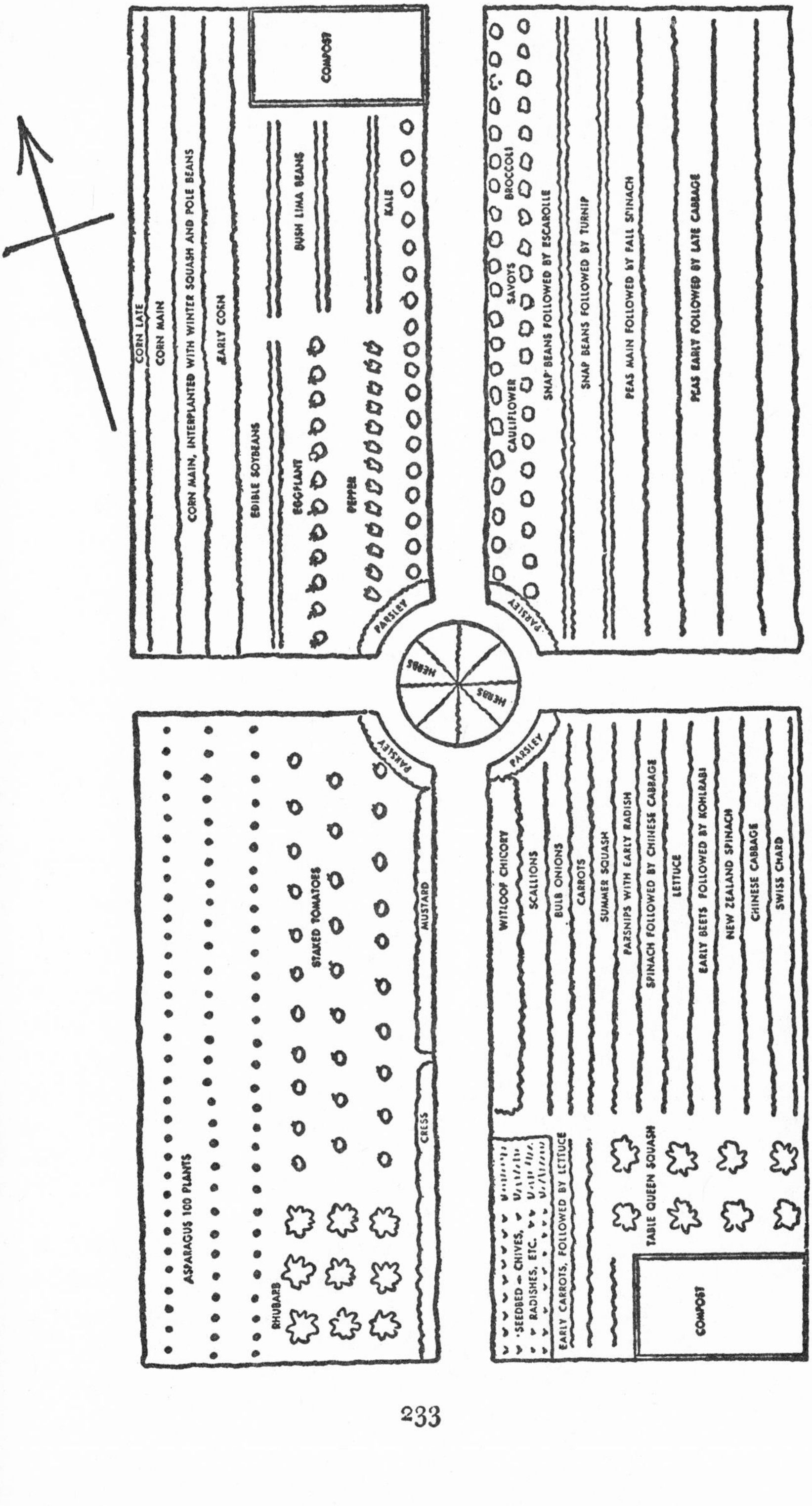

GARDEN PLAN 50' × 100'

Top-left plot:
CORN LATE
CORN MAIN
CORN MAIN, INTERPLANTED WITH WINTER SQUASH AND POLE BEANS
EARLY CORN
EDIBLE SOYBEANS
BUSH LIMA BEANS
EGGPLANT
PEPPER
KALE
COMPOST

Top-right plot:
BROCCOLI
SAVOYS
CAULIFLOWER
SNAP BEANS FOLLOWED BY ESCAROLLE
SNAP BEANS FOLLOWED BY TURNIP
PEAS MAIN FOLLOWED BY FALL SPINACH
PEAS EARLY FOLLOWED BY LATE CABBAGE

Center:
PARSLEY
HERBS
PARSLEY

Bottom-left plot:
ASPARAGUS 100 PLANTS
STAKED TOMATOES
RHUBARB
PARSLEY
MUSTARD
CRESS

Bottom-right plot:
WITLOOF CHICORY
SCALLIONS
BULB ONIONS
CARROTS
SUMMER SQUASH
PARSNIPS WITH EARLY RADISH
SPINACH FOLLOWED BY CHINESE CABBAGE
LETTUCE
EARLY BEETS FOLLOWED BY KOHLRABI
NEW ZEALAND SPINACH
CHINESE CABBAGE
SWISS CHARD
PARSLEY

- SEEDED — CHIVES,
- RADISHES, ETC.
EARLY CARROTS, FOLLOWED BY LETTUCE
TABLE QUEEN SQUASH
COMPOST

233

might be used for two plants of eggplant and two or three of sweet pepper.

LAST ROW: Specialties or trial materials. If you wish summer squash, I would plant two or three hills of two varieties at the ends of the tenth and eleventh rows. This gives four feet which will accommodate the hills. Cucumbers might be placed in this same manner by shortening these two rows.

Spinach may be planted in the last few rows. And strawberries may be substituted for some of the other things mentioned in the tentative garden which I have just given you. As soon as any of the crops are harvested and there is time to plant something else, the ground should be put to use. You may want a row of different kinds of herbs in occasional years. There is also a possibility of having plants ready in pots to set in, when a crop is removed, thus making it possible to mature a crop which otherwise would be too late.

If more ground is available, there is always the possibility of including more crops for canning and storage as well as some of the cane-fruits and white or sweet potatoes. By checking up on each crop that is desired, it is possible to work it into a plan where it will not interfere too much with the other crops. There is also the possibility of mixing flowers in with the vegetables. Most of the annuals will fit into the above scheme. If space is too limited, tomatoes may be staked on poles, so that more may be grown in the same space or part of the space used for something else.

How To Select Varieties

There probably is no one variety which is perfect under all conditions. Varieties differ as to the number of days required to mature them. It would be foolish to select a late-maturing tomato for the northern states where it probably would not ripen its first fruit until the first fall frost. Conversely, it would be wasted effort to grow a tomato in New Jersey which is a big yielder in northern Wisconsin, because the quality would be inferior to a later variety that could be grown in New Jersey. A pepper variety which was developed in Massachusetts and produces beautifully large fruits there, is practically worthless in southern New Jersey because it forms small fruits of poor quality. There are many of our vegetable varieties which are suited to certain localities, but are highly unsuited to others. The kitchen gardener must rely upon the seed houses. Local dealers usually stock seeds suited for the locality. The safest procedure for the grower is to make a practice of buying seeds through a well-known seed house which is located in the general area. People in New England should buy from seed companies in that area. People in the southeast should patronize their local seed companies. There is no objection for one to send an order to a distant seed house, but he should not be disappointed if his plants do not come up to expectation. Experience should dictate in those cases. (See list of seed houses on pp. 303, 304.)

Then there is the matter of selecting varieties. If one buys seed every year, the first job is to get a list of recommended varieties from the local county agricultural agent, usually located at the county seat in the post office building, or from the Department of Vegetable Crops at the State Experiment Station. (See list of State Agricultural Experiment Stations on page 302.) The varieties they recommend include the best they have found in their trial comparisons. They do not include the newest creations, which often turn out to be an old variety under a new name. One must realize that it takes years of patient breeding to produce a worthwhile new variety. Reliable seed companies follow a system of rigid plant and seed selection for continuous improvement of their old varieties, and some of our oldest varieties are still our best ones.

So when you get the list from your own government agency, send for a seed catalogue or two and sit down for an enjoyable evening to order your seed. If you see something that is not on the list but sounds good, include a small packet, but don't plant much area to it. A few plants will tell you whether it is worth while. A seed catalogue gives the number of days which are required to produce the edible portion from the time seed is sown. You must figure your growing season from early to late frost. (See Frost Table, p. 297.) Also it tells you whether it is a warm- or cool-season crop. It is a good idea to get as much information as possible from the catalogue. Generally speaking a packet is all the seed one needs for a family of 4 to 7 people. Beans and sweet corn might be needed in greater quantity if you restrict yourself to one variety.

By getting different seed catalogues occasionally, you can look for things that you have not previously tried. It adds to the variety. There are a lot of possibilities, for instance among the varieties of pumpkins and squashes. One gardener who tried out a few hills each of 20 varieties of muskmelon found there were only a few that he liked. But for the main part of the garden, the standard or commercial varieties are usually best. Golden bantam sweet corn is an exception which proves this rule. It has a quality and flavor that no other corn has.

I would suggest the possibility of saving your own seed. It is not as difficult as it sounds. Seeds of beans, corn, okra, and other varieties which produce seed in pods are picked when ripe, shelled, placed in bags and dried, after which they may be stored in a dry cold place. Pepper seed is taken out of the ripe fruit and dried. Tomato seed is taken from the ripe fruit and placed in a glass jar with its juice. It is permitted to ferment in its juice for two days, after which the seed is removed, washed, and dried. Cucumbers are handled in a similar manner. Melon, pumpkin and squash seed are taken out of the fruit and dried. Members of the cabbage family produce seed in cylindrical pods, easily saved. Lettuce and endive seed is produced in small heads and is picked when ripe and dried. It is easily rubbed out. Some plants, like carrots, beets, celery, and several other crops, produce seed the second year. They are not so easy to handle.

There is a good opportunity to improve varieties by saving seed. If you save the seed from the very best plants, you gradually improve a variety and your seed is an improvement over anything you can buy. The seed from one tomato fruit will give you all the plants you need. Two ears of corn will produce enough seed. Many new varieties have been developed by starting in this manner. This is well worth considering during these times when seeds are scarce. It would insure a supply of good seed.

When selecting varieties, the gardener can either use one variety and make successive plantings to get a succession of the same vegetable, or he can pick a number of varieties having different times of maturity and plant them at one time. For instance, Golden Bantam or any other variety of corn may be planted at weekly intervals, or the following varieties may be planted at one time and will mature in 72 to 120 days: Alpha, 72 (white); Golden Early Market, 76, Golden Sunshine, 80, Carmel Golden, 85, Golden Cross Bantam, 88, and Bantam Evergreen, 95 (all yellow varieties); Stowells Evergreen, 105, and Country Gentleman, 110 to 120 (white varieties). The same thing may be done with radishes, cabbage, celery, beans, and many other vegetables which the gardener will find in studying the seed catalogue. This method requires more space and more seed; therefore, it is more costly, but probably will require less labor. The disadvantage is that the varieties are not all of equally good quality. In sweet corn, successive plantings of Golden Bantam will insure a uniformly high quality corn. There are many hybrid varieties on the lists which may be used in a similar manner, if the older varieties cannot be grown because of wilt. In beans, this does not apply. There is much, therefore, that can be done by studying a seed catalogue.

Growing Seedlings for Transplanting

The first important step toward a successful garden is to have the right kind of a plant to set in the soil. Many people depend on buying plants.

Such plants have usually been crowded in shallow flats and are so hard and stunted by the time the gardener gets them, that they do not start off readily and, if a dry spell should occur about the time the gardener puts them into the ground, they never do get started. Bugs are liable to eat them up before they even start to grow. A plant should be grown in such a way that it is stocky—not too succulent—so that it will not wilt at the least provocation. It should be dark green in color—beautiful to look at.

Not all crops, of course, are grown from transplanted seedlings. The seeds of hardy plants, such as radish, are generally sown outdoors in the place where they are expected to mature. But seeds of tropical and warm-climate plants, such as eggplant and tomato, of half-hardy and tender annuals for early-season crops, and of hardy perennials are best sown under glass weeks before they could safely be sown out-of-doors. The seedlings are started in pans, flats, and nursery beds, then transferred to other flats or seed beds, or to greenhouse benches, hotbeds, or coldframes, until the seedlings and the weather have arrived at the proper condition for transplanting to the garden.

FERTILIZATION OF VEGETABLE PLANTS FOR SEED: The gardener who wishes to grow his own seed for planting or who includes in his garden vegetables whose edible portions consist of seeds, should know something about the types of plants from the standpoint of fertilization. This factor must often be considered in determining the best arrangement of rows or beds in the garden and the treatment of the plants under certain weather conditions. (See, for instance, CORN: SWEET CORN and TOMATO in Part I of this book.)

Generally, for a plant to produce seed or fruit it is necessary that pollen grains be produced which, when deposited on the stigma of the flower, will germinate and grow down through the style into the ovary where the nucleus of the pollen grain will unite with the nucleus in the ovule to bring about fertilization. The location of the pollen and ovule-producing organs is, therefore, of vital importance.

The manner of flower production varies considerably among different types of plants. The common form is the hermaphroditic or monoclinous flower arrangement in which the sex organs are produced in the same flower. All plants belonging to the Tomato family, including eggplant, pepper, and potato, have such a flower arrangement.

Plants which produce their sex organs in separate flowers but on the same plant are considered monoecious or diclinous. Practically all the plants belonging to the *Cucurbitaciae* have this type. This includes cucumber, squash, melons, pumpkins, and gourds. The pistillate flower forms the fruit and has the small fruit in evidence when the flower opens. The staminate or male flower contains only the stamens. Corn has this type of flowering. The tassel has the staminate flowers which produce the pollen, while the ear contains the pistillate flower. Every pistillate flower has a silk which is both stigma and style.

Another form is dioecious, where the pistillate and staminate flowers are produced on separate plants, so that we.have male and female plants. This is not so common. Asparagus and spinach have this type of flower arrangement.

Wherever it is important for the gardener to know what type of flowering plant a given vegetable or herb is, the necessary information has been given in the entry in Part I or II of this book. (See, for instance, Cucumber in Part I.) Such knowledge is often especially important for greenhouse culture. Pollination of tomatoes, for instance, normally effected outdoors by natural means, must be accomplished in the greenhouse by hand—if the air is dry, merely by jarring the vines to scatter the ripened pollen. This method would not be possible if the tomato were a dioecious plant.

Seedlings grown in greenhouses or similar artificial plant-growing devices also demand that special care be given to maintaining the optimum conditions of growth: soil, watering, ventilation, nutrients. Success depends upon how well such conditions are provided by the grower.

PREPARING THE SOIL: A good soil is necessary to grow a good plant. Any good garden soil, if it grows good crops, can be used to grow good seedlings. The secret of getting a good seedling-soil is to dig it in the fall, place it in flats, heaping full, and leave it out where it will freeze

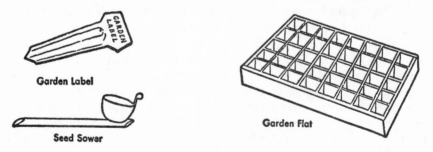

Garden Label

Seed Sower

Garden Flat

and thaw all winter. There are several things that can be done to such a soil before it is placed in the winter flats. Every gardener should have a bag of pulverized magnesium-limestone in his tool-shed. With every bushel of soil a good big handful of the limestone should be mixed; no other fertilizer should be added. The flats should be placed where they will not be disturbed throughout the winter but where the soil will freeze. In the spring, the soil is taken in and allowed to dry out. It should not be handled while it is wet. It should be dry enough to fall apart when a handful is squeezed. It can then be pulverized for the seed flats.

PLANTING THE SEED: The soil in the flat is leveled off with a stick and then packed with a board. This will lower the soil about a half inch. It is then marked off in small furrows, about 2 inches apart and just deep enough to accommodate the seed. After the seeds are placed in the furrows, it is a good practice to sprinkle some pit-sand over them to a depth of a quarter to one-half inch. This sand should be free of

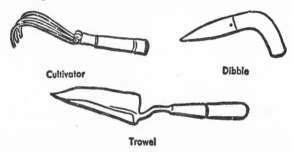

Cultivator

Dibble

Trowel

stones and mixed with limestone—a handful to a gallon of the sand. This will do much to help the seeds to germinate. The sand is porous and will permit plenty of air to get to the seed. It is loose and makes it easy for the seedlings to get through. Most important, it keeps the soil around the seedlings dry, so that the damping-off fungi cannot get started. This treatment is less necessary, of course, in the light sandy soils than in the heavy loam soils. The depth at which the seed is planted depends on its size. The general rule is to make the depth of planting about four times the thickness of the seed. Very fine seeds are barely covered with soil. The soil should be watered just enough to keep it moist.

WATERING SEEDLINGS: One of the greatest mistakes that the plant grower makes is to water too much. The soil should be kept moist but not wet. When the seeds have germinated and the seedlings have made the first true leaves, they are ready to be spotted. In most cases, they are spotted to similar flats or to pots. It is here that the watering becomes really important. After the seedlings have been spotted to flats in moist soil, they need not be watered for a day or so. This will encourage the roots to become established. After the plants are established, the soil should be watered only when the ground is dry and then the hose should be held close to the ground, so that the water flows out slowly and floods the ground. The leaves should never be made wet.

This precaution is taken to keep leaf-diseases from getting a start. The flats should be watered heavily when they are watered: they should never be sprinkled. If the seedlings wilt too much, it is better to water the walls and walks around the plants, to increase the moisture in the

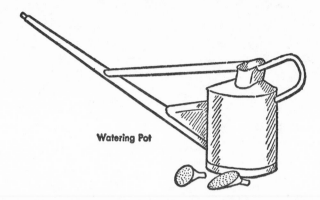

Watering Pot

air, than to water directly. Dry air causes the seedlings to wilt even when they have plenty of water. Seedlings will wilt after a period of cloudy weather, because they tend to get soft when they cannot get sunlight. Plants need sunlight to be sturdy, and during cloudy weather they should be grown very slowly by withholding water and keeping the plants cool. Plants make their growth during the night so that they should not be watered in the afternoon. The best time for watering is early in the morning before the sun gets too hot. Plants should be watered only on sunny days.

GROWING-TEMPERATURES AND VENTILATION: Temperatures and ventilation vary with the plants that are to be grown. Lettuce, members of the cabbage family, and onions, if they are being started early, should be grown at a night-temperature of not over 50 degrees. Tomatoes, eggplant, and peppers should be grown at temperatures close to 60 degrees. In view of the fact that seedlings make most of their growth at night, it is essential that the temperature be controlled at this time. They also make some growth during cloudy weather, for which reason the temperature on sunless days should not be too high. On bright sunny days, the temperature may be 20 degrees higher, because at this time the plants are storing up large quantities of sugar and starch which serve as a source of energy to make it possible for them to grow during the night.

Ventilation is one method of controlling the temperature and it promotes circulation of air around the leaves. If the ventilation is not good, water tends to collect around and on the leaves, thus making an ideal place for disease-producing organisms to grow and infect the plant cells. Most growers make the mistake of closing down the ventilators or sash during the late afternoon in order to conserve heat, and then wonder why the plants become spindly. Too rapid growth always results in spindly plants, due to the fact that there is not sufficient synthesized material from the day before to make the plants both tall and stocky.

SPECIAL PLANT-GROWING METHODS: Such plants as the cucumber and melon, which are easily affected by the damping-off fungus which causes the plants to tip over at the surface of the ground, may be planted in sifted coal-cinders. Everything that will go through an ordinary coarse mosquito bar is packed into a flat and the seed is sown as in soil. These cinders are sterile, and there is sufficient food in the large seed to keep them growing until the first true leaf is formed, at which time they should be transplanted to the soil. Large seeds may also be sown in sawdust. This produces very vigorous roots which will withstand considerable rough-handling. Sawdust and sifted cinders do not contain much nutrient material, and it may be advisable to apply a nutrient solution such as is recommended for soilless culture in the chapter on that subject.

Those plants which should not have their roots disturbed too much when they are set into the soil may be planted in veneer bands. These are thin veneer wood strips, 4 inches wide and 10 inches long. They are folded to make a box without a bottom and filled with good soil. The seedlings are set in these, or the seed may be sown in directly. The bands are all packed into a flat which holds them together. When it is time to transplant them, the veneer can be unfolded and the plant set into the garden soil without disturbing the roots. The veneer band may be dried and used again. Melon and cucumber seed are often sown in half eggshells filled with soil. When it is time to transplant them, the shells are merely crushed in the hand and the whole thing is set in the soil.

Sand culture may be used to grow seedlings. Flats are used just as for soil, and the unpacked, preferably a yellow, sand should fill the flat. The sand is then packed, furrowed as for soil, and the seed is sown. The sand is then smoothed over, and enough water is applied to soak the sand. The nutrient solution is not added until the seed has germinated and then it is applied once a week. The following solution is good for the purpose:

Baking Powder,	1 teaspoonful	} In one gallon of water, and if the seedlings tend to grow too slowly, add a teaspoonful of washing ammonia.
Epsom salts,	1 teaspoonful	
Saltpeter,	2 teaspoonfuls	

This solution has given good results and people who have used it tell me that, occasionally, it is advisable to use double the prescribed amount. This is especially true if the plants are growing in an abundance of bright light.

In making flats, care should be exercised not to make the bottoms tight. They should be made with one-half-inch material; the bottom boards should not be over three inches wide, so spaced that at least a quarter-inch crack is left between them. If this is not done, the seedlings will get too much water and too little air around the roots to grow. The size of the flat may be 16 by 20 or 24 inches and 3 inches deep. These same flats are used for spotting the small seedlings. A board with prongs 2 inches apart and 2 inches long is handy for marking off the flats and making holes in which to set the seedlings. Seedlings should be set slightly deeper than the seeds in the germination flat. The seedling flat may then be set into the coldframe. Seedlings may, of course, be transplanted directly to the coldframe soil, but this is not so handy when it comes to taking them into the garden. It is easier to carry the flat to the garden than to have to dig the plants out of the coldframe soil.

Greenhouses, Hotbeds, and Coldframes

The gardener who wishes to grow his own seedlings and to provide for early-season crops of the tender vegetables must, of course, be provided with a plant house or other plant-growing structure where growing conditions may be artificially maintained. His growing equipment, however, may be used for several purposes other than to start seedlings in advance of the outdoor season. It may be used, for instance, to shelter seedlings of hardy plants through the winter until they can be planted in the spring, to store hardy and semi-hardy plants through the winter months, to store hardy bulbs planted in flower pots or flats during their root-forming periods, and to propagate plants from cuttings, especially during summer.

The greenhouse, of course, has the widest variety of uses, because temperature and humidity can be controlled to simulate any natural growing-condition throughout the winter. Fruits, flowers, and vegetables can actually be produced out of season. Fresh asparagus, rhubarb, salad greens, or strawberries, for instance, can bring variety and luxury to the mid-winter table.

The hotbed and the coldframe differ chiefly in that the former is artificially heated and so can be used earlier in the spring and later in the fall. As its source of heat dissipates or is removed, the hotbed becomes, to all effects and purposes, a coldframe. The gardener should know how to place, construct, and heat such plant-growing structures.

LOCATION

The equipment for growing plants should be as portable as possible, unless it is to be used also for other purposes. Permanent structures, in which plants are to be grown all summer even after the seedlings have been set in the garden, should be carefully planned. A lean-to greenhouse or plant house is a fine thing, but must be placed where it is protected from north and west winds and have full exposure to sunlight. It is usually located close to the dwelling, for easy access to the basement water faucet and, if possible, to permit the attachment of a greenhouse radiator to the central heating system. Otherwise it will be necessary to install a separate heating system. If the greenhouse is so large as to require a separate heating installation in any event, it will soon develop into a white elephant.

The location of hotbeds and coldframes is perhaps even more important than of the greenhouse. They should be provided with protection from all cold winds, have full exposure to the sun, and be located in areas where there is no danger from air pockets or wet soil. In most cases, there is not much choice of location; if the yard tends to be too low, it may even be necessary to build the frames a foot or two above the ground to get good drainage. A good location for a hotbed or coldframe is just outside the cellar window, where the heat from the cellar can be utilized to keep the frame warm.

This type of structure is ideal for the person who wishes to grow only a few plants. If possible, the sash should slope slightly downward to permit water to drain off readily; otherwise, water will drain through and drown out the plants. It may also be necessary to enlarge the window opening, because many of the plant-caring operations may have to be performed through it. A two-foot window will be deep enough. The width usually cannot be changed. If there is insufficient heat from the basement, a few light bulbs will make a good supplement.

Window boxes are very useful for growing plants. If a window box is built outside a south window and covered with one of the glass-substitutes, such as cellulose acetate, the covering can be arranged in such a manner that, when the window is opened, sufficient heat will be let in to keep the plants from freezing but the winds will be barred from entering the house. Window boxes can also be arranged on the inside of the window, but there is always the danger of getting too much heat from the room, so that the seedlings will grow too rapidly and become spindly. The temperature for most garden plants should not be over 60 degrees. A few tropical plants, such as artichokes, will of course require higher temperatures.

If plant-growing equipment is portable, so that it can be taken down after the plants have been grown, there is not much trouble in locating

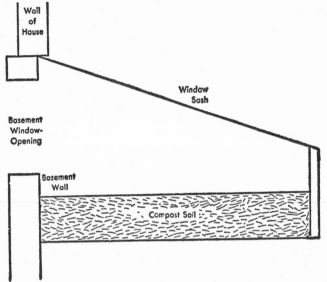

A Plant-Growing Frame Placed Opposite a Basement Window

it in the garden. Any permanent structure, such as a concrete frame, should be located in an out-of-the-way place where it will not become an eyesore when weeds grow up in it. In the small garden, such structures should be set to plants all summer, so that the space is not wasted. They are good places to grow certain vegetables which need protection against insects or other pests—melons and cucumbers, for example. Of course, it is always possible to have a permanent trellis in front of the frames, so that Scarlet Runner or pole beans may be grown up over it to act as a screen.

GREENHOUSE CONSTRUCTION

A small greenhouse should be just large enough to grow what plants are needed in the garden, unless it is primarily a hobby proposition or is large enough to require the services of a full-time man. A garden greenhouse should not have more than fifty square feet of bench area or approximately 100 square feet of floor area. The disposition of the area is quite important if one wishes to get the greatest amount of use from it.

The house may be any length, depending on the needs of the grower. The benches are two feet high and may be built either as solid benches or better still as slatted frames on which flats may be placed. If the flats are 12 by 18 inches, the benches will accommodate two rows of

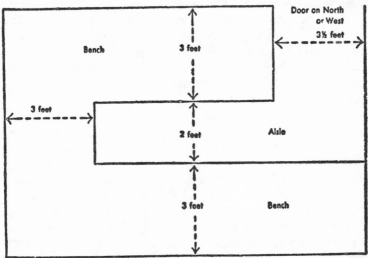

FLOOR PLAN OF A SMALL GREENHOUSE FOR PLANT-GROWING PURPOSES

them. The space under the benches may be used for storing flats or for forcing rhubarb or chicory. Soil may also be stored here, but it is better to store the soil out-of-doors. If the benches are built solid, a two-inch space should be left between them and the outer walls.

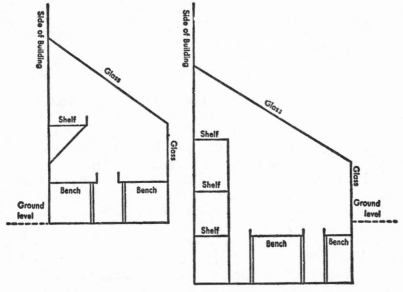

TWO LEAN-TO GREENHOUSES ON THE SIDE OF THE HOUSE OR OUT-BUILDING

House No. 1 sits on the top of the ground. House No. 2 sits over a basement so that the house may be entered from the basement and may be heated from cellar heat. The arrangement of benches is not compulsory. Either arrangement may be used. In the basement house, the glass starts at the ground level, giving light from two feet above the bench. Ventilators should be arranged along the top. These may be solid wood and three feet long. They need not be glass. Precautions must be taken to prevent ice from falling from the roof of the main building upon the glass of the lean-to's.

The sash-house is probably the most satisfactory kind of greenhouse. It is usually built with the eaves about a foot above and the floor three feet below the ground, so that the benches can be placed at about ground-level. The walls are built of concrete blocks and the only light is through the three- by six-foot sashes which are fitted to either side of a frame structure. The house is 16 feet wide on the outside and 14 feet 8 inches on the inside. The length is in multiples of three feet plus two inches for each sash bar, upon which the adjacent sashes rest. A cap is made to cover the ridge so that the sashes may slide underneath and the rain will not leak in. More detailed directions may be obtained from the local government agent.

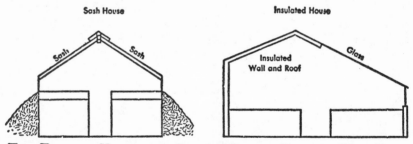

Two Types of Houses for Growing Plants, Showing Gable Ends

The advantage of the insulated house is the saving in heat. The roof is so pitched that the sun's rays will reach to the rear wall. The solid walls are painted white to reflect the light. The benches are 6 feet wide, which means that for some of the operations the grower must get on top of them; but for watering and general care, this is not necessary. A plank is usually laid across the bench on which the operator can rest his body while weeding. There are many details in the construction of plant-houses which the grower must work out for himself.

There are several methods used in heating the plant house. The most elaborate method is to place the pipe under the benches and heat from a hot-water or steam boiler. A cheaper installation is to run an 8-inch pipe under the bench, 2 feet from the wall all the way around, connected at one end with the smoke-pipe opening of the stove and terminating at the other end in the chimney. The pipe must be so placed as to make a gradual upward slope from the stove to the chimney. If the house is tight and not too large, this system will be satisfactory. Sometimes a foot-square flue, covered with sheet metal to get the maximum heat, is built the full length of the benches. An ordinary wood-burning stove will give sufficient heat. The stove should be placed in the corner most apt to be shaded, for that is usually a poor place to grow plants anyway.

CONSTRUCTION OF HOTBEDS AND COLDFRAMES

There are several ways of constructing and heating hotbeds and cold-frames. The old method is to build the hotbed with three- by six-foot sashes, laid over a frame six inches higher at the back than at the front and long enough to accommodate as many three-foot widths of sash as may be used. But if a person has need for only one sash, there is no reason why the frame should not be built so that the sash slopes widthwise rather than lengthwise. If manure is to be used to heat the beds, the inside depth should be 30 inches at the front and 36 inches at the back, above 18 inches of horse-manure, packed down and covered with 6 inches of soil. If the beds are to be heated by other means, the depth need be only one-half that distance. The soil should be excavated to the desired depth and the sides built up with inch-thick lumber nailed to two-inch-square corner posts.

Manure Hotbed

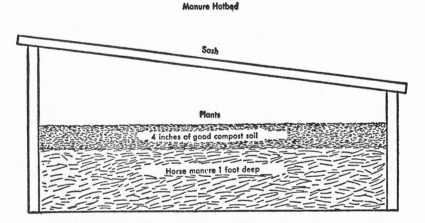

The walls may be made of 2 to 4 inches of concrete or 1½-inch boards. The distance between the soil and the sash should be at least 8 inches and at the upper end at least 12 inches. Instead of the manure, a floor may be placed just under the soil to form a basement compartment through which hot-water pipes may be run to furnish heat. Or hot-water pipes may be installed around the outer walls at the ground level. This system requires, of course, a source of hot water. This type of heat is controlled at its source while the manure-heat is controlled by opening the sash an inch or more to let some of the heat escape.

The old flue-heated beds, which have been much used in the past for growing sweet potato sprouts, have some advantages but are more bothersome because they must be fired and this requires considerable care as it is rather difficult to control this heat.

One of the newer methods of heating the hotbed is by the use of Mazda bulbs placed under the partitions between the sash. These are not costly to run and have the added advantage of giving the seedlings a permanent source of light—a great help in cloudy weather. This hastens the growth of the seedlings and helps to make them stocky. Dr. Alton Porter, of the Connecticut Experiment Station at Storrs, is responsible for having developed this method.

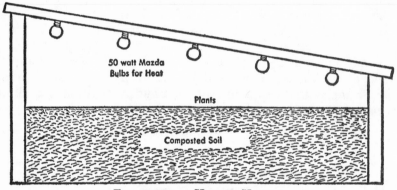

50 watt Mazda
Bulbs for Heat

Plants

Composted Soil

ELECTRICALLY HEATED HOTBED

Electrical heating-cable is also used to furnish heat. The cable is strung back and forth under 4 inches of soil and is near the bottom of a 4-inch layer of cinders. This can be installed by any one who has a source of electricity. It does a fine job but may be slightly more expensive than manure. Hot-water heat is probably the least expensive.

The cost of heating a hotbed depends on how well the frames are protected and how well they are insulated. It stands to reason that if you must heat the outdoors while you are accumulating enough heat to grow seedlings, it will cost much more than if you can depend on getting considerable heat from the sun and holding it in the frame by closing the ventilators to let out moisture and keep the temperature from going too high. But the ventilators should be closed before the beds cool off too much in the afternoon. It requires some judgment to maintain a good balance between the need to hold the heat in order to reduce the cost of heating and the need to release the heat when it gets high enough to cause the seedlings to become too succulent. Plant growth can, of course, be controlled by withholding water. Under no circum stances should the plants be watered after the noon hour. During very cold weather, mats made from rye-straw or salt-hay are placed over the glass to keep the heat in and the cold out. Old carpets or bags or even papers are useful for this purpose. Loose material is sometimes avail- able which may be thrown over the sash. With good insulation, the cost of heating the frames by whatever method is not apt to be prohibitive.

Making a Compost Heap

When the seedlings have reached the stage of growth in greenhouse, hotbed, or coldframe when transplanting to the permanent garden may be safely made, the garden plot must be ready to receive them. The debris of last year's crop must have been cleared away and the soil replenished for feeding the new growth. The subject of garden-prepar- ation and of fertilizers may well be opened with a discussion of the compost pile, for it may be used as the general receptacle for all the old-garden refuse and as a source of both the humus and other plant- food elements in the new-garden soil.

Setting up a compost soil-pile for the home garden is not only practi- cal but highly important from many angles. There are always many waste materials in the garden which many gardeners think they have to burn or carry off to the rubbish heap. But there is nothing in the garden which cannot be put into a compost pile. All rubbish that is left after plants are through producing fruit, any clippings from shrubbery or fruit trees or even hedges, leaves or lawn clippings, and even such garbage as is left after vegetables are prepared for the table should be placed in the compost pile. There is no reason why fruit rinds cannot be included. If materials such as these are used, however, they should be covered with some soil, and a bag of limestone should be handy so that a handful may be thrown over the pile for every four inches of material that is added. Furthermore, it is a good idea to add wood ashes if they are available either from outdoor or indoor fireplaces. If the lawn clippings are added, they should be spread out thinly as they add nitrogen to the mixture. Enough soil should be added to keep the mass well compacted. If it dries out too much, it is a good idea to add a little water to keep it moist. Twigs should be cut so that they will lie flat. Otherwise they may be the cause of the compost drying out, and this is not conducive to breaking down the fibrous material. It usually takes a year to disintegrate fibrous material.

Compost material is ideal for spading under when the garden is spaded in the fall or early spring. If it breaks down enough, it may be used for mulching material. It usually is not suited for growing seedlings unless it has lain for several years. If you plan to use some mixed fertilizer, the compost pile is a good place to add it, so that it will be mixed with the general mass when the compost material is spaded down. This will give the mixed fertilizer better distribution in the soil and make it more readily assimilable by the plants.

Other types of composts have been used, but it is a question whether, with the present methods of feeding plants, it is worth while to go to the trouble of making a special compost for the small garden, other than to utilize waste material as described. A real compost pile is made by digging up sod and placing 8 inches of this in a layer and covering with 4 to 6 inches of manure, then putting on another 6-inch layer of sod and more manure, until a height of at least 5 feet is reached. If the connective soil is a heavy clay 2 inches of sand should be upon the manure for each 6-inch layer of soil. The manure should be sprinkled with superphosphate at the rate of a pound to a square yard of manure as it is spread on the compost pile. The size of the compost pile is determined by the amount of compost wanted. If a cubic yard is wanted, a pile with a yard-square base should, because of shrinkage, be built to about 4½ feet high. The top of the pile should be covered with 4 inches of sod-free soil. The pile should be moist to start with and should not

Spading Fork

be covered. The top should be flat to collect moisture from rain but should not sag so much in the center that excessive water cannot run off. After six months, the pile should be turned to mix the manure and soil, and at this time 5 pounds of pulverized magnesium limestone should be added to each cubic yard, and thoroughly mixed with the compost. If the soil is very heavy and quite acid, 10 pounds of limestone should be added. A second turning of the pile is made at the time the compost is to be used.

If a grower needs only a small amount of compost soil, it may be made to suit his needs in an unused place in the garden. The square yard or so is covered with 2 pounds of limestone and a heavy application of manure or an organic fertilizer-mixture is applied. If the soil seems to be low in organic matter, that is, if it feels gritty when rubbed between the thumb and forefinger, some organic material such as straw, hay, weeds, sawdust, or other material is spaded in. Weeds are then permitted to grow and are cut down just before they go to seed. In the fall the soil is again spaded and may be piled up for use. It should be permitted to freeze during the winter. This makes good soil for greenhouse beds for growing any kind of plants. It may be necessary to screen it before it is placed in flats. This also makes a good potting soil for plants.

The question often is asked whether muck or peat soils can be used for growing plants. If the material is well decomposed, and a good weed growth has been observed on it, it is ideal for growing plants, but it should be used as a source of organic matter to mix with a mineral or regular soil or with an equal volume of sand. It may hold too much moisture. Most plants that are seen growing on these muck soils have a fondness for moisture and do not object too seriously to poor aeration. That is not true of most of our garden plants. They do not tolerate wet feet or poor air conditions. The better the aeration, the better the root growth and consequently the better the plant. We have to start from the bottom in growing plants. Too many of us admire the flowers and never think about the roots. We cannot have nice flowers without first having nice roots. In sections where the soil is naturally acid, muck soil will probably be acid and heavy applications of pulverized limestone should be made on it. Ten to twenty pounds should be added to a cubic yard. This should be thoroughly mixed and the soil permitted to remain in a pile for several months before it is used. If the muck soil or peat comes from an area where limestone soils surround it, there is probably plenty of lime in it.

Judging and Improving the Soil

Before a plan of procedure is adopted for fertilizing the garden soil, some estimation should be made as to the type of soil available and how it was formed. Of course, the gardener can send in a pound sample to his County Agricultural Agent or his State Experimental Station and have an analysis made for lime-requirements and fertility-level. After all, the gardener is only concerned with getting good crops off the soil, and if it is in a good stage of fertility he may not need to add anything. The only things he wants to add to his soil are those which are lacking. The fertilizer simply adds the same kinds of material as those already in the soil—but there in insufficient amounts.

The first question to determine is whether the soil was formed in its present location or was hauled in and piled, perhaps, over a lot of tin cans, tar, and other refuse. Or is it a fill over a deposit of black muck—

a condition to be suspected particularly in real-estate developments where houses are built on low-lying land, with yards filled in later. Filled-in soils can be made into good gardens, but it is necessary to do considerable work and usually to add much lime and organic material to get it into condition. It is a good rule to assume that the more clay in the soil, the more lime should be added. On naturally formed soils the surface soil should be red or brown, while the subsoil is usually a clearer red or brown. The more organic matter the soil contains, the darker the soil is apt to be. In some cases this is a good indication that the soil is good and fertile, but in other cases it may indicate poor drainage and relative unsuitability for a garden.

If it is impossible to have an expert test made of the soil, there are certain rough tests the gardener himself can make. A small package of blue litmus paper can be obtained from the drugstore for a nickel and used to determine whether the soil is sour or sweet. A handful of moist soil is rolled into a ball; the ball is carefully broken open and a piece of the litmus paper is placed between the two halves, which are patted together again; the ball is then laid aside for ten or fifteen minutes. A similar ball should be made from the subsoil, that is the soil below the level usually spaded or plowed. In ten to twenty minutes the balls of soil are again broken open and the color of the litmus paper observed. If the paper has been thoroughly moistened by the soil, the color will tell how much lime is needed. If the color is still blue, practically no lime is needed. If the soil has colored the paper a deep red, it is an indication that the soil is very acid or sour and considerable lime must be added. For a heavy soil, one that contains considerable clay, this means that four or five tons of limestone to the acre are needed. This amount, however, should not be put on at one time. A ton to the acre should be applied and plowed under, while an additional ton to the acre should be applied to the surface and worked in. In a year another application should be made. The applications are continued until the litmus paper shows only a very slight change from the blue.

The pH scale (p for parts, H for hydrogen ion concentration) is used to measure the active, though not the total, acidity or alkalinity.[1] Technically it is the logarithm of the reciprocal of the gram ionic hydrogen equivalent per liter; in water the equivalents of H and OH ions are each 10^{-7}; pH 7 therefore represents neutrality. This scale is graduated from 1 to 14, the middle or neutral point, as in purified distilled water, being 7. Numbers below 7 indicate acidity; above 7, alkalinity. Vinegar has a pH value of 3, from the acetic acid it contains; and

[1]This explanation of pH is reprinted from *A Manual of Home Vegetable Gardening,* by Francis S. Coulter, by permission of the publishers, Doubleday, Doran and Co., Inc.

ammonia, a strong alkali, registers pH 11; but though such ordinary substances may be near one or other end of the scale, a range of pH 4.5 to pH 8 covers all the reactions of cultivable soils, thus

pH	Soil Reaction	pH	Soil Reaction
4.5	Very acid	7.0	Neutral
5.0	Acid	7.25	Slightly alkaline
5.5	Medium acid	7.5	Medium alkaline
6.0	Slightly acid	7.75	Strongly alkaline
6.5	Very slightly acid	8.0	Very strongly alkaline

It will be noticed that there are 2.5 units on the acid side and only one unit on the alkaline side, within the limits of plant growth. The scale being logarithmic, each unit on it represents a tenfold change in acidity or alkalinity. Thus compared with a soil of pH 6, one of pH 5 is ten times as acid and one of pH 4 is a hundred times as acid.

Most garden vegetables thrive better in a soil that is slightly acid, where plant food is likely to be better balanced than in alkaline or even neutral soils. Few can tolerate sour alkaline soils, and undue acidity may be accompanied by toxic compounds of aluminum, iron, etc.

So many factors condition the growth of a plant that it is not practicable to attempt any more than a rough classification as to their soil pH preferences. Such is the following, issued by the Connecticut Experiment Station:

pH 5.0 to 5.6	pH 5.2 to 6.0	pH 5.6 to 6.8	pH 6.0 to 7.2
Potato	Eggplant	Beans	Beet
Sweet Potato	Pepper	Carrots	Broccoli
Watermelon	Tomato	Corn	Cabbage
		Parsley	Cucumber
		Parsnip	Endive

pH 5.6 to 6.8	pH 6.0 to 7.2	pH 6.4 to 7.6
Pumpkin	Leaf Lettuce	Asparagus
Salsify	Muskmelon	Cauliflower
Swiss Chard	Peas	Celery
Turnip	Radish	Leek
	Rhubarb	Head Lettuce
		Onion
		Spinach

To find out what kind of a soil you have, a handful should be dropped into a pint jar half-full of water. This should be thoroughly shaken and allowed to stand for ten minutes. The heaviest particles should be found on the bottom, while the lightest material will be on the top. If the liquid above the soil is clear and there is no fine material on the top of the soil, it is an indication that the soil is very light and low in fertility and that it should be handled more or less as a sand-culture so far as the application of plant nutrients is concerned. If there is an eighth-inch of very finely divided material covering the mass of soil and the solution above the soil is clear, it is an indication of a fairly good soil with an appreciable amount of lime or gypsum—a soil which will probably produce good crops without much additional fertilizer. And of course there will be many gradations between. Any considerable grayish turbidity in the solution above the soil will probably be due to organic matter. A reddish turbidity, caused by particles of suspended clay may indicate a lack of lime. On real sandy soils, a half ton of pulverized limestone may be sufficient, but it should be applied every year. Such soil does not hold lime very well. A heavy soil, when once thoroughly limed, will last for a number of years, depending on the treatment it receives. I saw a place on a large lawn where tennis courts had been marked out with hydrated lime 25 years before, and the lawn grass was growing enough better along the lines still to serve as markings if a court were again set up.

The preparation of a lawn should be started ten inches to a foot below the surface, though few lawns are made this way. If there is a clayey subsoil, at least two tons of hydrated lime should be plowed under to a depth of at least ten inches. If pulverized rock-phosphate can be obtained, a ton of this and a ton of magnesium hydrated lime should be broadcast and plowed under. Then a ton of pulverized limestone and a ton of superphosphate should be applied to each acre of plowed soil and thoroughly mixed in with some sort of a cultivator rather than a disc harrow. A disc harrow is a good pulverizing tool but it does not get the material down more than a couple of inches. After this treatment, the ground should be permitted to grow small weeds, which should be harrowed about three times. The grass seed should be sown about the first of September. Such a lawn will need very little fertilizer for many years. It should not be fertilized until the grass seems to be crowded out by weeds. Surface applications of lime and fertilizer, preferably in liquid form, will keep the grass in good condition.

There is very little difference in the preparation of the ground for a good garden and for a lawn. Roughly, 50 pounds to one thousand square feet (an area 10 by 100 feet) is equivalent to a ton to the acre. Phosphate fertilizers do not penetrate readily when placed on the surface in the dry form. For this reason they should be applied to the surface in liquid form or be plowed or spaded under to where the roots have access to them. Nitrogen and potash, as well as the other nutrient materials needed by plants, can be applied to the surface in liquid form with the assurance that they will reach the roots.

Soils that have had their origin in limestone rock and which are called limestone soils are naturally more fertile and do not require lime if wood-ashes can be thrown over them occasionally. Otherwise, a half ton of pulverized limestone applied every two or three years is sufficient to keep them productive. Such soils respond well to liquid fertilizers.

Shale soils which have fragments of red shaly material in them and which have a rocky subsoil are good soils if they can be kept moist. They dry out very badly during the summer. They usually need considerable liming-material and should be well supplied with organic matter. I planted a rose bed in such a soil one time. I used a pick and shovel and dug a trench three feet wide and two feet deep and, after mixing a 12-quart pailful of limestone to every ten feet, I mixed a six-inch layer of spent licorice-root with the soil. I thoroughly pulverized the soil as I mixed the material and put the whole thing back in place. The bed was six inches higher than the original soil level. It is now seven years later, and the roses are still growing fine—the only things in the garden that are. The beds are level with the surrounding soil now and the roses need more attention. It would be advisable to dig up the bed and re-set the plants after treating the soil with some organic material and some phosphate and limestone. It seems like a lot of work at the time, but the satisfaction one gets from the results makes it very much worth while.

If the garden spot is low and wet, it must be drained before it can be used for a successful garden. If the level of the ground-water is two or three feet below the surface, it is of course possible to grow certain vegetables and flowering plants without draining. Many plants can be grown by raising the soil into beds with a two-foot-wide depressed path between them. Such soils should be limed to a depth of several feet to improve aeration. Such soils should not be given any manure or other compost material. All the nutrients should be added in the chemical, inorganic form rather than as natural manures.

Soils that have been filled in over cans or other refuse are a headache to the owner, and no person who is really interested in a good garden or lawn should be guilty of buying such a place. The fills are usually subsoils dug out of a pit and perhaps covered with a couple inches of loam soil. They never seem to come to a resting place, but keep settling as the material underneath decays or rusts out. However, by continuously liming and adding superphosphate and plowing or spading under the accumulating weed and plant refuse, such soils can gradually be developed into a soil that will hold moisture and produce a fairly good growth. The surface soil will gradually accumulate organic matter and moisture relations will gradually improve. Thus, even poor soils will, with the right treatment, develop into good garden soils; the right treatment is largely one of getting enough limestone mixed with the soil so that the plant roots may forage for nutrients. Any organic material that can be mixed in, such as sawdust, green crop refuse, or partially decomposed compost material, will help to make it a better soil. Wood ashes do much to improve such soils. Nothing should be permitted to go to waste in a garden. If it is vegetable matter, it should be returned to the soil. The soil is a wonderful agent to reduce refuse to its elemental forms and to sterilize the material to make it harmless to plants or humans. As a youngster, I used to put mud on a cut or wound as well as on bee stings. It is surprising that so many people have lived through this kind of treatment and have not suffered or died from blood poisoning. The only conclusion that we can come to is that the soil is a natural sterilizer—a conclusion which recent scientific investigations have confirmed. Apparently the microflora in the soil are responsible for this action, but we must keep in mind that microflora are also plants which require proper soil conditions for their fullest development and that limestone seems to be an aid in maintaining such suitable conditions.

Kinds of Liming and Fertilizing Materials

There is much confusion regarding what liming materials should be used on the garden soil. Billions of tons of bedded limestone rock deposits were formed during past geological eras by the settling of carbonates of calcium and magnesium in the shallow water which formerly covered much of our present garden soil. This accounts for the areas known as limestone areas. If one were to drive from Philadelphia to Chicago and on to Seattle, one could almost pick out the dividing line between the areas where the soil was formed from limestone and where it was formed from acid-producing rocks by the appearance of the farm buildings. Limestone soils are fertile soils and farms located on them have thrifty, prosperous-looking buildings, and even the animals are better looking. Most anyone living on such soils can make farming a profitable venture, but it takes a good farmer to make a respectable living on non-limestone soils. Those farmers who are successful on acid soils use large quantities of lime.

Either high-calcium or high-magnesium lime rock is ground to various degrees of fineness, the finest grade being pulverized limestone. In order to get plastering lime (or hot lime) for the building trades, this same limestone is burned to drive off the carbon dioxide (the gas which plants convert into sugar in their leaves). This slacks with the evolution of much heat to form the hydrated lime which we refer to as agricultural lime. However the hot lime is also ground fine and applied to the soil unslacked. One ton of this will go as far as two tons of the original pulverized limestone. The hydrated lime is about 30 percent more efficient than the pulverized limestone. Thus any given limestone can be used and is available in three forms, and as there are two types of limestone, there are available six kinds of liming materials. The burned lime, when ground fine, must be used at once, as it will take on water very rapidly in storage, and is therefore not very practical for the gardener. The hydrated lime must be used with some caution because, if it is applied just before a crop is planted, it may depress the growth for several weeks. It should be plowed under several months before the crop is to be planted. However, this limestone is safe at any time and, in view of the fact that it is priced so that you pay for what you get, it is to be recommended for the small gardener.

There are other liming materials which may be used. Ground oyster shell is similar to ground limestone but is less efficient than the pulverized limestone. It is much better suited for poultry feeding than for liming the soil. Wood ashes have been mentioned. Wood ashes from the limekilns where the limestone is burned are as valuable for lime as pulverized limestone itself, and contain also some potash, phosphorus, and many minor elements. The use of wood ashes from a fireplace where they have not been leached by rains is ideal for the garden, but ash should be used sparingly around plants which are growing rapidly. When the plants are dormant, wood ashes may be used freely.

Slags and by-product limes are also available in certain localities. The slags are very valuable. Basic slag contains phosphorous in addition to much liming material. It is worth as much as hydrated lime. The slag produced at our steel mills is usually calcium- and magnesium-silicate slag. Limestone is thrown into the furnaces. with the steel and, when it is molten, is poured off and cooled in water and comes. out as a crumbly mass containing many minor elements as well as calcium and magnesium. It is fine material to use and is worth even more than pulverized limestone if the soil is low in minor elements. It may be used more freely than limestone, as it does not raise the pH or sweeten the soil as rapidly. I have seen some results with this material that approached a miracle. Many industrial. by-products of this kind are very valuable. People consider them worthless only because they know nothing about them. We have paid little attention to these materials, because the abundance of raw materials was so great that we were willing to let industrial by-products go to waste. And those who have attempted to utilize them have generally found the price prohibitive, at least compared with the cost of raw materials. However, we shall probably come to use more and more of the by-product limes. When they can be bought reasonably enough, they are as good as anything we can use. Of course, some by-product materials are in a chemical form which the plants cannot utilize. The soils, too, in many cases, contain considerable material unavailable to the plants, and it would be silly to add more. Our problem is to find out how to make the material in the soil available to our plants. When we do that, we will have accomplished much in the economical production of food plants. Up to the present we have taken the easy road, which meant buying expensive plant-foods and ignoring the potential storehouse in the soil.

Gypsum or land-plaster is a valuable material to add to the soil, but since it makes up at least one-half of the superphosphate used in mixed fertilizer, we have not paid much attention to it. It adds calcium to the soil but it does not sweeten it. As a matter of fact, it probably makes it more acid. But it has a good effect in improving drainage and aeration in the subsoil. People often confuse gypsum and plaster of Paris. The latter is really a calcinated gypsum; true gypsum does not harden in the soil as does plaster of Paris.

Gardeners are using more and more of the chemicals that are offered for sale as plant-food materials or plant nutrients. Anything which, being added to the soil, will gradually become available for plant-needs by dissolving in water so that it can enter the roots of plants, serves as a plant nutrient or a food material. The early American Indian buried a dead fish near the hill in which he planted his corn seed. He knew his corn grew better when he did that. He was fertilizing his corn just as effectively as though he took chemical fertilizer out of a bag and scattered it around the place where the seed was planted. The fish decayed in a short time and released some of practically every plant-food element needed for plant growth. Had he buried a large handful of lawn clippings with the seed, he probably would have gotten almost as good results. Or he might have poured a quart of milk over the seed as he planted it, and that would also have fertilized the seed.

Practically everything we use, except iron and steel, glass and quartz sand, will in some form serve as a fertilizing material. The question is, how good is the material in terms of a fertilizer? A young corn plant eight inches tall makes a good fertilizer, because it contains large quantities of plant nutrients; and, because it is green and succulent or tender, it will decay within a few weeks after it is turned under the soil and will release all the food-elements so that another growing plant may use them to make the same kind of growth. In other words, it makes good fertilizer. But suppose the same plant is permitted to grow to maturity and produce an ear of corn and ripen the seed. If, when the ear is removed, the leaves and stalk are turned under the soil as fertilizer, plants will not grow so well upon it. First of all, the stalk has been robbed of much nutrient material by the ripening seed; secondly, it is too tough to break down quickly and so releases its remaining nutrients too late for use by the growing plant. But it does add humus to the soil which, during the following years, may be more beneficial to the growing plants than the small succulent plant which gave up its nutrients immediately.

We must always consider both the long-term and the short-term uses of fertilizing materials. Such materials as the fish and the cornstalk are called organic fertilizers, in contrast to such things as baking powder, epsom salts, or saltpeter, which are called inorganic fertilizers. Such inorganic chemicals, which are generally the components of the prepared fertilizers which you buy, are quite soluble in water and for this reason are available to be taken into the roots ten minutes after they have been applied to the soil. If you want something that will act quickly, but which may be a little dangerous because you might use too much, use the pure salts. If you want something that is slow to act but will carry over for a long time and will be much safer to use, organic materials are better suited. Both are often used in a mixed fertilizer.

Plants take a large number of nutrient materials from the soil to complete their growth. Some of these nutrients are used in extremely minute quantities (a pound of boron will grow an acre of cabbage), while others are used in large quantities. One is fully as important as the other. If the pound of boron is missing from the soil, it is impossible to grow a crop of cabbage, even though all the other materials are present in abundant quantities. If any of these nutrients are not present in the soil, they must be added by the gardener before he can hope to grow good garden plants. Generally speaking, however, if manure and lime, or a mixed fertilizer and lime, are added to the soil, good crops will result, even though some of the essential nutrients have not been supplied by the gardener. The soil contains a large potential supply of many of the minor materials, and these become gradually available through chemical changes which it is the gardener's task to foster by proper manipulation of his soil. These changes are known to be stimulated by certain cultural practices recommended for the several crops in the encyclopedia-entries proper. Each cultural practice is based on the fundamental principle that the promotion of chemical changes in a certain direction will promote better plant growth.

Mixed fertilizers are designated by three figures. For instance, a 5-8-7 fertilizer contains 5 pounds of nitrogen, 8 pounds of phosphoric acid, and 7 pounds of potash in each 100 pounds. There may be a hundred or more fertilizers on the market, each one with its own formula, such as 2-8-10, 3-8-10, 3-12-15, 4-8-7, 4-12-4, 5-10-5, 8-16-8, 10-20-10, 13-26-13, 11-52-17, 23-27-17, and many others. It is seen that each one contains more units of plant nutrients than the previous one, and therefore each one is worth more than the previous one. A 2-8-10 mixture has 20 units, a 10-20-10 has 40, and a 13-26-13 has 52. When a person buys fertilizer he pays according to the number of units—or should pay that way, if he is to get his money's worth. This is very confusing to the gardener who buys his nutrients in packages and sees a big package for a quarter and a package half the size for a dollar. And yet the dollar package may be more economical to buy. Commercial growers buy their fertilizers on this basis because it assures them of a square deal; if a 100-pound bag or package is labeled 5-10-5, it must, under the State law, contain 5 pounds of nitrogen, 10 pounds of phosphoric acid, and 5 pounds of potash. No fertilizer dealer can cheat on this basis. The same is true of small-package materials, but these are sold by name rather than by formula and, unless the consumer inspects the formula (usually found in the fine print where it is difficult to read) he may get cheated, in which case he has nobody to blame but himself. A material sold as fertilizer without carrying the formula on the label should be eyed with suspicion. There is some good in every fertilizer sold, providing it has some plant nutrients in it, but a 10-20-10 mixture is worth twice as much as a 5-10-5 under any circumstances. However, a 5-20-15 may not be worth twice as much as a 5-10-5, even though it contains twice as much nutrient, unless the soil requires a large amount of potash. There are very few places where such a fertilizer is needed and, generally speaking, it would not be worth much more to the grower than the 5-10-5. Because nitrogen is so important in the growth of vegetable plants, a 10-10-5 might be worth twice as much as a 5-10-5, even though it does not contain double the amount of nutrient materials. In general, however, a fertilizer that approaches a 1-2-1 ratio, such as a 5-10-5 or a 10-20-10 or a 7-14-7, seems to give good results for most garden plants. If you decide to use 10 pounds of a 5-10-5, you can get along with 5 pounds of a 10-20-10 or 3.8 pounds of a 13-26-13.

The nutrient needs of plants include such materials as nitrogen, phosphoric acid, potash, sulphur, calcium, magnesium, iron, boron, manganese, and many others. The first four we get in most of our mixed fertilizers, while calcium and magnesium (which are probably more important) are supplied when we add lime to the soil. Thus, the reason for liming the soil is not merely to make it sweet but, what is much more important, to make it fertile; we cannot have a fertile soil unless calcium and magnesium ions are literally swarming all through the soil-solution that bathes the roots. We hear much about the importance of calcium in the human diet, and we depend on plants to take up this calcium so that we can get it in the plant-foods we consume. The peculiar thing is that plants will make a fair amount of growth with a small amount of calcium—too little to satisfy the needs of humans. In growing vegetables in a garden, we are interested in their food-value more than their color or flavor, and therefore we want to prepare the soil in such a manner that we are assured of a product that is really going to do us some good. So, before we think about applying the fertilizer, we want to make sure that the soil has all the lime that it will hold.

Knowing the importance of nutrients to the growth of plants, we are ready to evaluate the various materials that are used for fertilizer. Gardeners are always in a quandary as to the value of some materials for the garden. They should evaluate each material according to the amount of nutrient material it would supply to the growing plant.

If the soil in which a plant grows contains a pound of nitrogen and the plant needs four pounds of nitrogen, we must add the additional three pounds to the soil. If we apply it in the form of a mixed fertilizer that contains 3% nitrogen, we would have to use 100 pounds of the mixture. If we add manure which contains 1% nitrogen, we would have to use 300 pounds, and if we had tankage that contained 9% nitrogen, we would have to add 33 1/3 pounds of it. In other words any material that is used on the soil is applied according to its chemical content. If we have urea that contains 44% nitrogen, we would need only 7 pounds of the material, and yet gardeners will make the mistake of using indifferently either 50 pounds of the urea or 50 pounds of mixed fertilizer or manure. The urea will burn the plants while the manure will not add enough nitrogen. Whatever is used, therefore, must be used according to the percent of nitrogen, phosphorus, or potash that it contains. Ground bone is often used to good advantage around shrubbery. It has a low nitrogen-content which becomes available only with decay, while the phosphoric acid becomes available very slowly. Although shrubbery needs only small quantities of plant nutrient, it is practically impossible to get too much ground bone in the soil. Fast-growing plants need more artificially applied nutrients, while very slow-growing plants, such as boxwood, need none at all.

In general, animal manures make very satisfactory fertilizers for most vegetable crops and any other plants in the home garden. Chicken manure is usually high in nitrogen and potash and very low in phosphorus, so that, if it is used, one pound of superphosphate is usually added for each five pounds of manure. This makes a good fertilizer but it should not be put on close to the plants. It is very active and may burn the roots. For this reason, it is spaded under instead of being placed on the top of the ground. That brings up the question as to where the fertilizer should be placed. Any dry applications of fertilizer,

Fertilizer Spreader

or manures of any kind, should be spread evenly over the ground and spaded under. There is no reason for placing any kind of dry fertilizer on top of the ground. The reason is evident. It is slow to penetrate and does not reach the roots except during very heavy rainfall. The two or three inches of surface is continually cultivated, so that the roots do not have a chance to feed there. Furthermore, this layer of soil dries out quickly and plants cannot absorb nutrients from dry soil. If fertilizer is placed deep, there is always moisture to make it easily accessible to the roots. The same is true of liming materials.

The most satisfactory method of applying plant nutrients in the garden is to dissolve them in water and pour the fluid around the plants from a sprinkling can or other container.

Growing Vegetables with Liquid Fertilizer

One of the greatest and most recent developments in the culture of garden plants is the application of nutrients in water. Many materials which will dissolve in water will not dissolve in the soil moisture when applied dry to the surface of the soil around growing plants. For this reason, if the materials are first dissolved in water applied to the soil in solution, they will be much more quickly available to growing plants and can be applied as the plants need them. This method eliminates all danger of burning plants with fertilizer and makes the fertilization of garden plants much more effective. As a matter of fact, it has been used on trees, shrubs, lawn, flowers and vegetable plants with equal success.

The first requisite of this method, just as for dry fertilizers, is to make sure that the soil is properly limed. Then a large variety of mixtures may be used, if they will dissolve in water. Obviously, anything that will not dissolve in water cannot be used in a nutrient solution. The ordinary dry fertilizers can be used, but at least a third of the ingredients will not dissolve and must be thrown out, but that does not mean that the fertilizer is less effective. It simply means that some of the filler and some of the gypsum has not dissolved. All of the nitrogen and potash and some of the phosphorus will be dissolved in the water, while the insoluble materials, which also contain some phosphorus, can be scattered over the ground. Or, if the insolubles can be kept in suspension by constant stirring as they are applied to the soil, they will be of some help to the growing plants. The usual method is to place the fertilizer in an open mesh bag and hang it in a barrel of water. Not over a pound of the fertilizer should be dissolved in a gallon of water. In this way each gallon is equivalent to a pound of fertilizer, and can be diluted accordingly.

STARTER OR TRANSPLANTING SOLUTIONS

Starter or transplanting solutions are no different from side-dressings in composition, but they are used in much lower concentration. Starter or transplanting solutions can be made from a wide variety of fertilizer materials, but they must have certain essential properties to be really successful. Because they are placed in direct contact with the plant roots or seed, they must be made as sweet as possible. The mixtures mentioned in the above table are apt to be acid, and a handful of lime should be mixed in each 50 gallons of the solution. For small lots of the material, where only a few gallons are made up, a tablespoonful of washing ammonia to a gallon of the solution will sweeten it sufficiently to prevent injury to the roots or the seed. The solution is applied to the roots of the seedlings before they are covered with soil, when they are being transplanted to the garden soil. A half pint of the solution is poured around the roots and the soil is then filled in loosely. It should not be packed, as this will puddle the soil and prevent the plant from making a quick start.

The two following mixtures have given excellent results both as starter solutions and as side-dressing materials. They are highly concentrated and easily soluble, which makes it possible to dump the dry mixture into the water in the correct proportion and use it immediately.

Ingredients	13–26–13	10–20–20
"Ammophos" (11–48)	11 parts	9 parts
Muriate of potash (60%)	4.4 parts	7 parts
Sulphate of ammonia (20.5%)	1 part	1 part
Nitrate of soda (16%)	1 part	1 part
"Uramon" (42%)	2.6 parts	2 parts

These mixtures are sweet when made up and do not have to be corrected for acidity for a transplanting solution. They have given excellent results on limed as well as on acid soils. For transplanting solution, two to three pounds of either of the above mixtures are dissolved in 50 gallons of water, or a heaping tablespoonful to a gallon of water. A starter solution made with 5 to 10 pounds in 50 gallons of water can be applied directly to the seed as it is planted and before it is covered with soil. It has given excellent results.

SIDE-DRESSING SOLUTIONS

For side-dressing purposes, a solution of 10 to 25 pounds of the above mixtures in 50 gallons of water has been used with good success. Two hundred gallons of solution are needed to fertilize an acre of ground. The solution is distributed along the rows of plants in furrows just at the outer edge of the plants. If more than two applications are made, they should be at two-week intervals and three weeks after the plants or seed have been placed in the ground. The solution is placed in a furrow so that the solution will make contact with the moist soil. If it is placed on dry soil it will not be so effective in stimulating the growth of the plants.

Short-season crops, like snap beans, sweet corn, and lettuce, require only one side-dressing, and that should be applied soon after the plants are well established. Long-season crops, like tomatoes, cabbage, Lima beans, and carrots, should have at least two side-dressings and possibly a third. If the plants seem to be growing vigorously, they may not need the third application.

Lawns may be fertilized by dissolving the mixture in a concentrated solution at the rate of a pound to a gallon of water and running it through a hose while sprinkling the lawn. This can be done by attaching a small, inexpensive pump to the spigot before the hose is attached. By means of a rubber tube which is placed in the solution, it is sucked into the stream of water and diluted. A half pound of mixture to 100 square feet is sufficient for a feeding. By measuring off the lawn in squares or strips and watching the liquid as it is taken into the hose, an accurate application can be made. A half pound of 9-9-6 to 100 square feet is a good feeding. Pulverized limestone at the rate of 5 pounds to

100 square feet should also be applied once during the year. The best time to apply this fertilizer is in the latter part of the summer or early fall. The grass should not be cut short at this time.

For trees and shrubs, the fertilizer is mixed at the rate of a half-pound to a gallon of water and three gallons are applied to a fair-sized tree by sprinkling it just under the outer branches. In a dry season, it may be poured into holes made with an iron rod, but the solution should be more diluted for this purpose. The holes should be two feet apart in each direction but under the outer rim of the branches. Three times as much water should be used.

For shrubbery or perennial plants in the border, a teacupful of the concentrated fertilizer or three teacupfuls of a six- to nine-percent (based on the nitrogen content) mixture should be dissolved in a sprinkling can of water and poured around the plants. It should not be sprinkled over the foliage, as it might cause some burning. It can, of course, be washed off with water. For shrubs, it should be sprinkled all over the ground under the branches or foliage.

NUTRIENT SOLUTIONS FOR WARTIME

If the ingredients suggested above for starter and side-dressing solutions are unavailable because of wartime priorities, good nutrient solutions may be made by dissolving various proportions of superphosphate, sulphate of ammonia, and muriate of potash in water. The following table shows the ratios of each required for five different mixtures. The formula at the head of each column indicates the ratios of nitrogen, phosphoric acid, and potash produced by the particular combination of the salts in the proportions indicated. Since muriate of potash releases three times as much potash as equal amounts of ammonium sulphate and superphosphate release nitrogen and sulphuric acid, respectively, the salt proportions must vary from the nutrient ratios, as follows:

Ingredients	3-15-6	6-12-6	6-9-15	9-9-6	4-12-12
Sulphate of Ammonia	3 parts	6 parts	6 parts	9 parts	4 parts
Superphosphate (20%)	15 parts	12 parts	9 parts	9 parts	12 parts
Muriate of Potash (60%)	2 parts	2 parts	5 parts	2 parts	4 parts

The Amounts of the Above Mixtures to Use in 50 Gallons of Water

	3-15-6	6-12-6	6-9-15	9-9-6	4-12-12
For a transplanting solution	12 lbs.	6 lbs.	6 lbs.	5 lbs.	9 lbs.
For a side-dressing solution	25 lbs.	15 lbs.	15 lbs.	10 lbs.	20 lbs.

The foregoing materials are available even during times of emergency, and are about the only materials that can be depended on, although there are other synthetic salts which would serve the purpose better if they were not needed for war purposes.

COMPARATIVE RESULTS OF DRY AND LIQUID FERTILIZERS

Experiments to determine the relative advantages of dry and liquid fertilizers have produced some surprising results, as illustrated by the comparative yields of sweet potatoes under both types of treatment. With dry fertilizer, the average yield of sweet potatoes is slightly more than 125 bushels an acre. If one were to go along a row and weigh the tubers on a few hundred plants, he would find that many would have no salable tubers while some would have ten pounds and all gradations between. The plants, theoretically, all have the same ability to produce ten pounds of tubers, but something has happened between the time the plants were started in the plant-bed and the time of harvesting to reduce the yield. There are so many controllable factors that might have this effect that it is not difficult to see how our average yields may be increased.

For instance, on a certain soil without any fertilizer or water the yield was 84 bushels. Setting the plants with water increased the yield to 97 bushels, while a starter solution on the plants when they were set boosted the yield to 180 bushels. Two side-dressings of liquid fertilizer increased the yield by 104 and 74 bushels respectively, bringing the yield up to 358 bushels. As yet nothing had been done but to add plant food. Mulching the plants with cut-up corn stalks boosted the yield by 74 bushels. There was an increase in yield of 131 bushels when a little limestone was placed in the bottom of the furrow under the row of plants. So far, the highest yield from this group of experiments was 485 bushels of good salable potatoes.

Even more startling results have been obtained with liquid fertilizer on small plots subject to more complete control. An average of one pound of tubers per plant would amount to slightly better than the average dry-fertilizer yield—135 bushels to the acre. An average of ten pounds per plant would mean the almost unbelievable yield of 1,130 bushels per acre, and yet, on experimental plots, slightly more than ten pounds have been produced on individual plants. Entire quarter-acre plots have been made to yield an average of five pounds to a plant, or 565 bushels per acre. This was possible because liquid fertilizers can be made available to the plants in the precise amounts and at the precise times required for optimum growth under varying soil and weather conditions. Even in the ordinary garden, this procedure is more economical, injures the plants far less, and increases the yield by at least

75 bushels to the acre more, than any known method of using dry fertilizer. The transplanting solution alone has been responsible for increases in yield greater than many growers can get with a ton-to-the-
acre of dry fertilizer.

Growing Plants by Soilless Culture Methods

No discussion on the growing of vegetables in the small garden is
complete unless it includes directions on how to grow vegetables without soil. The plants may be grown in out-of-the-way places where it
would be practically impossible to plant them in the soil. Of course,
soil may be placed in containers and set in obscure corners, but since it
is a chore to care for them anyway, one may as well have the extra fun
of growing plants that are practically made from chemicals. The difference between soilless culture and liquid fertilizer is not great, except
that in the former every single element must be included in rather
exact proportions, while in the latter the soil may be relied upon to
supply the "trace elements" and to correct the proportions of the large-
quantity nutrients.

Plants may be grown in any medium that will anchor the roots, providing the necessary growth-promoting substances are supplied in an
available form. All the elements that plants ordinarily take from the soil
are soluble in water. The amounts of these substances that are dissolved
in a given volume of water will determine the concentration of the
solution. The optimum concentration varies with the temperature in
which the plants are growing, with the amount of water vapor that is
present in the air, the time of the year, the intensity and quality of
the light, and the kind of plant that is to be grown. Tomatoes, for
instance, require a large amount of sunlight and must have a more
highly concentrated solution in the winter than in the summer. In
other words, when plants give off a lot of water through their foliage,
they will wilt if the amount of salts in the solution in which they are
growing is too high. Under conditions where plants tend to grow too
soft, they can be made to produce a harder, firmer growth by concen-
trating the solution. This, however, requires some experience, and the
novice should follow directions rather closely until he learns the art of
growing plants. Knowing this art is far more important for success with
the soilless-culture methods than with the method of applying nutrient
solutions through the soil. Woody plants which grow slowly are much
more easily grown than plants which grow rapidly. Rapid-growing
plants take so much out of the solution that they bring about rapid
changes in the reaction of the solution; for this reason the solution must

be changed with a frequency proportioned to the rapidity of plant growth.

It is a far simpler task to grow plants by the soilless-culture method out-of-doors during the summer than to try to grow them in an over-heated living room during the winter months when sunlight is at a premium. Plants that require a large amount of sunshine are naturally more difficult to grow in the house than plants that can grow in the shade. Most people want to grow tomatoes in the house in the winter, because they like to see the red fruit. Yet this is probably the most difficult plant to grow in the house by the soilless-culture methods. It is a fairly simple matter to grow a flowering plant and have it produce flowers, but so much depends on the composition of the plant as to whether the flowers will set fruit, that it is pretty much of a gamble. Any fruiting plant should have a night temperature of 60 degrees Fahrenheit, a humidity of over 40 per cent, and plenty of sunlight most of the day. In a house, the temperature is likely to be 10 degrees too high, the humidity 10 percent too low, and the amount and duration of sunlight available through the window where the plant is placed, too little.

Plants growing in shade usually are spindly. That is one of the difficulties with growing plants in the house, unless special precautions are taken as to temperature and humidity. It has been my experience that plants will grow much better in the house when the heating system is shut off. When the plants grow spindly, the older leaves drop off. They usually turn yellow before they drop off. This is usually due to too little sunlight rather than deficiency of nutrients, but it may be due to the illuminating gas from a cook stove. Unburned gas or partially burned gas is poisonous and will cause the leaves to turn yellow and drop off. People who change from gas cooking to electricity realize all of a sudden that they are able to grow plants with much less trouble. Wood stoves never give any trouble.

MAKING UP A NUTRIENT SOLUTION FOR SOILLESS CULTURE

A complete nutrient solution may be made from three salts: primary potassium phosphate, calcium nitrate, and magnesium sulphate. These salts are used in various proportions, but a combination that has given good results with most plants is made as follows:

> Primary potassium phosphate—2 parts
> Calcium nitrate—8 parts
> Magnesium sulphate—5 parts

A level tablespoonful of this mixture will, when added to a gallon of water, make a good solution for most purposes. If plants do not seem to grow well enough, a half tablespoonful more may be added. In addition, a crystal of ferrous sulphate the size of a small pea should be added. Boron and manganese are also needed in very minute quantities, if water is used in which these are lacking. Well-water may not have it, although pond-water, which is the usual source of city water, usually has enough for practical purposes. Otherwise a teaspoonful of borax and 2 teaspoonfuls of manganese sulphate should be dissolved in a quart of water and kept in a quart jar to serve as the stock solution. A tablespoonful of this in a gallon of nutrient solution will supply all the boron and manganese needed. This will make a good clear solution and the nutrients will all dissolve.

If you have difficulty obtaining these salts, a tablespoonful of a regular mixed fertilizer, such as a 5-10-5, plus a half teaspoonful of epsom salts and a teaspoonful of washing ammonia, in a gallon of water, will make a good solution that will be turbid or cloudy. The "grocery-store mixture" will also grow good plants, but it will not make a clear solution. It is made as follows, and the ingredients can be bought in the ordinary grocery store:

Baking powder—1 teaspoonful	
Epsom salts—1 teaspoonful	
Saltpeter—1 tablespoonful	to the gallon of tap water
Washing ammonia—1 tablespoonful	

The "grocery-store mixture" has been used to grow commercial crops of radishes, snap beans, beets, and carrots on pure sand. It should be applied at least once a day, except in dark cloudy weather when it may not be needed more than twice a week. If the plants are growing in coarse gravel, it need not be used more than half as often. If the drainage water is saved, it may be used over and over simply by making up to the original volume with water. It may not be necessary to change the solution more than once a month. When this type of culture is used during the summer in the open, tanks must be covered with a screen to prevent mosquitoes from laying their eggs in the solutions. Even in the house, the solutions may have to be changed every two weeks to prevent mosquitoes from breeding in them.

TYPES OF SOILLESS CULTURE

CINDER CULTURE: Cinders can be used to good advantage for anchoring plants. The cinders are obtained from hard or soft coal. They are sifted to get rid of the clinkers as well as the very fine ash. The ash can be washed out by placing the cinders in a tub or pail and running water through them from a garden hose. If the nozzle is shoved down to the bottom of the container and the water allowed to flood the cinders, the ash will come to the top and flood over the sides of the pail. In growing the plants, precautions should be taken against the cinders becoming too acid. When they get too acid, a little limestone will correct the condition.

SAND CULTURE: Fine sand makes a good medium, but should not be used during the winter. If it is too fine, the plants will not get enough air. A medium sand that is good for plastering is fairly good. White sand is ideal. Yellow sand may have to be saturated with nutrient solution a week or so before the plants are set in; otherwise it may make the phosphorus unavailable. Red sand should not be used unless it has been mixed with lime and permitted to stand in a moist condition for a week or two, in order to correct the acidity on the sand particles.

GRAVEL OR CRUSHED STONE: These are both satisfactory materials. Gravel sifted from sand that has particles the size of small peas is a good medium, but may have to be watered every day or even twice a day to keep the plants from wilting. Crushed stone, except limestone, is often used and makes a fine medium. The material is usually graded and only the finer particles used. Coarser materials are not very satisfactory, as they do not hold water long enough.

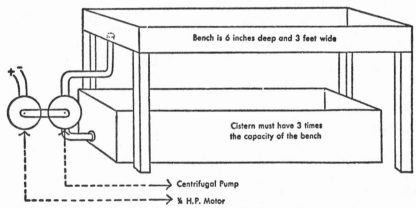

Bench is 6 inches deep and 3 feet wide

Cistern must have 3 times the capacity of the bench

Centrifugal Pump

¼ H.P. Motor

A GRAVEL CULTURE BENCH WHICH IS FED BY SUB-IRRIGATION

The solution is forced up through the bottom of the bench and when the gravel is flooded, the motor shuts off and the solution flows back through the pump to the cistern. The number of feedings a day depends on the coarseness of the material. Coarse gravel may have to be flooded twice a day when evaporation is rapid.

WATER CULTURE: This is sometimes called *Hydroponics*. It has been given a tremendous amount of publicity in the press, and yet it is probably the most difficult method to use, because it is not natural for garden plants to grow with their roots in water. The problem of aerating the water so that the roots will develop normally is especially difficult to overcome. If it were not so difficult to grow plants in water, this method would offer great possibilities, because it is so much easier to conduct water than to transport gravel, sand, and soil.

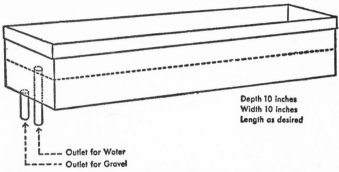

Depth 10 inches
Width 10 inches
Length as desired

L___ Outlet for Water
L____ Outlet for Gravel

A TROUGH FOR WATER, CINDER, GRAVEL, OR SAND CULTURE

For water culture, an overflow pipe in one end keeps the depth to six inches of water when the seedlings are started and permits it to be lowered to four inches as the seedlings get larger. For cinder, gravel, or sand culture, it is provided with a drainage pipe which permits the solution to flow back to the solution tank. This must be flush with the bottom, so that all the solution flows out. It is filled to the top with the gravel or other media and flooded once every day or two days with the solution.

When used for water-culture a quarter-inch mesh tray two inches deep is placed in the top of the trough in which sphagnum moss is placed to hold the roots and stems of the plants. The seed may be planted in the moss but it must be kept moistened while the seeds are germinating. There should be from two to three inches between the bottom of the tray and the surface of the water.

WATER VAPOR METHOD: This is one of the newer techniques and has many possibilities. The method consists of spraying the roots of plants with a fine mist of solution. The roots absorb the water and nutrients from air which is practically saturated with fine water particles. The plants are placed in small openings just large enough to permit the stem to grow to maturity and are held in place with cotton. The growing box must have a watertight bottom to serve as a tank. The solution is drawn out of the tank and forced through an atomizer-nozzle, so that it hits the roots. The roots thus get plenty of air.

This tank is eight inches deep. It has a solid cover with one-inch holes on ten-inch centers bored through it to accommodate the plants. The solution is not over an inch deep in the bottom of the tank. Nozzles in

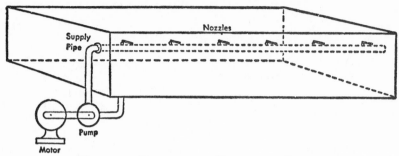

TANK FOR WATER-VAPOR FEEDING OF PLANTS

the half-inch supply line which extends through the sides of the tank eject a fine mist. The pump motor need not be more than 1/125th of a horse power.

CONTAINERS IN WHICH TO GROW PLANTS

Glazed flowerpots make good containers, but must have some kind of a pan underneath to collect the drainage water. The technique is to cover the opening in the bottom with a small wad of glass wool, so that the sand or gravel will not run out. The solution can then be poured on once a day and permitted to drain through, or it may be dripped from a glass tube which conducts the solution from a solution tank. For water-culture methods, glass jars may be used. See illustration for details.

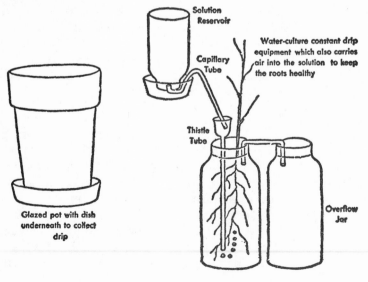

Solution Reservoir

Water-culture constant drip equipment which also carries air into the solution to keep the roots healthy

Capillary Tube

Thistle Tube

Overflow Jar

Glazed pot with dish underneath to collect drip

Watertight window boxes are also used to good advantage and are much less difficult to handle. These may consist of one tank above another, or a tank mounted on the window box by means of a hinge. See illustration.

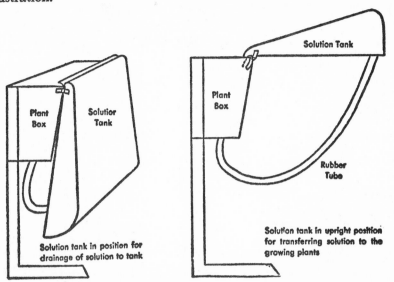

A SHEET-IRON WINDOW BOX USED FOR GRAVEL CULTURE

For out-door plantings, tanks of various sizes and shapes are used to good advantage. They should be screened from mosquitoes, which would otherwise breed in the solution. These tanks or troughs are made from metal, wood, or concrete. If they are used for sand, gravel, or

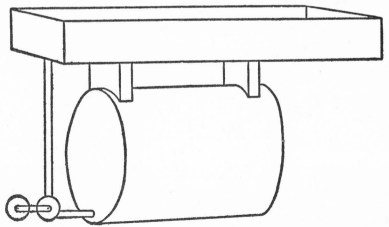

A SMALL GRAVEL OR WATER-CULTURE BENCH UTILIZING A 50-GALLON BARREL FOR A CISTERN

cinders, they have a hole at one end of the bottom through which the solution will drain, or a pipe may be attached through which the solution may be drained to a second tank. The solution is usually pumped back to a feeding tank and permitted to re-begin its circuit through the gravel around the plants by means of gravity, or it may be pumped directly to the gravel box.

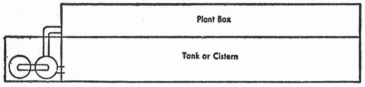

A SMALL PORTABLE EXPERIMENTAL UNIT FOR GRAVEL CULTURE

For large installations, the solution is held in cisterns under the benches or in some remote corner, from which it is pumped into the benches from the bottom until the medium has been thoroughly saturated. The pump is then shut off and the solution flows back into the tanks by gravity. There is no reason why a series of tanks cannot be so arranged that the solution will drain from one to the other into a cistern from which it is pumped back to the original or upper tank. Of course, such an arrangement would place some restrictions on the size

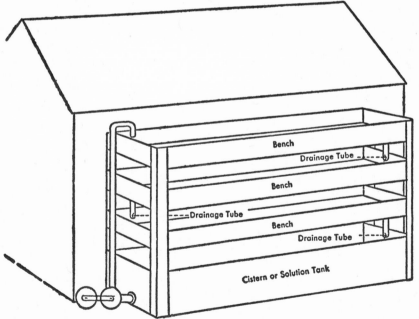

GRAVEL CULTURE EQUIPMENT ON THE SIDE OF A BUILDING

of the plants which could be accommodated, but if the tanks are not too wide, the sun will reach to their back ends and make it possible at least to grow low-growing plants. The illustration shows such a piece of equipment as it would be mounted on the side of a small building. Three benches, four to six inches deep and a foot wide, built above a cistern in which the nutrient solution is stored. There is at least a foot of space between the benches. The lower one may sit on the solution tank. The solution is pumped into the upper bench where it must seep to the far end to drain into the bench below. This equipment may be used for growing any low-growing plants or such plants as might hang down over the edge for a short distance.

Mulching the Garden

Few people appreciate the many advantages of using mulching materials on the garden. In addition to saving labor, preserving moisture, and protecting the soil, a mulch can actually serve as a source of fertilizer. So much has been written about the advantages of a dust mulch that many gardeners have been given the idea that a mulch has but one purpose—to conserve moisture, but this is only one of the benefits that may be obtained. A mulch may be credited with all of the following:

1. It prevents weeds from growing, because it shades the ground. Weed seeds do not germinate under the mulch. However, it will not prevent perennial weeds, those that produced a fleshy root the previous year, from coming through. The ground between the plants should be free from weeds when the mulch is placed.

2. It makes more fertilizer available to the growing plants. It actually gives plants a chance to grow in more soil, because the surface soil is not disturbed by cultivation. The roots can grow up near the surface where the fertilizer is placed. Fertilizer should be placed deeper, just as manure is plowed under.

3. It prevents the soil from becoming puddled. Any soil that has over ten percent clay will become puddled at the surface. When a heavy rain beats down on it, the soil has all the air driven out of it, and when it dries it is as hard as a brick. Any protective covering will prevent this. Thus the roots can get more air, which they need.

4. It holds moisture in the soil. Any covering will prevent the soil from losing moisture. However, this probably is not as serious a factor as most people are led to believe.

5. It keeps the soil from becoming excessively hot during bright sunny days. There may be a difference of ten to fifteen degrees between the soil in the mulched plot and the unmulched plot. This is

a handicap, however, if the soil is mulched too early in the spring, before the ground has had a chance to become warm.

6. It prevents tomato fruits from cracking and improves the quality immensely, because it makes conditions in the soil uniform from day to day. This results in a steady uniform growth, always desirable.

7. A mulch may serve as a source of plant nutrients, if the material that is used will break down during the season. This could be one of the greatest advantages of a mulch and will be discussed in greater detail later.

Materials that are suitable for mulching vary tremendously in composition and should be used according to the effect that is to be obtained. Obviously, material that has a large amount of weed seeds in it should not be used, as the seeds will infest the ground and cause no end of trouble. The following materials have been used to good advantage:

LAWN CLIPPINGS: These are always available for the small garden, but usually the quantity is not great enough to cover the ground. Lawn clippings are an excellent source of plant nutrients; because they are so succulent, they will gradually break down, permitting the nutrient salts to leach into the soil. The plant roots, being close to the surface because of the mulch, will be quickly benefited by them. The clippings should be spread out thinly, not over a half-inch thick, and used several times during the growing season. They are excellent for close-rowed crops, like carrots and onions; also for roses and delphiniums.

WEEDS: If you use mulches you do not have any weeds, but so often there are weeds in fence corners, vacant lots, and waste ground that make a voluminous succulent growth. If these are cut before they form seeds, they are ideal for mulching materials, as they break down easily during the season and serve as a good source of nutrient material while doing their ordinary duties as a mulch. As this material is rather coarse, it should be used between vigorous or large-growing plants such as tomatoes and cabbage. Farmers who have any acreage of waste land on which they could cut weeds, would find it worth while to apply lime and fertilizer to the weeds so that they would make even better mulches.

STRAW: Straw is usually that part of the grain crop left after the threshing. In some sections there are large quantities of this type of material. It does not have much nutrient material in it and does not break down very rapidly, but for all that it is very good mulching material. If plowed under after the crop is taken off, it adds to the organic matter in the soil. It is probably the cheapest material that can be bought for the purpose. As it comes from the threshers, it is long and rather difficult to handle and therefore its use is restricted to crops where it can be placed without too much difficulty. It may be used for trees, potatoes, tomatoes, and strawberries. If it is cut up into inch-lengths, it may be used for the lower-growing plants. Oat straw is softer and will make a better mulch than wheat or rye. Barley straw makes a good mulch, but it has barbs in it which irritate the skin, and when one walks between the plants, these barbed awns get into stockings and become very uncomfortable.

The one objection to straw mulches is the fire hazard. Cigarette butts cannot be dropped around the garden if a straw mulch is being used. Other mulches are safe from this point of view, unless they become very dry and the wind happens to be strong enough to keep the flame going. Paper mulches have been used but they are liable to do as much harm as good. They are usually good for dry years, but shut off too much air in wet weather.

Corn Stalks: This material is very coarse and cannot be used unless it is run through a shredder or cutter and reduced to pieces an inch or less in length. In such condition, it makes a fine mulching material and should be used on sandy soils for most crops. If sweet-corn stalks are cut immediately after the ears are removed, they will contain an appreciable amount of nutrient material which will become available to the growing plants.

Salt Hay or Marsh Hay: This makes a very good mulching material, but will remain intact for several years. It does not break down readily even when it is plowed under. It is excellent for strawberries and blueberries and other coarse-growing plants. If cut into short pieces, it may be used for any crop.

Peat Moss: This makes a good mulch for the flower and shrub garden, but it is usually too expensive for general purposes. It does give a better appearance to the garden than straw or similar material. Leaf-mold makes a good material for mulching, but it does not save so much time, as the weeds will usually grow through it. It is excellent from the standpoint of adding nutrients to the soil and a fine material to use around perennials and narrow-rowed vegetables. At least an inch-layer of these two materials should be used.

Sawdust: Sawdust or shavings are good for mulching purposes, but should be mixed with limestone before they are applied. For azaleas and rhododendrons, however, they should be used without lime-mixture. They are very easy to spread because they are so fine. They may be used for any purpose. If sawdust or shavings can be composted with some lime and fertilizer, they make the finest kind of material for mulching purposes. An inch of this material is sufficient.

BAGAASE: This material comes from sugar cane after the juice has been squeezed out. It is usually finely shredded and is often used by poultry growers as litter, because it has the capacity to absorb large quantities of water If it is available and not too expensive, it is fine in the general garden, but is not so good for strawberries, because it tends to stick to the berries when they are covered with dew.

HAY: Cured hays are very good for mulching material. It is often possible to buy spoiled hay, unfit as food for animals, but still excellent for a mulch. The advantage of such material is that, when it becomes moist, it begins to break down, and by the end of the season will be practically used up. It furnishes an abundance of nutrient material to the growing plant. Clover and alfalfa hays have a large amount of protein in them. As the mulch breaks down, the protein disintegrates and the freed ammonia seeps into the soil to serve as food for bacteria which are responsible for changing it over to nitrate nitrogen, a valuable nutrient for plants. Grass hays, such as timothy, orchard grass, redtop or quack grass, are good for mulches, but are more resistant to decomposition. They will last longer because they contain less nitrogen, but will add more organic matter to the soil. The one objection to hay is the fact that it is often cut so late that any weeds which may be present will have gone to seed. These, of course, will infest the ground. I once tried a hay which had a large amount of sour dock in it. The seed infested the ground and germinated late in the summer. The following spring, when I spaded the ground, I was amazed to see a solid carpet of sour dock plants. They were easily killed by spading them under, but they could have given considerable trouble under other circumstances. Quack grass is a bad weed because its prolific mass of rootstocks will send up plants wherever they are broken. It requires a tremendous amount of work to get rid of them, as the plants will grow right through a mulch. The grass must be cut before the seed is formed, if it is to be used for a mulch.

BY-PRODUCTS: Spent licorice root is sometimes available for mulching material and is very good for the purpose, but it adds very little nutrient material to the soil. It is fine for adding organic matter to the soil when it is turned under. Tobacco stems are often used and are alleged to be valuable as an insecticide for the plants which are mulched with them. Although they usually have the active ingredients taken out of them, they may still have some slightly repellent effect. At any rate, they make good mulching material, as they are usually finely divided. Peanut hulls are also good, because they are small enough to be easily filled in around growing plants. Shredded paper is sometimes available, but it is apt to pack down into a solid layer which may exclude the air as badly as the ordinary paper mulch. Dried manures as well as strawy, fresh manures are used and are excellent as fertilizers but have some disadvantages as mulches. They are apt to be messy to walk in and, if dried, may be too expensive for the garden. Dried manures have their place in mulching shrubbery. Sludges are often available but, whether dried or wet, are very unsatisfactory. If they are used, they should be spaded under for fertilizer. Leaves make fair mulching material, as is evidenced by thickets where a natural mat of dead leaves may always be found. They may be a little difficult to keep in place when first applied, but will soon settle down. For most vegetables and flowering plants, sufficient liming material should be available in the soil, as some leaves tend to build up soil-acidity. Leaves might better be composted with some lime for six months before they are used as a mulch. Rotten logs, if sufficiently decomposed to be broken to pieces, make good material, if available. Some kinds of bark contain considerable tannin, but can be used for a mulch if mixed with limestone. If the material has a strong aromatic odor, it will be improved with limestone.

Joys and Problems of Mulching

Mulching material makes it possible to have a garden and go on a vacation at the same time. It is rather disconcerting to plant a garden and have it free of weeds up to the time you start on a month's vacation, and come back to find that the weeds have taken complete possession. This will happen particularly if there has been considerable rain. I once left a garden, one-half mulched, the other half freed of weeds by cultivation. I asked a friend of mine to look after it. When I came back, there were pigweeds so high between the drive and the garden that I couldn't see over them. It had rained so much that it was impossible to keep the weeds down. I took a scythe and started mowing, and all of a sudden came to the mulched part of the garden, still in fine condition. Although there was an occasional weed as big as a tree, the garden gave us vegetables for the remainder of the summer. The unmulched part of the garden, however, was a total loss: the weed-pulling so disturbed the vegetable roots that the plants stopped growing; the plants were so spindly from shading that no fruit had set on the tomatoes; the corn was lacking ears; cabbage did make some small heads, but the other things had been crowded out. Now, I plan my plantings according to when I take my vacation and anything that I can mulch, I do. A friend of mine once said that my back yard was so nice during the summer, it was a shame that I couldn't enjoy it. The more I thought of it, the funnier it sounded. Mulch in the garden has made it possible to enjoy my back yard. Too many people get only a worm's view of their gardens, because they spend so much time on their hands and knees getting rid of weeds.

The method of using a mulch depends on the size of the material and the crop to be planted. Potatoes can be planted and immediately covered with a straw mulch. The plants will come up through the straw. Tomatoes may be set through the mulch, or the material may be worked around the plants. If they are set very early, it may be desirable to let the soil get warm before the mulch is applied. This is especially true if the soil is heavy. On the light sandy soils, the mulching material should be applied as soon as possible. Liquid fertilizer should be used and can be poured through the mulching material. Strawberries are mulched during the late fall by covering the whole plant. In the spring part of the mulch is removed and the remainder is raked to the center between the rows. Blueberries can be grown on high ground if a four-inch layer of salt-hay mulch is applied between the plants. The yields may be even better than in low ground. Muskmelons should be mulched when they are set in the garden, but squashes and pumpkins do not need a mulch, as the leaves soon shade the ground sufficiently to keep weeds from starting. Snap beans grow so quickly that it is hardly worth while to apply a mulch. Lima beans, pole beans, and sweet corn should be mulched after the plants are up.

Enough mulch should be applied to keep weeds from growing through; therefore, if coarse materials are used, a thicker mulch-layer must be made than if finely divided materials are used. A ton of straw will usually mulch a small garden, as three tons will mulch an acre of tomatoes.

When it comes to choosing the material, the price is usually the determining factor. However, where any appreciable amount of mulch is to be used, it may be well to keep in mind that plants which tend to grow too rapidly should be mulched with straw or material that is low in nitrogen. For plants that tend to grow slowly, green grass or clover hay will be much better both as a mulch and as a source of nutrients.

Controlling Weeds in the Garden

Even though a mulch seems to be the last word in the control of weeds, there are times when a mulch cannot be used or is not available.

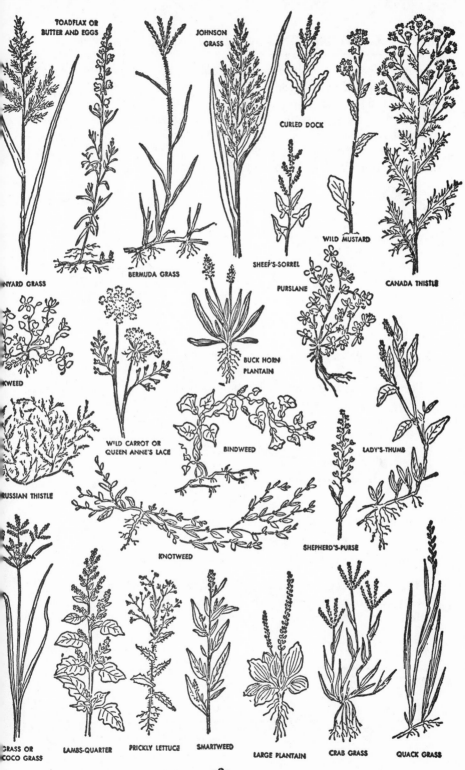

TOADFLAX OR BUTTER AND EGGS

JOHNSON GRASS

CURLED DOCK

WILD MUSTARD

SHEEP'S-SORREL

BERMUDA GRASS

PURSLANE

CANADA THISTLE

NYARD GRASS

KWEED

BUCK HORN PLANTAIN

WILD CARROT OR QUEEN ANNE'S LACE

BINDWEED

LADY'S-THUMB

RUSSIAN THISTLE

KNOTWEED

SHEPHERD'S-PURSE

GRASS OR COCO GRASS

LAMBS-QUARTER

PRICKLY LETTUCE

SMARTWEED

LARGE PLANTAIN

CRAB GRASS

QUACK GRASS

281

The main reason for cultivating or hoeing in the garden is to kill weeds. The best type of cultivating equipment is that which will shave off the weeds at the surface or just below the surface. The only equipment that is needed is a hoe, a round-pointed shovel (a square-pointed spade is nice to have for certain _urposes, but is not necessary), a Boston shove-hoe, which comes in various widths (or a wheel-hoe, if you want to spend the money), and a good garden rake. Anything beyond this is for

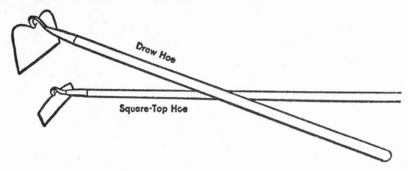

special jobs. A ball of jute twine may be an asset for making straight lines.

The best time to kill weeds is when they are just through the ground.

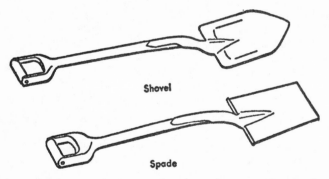

At this time the garden rake or the shove-hoe can be used, and the whole garden can be weeded in an hour. Every day the weeds are permitted to grow adds an extra hour to the job, until you get to the point

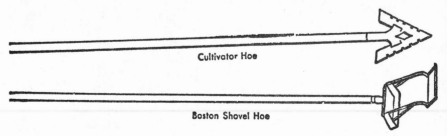

where they must be pulled to get rid of them. When weeds have to be pulled, it disturbs the roots of the vegetable plants. I had an experience that convinced me that it is bad practice to disturb the roots of vegetables. I had ten rows of sweet corn, and the only time that I could work in the garden was on Saturday afternoons. I started to clean out the weeds by hoeing, for they were already two to three inches high.

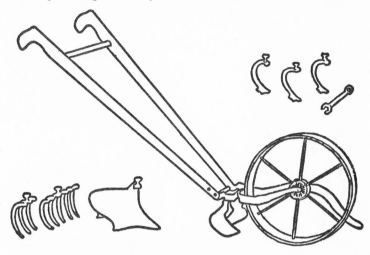

Wheel Cultivator and Attachments

When I had finished five rows, it started to rain and I had to leave the other five rows until the following Saturday. By that time the weeds were too big to be hoed, and it was necessary to pull them. I did what I thought was a good job and left the weeds between the rows. A week later, these five rows were turning yellow and, in spite of anything I

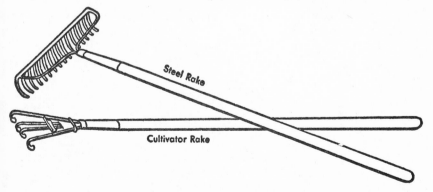

could do, it took two weeks before they turned green again. By that time, they had been checked so badly that they failed to produce ears;

the five rows were a total loss. I saw this happen to a commercial grower who decided to do a thorough job of cultivating. He cultivated close and deep and cut a large number of roots. His corn also turned yellow and he got no ears. I have since noticed that when weeds get a start like that, it is safer to cut them off at the surface of the ground. It is better to let them grow than to pull them out. Of course, they should not be permitted to get that large. But they sometimes do in spite of the best intentions.

Annual weeds, those which come up from seed and complete their life cycle the same summer, are easy to kill, and the garden rake will usually take care of them if the soil is not too hard. But weeds that have fleshy roots or underground stems are more difficult to get rid of. If a gardener has the misfortune to start his garden in a patch of quack grass, he is in for trouble as most mulching materials will not help him

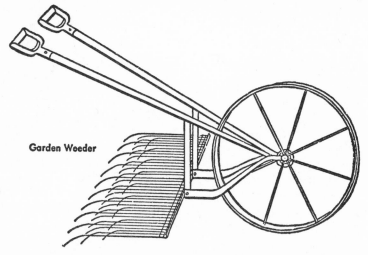

Garden Weeder

much. A sharp hoe is the only solution, or, if he can dig out most of the white stem-like roots, he will weaken the weed enough so that persistent hoeing will kill it. These root-stems are stored with energy provided for them by the leaves, and every time the leaves have a chance to grow for a week or so, the roots will store up a fresh supply. The idea is to keep the young leaves from growing. Usually, if they are hoed off three or four times, they will be so weakened that they will die out. Canada thistles must be treated in a similar manner. Bindweed or wild morning-glory makes large fleshy roots that will keep sending up young plants all summer. This is the most persistent weed of all. It should be dug up by deep cultivation followed by careful hoeing.

Cultural Practices in the Garden

Cultivation of vegetable plants is primarily to kill weeds. If there are no weeds, there is no reason to cultivate. The ground should have been properly prepared before any seeding is done; after that, simply shaving the weeds off at the surface of the ground is sufficient.

We hear a lot about maintaining a soil mulch, but this is another practice which was made to give the gardener work to do rather than to help make the plants grow. If there are no plants growing in the ground, and there are no tree roots penetrating the soil, the moisture will remain for a long time. Plant growth, rather than evaporation, dries the soil. A lawn dries out rapidly because the numerous plants are pumping water out by the ton. Any plant that is growing acts as a pump. The roots, if given a chance, will penetrate downward 2 or 3 feet or more and will grow out from the main taproot an almost equal distance. They are thus capable of drawing moisture from a large area, and so the soil is dried out. Few people realize the extent of the root system. A small radish seedling that is sending out its first true leaves

Fork for Loosening the Soil

may have a root a foot long. It gets its water deep in the soil. This is the reason why it is so important to have the subsoil in good condition. Roots do not grow extensively, however, unless they have conditions to their liking. As plants grow, they make a mat of roots between them; the proper distance between plants is determined, not only by the *Lebensraum* required for above-ground growth, but also on the area demanded by the roots for exploration. Soils that dry out easily cannot support as heavy a growth of plants as well-aerated soils that hold an abundance of water.

Applying water during dry weather is a tricky practice that may do as much damage as good. Water should be applied as rapidly as may be possible without washing the soil. Enough water should be applied to soak the soil to a depth of 4 or 5 inches.

Most gardeners make the mistake of sprinkling the plants, and figure that when they have wet the foliage they have watered the plants. This does more damage than good. It does not actually water the roots and it keeps the leaves moist all night so that diseases can get a start and grow. A sprinkler should only be used on grass, unless it is one of the coarse ones that will apply an inch of water in two hours. That means an actual inch of water all over the ground. A better method is to place the garden hose right on the ground or in a flat pan so adjusted that, as it overflows, the water runs over on all sides. By using a hoe and making an occasional shallow furrow here and there, the water can be directed between the plants where it will soak down and really wet the roots. It has been my experience, however, that it is not necessary to water plants except when they are transplanted. A transplanted seedling does not have the same relationship to the soil as one which has developed where it is to grow permanently. Its roots are all near the surface and must be given some help in the way of water if it is to live. However, other plants in the garden rarely need water, and if it gets too dry for them to grow, so much water is required that the average person could not pay the water bill. It is cheaper to buy the vegetables. This is just another reason why a mulch is worth while. But a mulch should cover the whole area; it does not preserve the water supply if it merely covers a small area and there is bare ground around it.

Transplanting seedlings is not a simple practice. When the seedling is removed from the soil many of the roots are broken off. The balance

Sprinkler

between the roots and the leaves is thrown out of adjustment. For this reason some of the leaves should be pulled off or cut off, or they will dry up. This is not so serious, except that it removes considerable water from the stem, which the roots are not in a condition to replace. If the leaves are cut off, the stem will remain full of water, and a new growth from dormant buds will start out after the roots are established. The development of the new roots depends on the amount of air around the taproot. If the seedling is set with water and the soil is packed down hard, the roots will not get enough air, and it will take some time for them to get started. If, however, the soil is dry and the plants are set with water but the soil is not packed around the roots, there is ample opportunity for the air to be drawn into the soil as the water drains out, and the plant growth will start out quickly. The best transplanting is done where the soil is moist but not wet, and the water is applied around the plant a few moments later. Tomato plants need a great deal of air, and if they are set in a mud pack they may never recover. Cabbage plants, on the other hand, can be transplanted in mud and will start out rapidly, because they do not need so much air. There are many plants that are finicky about too much water. Thus, unless a starter solution is used with care, it may not start plants off as quickly as one would expect. The plant should be set in a hole, the starter solution poured around the roots, and then the soil sifted in gradually without any packing or tamping.

Another practice which the grower is burdened with is the hardening of plants before they are transplanted. If seedlings are grown properly, there is no need to harden them. But if plants are grown so rapidly that they become soft and succulent, they are difficult to transplant. They wilt and chill easily. Such plants must be hardened before they may safely be transplanted from the warm environment of the greenhouse or hotbed to the field at a time when the temperatures may still be close to freezing for several nights. The reason plants are so often frosted after they are set in the field is that the water relations between the soil and the plant have not been re-established. I have seen tomato plants which were grown from seed in the field live through a frost without a casualty, while the transplanted seedlings were killed to a plant. And the seedlings grown from seed in the field were softer than the transplanted seedlings. Growers have told me that if they can get their seedlings transplanted a week before a frost occurs, the plants will usually live through it. The reason for growing seedlings for transplanting to the permanent place is to get them to mature early. It means a difference of two or three weeks. Plants which are set from pots where the roots are not disturbed will keep on growing with very little effect from the transplanting. This is particularly true if they have been well fed with liquid fertilizer. Very often, it is possible to feed plants enough in the pots so that they will need no additional plant nutrients when they are set.

There are various devices on the market for the protection of plants when they are first set in the field. Any kind of shade for a day or two will help to get them established. Hot caps, which consist of a semitransparent paper made into a cone, protect plants against strong, cold winds. Quarter- or half-bushel baskets make a good protection for them. Growers sometimes use panes of glass with a board or two for a frame. The glass-substitutes are good for making plant protectors.

Pruning plants helps to produce the right kind of growth. When a tomato plant is staked in the field, the lateral branches which come out at the base of the leaves are pinched off. The main stem carries five or six clusters of fruit. If the branches were permitted to develop, they also would have several clusters of fruit, but they would have to be supported by some means. So the plants are grown closer together and the branches are pruned off.

Pruning means to remove some foliage from the plant. I have seen tomato plants set in the field with all the leaves removed, and they started to send out new growth even more quickly than plants set with all their leaves. Whether pruning is an advantage depends on the chemical composition of the plants. A hard plant with stiff and brittle leaves will be benefited by the removal of some of them when it is set in the ground. Very soft plants, which are dark green and wilt easily, might be at a disadvantage with the leaves removed. This is due to the fact that the hardening influence comes through the leaves, while the softening influence comes through the roots. If roots are destroyed in transplanting, the absorption of nutrients and water is reduced while the leaves go right on making sugar and starch which tends to make them hard and brittle. Thus, pruning and moderate shade for a few days may help to get the plants established. It tends to balance the leaf and the root products—in other words, to balance the sugars and starches with the proteins. The whole art and science of plant growing consists of maintaining a proper balance between these two chemical processes. Everything the gardener does affects in some way this balance between the leaf products and the root products.

Shading tends to emphasize the root products. The same is true of an abundance of water, an abundance of nutrients, pruning, leaf-eating insects or bugs, or anything that impairs the efficiency of the leaves as a manufacturing establishment. Such things as root lice, soil diseases, acid soil, lack of nutrients, a lack of air, or anything that impairs the efficiency of the roots tends to throw the balance in the opposite direction. When the balance is thrown too far in one direction or the other, we do not get the yields of vegetable products that we expect. For instance, we have what are called wine years in the grape industry. Wine made in certain years is much better than in others. If we have weather conditions that tend to cut down the quantity of leaf-produced sugar and starch, we have a poorly flavored wine. If we have a wet, cloudy summer, we may get a large amount of foliage in tomatoes or peppers and very little fruit. We blame the period of the moon in which they were planted and let it go at that. The trouble is that the chemical balance in the plant has been thrown over so far in the direction of the root products (proteins) that there is not enough sugar to go around, so there may be a large number of flowers but no fruit. I have seen watermelons growing on a compost heap, because it was thought to be a good fertile place to grow them. The vine growth was wonderful but there were no watermelons. Occasionally, in a very dry summer, it is possible to get some melons in such an environment because there is not enough water to permit the plant to use up all the sugar and starch that is manufactured in the leaves.

Pruning shrubbery has a stimulating effect, because it reduces the starches and makes what proteins are formed in the roots go farther. It is the proteins that make it possible for the plant to grow large leaves and large plants. Adding nitrogen to the soil makes it possible for the plant to make more protein, and adding lime, phosphorus, and potash to the soil makes it easier for the plant to build protein from the nitrogen.

The prevailing temperature has much to do with this chemical balance or composition of the plant. If it stays cold, the tendency is for the sugar and starches to build up at the expense of the protein. If the temperature is too high, it tends to burn up these sugars and starches and the proteins are favored. If we want to accumulate starches and sugars, as in potatoes, we want cool weather between the period of full plant growth and the time of harvest. The same condition also favors the set of fruit and is necessary for a large yield. On the other hand, if we want a good leaf quality in lettuce or spinach, we do not want too much of the starch and sugar but more of the protein. This is favored by a higher temperature, keeping in mind that each species of plant has an optimum temperature range beyond which the proper balance between starches and proteins cannot be maintained. Very few of us pay any attention to the chemical composition of the plant when we carry out our cultural practices, but we affect it none the less. If we will keep in mind that a soft, succulent, dark-green plant is better for a leaf-growth than it is to set seed or fruit, and that a harder, less-succulent, bronzy-green or light-green foliage is better for setting fruit or seed than it is for a leafy product, we can decide whether we should feed the plants more to make them more succulent or save our money and get a better yield of fruit. We will then take a keener interest and accomplish more with our garden plants. It takes time to get into this frame of mind, but experience will soon simplify the thing so that it will become second nature. When the grower has arrived at the point where he no longer needs to ask questions but can reason out the right procedure for any situation as it arises, he has become a scientific gardener.

Controlling Garden Pests

There are two general types of insects that may bother plants in the garden, those that eat the foliage or other plant-parts, and those that suck the juices. An insecticide that will kill one type may not kill the other. The stomach poisons, naturally, are used primarily for the leaf-eating insects; the contact poisons, for the juice-sucking insects. Some insecticides will serve both purposes.

Cutworms are most serious when plants are first set in the field. They will either eat the stem near the ground, causing the plants to tip over, or they will eat the foliage or stems higher up the plants. Worms that cut the plants off near the ground are the most damaging. They work at night, and if the ground is carefully scratched around the base of the plant, the worms can be found. A few plants can be protected by wrapping paper two inches high around the stems. The lower end need not be buried more than a half-inch. Cutworms are best controlled by making a bran mash and scattering it around the plants when they are set out. The mash may be made as follows:

> 5 pounds of dry bran.
> 1 tablespoon of arsenate of lead or calcium arsenate.
> 1½ pints of water.
> ½ pint of molasses.
> Mix thoroughly and spread lightly around the plants.

There are many worms which eat the leaves, especially of plants of the cabbage family. These can be killed with a rotenone dust. This dust or its equivalent can be bought ready made. Bean beetles can be controlled by dusting the same rotenone dust upon the bean plants from the under side of the leaves. Asparagus slugs, potato beetles, cucumber beetles, and certain other leaf-eating bugs can also be controlled by the rotenone dust.

Plant lice or aphids are easily killed with nicotine spray or dust. Nicotine sulphate, sold as Black-Leaf 40, makes a fine spray for the purpose.

Cucumber beetles, which are found on melons and squashes as well as cucumbers, may be controlled by a lime dust scattered over the foliage. A rotenone dust will also kill them.

Duster

Leaf hoppers and flea beetles may be repelled with a copper-lime dust or Bordeaux spray.

Thrips on onions may be repelled by scattering flaked moth balls or naphthalene flakes along the row at the base of the plants.

Red spiders are sometimes very bad in dry weather and are very

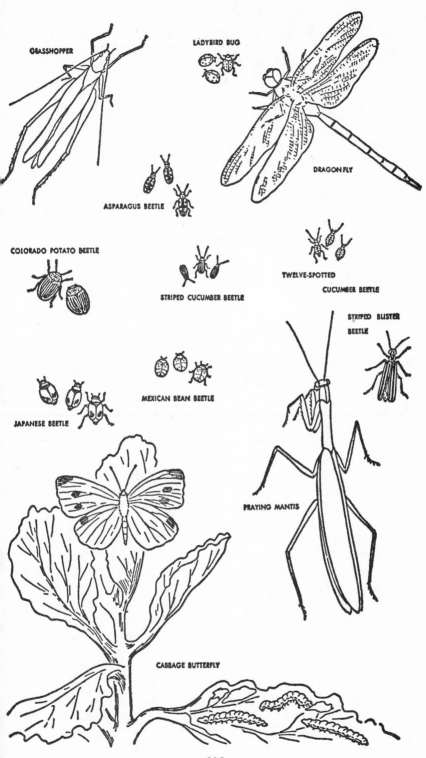

GRASSHOPPER

LADYBIRD BUG

DRAGON FLY

ASPARAGUS BEETLE

COLORADO POTATO BEETLE

STRIPED CUCUMBER BEETLE

TWELVE-SPOTTED
CUCUMBER BEETLE

STRIPED BLISTER
BEETLE

JAPANESE BEETLE

MEXICAN BEAN BEETLE

PRAYING MANTIS

CABBAGE BUTTERFLY

difficult to kill. If they become too bad it is probably more economical to plow the crop under or harvest it at once. Sulphur is sometimes dusted on the foliage, but I question whether it is practical.

Plant diseases are not a serious consideration in the garden. They do some damage at times but the control measures are usually so costly and messy to use in the small garden that it is not practical to do much about them. An ounce of prevention is worth a pound of cure. That ounce of prevention is good soil-preparation with plenty of lime and organic matter incorporated with the soil. If plants are grown reasonably rapidly, but not too soft, and with an optimum amount of water and fertilizer, diseases will not be very prevalent. A well-grown plant has an abundance of resistance which will go a long way to ward off diseases.

For more specific suggestions relating to particular plants, see the alphabetical entry by name of vegetable in the first section of the book.

Storing Vegetables for Winter Use

Storing vegetables is very much worth while, because it is possible to grow a much larger quantity of garden produce than is used at the time it is ready for harvest. Some crops are stored in basements, while others are best stored in the open ground. In the temperate regions where the winters are not so severe, much can be stored in pits and temporary storages out-of-doors.

Whether a crop will keep well depends somewhat on how it is grown and how mature it is when it is harvested. Weather conditions at the time of harvest have a big effect on the keeping-qualities of vegetables. Some crops must be stored with their roots in the soil while others may be removed from the vines.

Perishable crops cannot be stored and must therefore be canned, preserved, or dried. Many of the perishable crops can best be preserved by freezing and, as soon as thawed, prepared for the table just as though they were taken from the garden. The small, portable freezing-units are a great help, as many fruits and vegetables may be frozen as they come from the·garden and there need be no other expense in connection with the process. Such crops as berries, asparagus, beans, sweet corn, peas, spinach, Swiss chard, and especially strawberries keep perfectly if frozen. They cannot be kept in any other way without some form of canning.

Roots such as carrots, beets, rutabaga, and turnips can be stored in a cool place where the air is not too dry. For this reason they should be stored in a regular storage-cellar. They will keep well providing they have been properly matured. They should not be harvested until the ground has cooled off, but should be left in the ground after there is sufficient frost to injure the tops.

These roots are the means by which the plants are able to live from one year to the next. Low temperature causes the storage cells to fill up with sugar and starchy materials, and the more that can be stored in the cells, the less water they will contain and the better they will keep. Anything that is placed in storage with an abundance of water in the tissue will not keep well. Grain can be stored so well because it has so little water in it. As soon as the water-content is a little too high the grain spoils. Vegetables that are stored with too much water will shrivel badly and lose much of the energy that was stored there by the plant. Crops that are dug during warm, muggy weather have less energy stored in them and therefore do not keep well. Root crops grown with too much nitrogen or too much fertility or an abundance of water will not keep well, because sufficient starch will not have been stored in the cells. Most of these root crops will be better if dug after there has been considerable freezing, than if they are dug too early.

Very often, root crops such as these are stored in pits in the garden. This can be done because they are not damaged even though they are frozen, but they must be used as soon as they have thawed out. These pits consist of a trench several feet deep in a well-drained spot where the roots can be piled and covered with straw of some sort, usually about a foot deep and then a four-inch layer of soil placed over it. Roots will keep better in such a pit than if placed in a storage room in a basement.

Parsnips may be stored in such pits with the other root crops, but they are much better if they can be left in the ground until after the ground has frozen. In order to make them accessible during the winter, they are covered with straw to keep the ground from freezing too deep. A slight crust can be broken in order to dig a half dozen for a meal. They must be eaten before they start to grow in the spring.

Celery may be stored in pits and covered with a foot of straw weighted down with boards. However, it will be much handier if the storage room in the basement has a dirt floor or has a bin with sand in it in which the roots of the celery may be set. The sand should be kept moist. If the temperature can be kept below 40 degrees, celery will keep very well. It is better if the storage cellar has some light for this particular crop.

Cabbage may be stored in pits with the roots in moist soil, but it will keep very well in storage with celery if the heads are placed in large paper bags and hung by the stems from the ceiling. Needless to say, all diseased leaves should be removed before it is placed in storage. It is time wasted to try to store poor produce.

Brussels sprouts can be stored for short periods if the temperature can be kept below 40 degrees. They should be left on the stems and the stems hung up as for cabbage. The smaller sprouts will continue to grow if given a chance, so the larger sprouts ought to be used first. Cauliflower may be stored for two weeks, but a better practice is to dig plants from the garden which are late in forming a head and setting them close together in a coldframe where they can be protected by sash or straw and continue to grow. They may be stored until January by this method. Broccoli can be stored in the same manner, but the buds must be kept cut off when ready, or they will bloom and be unfit for use.

Kohl-rabi can be harvested and stored on shelves in the storage room in the cellar. It should be stored at low temperatures. It can be kept for several months.

Green cucumbers may be stored for a few weeks, but they soon become bitter, and it is a question whether they might not better be placed in the refrigerator for a short time.

Muskmelons and cantaloupes may be kept for some time at low temperatures, but they must be in the early stage of ripening before they are removed from the vines. The early varieties can be kept for a month. The late varieties, such as the honey-dew and cassaba melons, may be stored for several months, providing they are mature when placed in storage. Occasionally, these late-maturing melons may be removed from the vines even before they are entirely ripe, if they have not been frosted, and stored in hay or straw, where they will continue to ripen. The temperature should not be below 55 degrees for ripening, however. They may be stored at a lower temperature if they are ripe when stored. They should be placed on shelves in the basement proper, where the temperature is 50 degrees or even higher, rather than in the regular storage room. The rind should be hard and have a hollow ring when snapped with a finger. They should not be punctured with the thumbnail as they will start to decay at the spot. They may be kept for several months.

Pumpkins and winter squash should be piled in the open, where they are exposed to sunshine, until freezing weather, when they are placed in permanent storage. They must be protected against frost on cold nights. When placed in storage, they should not be bruised and should not be piled more than two deep. They are better if placed singly on shelves. The temperature should be between 60 and 70 degrees for three or four weeks, after which it may be dropped to 50 degrees. A higher temperature will do no damage.

Onions as well as any other bulbs should be well cured and dried before they are placed in storage, and then they may be kept at temperatures between 40 and 60 degrees Fahrenheit. The lower temperature is better if they start to sprout.

White potatoes should be stored at a temperature of 35 to 40 degrees if possible, but they should not be frosted. If the temperature is too high, they will shrink and the sprouts will start to grow from the eyes.

Sweet potatoes are difficult to store. Only well-matured tubers should be stored. They should be carefully handled so that they are not bruised when they are placed in baskets. They must be cured at a temperature of 70 degrees for several weeks, after which the temperature is carried at around 60 degrees. They should be kept in a place where there is good circulation of air around the baskets. They must not be handled when once placed in storage. The least little bruising will cause decay to set in. Dahlia tubers should be handled in a similar manner.

Tomato, pepper, and eggplant fruits should be stored on tables or shelves in single layers. In this manner ripe fruits may be kept at temperatures around 40 degrees for some time. Green tomatoes should be stored at a temperature of 55 to 60 degrees, if they are to be ripened. Tomato plants with green fruits may be pulled out by the roots and hung in a basement. The fruits will ripen.

Parsley and chives should be planted in eight-inch pots and kept in the basement window after frost.

Watermelons may be stored in the storage room with celery and cabbage. They should be kept on shelves.

The construction of the storage cellar requires some planning. It should be accessible from the outer entrance of the cellar or basement. It should have a ventilating window, which should be open to let in cold air during the night and be closed during the day. There should be some arrangement for opening and closing the window from the outside, so that it is not necessary to go to the basement. Too many trips will make it easy to forget the ventilation problem in the storage cellar.

Another type of storage cellar would be an addition to the regular cellar, perhaps dug under the porch, but with a door into the basement. The size of the storage cellars varies, but one designed for shelves on both sides should be 8 feet wide; one for a single wall of shelves, 5 feet wide. The depth will depend on the amount of material to be stored. If much canning is done, the canned fruit and vegetables should have a special shelf in the storage room. Perhaps the most satisfactory arrangement to accommodate both low- and high-temperature vegetables would be a double compartment with insulation only around the low-temperature part. The following floor- and wall-plan is a suggestion:

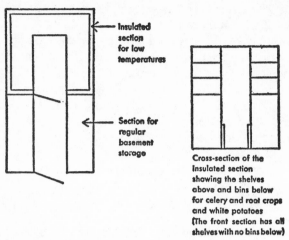

Insulated
section
for low
temperatures

Section for
regular
basement
storage

Cross-section of the
insulated section
showing the shelves
above and bins below
for celery and root crops
and white potatoes
(The front section has all
shelves with no bins below)

The shelves should be 2 or 3 feet wide with a 2-foot space between them. The bins need not be over a foot high and the space between the floor and the first shelf should be 3 feet, leaving a 2-foot space on the wall just beneath the first shelf for hanging up cabbage.

If the walls are not made of concrete blocks, they should be made of a double-shell of boards attached to and separated by 2 x 4 studding. The space between the boards should be filled with some insulating material such as sawdust. Even old paper may be packed in, but there is some danger of mice and rats getting in and even some danger of fire. The studding should be placed on concrete to prevent termites from getting a foothold. If soil is placed in the bins, the wood sheeting on the inside should be covered with a cement paint or some metal sheeting to prevent moisture from decaying the wood.

If the cellar for storage purposes is built as an addition, the walls must be made of concrete and should be insulated to avoid any danger of freezing the vegetables, although if it is underground, there is little danger of this. The arrangement of the shelves is the same as for an inside storage. Hot-air furnaces will not heat the basement so much as a water or steam boiler, and, in that case, it may not be necessary to have the high-temperature room separate from the basement. A curtain over some shelves to confine the moisture there may answer the purpose, especially for squash and pumpkins.

Table of Spring and Fall Frost Dates

State	Agricultural Experiment Station	Average date of last frost	Average date of first frost	Days of grow-ing season
Alabama	Gadsden	March 31	Nov. 2	216
	Mobile	Feb. 7	Dec. 5	302
Arizona	Prescott	May 13	Oct. 7	147
	Tucson	March 16	Nov. 20	249
Arkansas	Fayetteville	April 3	Oct. 24	204
	Hope	March 25	Nov. 4	224
California	Chico	March 31	Nov. 20	234
	Santa Monica	Jan. 20	Dec. 26	339
Colorado	Denver	May 10	Oct. 5	148
	Grand Junction	April 20	Oct. 10	173
Connecticut	Hartford	April 20	Oct. 14	177
	New Haven	April 15	Oct. 23	191
Delaware	Newark	April 20	Oct. 17	180
	Dover	April 17	Oct. 23	189
Florida	Jacksonville	Feb. 20	Dec. 1	284
	Tampa	Jan. 15	Dec. 20	339
Georgia	Cornelia	April 15	Oct. 19	187
	Valdosta	March 14	Nov. 11	242
Idaho	Coeur D'Alene	May 12	Oct. 14	155
	Boise	April 28	Oct. 12	167
Illinois	Rockford	May 7	Oct. 11	157
	Anna	April 5	Nov. 1	210
Indiana	South Bend	May 6	Oct. 11	158
	Evansville	April 4	Oct. 27	206
Iowa	Osage	May 10	Sept. 25	138
	Osceola	April 25	Oct. 10	168
Kansas	Leavenworth	April 1	Oct. 18	200
	Winfield	April 15	Oct. 22	190
Kentucky	Louisville	April 11	Oct. 22	194
	Paducah	April 7	Oct. 24	200
Louisiana	Shreveport	March 6	Nov. 12	251
	New Orleans	Feb. 18	Dec. 5	290
Maine	Presque Isle	May 31	Sept. 18	110
	Portland	May 5	Oct. 11	159
Maryland	Towson	April 15	Oct. 22	190
	Salisbury	April 20	Oct. 20	183
Massachusetts	Amherst	May 12	Sept. 19	130
	Fall River	April 22	Oct. 23	184
Michigan	Traverse City	May 10	Oct. 9	152
	Detroit	April 29	Oct. 13	167

Table of Spring and Fall Frost Dates

State	Agricultural Experiment Station	Average date of last frost		Average date of first frost		Days of growing season
Minnesota	Two Harbors	May	19	Sept.	27	131
	Worthington	May	10	Sept.	30	143
Mississippi	Tupelo	March	31	Oct.	28	211
	Biloxi	Feb.	22	Nov.	28	279
Missouri	St. Joseph	April	11	Oct.	14	186
	Springfield	April	13	Oct.	20	190
Montana	Moccasin	May	21	Sept.	20	122
	Bozeman	June	1	Sept.	11	102
Nebraska	Alliance	May	12	Sept.	25	136
	Omaha	April	14	Oct.	16	185
Nevada	Lovelock	May	13	Sept.	23	133
	Las Vegas	April	1	Nov.	6	219
New Hampshire	Errol	June	1	Sept.	5	96
	Concord	May	11	Oct.	1	143
New Jersey	Charlotteburg	May	12	Sept.	26	137
	Vineland	April	21	Oct.	20	182
New Mexico	Santa Fe	April	23	Oct.	19	179
	State College	April	9	Oct.	26	200
New York	Buffalo	April	28	Oct.	22	177
	Cutchogue	April	20	Oct.	29	192
North Carolina	Winston-Salem	April	14	Oct.	24	193
	Wilmington	March	22	Nov.	14	237
North Dakota	Langdon	June	1	Sept.	12	103
	Fargo	May	20	Sept.	27	130
Ohio	Cleveland	April	16	Nov.	4	202
	Cincinnati	April	9	Oct.	23	197
Oklahoma	Woodward	April	7	Oct.	30	206
	Oklahoma City	March	29	Nov.	4	220
Oregon	Milton	April	17	Oct.	24	190
	Medford	May	7	Oct.	14	160
Pennsylvania	Erie	May	1	Oct.	11	163
	Philadelphia	April	21	Nov.	1	194
Rhode Island	Providence	April	16	Oct.	19	186
	Kingston	May	1	Oct.	14	166
South Carolina	Greenville	March	30	Nov.	6	221
	Charleston	Feb.	20	Dec.	11	294
South Dakota	Aberdeen	May	15	Sept.	23	131
	Yankton	May	2	Oct.	7	158
Tennessee	Cedar Hill	April	9	Oct.	25	199
	Knoxville	April	2	Oct.	29	210
Texas	Lubbock	April	9	Nov.	2	207
	Eagle Pass	Feb.	27	Nov.	26	272
Utah	Salt Lake City	April	20	Oct.	19	182

Table of Spring and Fall Frost Dates

	St. George	April	19	Oct.	14	178
Vermont	Burlington	April	29	Oct.	8	162
	Bennington	May	15	Oct.	4	142
Virginia	Lynchburg	April	9	Oct.	27	201
	Norfolk	March	25	Nov.	16	236
Washington	Seattle	March	15	Nov.	20	250
	Walla Walla	April	10	Nov.	1	205
West Virginia	Terra Alta	June	8	Sept.	26	110
	Point Pleasant	May	23	Oct.	16	146
Wisconsin	Grantsburg	May	22	Sept.	19	120
	Milwaukee	April	26	Oct.	18	175
Wyoming	Powell	May	18	Sept.	20	125
	Torrington	May	20	Sept.	24	127

Information for Planting Vegetables

Vegetable	Seed or plants for 100 ft. of row	Distance between: Rows	Distance between: Plants	Planting before or after frost	Days to harvest time	Yield per 100 ft. of row.
Asparagus	50 pl.	4 ft.	2 ft.	Before	2 yrs.	30–50 lbs.
Beans:						
Snap-bush	12 oz.	2 ft.	3 in.	After	40	2 bu.
Snap-pole	12 oz.	30 in.	2 ft.	After	60–100	3 bu.
Lima-bush	12 oz.	30 in.	10 in.	After	110	2 bu.
Lima-pole	12 oz.	3 ft.	3 ft.	After	110	2 bu.
Beets: early	1 oz.	15 in.	2 in.	Before	50	2 bu.
late	1 oz.	15 in.	2 in.	Before	60	2 bu.
Broccoli	50 pl.	2½ ft.	2 ft.	Before	70	30 bu.
Brussels sprouts	50 pl.	2½ ft.	2 ft.	Before	100	30 qts.
Cabbage	50 pl.	2½ ft.	2 ft.	Before	100	50 heads
Cantaloupe or Muskmelon	½ oz.	5 ft.	4 ft.	After	100	150 melons
Carrots	1 oz.	15 in.	2 in.	Before	70	2 bu.
Cauliflower	50 pl.	2½ ft.	2 ft.	Before	100	50 heads
Celery	200 pl.	2½ ft.	6 in.	Before	120	200 plants
Corn	¼ lb.	3 ft.	2 ft.	After	70	100 ears
Cucumber	½ oz.	5 ft.	4 ft.	After	70	200 fruit
Eggplant	50 pl.	3 ft.	2 ft.	After	100	150 fruit
Dandelion	½ oz.	15 in.	6 in.	Before	100	2 bu.
Endive	½ oz.	15 in.	6 in.	Before	70	200 heads
Kale	50 pl.	3 ft.	2 ft.	Before	70	60 bu.
Kohlrabi	100 pl.	2 ft.	1 ft.	Before	60	2 bu.

Information for Planting Vegetables

Leeks	1 oz.	15 in.	2 in.	Before	100	300 plants
Lettuce:						
Leaf	½ oz.	15 in.	10 in.	Before	70	100 heads
Head	½ oz.	15 in.	12 in.	Before	60	100 heads
Okra	1 oz.	2½ ft.	1½ ft.	After	90	500 pods
Mustard greens and collards	1 oz.	1 ft.	2 ft.	Before	70	100 plants
Onions: sets	1 qt.	1½ ft.	3 in.	Before	50	140 bunches
seed	1 oz.	1½ ft.	3 in.	Before	110	2 bu.
Parsley	½ oz.	15 in.	4 in.	Before	70	75 bunches
Parsnips	½ oz.	15 in.	4 in.	Before	140	2 bu.
Peas	1 pt.	18 in.	1 in.	Before	50	2 bu.
Peppers	50 pl.	2 ft.	2 ft.	After	120	5 bu.
Potatoes (white)	½ bu.	3 ft.	15 in.	Before	100	3 bu.
Pumpkins	1 oz.	5 ft.	4 ft.	After	75	40 to 100
Radishes	½ oz.	15 in.	1 in.	Before	50	100 bunches
Rhubarb	25 rts.	4 ft.	4 ft.	Before	1 year	250 stalks
Rutabagas	½ oz.	15 in.	4 in.	Before	50	2 bu.
Salsify	½ oz.	15 in.	2 in.	Before	140	500 roots.
Spinach	½ oz.	15 in.	3 in.	Before	65	3 bu.
Squash	1 oz.	4 ft.	4 ft.	After	60 to 120	75 to 150
Sweet potatoes	80 pl.	2½ ft.	15 in.	After	140	3 bu.
Tomatoes	25 pl.	4 ft.	4 ft.	After	120	4 bu.
Turnips	½ oz.	15 in.	2 in.	Before	50	2 bu.
Watermelon	1 oz.	6 ft.	6 ft.	After	110	40 melons.

GLOSSARY

Aeration: the process of free movement of air through soil, sand, or other media.

Annuals: plants that complete their life cycle in one year—that produce seed the same year the plants start to grow from seed.

Axil: the point where a leaf is attached to the stem of a plant.

Biennial: a plant that requires two years to produce seed from the seedling stage.

Carbohydrate: any chemical substance such as sugar or starch that contains only carbon, hydrogen and oxygen in definite proportions.

Compost: a mixture of soil and plant refuse in which the plant material is partially decomposed.

Colloidal: any material in a semi-solid condition which will react chemically, such as the casein in milk.

Corolla: usually the colored petals of a flower.

Corymbs: a form of flower head in which the florets are arranged on the same plane or in a convex head.

Cotyledons: the two halves of a seed which usually form the first seed leaves, as in a bean. In peas they stay underground.

Cross-fertilization: the process whereby the stigma of a flower receives pollen from the flower of another plant to fertilize its ovules in the ovary.

Crown: the part of a plant which forms the union between roots and stems or roots and leaves.

Diclinous: having the stamens and pistils produced in separate flowers on the same plant, as in cucumbers. See monoecious.

Dioecious: having the stamens and pistils produced on separate plants, as in asparagus.

Drills: small shallow furrows in which seeds are sown.

Entire: having the margins free of indentations—used in reference to leaves.

Female Flowers: those containing only the female elements, the pistils and ovules.

Fertilizer: a mixture of materials containing mineral salts which, when applied to the soil, serve as necessary nutrients for plants.

Flats: shallow wooden trays in which soil is placed for the purpose of growing small plants.

Germination: the initial growth of the embryo plant in the dormant seed, resulting in the rupture of the seed coat and the emergence of the root and sprout.

Gypsum: land plaster or calcium sulphate.

Heavy soil: one that contains enough silt and clay to make it dense and finely textured.

Hermaphroditic: having both sex organs in the same flower; perfect, monoclinous.

Inflorescence: the flowering part of the plant.

Leafstalk: a structure, such as celery, which supports the leaves.

Leguminous: belonging to the pulse or sweet pea family; being capable, by means of its associated bacteria, of using nitrogen from the soil air.

Liming: the process of broadcasting one of the many lime compounds on the soil.

Loam: a soil consisting of a comparatively large amount of finely divided material, or one consisting of a friable mixture of organic matter, clay, and sand.

Male Flowers: those containing only the male element or stamens.

Monoclinous: see Hermaphroditic.

Monoecious: see Diclinous.

Nodules: the small tubercles or swellings on the roots of legumes, which harbor bacteria enabling the plant to use gaseous nitrogen from the air.

Nutrients: the essential elements in a fertilizer, on which plants depend to make their growth.

Oppositely: with the leaves arranged on opposite sides of the stem, directly across from one another.

Palmately: broad, flattened, with regular margins—said of leaves.

Panicles: a form of inflorescence which is branched and on which the individual flowers are attached by short stems.

Perennial: a plant that lives from year to year without re-seeding.

Perfect: see Hermaphroditic.

Pinnate: finely divided—said of leaves.

Pistillate: being a female flower; containing only the pistil.

Pollination: the process of depositing pollen from the stamens onto the stigma of the pistil; fertilization of flowers.

Protein: a chemical compound containing carbon, hydrogen, oxygen, and nitrogen in certain proportions.

Pubescence: the numerous fine hairs covering the surface of some leaves or fruits, as in the peach.

Puddling: compacting a wet clay soil by driving out water and air. Heavy soils may be ruined if worked too wet.

Pupate: to change from a larva to an adult insect.

Raceme: a form of inflorescence where the flowers are attached to a central axis by means of short stems.

Rhizome: an underground root-like stem of a plant. New shoots may grow up from the rhizome, which also sends down roots.

Rootstock: the common term for a root-like underground stem or rhizome, refers to the part of the root used in plant propagation.

[The term "rootstalk" is also used to refer to a root-like underground stem, but the word "rootstalk" emphasizes the relation of the underground stalk to the main stalk, whereas *rootstock* is more specifically the part of the underground stem used for plant propagation.]

Seedstalk: the stem of a perennial plant which produces the seed. This is in contrast to a leafstalk.

Sex of Flowers: There are three types of flowering plants from the standpoint of sex: (1) those in which the male and female flowers are on different plants (*see* Dioecious); (2) those which have both male and female flowers on the same plant (*see* Diclinous); and (3) those which have both the male and female elements in the same flower (*see* Hermaphroditic).

Side-dressing: the act of applying fertilizer along the row beside the plants.

Staminate: being a male flower; containing only stamens.

Starting Solution: water containing a small quantity of plant nutrients which is poured on roots of plants or seed when they are planted, to promote a quick start.

Stolon: a modified stem which grows along the top of the ground, such as a runner on a strawberry plant.

Spotting: the act of transplanting very small seedlings from one flat to the other or to a ground bed.

Subsoil: term commonly used to designate the soil just below the plowed or cultivated area; more accurately, the deeper soil.

Taproot: the main central root from which lateral roots originate.

Trace-elements: mineral nutrients which are needed by plants in very minute quantities.

Transplanting Solution: a more restricted term than starter solution. Refers to a solution poured on the roots of plants when they are transplanted.

Tuber: a modified stem-structure formed on plants to serve as a storage organ. A white potato is a good example.

Vitamin: a complex chemical compound, sometimes resembling a carbohydrate, sometimes a protein, which is formed by plants and is needed in very minute quantities by humans to maintain normal health.